Between Samaritans and States

This book provides the first book-length, English-language account of the political ethics of large-scale, Western-based humanitarian INGOs, such as Oxfam, CARE, and Doctors Without Borders. These INGOs are often either celebrated as do-gooding machines or maligned as incompetents "on the road to hell". In contrast, this book suggests the picture is more complicated.

Drawing on political theory, philosophy, and ethics, along with original fieldwork, this book shows that while humanitarian INGOs are often perceived as non-governmental and apolitical, they are in fact sometimes somewhat governmental, highly political, and often "second-best" actors. As a result, they face four central ethical predicaments: the problem of spattered hands, the quandary of the second-best, the cost-effectiveness conundrum, and the moral motivation trade–off. → *synthesise*

This book considers what it would look like for INGOs to navigate these predicaments in ways that are as consistent as possible with democratic, egalitarian, humanitarian, and justice-based norms. It argues that humanitarian INGOs must regularly make deep moral compromises. In choosing which compromises to make, they should focus primarily on their overall consequences, as opposed to their intentions or the intrinsic value of their activities. But they should interpret consequences expansively, and not limit themselves to those that are amenable to precise measurements of cost-effectiveness. The book concludes by explaining the implications of its "map" of humanitarian INGO political ethics for individual donors to INGOs, and for how we all should conceive of INGOs' role in addressing pressing global problems.

synthesise

Finest
TARGET

Between Samaritans and States

The Political Ethics of Humanitarian INGOs

Jennifer C. Rubenstein

OXFORD
UNIVERSITY PRESS

OXFORD

UNIVERSITY PRESS

Great Clarendon Street, Oxford, OX2 6DP,
United Kingdom

Oxford University Press is a department of the University of Oxford.
It furthers the University's objective of excellence in research, scholarship,
and education by publishing worldwide. Oxford is a registered trade mark of
Oxford University Press in the UK and in certain other countries

First published 2015
First published in paperback 2016

Published in the United States of America by Oxford University Press
198 Madison Avenue, New York, NY 10016, United States of America

British Library Cataloguing in Publication Data
Data available

Library of Congress Cataloging in Publication Data
Data available

ISBN 978-0-19-968410-6 (Hbk.)
ISBN 978-0-19-877869-1 (Pbk.)

For Pete and Zora,
my loves,
Old and New.

Acknowledgments

Help can sometimes go terribly wrong. In writing this book, I received truly excellent help. I am deeply grateful.

This book began as a PhD dissertation in the Political Science department at the University of Chicago. I doubt that a single sentence of the dissertation remains. However, the support that I received in writing the dissertation was integral to the book it eventually became. I thank my dissertation committee—Charles Larmore, Jacob Levy, Patchen Markell, Lisa Wedeen, and Iris Marion Young—for insightful and patient guidance during this process. Since my second year of graduate school, Jacob, in particular, has been unrelentingly generous in providing substantive feedback, encouragement, good advice, and friendship. I can only hope to be half the advisor to my students that he has been to me. Because I lived away from Chicago during the time I was writing my dissertation, I saw Iris only rarely. But in the years since her death, I have found that hers is one of the voices that has stuck with me most, pushing me to make my work clearer, more analytically rigorous, and more politically relevant. I am so thankful that I had the opportunity to learn from her. I am sure that this book is not up to her standards. I wish she were here to tell me why.

In researching and writing the dissertation I also received, and am grateful for, generous institutional support, in the form of a Social Science Research Council International Dissertation Field Research Grant, an Aspen Institute Nonprofit Sector Research Fund Award, and a United States Institute of Peace Jennings Randolph Program Peace Scholar Award. Writing the dissertation would have been much harder—and much less fun—without Yasmin Dawood, Sujatha Fernandes, Chad Flanders, Breena Holland, and Margaret Litvin.

I also wish to thank the organizations that generously hosted me while I was doing my fieldwork: MSF-France, MSF-Belgium, MSF-Holland, the International Rescue Committee, and Oxfam-GB, as well as aid workers from those organizations who allowed me to interview them. Many aid workers and NGO managers, despite having much better things to do, sat down with me and thoughtfully answered myriad questions about difficult topics, often listening patiently to my first question in labored French before responding in perfect English. Several of these organizations were also very generous in allowing me to observe meetings, join group dinners, and read through old files. Fiona Terry not only spoke with me directly and at length herself, she also helped to open doors for me at several organizations. Simon Worrall, then of the International Rescue Committee, was an insightful and generous host in northern Uganda. Watching him in action deeply informed my understanding of what it means to be an excellent aid worker.

I wrote (and re-wrote) this book during a postdoctoral fellowship in the Society of Fellows in the Liberal Arts at Princeton University and as an assistant professor at the University of Virginia. At Princeton, Mary Harper and office-mate extraordinaire Margot Canaday made three years of world-class intellectual stimulation and copious free cheese somehow seem worth it; Chuck Beitz was a wonderfully welcoming presence in the Princeton Politics Department. At UVa, my Politics department colleagues, especially Lawrie Balfour, Colin Bird, George Klosko, David Leblang, Lynn Sanders, Denise Walsh, and Stephen White, and former colleagues Chris Lebron, Melvin Rogers, and Vesla Weaver, provided a wonderfully supportive environment in which to work.

Upon my arrival at UVa, I had the good fortune to stumble into an epically fantastic writing group. For the last several years, the members of this group—Jennifer Petersen, Allison Pugh, and Denise Walsh—have provided immensely helpful feedback, professional advice, and much-needed camaraderie, as well as warnings against yelling about steak, which, I fear, I have not sufficiently heeded.

I presented portions of this book at numerous meetings of the American Political Science Association and Association for Political Theory, as well as at smaller conferences or workshops at Brown University, Fordham University, George Washington University, Harvard University, Princeton University, The Norweigan Center for Human Rights, the Prato Conference on Political Justice, University of Virginia, Washington University of St. Louis, and Wellesley College. I am very grateful to the organizers of, and participants in, those events for generous feedback. In these contexts and others, a few people provided especially extensive comments that made this book far better than it otherwise would have been. They include Michael Barnett, Jeff Flynn, Kristen Gelsdorf, Jacob Levy, Colleen Murphy, Andrew Sabl, Charles Matthews, and Alex Van Tullenken. Colin Kielty, Molly Scudder, and Claire Timperley were wonderful graduate research assistants. Colin, especially, provided help that was orders of magnitude greater than RAs typically provide; he read every chapter, most of them several times, and offered excellent substantive comments on each. The entire book is significantly better because of his input. Dominic Byatt was as supportive and patient an editor as one could hope for. Of course, none of these generous people are responsible for the book's shortcomings and errors; these remain mine alone.

Chapter 5 of this book, "The Quandary of the Second-Best," is a revised version of "The Misuse of Power, not Bad Representation: Why it is Beside the Point that No One Elected Oxfam," published in the *Journal of Political Philosophy*. I am grateful for permission to reuse this material here. Oxford University Press and I acknowledge the permission granted to reproduce the copyrighted material in this book. I made a significant effort to trace copyright holders and obtain their permission for the use of copyrighted material. I and OUP apologize for any errors or omissions; we welcome notification of any corrections that should be incorporated in future reprints or editions of this book.

In writing this book, I also received help of a more personal nature. I could not have started, let alone finished, this book without the steadfast love and support of my mom, Alice Rubenstein. While my dad, Jerry Rubenstein, is no longer with us, his love of wordplay and facility with language inspired me deeply—although perhaps not deeply enough; the reader will have to judge this for herself. I am also grateful to the rest of my family, especially my stepdad, Andy Steinbrecher, my stepmom, Eve Rubenstein, my sister, Heather Collins, and my brother-in-law, Brendan Collins, for putting up with the profoundly un-fun, sorry-I-can't-gotta-work-on-the-book version of me for way too long. My hero and grandmother, Gertrude Kleinberg (age 100), has been not only a breathtaking exemplar of fortitude and insightfulness; she has also kept me on track by continually asking whether the book is finished already. During and after a serious illness, Kathryn Korbon and Stefan Gorsch helped me to not only regain my health, but re-enter my life. Conversations with Dr. G., ostensibly about oncology, also informed my thinking about substantive themes of this book, including the role of uncertainty in decision-making, the difference between active and passive risk-taking, the power of photography, and what it means to treat people with respect in a medical setting. Kristi Morris gave me the greatest gift in the world. Almost 20 years ago, DJODA Brigitte was a generous host and a remarkable friend. While we have not been in touch for a long time, I think of her often, and with gratitude. She taught me a tremendous amount.

This book would, quite literally, not have been possible without the hundreds of millions of poor, marginalized, and disaster-affected people in the world today—both those that INGOs try to assist, and those they overlook or knowingly pass over. It would be odd to say that I am grateful to them. But this is the place to explicitly acknowledge the troubling connection between their fate and my own: if not for them—and in particular, if not for their misfortune and the active and passive injustices perpetrated against them—I would have no subject. I hope that in some small way, this book will help to undermine the prospects for a sequel.

For about the last 23 years, Pete Furia has been making me laugh, think, and notice the sun glinting on the pyrocantha. Our daughter, Zora Raye Rubenstein Furia, has been doing the first two of these things since 2012. This book is dedicated to them.

Contents

Contents

List of Figures

A medical act leaves a political trace.

—French Consul in Erbil, Iraq,
cited in Abu Sada, *In the Eyes of Others*

1

Introduction

Yes, the abuse must be stopped but by whom, with what techniques, with what unintended effects, and above all, unfolding what possible futures?

—Wendy Brown[1]

In 1994, after the Tutsi-dominated Rwandan Patriotic Front (RPF) routed the Hutu-dominated Rwandan Armed Forces (FAR) to end the Rwandan genocide, almost two million Hutus, including both civilians and "ex" members of the FAR, streamed out of Rwanda and into camps in Burundi, Tanzania, and what was then Zaire. The camps in Zaire soon became highly militarized. The putatively "ex"-FAR, seeking to regroup and rearm, stole vast quantities of aid intended for civilians; they also used the civilians in the camps to garner international sympathy, and as human shields. The international non-governmental organizations (INGOs) working in the camps, including Oxfam, CARE, and Doctors Without Borders (also known as Médecins Sans Frontières, or MSF), knew that this was happening. They therefore faced a wrenching question: Should they continue to provide water, medical care, and other services in the camps, knowing that in so doing they were enabling the "ex"-FAR to gain strength, or should they withdraw, thereby depriving legitimate refugees of needed services?[2]

This situation is just one instance of a type of ethical predicament that humanitarian INGOs regularly face: How should they respond when their well-intended and (in some ways) beneficial actions, such as providing food, water, and shelter to displaced people, are partially redeployed by third parties for what INGOs see as unjust purposes? This type of ethical predicament,

---

[1] Wendy Brown, " 'The Most We Can Hope For...': Human Rights and the Politics of Fatalism," *The South Atlantic Quarterly* 103.2 (2004): 451–63 (460).

[2] At least temporarily. Fiona Terry, *Condemned to Repeat? The Paradox of Humanitarian Action* (Ithaca and London: Cornell University Press, 2002), ch. 5. See Chapter 4 for additional discussion and citations.

in turn, is only one of several distinctive types of ethical predicaments that humanitarian INGOs regularly confront. This book is about these predicaments: situations in which basically well-meaning and competent large-scale humanitarian INGOs face extremely challenging ethical conflicts.[3] Because most large-scale "humanitarian" INGOs undertake a range of activities in addition to humanitarian aid, such as development aid and advocacy, the ethical predicaments they face range over these other activities, as well.[4]

In studying these predicaments, and in asking whether there are better and worse ways for INGOs to navigate them, this book starts from a conception of humanitarian INGOs that differs from several conceptions that are prominent in the public culture of "donor" countries such as the US.[5] In these countries, humanitarian INGOs are often portrayed as angelic good Samaritans, swashbuckling heroes, or "do-gooding machines," on the one hand, or as naïve miscreants "on the road to hell," or cold, narrowly self-interested, profit-driven corporations, on the other.[6] All of these portrayals suggest that there is little need for an account of humanitarian INGO ethics, either because humanitarian INGOs always act ethically, or because they have no interest in, or chance of, doing so.

In contrast, this book begins from a conception of large-scale, mainstream, Western-based humanitarian INGOs as organizations that do considerable good, but also have serious limitations and unintended negative effects.[7] Unlike good Samaritans, swashbuckling heroes, and do-gooding machines, they face extremely challenging ethical predicaments, but unlike naïve miscreants and coldly self-interested corporations, they wish to navigate these

---

[3] As I discuss further at the end of this chapter, this book focuses on large-scale humanitarian INGOs that are donor-funded, based in wealthy Western countries, and that provide humanitarian aid, in addition to whatever else they do.

[4] "Humanitarian" aid is typically defined as "assistance and action designed to save lives, alleviate suffering and maintain and protect human dignity during and in the aftermath of emergencies." However, "in practice it is often difficult to say where 'during and in the immediate aftermath of emergencies' ends and other types of assistance begin, especially in situations of prolonged vulnerability" (Oliver Buston and Kerry Smith, "GHA Report 2013," Development Initiatives: Global Humanitarian Assistance, 2013, 11). In contrast to humanitarian aid, development aid is "seen as sustainable, long-term and poverty-reducing" (Global Humanitarian Assistance. "GHA Report 2010." Development Initiatives, United Kingdom, 2010, 18–19 <http://www.globalhumanitarianassistance.org/wp-content/uploads/2010/07/GHA_Report8.pdf>).

[5] By "donor" countries I mean countries that are *primarily* donors rather than recipients of humanitarian aid. We should not overstate this distinction, however: even "donor" countries such as the US, France, and Japan have been recipients of international humanitarian aid, and many countries that are primarily recipients of aid also donate.

[6] Terje Tvedt, *Angels of Mercy or Development Diplomats? NGOs and Foreign Aid* (Trenton, NJ: Africa World Press, 1998); David Kennedy, *The Dark Side of Virtue: Reassessing International Humanitarianism* (Princeton: Princeton University Press, 2004); Michael Maren, *The Road to Hell: The Ravaging Effects of Foreign Aid and International Charity* (New York: Free Press, 1997).

[7] I cannot defend this picture of humanitarian INGOs explicitly here; to do so would make this a different book. However, readers who are skeptical might nonetheless find themselves persuaded of this picture based on the discussion that follows.

predicaments in an ethically sensitive way. While the underlying structure of humanitarian INGOs—in particular, the fact that they rely on voluntary donations from some to "help" others—generates very daunting ethical challenges, I conceive of humanitarian INGOs as having enough latitude or discretion that it is generally possible to identify meaningful differences among different courses of action that they could pursue. Thus, rather than render an account of humanitarian INGO ethics beside the point, the serious challenges that INGOs face—challenges that are built into their very structure as organizations—do not obviate the need for an account of humanitarian INGO ethics. On the contrary, they help explain why the need for an account of humanitarian INGO ethics is so pressing.

In explicating the ethical predicaments that INGOs face, this book engages more closely with empirical details about the world than is the norm in political theory and philosophy. But I want to emphasize at the outset that this is a work of political theory and political ethics—not anthropology, journalism, or aid worker memoir. In the chapters that follow, there is no ethnography, only a few good stories, and exactly one mention of a wild dance party.[8] Indeed, while I aim to show that important theoretical and ethical insights can be gleaned from working "closer to the ground" than is the norm in the field of political theory, I also want to persuade anthropologists, journalists, and aid practitioners that there is value in working at a somewhat higher level of abstraction than is their usual practice.

1.1 A Cartographic Approach

I focus on four main questions surrounding the ethical predicaments that humanitarian INGOs face. First, *what kind of actors are humanitarian INGOs?* Despite their significant diversity, can they be characterized as a distinctive type of actor? I argue that large-scale, Western-based, donor-funded humanitarian INGOs share three features that render them, despite their significant diversity, a distinctive type of political actor. First, these putatively "non-governmental" actors in fact engage in governance, albeit to a limited degree.[9] Humanitarian INGOs are "between Samaritans and states"

---

[8] Discussion of wild dance parties is prevalent in memoiristic and documentary accounts of life as an expatriate aid worker. See Kenneth Cain, Heidi Postlewait, and Andrew Thomson, *Emergency Sex and Other Desperate Measures: A True Story from Hell on Earth* (New York: Miramax, 2004), and Doctors without Borders, *Living in Emergency*, film by Mark Hopkins, 2008.

[9] On governance outside of the nation-state, see James N. Rosenau and Ernst Otto Czempiel, *Governance Without Government: Order and Change in World Politics* (New York: Cambridge University Press, 1992); Rodney Bruce Hall and Thomas J. Biersteker, *The Emergence of Private Authority in Global Governance* (New York: Cambridge University Press, 2002); David Held and Mathias Koenig-Archibugi (eds.), *Taming Globalization: Frontiers of Governance* (Malden,

in that they (a) engage in governance far more than the prototypical individual good Samaritan, that is the private individual who offers spontaneous assistance when she comes upon someone in need of help, but (b) also differ from full-fledged governments in important ways.

Second, although some humanitarian INGOs claim to be "neutral" or to "stay out of politics," they are, in fact, highly political. Even when they are not engaged in governance, they are political in the sense that they have effects—often unintended and negative—that are themselves political or that happen as a result of political dynamics from which humanitarian INGOs cannot extricate themselves. Humanitarian INGOs are also political in the sense that they help to shape widely shared understandings that themselves have political effects.

Third, humanitarian INGOs are often "second-best" actors, in the sense that they undertake activities, including but not only governance activities, that other actors could potentially perform better. The account of humanitarian INGO ethics offered in this book is to a large extent an elucidation of the ethical predicaments that humanitarian INGOs face as a result of having these three features—that is, of being somewhat governmental, highly political, and often second-best. It is because humanitarian INGOs are somewhat governmental and highly political that the account of humanitarian INGO ethics offered here is an account of humanitarian INGO *political* ethics.

As somewhat governmental, highly political, and often second-best actors, *what types of ethical predicaments do humanitarian INGOs regularly face?* This is the second main question addressed in this book. I argue that humanitarian INGOs regularly face at least four important types of predicaments: the *problem of spattered hands, the quandary of the second-best, the cost-effectiveness conundrum*, and *the moral motivation tradeoff.* I describe these predicaments in detail below. The important point for now is that this book offers a "map" of these predicaments: just as a topographic map of a terrain shows the mountains, deserts, and rivers that travelers crossing that terrain must navigate, my map of the ethical predicaments that humanitarian INGOs face highlights the various ethical responsibilities and practical constraints that they must navigate. Maps can help travelers decide what route to take, but they do not replace travelers' own judgment. The same holds for the map offered here: it offers conceptual descriptions with normative implications, but it is not narrowly prescriptive.

Is it possible to identify better and worse "routes" for INGOs to take in navigating this terrain? That is, *are there better and worse ways for them to respond to the ethical predicaments they face?* This is the third question addressed in this

MA: Polity Press, 2003); Thomas Risse (ed.), *Governance Without a State? Policies and Politics in Areas of Limited Statehood* (New York: Columbia University Press, 2013).

book. I argue that there are some general (and specific) things that we can say about better and worse strategies for INGOs to take in navigating particular kinds of ethical predicaments. Moreover, as just noted, some ways of conceptualizing these predicaments bring the normative differences among different strategies into view better than others. However, most "routes" require at least some moral sacrifice or compromise. That is, the question that INGOs face is generally not "how can we avoid all moral compromise?" but rather "*which* moral compromises should we reject, and which should we grudgingly accept?"

The normative standards that I bring to bear in answering this question are democratic, egalitarian, humanitarian, and justice-based norms. Because these norms are very abstract, asking how INGOs might navigate the predicaments they face consistently with these norms amounts to asking three more specific questions: Which norms are relevant to a given INGO activity? How should those norms be interpreted and specified for the context of that activity? How do relevant specifications of relevant norms support or conflict with each other?

In very broad terms, I argue that for humanitarian INGOs,[10] navigating the ethical predicaments they face in a way that is as consistent as possible with relevant specifications of democratic, egalitarian, humanitarian, and justice-based norms requires putting significant weight on the overall consequences of their activities.[11] Sometimes this means following "rules of thumb" that capture what the best consequences are likely to be; sometimes it means making more context-specific practical judgments with an eye toward their likely consequences. Engaging in these forms of judgment, in turn, requires developing the sensibilities, orientations, and capacities necessary to do so.

This argument diverges dramatically from several important alternatives. One is the view, seemingly widely held in donor countries (and consistent

---

[10] Philosophers sometimes distinguish between "standards of rightness" that are used by third parties to evaluate what some actor is doing and "decision procedures" that are used, or that motivate, the actor herself. Some approaches to decision-making, such as utilitarianism, are sometimes said to function better as standards of rightness than as decision procedures. One might therefore ask whether I am interested in standards of rightness or decision procedures for evaluating how INGOs navigate the ethical predicaments they face. The answer is that I am interested in both. There are significant drawbacks, in the form of reduced transparency and accountability, if one adopts an approach to decision-making that functions well as a standard of rightness for external evaluation by third parties but that cannot also be used as a decision procedure by the actors involved. As the invocation of democratic norms suggests, I am interested in how INGOs can conceptualize and navigate the ethical predicaments they face so as to facilitate open discussion and debate among INGOs and their various interlocutors.

[11] Within the context of constraints imposed by ordinary moral norms. While INGOs sometimes face very extreme situations in which, for example, lying and causing harm are plausible responses, here I just mean to suggest a focus on consequences, not a narrow utilitarianism that allows all violations of moral norms so long as overall utility is maximized. For a broad philosophical defense of "rule-consequentialism," see Brad Hooker, *Ideal Code, Real World* (New York: Oxford University Press, 2000).

with the perception of INGOs as good Samaritans and heroes mentioned above), that what matters about INGOs are their intentions. On this view, INGOs' intentions are both intrinsically important and evidence that their actions will have good consequences; that is, INGOs' good intentions are assumed to yield good outcomes. Another alternative to the argument presented here is the view, endorsed by some aid practitioners, that INGOs' actions are intrinsically valuable, apart from their effects. While such actions presumably must be motivated by good intentions, it is the action itself that matters. As one aid worker put it, "I do not care if we can or cannot know that humanitarianism has improved the lives of others in need. I know that I must act."[12] This view is often connected to the concept of the "humanitarian imperative," or the idea that there is an "obligation to provide humanitarian aid wherever it is needed."[13]

While I argue that the overall consequences of INGOs' acts and omissions are of paramount importance, compared to their intentions and the intrinsic value of their activities, I diverge from "political humanitarians" who think that humanitarian aid should always be leveraged in the service of broader political aims, such as women's rights or democracy.[14] Not only are such efforts often self-undermining in even consequentialist terms, they are not sufficiently pluralistic about sources of value. I also diverge from philosophical proponents of "Effective Altruism," who suggest that INGOs should maximize good outcomes by undertaking activities the effects of which can be measured accurately and cheaply.[15] Among other things, this approach can lead to an overly narrow focus on technical interventions rather than political activity (the effects of which are difficult to measure).

Instead, I argue, INGOs should focus on consequences, but interpret consequences expansively, to include even those that are difficult or impossible to measure or commensurate precisely; in other words, INGOs should

---

[12] Cited in Michael N. Barnett, *Empire of Humanity: A History of Humanitarianism* (Ithaca, NY: Cornell University Press, 2011), 238.

[13] International Committee of the Red Cross, *Red Cross Code*. As I discuss in later chapters, the concept of the humanitarian imperative is ambiguous. The full text of the Code demonstrates this, with its slippage among the right to receive aid, the right to offer it, the duty to offer it, and the need for "unimpeded access" to aid recipients.

[14] Hugo Slim, "Claiming a Humanitarian Imperative: NGOs and the Cultivation of Humanitarian Duty," *Refugee Survey Quarterly* 21.3 (2002): 113–25.

[15] See the Effective Altruism website <http://effectivealtruism.org/>; Toby Ord, *Moral Imperative toward Cost-effectiveness in Global Health* (Washington: Center for Global Development, 2013) <http://www.cgdev.org/content/publications/detail/1427016>. See also the website of Giving What We Can <givingwhatwecan.org> and Givewell <www.givewell.org>. Ord and MacAskill, two founders of the Effective Altruism movement, are quite aware of and concerned about what they term "measurement bias" (personal communication, April 2014). However, they nonetheless are focusing for now on activities the outcomes of which can be measured accurately and cheaply. Givewell also appears to be somewhat attentive to this concern; it endorses some charities that are riskier because they work with governments but have the potential to do a great deal of good.

acknowledge that the tension between what is valuable and what is measurable is a constitutive challenge of humanitarian action. Thus, while the aforementioned four norms can be seen as intrinsically valuable or valuable because of their effects, I argue that they should be specified for humanitarian INGOs in ways that emphasize their effects, broadly construed. So for example, democratic norms are valuable because of their effects, but these effects include enhancing individuals' self-respect.[16]

The fourth main question addressed in this book is: *How does close study of humanitarian INGO political ethics broaden our understanding of democratic, humanitarian, egalitarian, and justice-based norms?* As I noted above, the question of how INGOs should navigate the ethical predicaments they face is in part a question about how to specify these norms for the context of humanitarian INGOs. This effort at specification, in turn, can enrich our understanding of these norms themselves. For example, I will argue that because of the deep structural inequalities that characterize INGOs' relationships with domestic NGOs in aid-recipient countries, "partnership" is often a poor specification of egalitarian norms in the context of humanitarian INGOs; likewise, because INGOs are second-best actors, "excellent representation of poor and marginalized people" is often a poor specification of democratic norms. Seeing the conditions under which partnership is not an appropriate instantiation of equality and good representation is not an appropriate specification of democratic norms deepens our understanding of egalitarian and democratic norms more generally.

In taking up these four questions, I aim to address themes of interest to academics and aid practitioners; I also hope to address concerns raised by at least some aid recipients. Summarizing a multi-year study of perceptions of humanitarian action in twelve aid-recipient countries, Antonio Donini et al. write that there is widespread acceptance of humanitarian action in principle, but when it comes to humanitarian practice:

> The nuances are different but the message is the same: the provision of aid is a top-down, externally driven, and relatively rigid process that allows little space for local participation beyond formalistic consultation. Much of what happens escapes local scrutiny and control. The system is viewed as inflexible, arrogant, and culturally insensitive.[17]

---

[16] For clarity, I begin with the question of what kind of actors humanitarian INGOs are. However, the question of what ethical predicaments humanitarian INGOs face, and how they do and should navigate those predicaments, is to an extent epistemically prior to the question of what kinds of actors they are: it is in part by studying the predicaments they face that we learn about INGOs as actors.

[17] Antonio Donini, Larissa Fast, Greg Hansen, Simon Harris, Larry Minear, Tasneem Mowjee, and Andrew Wilder. "Humanitarian Agenda 2015: Final Report: The State of the Humanitarian Enterprise," Feinstein International Center, 2008, 11. The countries studied were Afghanistan, Burundi, Colombia, the Democratic Republic of Congo, Iraq, Liberia, Nepal, Uganda, the occupied Palestinian territory, Pakistan, Sri Lanka, and the Sudan. The exceptions cited in the

Donini et al.'s findings suggest that whether and how INGOs can effectively provide humanitarian aid in a way that treats aid recipients as moral equals is an important and relevant question for many aid recipients.

1.2 A Map of Humanitarian INGO Political Ethics

As I noted above, humanitarian INGOs have three main features that make them a distinctive type of actor and help to shape the distinctive ethical predicaments they face. First, humanitarian INGOs engage in governance, albeit to a limited degree. While "governance" is a broad term, I focus on two forms of governance in particular: conventional governance and global governance.

Humanitarian INGOs regularly serve governance functions roughly analogous to those served by conventional domestic governments.[18] These include being the sole or almost sole providers of basic goods and services to millions of people—sometimes the entire population of a given geographic area—shaping the rules of coercive institutions, and making large-scale decisions about resource use that have public effects. For example, in the Rwandan refugee camps in Zaire described at the outset of this chapter, Oxfam was the primary source of clean water for tens of thousands of people. As Cohen, Küpçü, and Khanna write, with only some exaggeration:

> This armada of nonstate actors [a "hodgepodge of international charities, aid agencies, philanthropists, and foreign advisors"] has become a powerful global force, replacing traditional donors' and governments' influence in poverty-stricken, war-torn world capitals. And as a measure of that influence, they are increasingly taking over key state functions, providing for the health, welfare, and safety of citizens.[19]

In addition to engaging in conventional domestic governance activities, humanitarian INGOs also engage in global governance. They do this in two main ways: by *causally* influencing other international and supranational institutions, such as the World Bank, and by helping to *constitute* the

report are Maoists in Nepal (who viewed humanitarian aid as "imperialistic") and the Taliban (although as of 2008 even the Taliban had come to accept the ICRC).

[18] See Chapter 3 for full discussion. Humanitarian INGOs spent at least $8.6 billion in 2011 on humanitarian aid alone, although this is likely to be a severe underestimate. See Velina Stoianova, *Private Funding: An Emerging Trend in Humanitarian Donorship* (Wells, UK: Global Humanitarian Assistance, 2012), 7.

[19] Michael A. Cohen, Maria Figueroa Küpçü, and Parag Khanna, "The New Colonialists," *Foreign Policy*, June 16, 2008 <http://www.foreignpolicy.com/articles/2008/06/16/the_new_colonialists>.

"international humanitarian order," which can itself be seen as a global governance institution.[20]

Even when they are not engaged in conventional or global governance, humanitarian INGOs are highly political. "Political" is an even broader term than "governmental," but again I mean it in two very specific ways (without denying that INGOs can also be political in other ways). First, despite the claims of many INGOs to be "neutral" or to "stay out of politics"—and despite their, in many cases, sincere efforts to do so—they have a wide range of effects, often negative and unintended, that are political themselves or that occur through political processes. For example, by providing resources that were then stolen by soldiers, the INGOs in the Rwandan camps in Zaire helped to empower the "ex"-FAR. Another way in which humanitarian INGOs are political is that they frequently exercise what I call "discursive power," or the power to help shape shared meanings. For example, the humanitarian INGOs working in the Rwandan camps in Zaire helped—in some cases intentionally, in others inadvertently—to create the impression, among donor country publics, that the individuals in the camps were all innocent victims of a cholera epidemic, rather than a mix of legitimate refugees and facilitators or perpetrators of genocide suffering in large measure as a result of the failure of foreign governments to stop the genocide.[21]

Finally, humanitarian INGOs are often second-best actors.[22] That is, they not only govern less than conventional governments and other global governance institutions as a descriptive matter, they also often govern, and perform other activities, *less well* than other actors as a normative matter. More precisely, even if humanitarian INGOs perform some functions better than other actors in the short term, they have less potential to perform these functions better in the medium and long term. There are various reasons for this. When it comes to conventional and global governance activities, INGOs are often second-best actors because of features that distinguish them from well-functioning democratic governments: they are not authorized by, or accountable to, the people most significantly affected by their actions; they cannot impose taxes; they do not have a monopoly on the legitimate use of force; and they are poor "mirrors" or descriptive representatives of people directly affected by their actions.

In some cases, humanitarian INGOs are *not* second-best actors, but instead what we might call actors of last resort: however poor their performance in

---

[20] Michael N. Barnett, "Humanitarian Governance," *Annual Review of Political Science* 16.1 (2013): 379–98. See also Jennifer C. Rubenstein, "Humanitarian NGOs' Duties of Justice," *Journal of Social Philosophy* 40.4 (2009): 524–41.

[21] Terry, *Condemned to Repeat?*, 171 and 193.

[22] By "second-best" I mean worse than first-best, not necessarily second- as opposed to third- or seventh-best. See Chapter 3 for further discussion.

absolute terms, there is no other actor waiting in the wings, willing and able to do what they are doing better than, or as well as, them. This appears to have been the case for the INGOs in the Rwandan refugee camps in Zaire, and helps to explain why their decision about whether or not to withdraw was so wrenching.

These features of humanitarian INGOs—that they are somewhat governmental (in both a conventional and global governance sense), highly political (in their unintended negative effects and due to their exercise of discursive power), and often second-best (although sometimes actors of last resort)—each generate particular ethical responsibilities for INGOs. These responsibilities, in turn, pull humanitarian INGOs in different and sometimes conflicting directions. It is the divergent demands of these different responsibilities, coming together in different configurations, that generate the four distinctive types of ethical predicaments that humanitarian INGOs regularly face—that is, the four treacherous terrains they must navigate: the problem of spattered hands, the quandary of the second-best, the cost-effectiveness conundrum, and the moral motivation tradeoff.

1.3 Four Ethical Predicaments

When humanitarian INGOs provide basic services to a population, knowing that the resources that they provide, or even their very presence, are being used by other actors for unjust purposes—as was the case for the INGOs in the Rwandan camps in Zaire—those INGOs face what I call the *problem of spattered hands*. While this ethical predicament can arise in a range of contexts, it arises most persistently and is best documented in the context of basic service provision by INGOs during or after violent group conflict.

As the term suggests, the problem of spattered hands is a cousin of the problem of "dirty hands," as described by moral and political theorists such as Michael Walzer.[23] According to Walzer, the problem of dirty hands arises when a "particular act of government . . . may be exactly the right thing to do in utilitarian terms and yet leave the man who does it guilty of a moral wrong."[24] (Walzer's main example is torturing a terror suspect to find a ticking bomb.) One might think that INGOs face precisely this problem: if staying in the camps was justified on utilitarian grounds, but

---

[23] Michael Walzer, "Political Action: The Problem of Dirty Hands," *Philosophy & Public Affairs* 2.2 (Winter, 1973): 160–80 (161); Michael Walzer, "Emergency Ethics," in *Arguing about War* (New Haven: Yale University Press, 2004), 33–50. See also C. A. J. Coady, "The Problem of Dirty Hands", *The Stanford Encyclopedia of Philosophy* (Spring 2014 edition), Edward N. Zalta (ed.), <http://plato.stanford.edu/archives/spr2014/entries/dirty-hands/>.

[24] Walzer, "The Problem of Dirty Hands," 161.

the INGOs that stayed contributed to injustices perpetrated primarily by others, then they were both doing what was right in utilitarian terms and guilty of a moral wrong. I argue, however, that the problem of spattered hands differs in subtle but crucial ways from the problem of dirty hands. While Walzer emphasizes a moral conflict between role-based utilitarianism and abiding by moral principles, humanitarian INGOs face a conflict between avoiding two injustices: contributing to violence and intimidation perpetrated by others, and "pulling the rug" out from under innocent civilians by depriving them of basic services on which they have reasonably come to rely. For this and other reasons, we get a distorted view of predicaments such as that faced by the INGOs in the Rwandan camps in Zaire if we view these predicaments as instances of dirty hands. Ironically, while Walzer is sometimes accused of being too accommodating of violations of moral principles in the name of overall utility (or more precisely, the survival of a particular nation or community), viewing the situation faced by humanitarian INGOs in the Rwandan camps as a case of dirty hands rather than spattered hands is likely to push them too far in the other direction, toward putting too much emphasis on their own moral purity. While INGOs rarely even have the opportunity to get their hands dirty, much less a justification for doing so, they sometimes have good reason to *allow their hands to be spattered*.

For the INGOs in the Rwandan camps in Zaire, one conceivable route out of their predicament was to band together and demand concessions from the "ex"-FAR.[25] More generally, an important challenge that arises in the context of spattered hands problems, as well as several other ethical predicaments that INGOs face, is that what any given INGO should do sometimes depends on what other INGOs (or other humanitarian actors) are doing. Yet for reasons including different philosophies, competition for funding, and the difficulty of sanctioning humanitarian actors that refuse to cooperate, coordination and collective action problems are an important feature of humanitarian INGOs' ethical terrain.[26]

The humanitarian INGOs in the Rwandan camps in Zaire were not second-best actors in any practically relevant sense: while other INGOs could have stepped in to provide the resources or services that they were providing, there would have been a significant delay. These other INGOs would most likely have been less adept than the INGOs they were replacing, and they would have contributed to injustice in the same

---

[25] While at one point fifteen INGOs did band together and threaten to leave the camps, this was only a limited effort at collective action and yielded only a moderate improvement in the situation. Terry, *Condemned to Repeat?*, 177 and 189.

[26] Garrett Cullity, "Compromised Humanitarianism," in *Ethical Questions and International NGOs*, ed. Keith Horton and Chris Roche (Dordrecht: Springer, 2010), 157–73.

way as the INGOs that withdrew. In many contexts, however, INGOs *are* second-best actors. In these cases, they face a very different type of ethical predicament.

For example, the INGOs Global Witness and the Enough Project played a major role in passing and implementing the Conflict Minerals Provision (Section 1502) of the Dodd-Frank bill in the US.[27] They helped to write the text of the bill, and shaped the lineup of speakers in a roundtable about how to implement it. The bill was intended to help reduce conflict in the Democratic Republic of Congo by regulating the flow of minerals from conflict-ridden areas. However, many Congolese and US-based experts and activists argued that the bill would not accomplish this goal and would have other deleterious effects. This outcome appears to have largely come to pass.

How should advocacy by Global Witness and Enough be normatively evaluated? Democratic theorists have suggested that INGO advocates such as Global Witness and Enough should be evaluated based on how well they "represent" poor and marginalized groups. This conceptualization of INGO advocates as "non-elected representatives" suggests that they should represent as well as possible. However, not only do these INGOs not claim to represent anyone, but the idea that they should be excellent representatives overlooks their status as second-best actors, and the corresponding possibility that, rather than represent as well as possible, they should instead step back and make way for other, "first-best" representatives. In other words, the representation lens overlooks the *quandary of the second-best* that INGOs regularly face: to what extent should they engage in some activity, such as advocacy, themselves, and to what extent should they step back and make way for other, "first-best" actors, such as Congolese NGOs?

I argue that rather than hold INGO advocates to the normative standard of "democratic representative" or "equal partner" (the standard that some INGOs prefer), we should instead conceptualize INGO advocacy as the exercise of power, and hold INGOs to the normative standard of *not misusing their power*. This enables us to describe the over-reaching of Enough and Global Witness in more perspicacious terms, as one of displacing other actors from the debate, not failing to represent as well as possible themselves. Just as we mischaracterize the situation faced by the INGOs in the Rwandan camps in Zaire if we view their predicament as a problem of dirty hands, we mischaracterize the issue raised by Enough and Global Witness by describing it as a matter of poor representation or unequal partnership.

---

[27] See Chapter 5 for citations and a fuller discussion.

In order to provide basic services in conflict settings, engage in advocacy, or undertake any other activity, humanitarian INGOs must make large-scale decisions about how to use their limited resources. This generates yet another type of ethical predicament, which I call the *cost-effectiveness conundrum.*

For example, in 2000, the town of Gulu, in northwest Uganda, was struck by an Ebola epidemic.[28] Médecins Sans Frontières, one of the few organizations providing health care in the area, decided to divert resources away from a basic health care program it was running in order to address the epidemic. One aid worker defended this decision on the grounds that "[a]lleviation of suffering, and dying in dignity was enormously important. *We know we saved very few lives.*"[29] But another asked, "[h]ow would you explain to a villager from the outskirts of Gulu the choice MSF made in addressing the problem of Ebola but not the health problems in his village?"[30]

In deciding whether to treat the Ebola victims, MSF confronted the cost-effectiveness conundrum: in their large-scale decisions about resource use, how much weight, if any, should INGOs place on doing as much good as possible (which, under conditions of limited resources, requires putting considerable weight on considerations of cost-effectiveness), and how much weight should they put on other considerations, such as prioritizing the worst-off, prioritizing victims of intentional brutality, or continuing to assist current aid recipients? According to traditional humanitarian principles, humanitarian INGOs should pay little or no attention to issues of cost-effectiveness; they should instead provide humanitarian aid based on "need alone." MSF goes further. It endorses an "ethics of refusal" which takes a principled stand against the logic of cost-effectiveness by providing a high level of medical care, even if only to a few people. Against both of these views, some political and moral philosophers, such as proponents of Effective Altruism, argue that INGOs should seek to maximally alleviate morally important harm, which requires putting considerable weight on considerations of cost-effectiveness.

Which of these approaches is most consistent with democratic, egalitarian, humanitarian, and justice-based norms? I argue that the need principle is implausible if interpreted narrowly, and impossibly vague if interpreted loosely. The ethics of refusal and the harm minimization principle are more promising, but still have serious limitations: the ethics of refusal replaces political judgment with political reflex, while the harm minimization

---

[28] Nathan Ford and Richard Bedell (eds.), *Justice and MSF Operational Choices* (Amsterdam: MSF, 2002). The rest of my account draws on this source. See also Peter Redfield, "Vital Mobility and the Humanitarian Kit," in *Biosecurity Interventions: Global Health and Security in Question*, ed. Andrew Lakoff and Stephen J. Collier (New York: Columbia University Press, 2008), 147–71.

[29] Ford and Bedell (eds.), *Justice and MSF Operational Choices*, 26, my italics.

[30] Ford and Bedell (eds.), *Justice and MSF Operational Choices*, 26.

principle replaces political judgment with technical judgment. Yet because INGOs making large-scale decisions about resource use engage in conventional governance and global governance, exercise discursive power, and are second-best actors, making these decisions well requires a form of political judgment that I call the *ethics of resistance.*

Finally, for INGOs to make large-scale decisions about resource use, they must have resources to use. In order for them to have resources to use, they must raise funds. This creates yet another distinctive ethical predicament for INGOs, one involving the activity of creating and disseminating visual images of famine and severe poverty to raise funds. For example, in 2003, the INGO Save the Children helped organize a publicity shoot for the Irish rock musician Bob Geldof during his visit to a therapeutic feeding center in Ethiopia.[31] The result was a front-page photograph in the British newspaper the *Daily Mirror* (see Fig. 7.1). While the publication of this photograph was very effective in raising funds for Save the Children, it was so stereotypical in its portrayal of Geldof as a white savior rescuing an African child that Save the Children refused to use it in its own materials. However, publishing the photograph in a newspaper with wide circulation was arguably *more* detrimental, in terms of its effects on perceptions of "Africa" among the British public, than using it in an INGO fundraising brochure.

Save the Children thus faced a conflict between raising funds and not using what are widely seen as morally objectionable images. This conflict is frequently described, including by some INGOs, as a "dilemma" of "need versus dignity." However, this standard description, part of a broader set of four assumptions that I refer to together as the "standard view," fails to grapple with several crucial features of INGOs' portrayal-related practices, including the diversity of the "bads" associated with these practices. The standard view therefore papers over differences among several ethical predicaments that humanitarian INGOs face, which I argue are better conceived of as versions of a *moral motivation tradeoff.* Viewing INGOs' portrayal-related practices from the perspective of this tradeoff is also suggestive of several strategies for reducing, albeit not eliminating, it—including what I call *critical visual rhetoric.*

While the problem of spattered hands, the quandary of the second-best, the cost-effectiveness conundrum, and the moral motivation tradeoff are not the only ethical predicaments that humanitarian INGOs regularly face, I focus on them because they significantly affect the basic interests of many people. They are also not adequately discussed in the existing

---

[31] See Chapter 7 for citations and a full discussion.

literature about INGOs: this literature offers examples of these predicaments, but it does not adequately characterize or analyze the predicaments themselves. In addition, studying these predicaments broadens and deepens our understanding of democratic, egalitarian, justice-based, and humanitarian norms. In particular, it expands our understanding of what it means—and whether it is even possible—for putatively non-governmental actors to abide by these norms when they undertake governance activities.

1.4 Eight Extant Alternatives

This book is, as far as I know, the first book-length, English-language account of humanitarian INGO political ethics. Yet it is not the first or only effort to conceptualize humanitarian INGOs with an eye toward their political role and ethical responsibilities. To the contrary, at least eight existing "maps" are prominent, seemingly plausible, or both. Of these eight maps, three are conceptions of INGOs' social role: that INGOs are, and/or should be, *rescuers* of the poor and disaster-affected people they seek to assist, *equal partners* with domestic NGOs based in the countries where they work, and *agents for their donors*. Two additional conceptions are not quite structured or substantive enough to be roles, but nonetheless focus on INGOs' responsibilities to poor and marginalized people: the views that INGOs are or should be *agents for their intended beneficiaries* and the idea that they should be *accountable to their intended beneficiaries*.[32] The sixth conception is the idea that *traditional principles of classical humanitarianism* such as "humanity" and "impartiality" offer a sufficient basis for an account of humanitarian INGO political ethics. Finally, some critics of INGOs suggest that developing an account of humanitarian INGO political ethics is beside the point, because INGOs are no better than *multinational corporations* and/or are *neo-colonial*.

All eight of these extant alternative approaches offer helpful insights that an adequate account of humanitarian INGO political ethics should incorporate. However, individually and together, they fail to either (a) offer an adequate account of humanitarian INGO political ethics, or (b) make a persuasive case that such an account is beside the point.

---

[32] Some commentators object to the term "beneficiaries" because it reduces the people INGOs aim to assist to their role as recipients and assumes that they do indeed benefit from aid. I think that the term "*intended* beneficiaries" avoids both of these problems, because while it identifies what is salient about people in a given context (that an INGO wishes to assist them), it does not assume that the INGO succeeded in doing so.

1.5 Democratic, Egalitarian, Humanitarian, and Justice-Based Norms

As I noted above, one aim of this book is to explore what it looks like for humanitarian INGOs to navigate the predicaments they face in ways that are as consistent as possible (or consistent enough) with democratic, egalitarian, humanitarian, and justice-based norms. By a "norm," I mean an abstract idea with normative content. A single norm can therefore be interpreted or specified in several different ways. Thus, not only can democratic, egalitarian, humanitarian, and justice-based norms conflict with each other, but different interpretations of the same norm can also come into practical conflict with each other. There is also some overlap among these norms.

While I wish to leave them as open as possible at the outset, by "democratic" norms I mean ideas related to self-rule and people having a say in decisions that significantly affect them; by "egalitarian" norms I mean norms connected to different forms of equality (of treatment, resources, status, etc.); by "humanitarian" norms I mean ideas connected to the value and dignity of every human life and the urgency of protecting individual human lives;[33] by "justice-based" norms, I mean ideas about what is fair or fitting, and treating people with dignity.

I focus on these four norms, in particular, because they are implicitly or explicitly endorsed by many humanitarian INGOs.[34] Asking what it looks like for these INGOs to act consistently with these norms therefore functions as a kind of immanent or internal critique, in which we hold INGOs to standards that they endorse for themselves. Importantly, though, not all humanitarian INGOs embrace all of these norms. For example, humanitarian INGOs that do not conceive of themselves as political actors often eschew, or claim to eschew, justice-based norms.

Insofar as particular INGOs reject particular norms, those norms function as the basis for an external critique, of interest to anyone who does care about those norms. However, one aim of this book is to show that, while they are not all relevant to every activity that INGOs undertake or every ethical predicament they face, these four norms are widely relevant to INGOs. In particular, I will argue that, because INGOs are somewhat governmental and highly political, justice-based norms are relevant to them.

Part of why these norms are more relevant to INGOs than they might initially appear to be is that, in asking what it would look like for INGOs

---

[33] Humanitarian norms are thus broader than the traditional principles of classical humanitarianism, discussed below and in Chapter 2.
[34] This sets them apart from other possible bases for evaluating INGOs, such as freedom or solidarity.

to "act consistently with" any of the foregoing norms, I mean not only *promoting* these norms in the world, but also, or alternatively, *enacting* them in their own activities. For example, many humanitarian INGOs want no part of "democracy promotion" in Iraq (or elsewhere) because, among other reasons, they feel that it compromises their ability to provide humanitarian aid. However, this is an entirely different issue from whether these INGOs do, or should, "enact" democratic norms in their own activities, for example by being transparent and consulting with the Iraqi people about their programs in Iraq.[35] Likewise, some humanitarian INGOs embrace neutrality and claim not to "do" justice, by which they mean that they do not promote political justice. But they still have a *prima facie* duty to not be unjust themselves, contribute to injustice perpetrated primarily by others, or "pull the rug out from under" aid recipients who rely on them for services. Likewise, INGOs can promote equality in a society, or they can enact equality by treating others equally in day-to-day encounters. I am not suggesting that enacting these norms is always a more relevant interpretation than promoting them, or vice versa; my point is only that both are possible, and that in claiming that these norms are highly relevant to humanitarian INGOs, I have both promoting and enacting in mind.

Democratic, egalitarian, humanitarian, and justice-based norms also provide a basis for engaging with criticisms of INGOs made by aid recipients. On the one hand, aid recipients' criticisms of INGOs can help to reveal that, or how, particular norms are relevant to INGOs. For example, aid recipients frequently state that INGOs' motivations, objectives, affiliations, and funding sources are very difficult to discern; they are mysterious outside forces. This criticism helps to drive home the relevance of democratic norms of publicity and transparency for INGOs. On the other hand, the foregoing four norms also help to identify conditions under which INGOs might be justified in rejecting, or indeed might be morally required to reject, the wishes of aid recipients, for example if their wishes violated widely accepted interpretations of those norms, such as non-discrimination based on ethnicity or race.

1.6 Contributions to Existing Literatures

In addressing the four questions articulated at the outset of this chapter, this book contributes to broader literatures on governance, the individual duty to help alleviate distant suffering, and political ethics.

---

[35] Enacting a norm can be a way of promoting it; for example, some argue that the US can best promote democracy by enacting it. However, enacting a norm can also diverge from promoting it, as when a pacifist refuses to take up arms to promote peace.

The idea that "non-governmental organizations govern" is not new.[36] However, the aspects of this idea relevant to the argument of this book have remained surprisingly under-developed. The literature on non-governmental humanitarian organizations governing—so-called "humanitarian govern-ance"—recognizes that humanitarian INGOs engage in global governance and "Foucauldian governance."[37] However, there has been surprisingly little acknowledgment that international organizations in general, and humani-tarian INGOs in particular, engage in what I am calling conventional govern-ance.[38] Yet humanitarian INGOs sometimes *do* engage in activities that can be fairly characterized as forms of conventional governance, and this turns out to be crucial for understanding the ethical and political terrain that they occupy.[39]

In addition to saying little about conventional governance, the exist-ing literature on non-state governance has also said surprisingly little about ethics. In particular, it has focused more on identifying institu-tional mechanisms for constraining the power of non-state actors that engage in governance than on elucidating the ethical predicaments these actors face, or considering how they should navigate those predicaments. Indeed, INGOs are sometimes treated not as global governance actors in their own right, but rather as tools for constraining other global govern-ance actors.[40] Thus, one broader aim of this book is to move beyond the insight that "non-governmental organizations govern," to disentangle the several different types of governance and related forms of power that

---

[36] James Bohman, "International Regimes and Democratic Governance: Political Equality and Influence in Global Institutions," *International Affairs* 75.3 (July 1, 1999): 499–513; William E. Scheuerman, "Global Governance Without Global Government? Habermas on Postnational Democracy," *Political Theory* 36.1 (2008): 133–51; Ole Jacob Sending and Iver B. Neumann. "Governance to Governmentality: Analyzing NGOs, States, and Power," *International Studies Quarterly* 50.3 (2006): 651–72; Thomas Risse, "Global Governance and Communicative Action," *Government and Opposition* 39.2 (2004): 288–313; Held and Koenig-Archibugi, *Taming Globalization*.

[37] Michael Merlingen, "Governmentality: Towards a Foucauldian Framework for the Study of IGOs," *Cooperation and Conflict* 38.4 (2003): 361–84; Sending and Neuman, "Governance to Governmentality: NGOs, States, and Power"; Mark Duffield, *Development, Security and Unending War: Governing the World of Peoples* (Cambridge: Polity Press, 2007). I have not used the analytic lens of Foucauldian governance here, in part because there has already been a lot of work in this vein, and in part because my previous attempts to do so have seemed to generate conversations that were more about Foucault than humanitarian INGOs.

[38] See previous footnotes and discussion and citations in Barnett, "Humanitarian Governance."

[39] Acknowledging that humanitarian INGOs engage in conventional governance is not only useful for developing an account of humanitarian INGO political ethics; it also highlights conti-nuities between debates about service provision by international NGOs and the privatization of service provision at the domestic level in donor countries (e.g. homeless shelters run by religious organizations).

[40] Allen Buchanan and Robert O. Keohane, "The Legitimacy of Global Governance Institutions," *Ethics & International Affairs* 20.4 (2006): 405–37; Michael Edwards, "'Does the Doormat Influence the Boot?': Critical Thoughts on UK NGOs and International Advocacy," *Development in Practice* 3.3 (1993): 163–75, conceptualizes them in both ways.

humanitarian INGOs exercise, and examine their political and ethical implications.

In addition to the literature on governance, there is also a vast literature in political and moral philosophy about what duties, if any, individuals have to help alleviate distant poverty and suffering.[41] With some exceptions, this literature—especially work written in the 1960s–1980s—adopted a conception of humanitarian INGOs as what I have called "do-gooding" machines: entities that automatically transform individuals' donations into good outcomes.[42] In this literature, "donate to Oxfam" is taken to be a kind of shorthand for "do good" or "rescue." The main question is, How much rescue effort are relatively well-off individuals obliged to undertake by donating to INGOs?, not What are the implications of the political and ethical complexities faced by INGOs for their donors? Given the focus on the former question, INGOs' negative or uncertain effects are seen as *releasing* individuals from the duty to donate, not *altering the content* of this duty.

Alongside the literature in moral philosophy that conceives of INGOs primarily as do-gooding machines, there is also a large literature by anthropologists, critical theorists, journalists, and aid workers that is very harshly critical of humanitarian INGOs. Far from treating INGOs as do-gooding machines, these authors argue that INGOs have serious negative effects, or even do more harm than good.[43] Like theorists of the

---

[41] The classic texts here are Peter Singer, "Famine, Affluence, and Morality," *Philosophy & Public Affairs* 1.3 (1972): 229–43; Peter K. Unger, *Living High and Letting Die: Our Illusion of Innocence* (New York: Oxford University Press, 1996); and Onora O'Neill, "Lifeboat Earth," in *International Ethics*, ed. Charles Beitz, Marshall Cohen, Thomas Scanlon, and John Simmons (Princeton: Princeton University Press, 1985), 262–81. More recent contributions include Richard W. Miller, *Globalizing Justice: The Ethics of Poverty and Power* (New York: Oxford University Press, 2010); Thomas Pogge, *Politics as Usual* (Cambridge: Polity Press, 2010); Thomas Pogge, *World Poverty and Human Rights*, 2nd edn. (Cambridge: Polity Press, 2008); Peter Singer, *The Life You Can Save: Acting Now to End World Poverty* (New York: Random House, 2009); and Deen K. Chatterjee, *The Ethics of Assistance: Morality and the Distant Needy* (New York: Cambridge University Press, 2004).

[42] For example, consider what the philosopher J. L. Lucas dubbed the "Oxfam Argument": the idea that "when there are people who are hungry or naked or in need of medical attention, it seems wrong to devote available resources to providing the very rich with pink champagne or for that matter the fairly prosperous artisans of our own country with a second colour TV," when one could instead donate the money to Oxfam. J. R. Lucas, "Against Equality Again," *Philosophy* 52.201 (1977): 255–80 (262).

[43] For example, Maren, *Road to Hell*; David Rieff, *A Bed for the Night: Humanitarianism in Crisis* (New York: Simon & Schuster, 2003); Philip Gourevitch, "Alms Dealers," *The New Yorker*, October 11, 2010 <http://www.newyorker.com/arts/critics/atlarge/2010/10/11/101011crat_atlarge_gourevitch?currentPage=all>; Emma Crewe and Elizabeth Harrison, *Whose Development? An Ethnography of Aid* (London: Zed Books, 1998); Tania Li, *The Will to Improve: Governmentality, Development, and the Practice of Politics* (Durham, NC: Duke University Press, 2007); Alexander de Waal, *Famine Crimes: Politics & the Disaster Relief Industry in Africa* (Bloomington: Indiana University Press, 1997); James Ferguson, *The Anti-Politics Machine: 'Development,' Depoliticization, and Bureaucratic Power in Lesotho* (Minneapolis: University of Minnesota Press, 1994); Adam Branch, *Displacing Human Rights: War and Intervention in Northern Uganda* (New York: Oxford University Press, 2011).

individual duty to alleviate distant suffering, although for starkly different reasons, these critics also tend to say little about the implications of the ethical challenges that INGOs face for donors to INGOs. In some cases, this is because they do not think that individuals should donate to INGOs.

More recently, some scholars have begun to examine the implications, for donors, of the ethical challenges that INGOs face. For example, Leif Wenar argues that because "poverty is no pond" (a reference to Singer's famous analogy between donating to poverty relief and saving a toddler drowning in a shallow pond), individuals looking to help alleviate poverty face a more epistemically and practically challenging task than Singer's analogy suggests.[44] Likewise, Thomas Pogge, as well as Singer himself in more recent work, have acknowledged some of these complexities, including that some INGOs are more cost-effective than others, such that donors must carefully choose which INGOs to support.[45]

Yet even these authors do not elucidate the implications, for donors and potential donors to INGOs, of the specific ethical predicaments described here. The final chapter of this book takes up this task. I defend a sea-change in how we conceptualize donating to INGOs: rather than putting money in a do-gooding machine, we should view donating to INGOs as roughly analogous to contributing to a political candidate running for elected office outside of one's district.[46] The moral risk, ambiguity, uncertainty, need for careful oversight, and concerns about illegitimate overstepping—together with the hope of helping make a better world—that feature in our conception of donating to a political candidate outside of our own district should also characterize our understanding of the political activity of donating to a humanitarian INGO.

One oft-made criticism of political ethics as a field of inquiry is that it is inherently conservative and biased toward the status quo: by focusing on existing actors and the possible courses of action actually available to them, political ethics fails to address the need for, and possibilities for achieving, more profound structural change. This allegation has special force in the context of humanitarian INGOs, because the issues that these INGOs address are so dire: even if INGOs developed and acted on the most perfect account of political ethics imaginable, the horrific problems they seek to address would remain. The account of political ethics offered in this book is intended

---

[44] Leif Wenar, "Poverty is No Pond: Challenges for the Affluent," in *Giving Well: The Ethics of Philanthropy*, ed. Patricia Illingworth, Thomas Pogge and Leif Wenar (New York: Oxford University Press, 2010), 104–32.

[45] Singer, *The Life You Can Save*; Thomas Pogge, "Moral Priorities for International Human Rights NGOs," in *Ethics in Action*, ed. Daniel A. Bell and Jean-Marc Coicaud (New York: Cambridge University Press, 2006), 218–56.

[46] This analogy refers to a presidential rather than a parliamentary system of government.

to function as an implicit counter-argument to these objections. I will try to show that an account of political ethics that is oriented outward in three ways—toward other actors and institutions, toward other sources of insight and knowledge, and toward the future—can contribute to, rather than resist, more transformative politics.

1.7 Scope of the Study, Fieldwork, and Methodology

This book focuses on a relatively small set of large-scale, mainstream, INGOs that are headquartered in wealthy Western countries, rely at least in part on donors for funds, provide humanitarian aid in addition to whatever else they do, and are not strongly religious.[47] This set of INGOs includes those that Michael Barnett calls the "gang of six"—CARE, Catholic Relief Services, MSF, Save the Children, World Vision, and Oxfam—along with several others.[48] While I focus on these INGOs, it is important to remember that they operate alongside and within "aid chains," comprised of a dizzying array of other humanitarian and development actors.[49]

While they share the traits just described, these humanitarian INGOs vary in terms of the percentage of their funding that comes from individuals

[47] On religiosity, there are certainly borderline cases. Here I only mean to acknowledge that there are some Islamic, Buddhist, Hindu, and Christian traditions of humanitarianism (e.g. Mother Teresa's order) that tend to have a quite different ethical orientation than that of the INGOs examined here—an orientation focused more on fulfilling religious duty than on alleviating suffering (Erica Bornstein and Peter Redfield, *Forces of Compassion: Humanitarianism Between Ethics and Politics* (Santa Fe, NM: School for Advanced Research Press, 2011), ch. 1), that is likely to significantly alter their own self-understanding of the moral issues they face. I consider World Vision, Catholic Relief Services, and Islamic Relief to fall within the ambit of this study, although in any given case, religious dynamics might help to shape the content or character of the ethical predicaments they face.

[48] Barnett, *Empire of Humanity*, 242, footnote 25. See also Glyn Taylor, Abby Stoddard, Adele Harmer, Katherine Haver, Paul Harvey, Kathryn Barber, Lisa Schreter, and Constance Wilhelm, "The State of the Humanitarian System 2012" (London: ALNAP/Overseas Development Institute), 27.

[49] As Watkins et al. write describing aid chains in a development context:

The donors distribute billions of dollars, euros, or yen to international NGOs (INGOs) that have headquarters in world capitals. These INGOs refine the donors' policies and programs, and select (or create) organizations to implement them. After retaining their overhead costs, the INGOs contract to distribute millions to multiple medium-sized NGOs in the capitals of poor countries; we call these national NGOs. These, in turn, take overheads and then provide smaller local NGOs with smaller amounts to do the work of actually implementing the donor visions in local communities.... The funding chain can be quite long: for example, from the European Community, to the Aga Khan Foundation–London, to the Aga Khan Foundation–Geneva, to the Aga Khan Foundation–India, to the Aga Khan Rural Support Program in India, to an NGO, Sadguru, and finally to villages.

(Susan Cotts Watkins, Ann Swidler, and Thomas Hannan,
"Outsourcing Social Transformation: Development NGOs as Organizations,"
Annual Review of Sociology 38: 285–315).

versus other sources, whether they are secular or (somewhat) religious, how explicitly political or "rights-based" they are, the number and geographic range of countries in which they work, the activities they undertake, and their areas of expertise.[50] These differences matter, and help to explain why a map of humanitarian INGO political ethics is preferable to a one-size-fits-all set of rules or principles for guiding INGO decision-making. That said, it is also worth noting that in many contexts, the differences among INGOs are often of little significance for aid recipients.[51] To the contrary, the public "faces" of INGOs are often very similar: big white 4×4s speeding along the road, and expatriates wearing logoed T-shirts, drinking beer in rented compounds with select locals.[52]

Most of the humanitarian INGOs that are the main subject of this book were founded in the mid-twentieth century as small organizations that undertook a single activity, typically involving the provision of a good or service. For example, Oxfam began as an effort by a small group of pacifists to send food to starving Greek children behind the Allied blockade during World War II; MSF began as a few doctors providing emergency medical care to civilians during the Biafran War.[53] Today, however, the largest INGOs employ thousands of individuals in dozens of countries to (try to) assist millions of people. They also undertake a wide range of activities, including not only humanitarian aid, but also development aid, reconstruction, disaster prevention, peace-building, livelihood support, advocacy, campaigning, and scientific research.[54]

This small group of now-large INGOs constitutes a significant portion of the humanitarian INGO sector as a whole, whether measured in terms of number of donors, amount of money spent, or number of people assisted. For example, in 2009, the five largest humanitarian INGOs accounted for 38% of spending by humanitarian INGOs overall; the nineteen largest INGOs (or

---

[50] Donini et al. ("The State of the Humanitarian Enterprise") distinguish among four types of INGOs: principled, pragmatic, solidarist, and faith-based.

[51] Caroline Abu-Sada (ed.), *In the Eyes of Others: How People in Crises Perceive Humanitarian Aid* (New York: MSF-USA, 2012). This is not to say that aid recipients never distinguish among INGOs, nor is it to deny that, if aid recipients had more information about these differences, they might care more about them.

[52] This is the case even though most humanitarian INGOs hire the vast majority—often over 90%—of their employees locally.

[53] Maggie Black, *A Cause for Our Times: Oxfam—The First Fifty Years* (New York: Oxford University Press, 1992); MSF, "Timeline."

[54] For INGOs that do both development aid and advocacy, such as Oxfam and CARE, humanitarian aid comprises less than 30% of their expenditures. Part of this dynamic of expansion is due to what Hugo Slim calls "ethics creep." "Surely," he argues, "one cannot cure a wounded man only to send him back into battle or heal a small child only to discharge her back into a malarial area with no health education and primary health care system. If one sees and knows the deeper causes of a person's sickness, one is duty-bound to address it. Not to do so is morally irresponsible. It is this ethical logic that made most relief NGOs become development NGOs. And it is a good logic." Cited in Barnett, *Empire of Humanity*, 25.

associations of INGOs) accounted for approximately 60% of overall INGO spending on humanitarian aid.[55]

I focus on these humanitarian INGOs not only because they are important, influential, and have significant features in common, but also because they face distinctive challenges—challenges that other actors, that might at first seem quite similar, do not face. For example, INGOs that do exclusively development work, such as the International Development Exchange (IDEX), do not face the challenges associated with working on the ground in conflict zones or allocating resources between emergencies and non-emergencies. I therefore exclude development-only INGOs from my analysis. Likewise, because they have more information about the situation "on the ground" than INGOs and are less likely to be seen as culturally imperialist,[56] NGOs based in aid-recipient countries are less likely to be second-best actors than INGOs, and so less likely to have to deal with the quandary of the second-best. I exclude them from my central set of cases for this reason. Foundations such as the Gates Foundation are excluded because they do not rely on on-going contributions from the general public, and so do not face the ethical challenges associated with the need to raise funds from the general public. Finally, I focus on actors (i.e. humanitarian INGOs) rather than specific cases (e.g. the 2010 Haiti earthquake), because doing so allows me to consider how INGOs allocate resources among different situations.

[margin note: excludes these. But that's not too bad]

This book draws on semi-structured interviews, participant observation, and archival research that I conducted over the course of nine months with the International Committee of the Red Cross (ICRC), MSF-France, MSF-Belgium, MSF-Amsterdam, Oxfam-UK and the International Rescue Committee (IRC) in 2001–2.[57] I also shadowed an IRC aid worker for two weeks in northern Uganda.[58] The goals of this research were to better understand the political and ethical predicaments that aid workers face, the considerations that

[margin note: METHODS]

---

[55] Taylor et al., "The State of the Humanitarian System 2012," 29; Global Humanitarian Assistance, "GHA Report 2009," Development Initiatives, United Kingdom, 2009 <http://www.globalhumanitarianassistance.org/wp-content/uploads/2009/07/GHA-Report-2009.pdf>

[56] This is not always the case. Sometimes foreigners are seen as "so foreign" that their presence is less culturally grating or offensive than people from the capital (Abu-Sada, *In the Eyes of Others*).

[57] I received approval from the University of Chicago's Institutional Review Board for this research. The ICRC is not an INGO, but it is largely responsible for developing the principles of classical humanitarianism.

[58] I spent most of my time in the Kiryondongo refugee settlement, where the IRC was providing a range of goods and services to 35,000 Sudanese refugees and 10,000 Ugandan nationals living nearby the settlement. The IRC was also providing water and sanitation services for several thousand Ugandans who had been displaced by the Lord's Resistance Army and were living in internally displaced persons settlements near the town of Lira; I also spent some time there. "Intense Grief and Fear in Northern Uganda" was at the top of MSF's list of "Top 10 Most Underreported Humanitarian Stories" for 2004 (MSF, "Top 10 Most Underreported Humanitarian Stories of 2004" <http://www.doctorswithoutborders.org/news-stories/special-report/top-10-most-underreported-humanitarian-stories-2004>).

inform their decisions about how to respond to those predicaments, and the constraints under which they operate. I therefore sought out experienced, thoughtful practitioners with a range of different perspectives, who could help me understand the issues that INGOs face, and who would be willing to speak with me in a forthright way, rather than a representative sample of all aid workers (or even all expatriate aid workers). In analyzing both interviews and written sources, I have tried to treat practitioners not as sources of data-points that might generate generalizable conclusions, nor as "informants" in the anthropological sense, but rather as empirically well-informed political and moral theorists in their own right, whose conceptual and normative arguments deserve respectful attention.[59]

For logistical and ethical reasons, I was not able to interview aid recipients. While even a few such interviews would likely have offered generative insights, they would not have come close to providing a full or complete picture of "what aid recipients think." Yet over the past ten years, there have been some very ambitious and sophisticated efforts to document and analyze aid recipients' perceptions of humanitarian aid—efforts that cover many countries and utilize locally or regionally based interviewers.[60] Even though there is something uniquely valuable, for political theorists, in having direct experience of the issues they study (more on which below), respect for the diversity, nuance, and specificity of aid recipients' views and perspectives is consistent with drawing on these secondary sources, rather than trying (and failing) to replicate them.

The fieldwork that I was able to do informs this book in several ways. Most obviously, it appears in quotations from my interviews with aid workers, and in discrete pieces of information gathered during the course of my research. However, the connections between the most important insights that I derived from my fieldwork and the fieldwork itself are less apparent: it was not only seeing, but literally being inside a refugee settlement, and the offices of an organization charged with administering several aspects of it, that pushed me to take seriously and develop the idea that humanitarian

---

[59] One implication of this approach is that, in selecting which counter-arguments or potential objections to address in this book, I discuss not only those that are likely to strike political theorists and philosophers as the strongest alternatives to my positions, and not only arguments made by aid practitioners that political theorists and philosophers are likely to find plausible once they hear them (but that they would not have thought of themselves), but also arguments that some aid practitioners find credible, but that few theorists and philosophers are likely to find persuasive.

[60] See Abu-Sada, *In the Eyes of Others*; Mary B. Anderson, Dayna Brown, and Isabella Jean, *Time To Listen: Hearing People on the Receiving End of International Aid* (Cambridge, MA: CDA Collaborative Learning Projects, 2012) <http://www.cdacollaborative.org/media/60478/Time-to-Listen-Book.pdf>; and Donini et al., "The State of the Humanitarian Enterprise" and related country reports. While it is not about aid per se, the World Bank's "Voices of the Poor" project is also relevant.

INGOs engage in governance. Likewise, speaking directly and at length with aid workers helped me understand why activities the value of which does not lie (only) with their consequences, such as standing on principle, acknowledging special responsibilities, symbolic action, "proximity," and solidarity, are often so important to humanitarian practitioners. Even though I was not always entirely persuaded by these conversations, I understand the significance of these sources of value much better than I would have if I had not undertaken fieldwork.

Doing fieldwork also helped me to at least begin to comprehend, both intellectually and on a more sensory, visceral register, the immense difficulties that refugees, internally displaced persons (IDPs), and other extremely poor and/or disaster-affected people face, as well as the fact that these difficulties do not exhaust the content and texture of their lives. It is terrible to live in an abandoned starch factory with hundreds of other displaced people, with no heat and virtually non-existent sanitation facilities, when the ground outside is covered in mud and you don't know where some of your family members are, or whether your house has been burned down. Yet these conditions, as horrible as they are, do not stop many people from thinking or caring about the overall trajectory of their lives: how they will finish school, whom they will marry.

My fieldwork also drove home the importance of issues of respect and esteem. For example, one day when I was in the IRC office at the Kiryondongo refugee settlement in northern Uganda, a thin young man walked in, incensed almost to the point of tears that a portable library had (he felt) been located for too long in an area of the camp far from where he lived, an area populated by a group of refugees who had been in the camp longer and had more power than the group to which he belonged. How, he asked, was he supposed to continue his education without access to books? It is easy to say that his concern is far less important than people not having enough food, shelter, and medical care to survive. Indeed, on almost any plausible measure it *is* less important. But to the young man standing there, eyes burning, in his button-down white shirt tucked into blue pants, it was incredibly important. No aid practitioner can do her job well without recognizing and acknowledging the depth of this man's frustration and humiliation; no account of humanitarian INGO political ethics will be plausible if it fails to do so, either.

Finally, doing fieldwork deepened my humility about the very enterprise of developing an account of political ethics for humanitarian INGOs. In particular, as I describe further in this book's conclusion, it suggested to me that, rather than a definitive or official map, the map of humanitarian political ethics offered here is best seen as a map within a map: a contribution to a larger, open-source, collectively generated map, of the kind created by the Kenyan organization Ushahidi.

1.8 Outline of the Book

The next chapter examines the eight extant alternative approaches to conceptualizing humanitarian INGOs mentioned above. I explain why none of these approaches obviates the need for a new account of humanitarian INGO political ethics, either by providing an adequate account or by showing that a new account is beside the point. Yet all eight of these approaches offer insights into humanitarian INGO political ethics that should be carried forward into a better account.

Chapter 3 offers a summary sketch of what I will argue is such a better account: a "map" of humanitarian INGOs as somewhat governmental, highly political, and often second-best. This interpretation of humanitarian INGOs suggests that they regularly face four ethical predicaments: the problem of spattered hands, the quandary of the second-best, the cost-effectiveness conundrum, and the moral motivation tradeoff. The next four chapters examine each of these predicaments in turn: the problem of spattered hands as it arises in the context of basic service provision by INGOs in conflict settings (Chapter 4); the quandary of the second-best as it arises in the context of political advocacy by INGOs (Chapter 5); the cost-effectiveness conundrum as it arises in the context of large-scale decisions about resource use (Chapter 6); and the moral motivation tradeoff as it arises in the context of INGOs' "portrayal-related practices" (i.e. creating, publishing, and facilitating the creation and publication of images of famine and severe poverty) (Chapter 7). In Chapter 8, I discuss how these four ethical predicaments intersect. I also summarize the answers suggested in the previous chapters to the four questions described at the outset of this chapter: What kind of actors are humanitarian INGOs? What ethical predicaments do they face? Are there better and worse ways for them to navigate these predicaments? What does this tell us about democratic, humanitarian, egalitarian, and justice-based norms more generally? I then briefly explore the implications of my map of humanitarian INGO political ethics for individual donors to INGOs. I conclude by explaining how my approach to humanitarian INGO political ethics avoids status quo bias, and how we might understand the map offered here as part of a larger, Ushahidi-style map.

In the chapters that follow, I draw distinctions, offer re-conceptualizations, deploy normative arguments, and otherwise try to make (one kind of) sense of a dauntingly complex terrain. Compared to the story about the young man at the IRC office, some of these arguments are rather dry. But I strongly believe, and hope to show, that they do as much work as that story—and possibly more—in helping people who are at some remove from INGOs and the issues they address to understand both. It is easy to care about the bookish young man. Compared to (for example) the distinction between providing aid based on need alone and maximally alleviating morally important harm, he practically leaps off the page, sparkling with life. But there are hundreds of millions of people in the world as badly off as him (perhaps more than a billion, depending on how one counts). Each of them could be described in a way that would make *them* sparkle and leap off the page. A central strength of analytic political theory is that it insists that we—that is, you, me, anyone doing analytic political theory—not discount those hundreds of millions of people, simply because they were not so described. The challenge of thinking in both of these registers at once—that of the earnest young man standing in the doorway of the IRC office, and that of the hundreds of millions of poor, marginalized, or disaster-affected people not standing there—has made a mark, hopefully visible, on every page of this book.

2

Eight Extant Alternative Approaches

Political judgment means, among other things, the ability to determine which analogies are useful . . .

—Raymond Geuss[1]

This chapter examines eight prominent and/or seemingly promising approaches to conceptualizing and normatively evaluating humanitarian INGOs. All offer important insights. However, none provides an adequate basis for an account of humanitarian INGO political ethics or shows that such an account is unnecessary—or so I shall argue. In particular, these approaches do not tell us what ethical predicaments humanitarian INGOs regularly face—nor, as a result, what it would look like for INGOs to navigate these predicaments in ways that are consistent with democratic, egalitarian, humanitarian, and justice-based norms. Elucidating the limitations of these extant approaches helps to reveal the distinctiveness of the ethical and political terrain on which humanitarian INGOs operate, and suggests why we need an account of humanitarian INGO political ethics that is attentive to this distinctiveness.

The task of this chapter, then, is to explain the limitations of these eight approaches to conceptualizing and normatively evaluating INGOs, while also gleaning the insights that they offer. Of these eight approaches, three are claims that INGOs occupy particular social roles: the roles of *rescuer* of the poor and disaster-affected people they seek to assist, *partner* of domestic organizations or governments in the countries where they work, and *agent for their donors*. Two approaches are not quite well-defined enough to be roles, but like the rescuer approach, they focus on INGOs' responsibilities to their intended beneficiaries: the idea that INGOs are *agents for their intended beneficiaries* and that they should be *accountable to their intended beneficiaries*.

---

[1] Raymond Geuss, *Philosophy and Real Politics* (Princeton, NJ: Princeton University Press, 2008), 98.

Yet another approach focuses on *traditional humanitarian principles*. The last two approaches are claims that an account of humanitarian INGO political ethics is beside the point because INGOs are *neo-colonial* and similar in important ways to *multinational corporations* (MNCs).

Some of these approaches have a highly positive valance, while others are deeply critical of INGOs. Some identify ethical standards to which INGOs should be held, while others suggest that there might not be anything INGOs can do to meet minimally acceptable ethical standards. Despite these differences, all eight of these approaches are similar in that they are misleading and/or insufficiently detailed maps. In particular, they all mis-describe, or fail to adequately describe, INGOs' activities, relationships, capacities, and/or effects. As a result, they do not provide an adequate basis for examining the ethical predicaments that INGOs face on account of those activities, relationships, capacities, and/or effects.

The next eight sections discuss the limitations and insights of each of the eight approaches just mentioned, in turn. The final section summarizes the insights that, I will argue, should inform an alternative account.

2.1 INGOs as Rescuers

"If somebody's drowning, you save them."

—MSF-Holland Head of Mission, Uganda[2]

The narrative associated with the social role of rescuer is that rescuers, acting alone or in small groups, swoop into situations of acute emergency, save as many people as possible, and then quickly withdraw.[3] People in donor countries often assume that INGOs do, and should, act consistently with this narrative.[4] Some INGOs have actively reinforced this assumption. For example, MSF's "central public image" is of "an emergency-room team, on call worldwide."[5] Likewise, in the world of academic philosophy, utilitarian philosophers such as Peter Singer have helped to buttress a conception of INGOs as rescuers through the examples they use in their work. For example, Singer

---

[2] Cited in Peter Redfield, *Life in Crisis: The Ethical Journey of Doctors Without Borders* (Berkeley: University of California Press, 2013), 13.

[3] This narrative is also often applied to emergency first-responders, fire fighters and ambulance crews. I suspect that upon closer inspection, these other types of actors also diverge from this narrative. See Jennifer C. Rubenstein, "Emergency Claims and Democratic Action," *Social Policy and Philosophy* 32.1 (2015): 101–126.

[4] See Chapter 1, footnote 5 for a discussion of the term "donor country." For an example of aid recipients construing INGOs as rescuers, see Caroline Abu-Sada (ed.), *In the Eyes of Others*, 41 (also discussed below).

[5] Redfield, *Life in Crisis*, 175.

famously draws an analogy between giving money to Oxfam or UNICEF and rescuing a toddler drowning in a pond.[6] The tradition of classical humanitarianism also helps to shore up the perception of humanitarian INGOs as rescuers, by suggesting that INGOs should try to save the lives of the worst-off individuals even when doing so is not justified on utilitarian grounds.[7]

While prominent and seemingly uncontroversial, the idea that INGOs are rescuers is descriptively inaccurate and/or question-begging, for seven main reasons. First, humanitarian INGOs *do much more than rescue*.[8] When philosophers discuss the "duty to rescue," they invoke examples such as pulling a drowning toddler from a pond, providing food and lodging to a traveler beaten and left lying on the road to Samaria, or calling the police upon hearing Kitty Genovese's screams—that is, activities that involve saving an individual from imminent death.[9] Yet very few large humanitarian INGOs limit their activities to preventing imminent death. Indeed, some INGOs, such as Oxfam and CARE, devote only a small percentage of their budgets to emergency operations.[10] Even INGOs such as MSF and the International *Rescue* Committee (my emphasis), that refer to themselves exclusively as "emergency" or "humanitarian" organizations, do much more than rescue. For example, MSF provides ongoing medical care to chronically underserved populations, and engages in advocacy, campaigning, witnessing (or *témoignage*) and epidemiological research.[11] The IRC states that it responds to "humanitarian crises" by "help[ing] people to survive and rebuild their lives...[and] restor[ing] safety, dignity and hope to millions who are uprooted and struggling to endure."[12] So while the philosopher Bernard Williams is correct that "the private relief agencies such as Oxfam"

[6] Peter Singer, "Famine, Affluence, and Morality." See also Singer, *The Life You Can Save: Acting Now to End World Poverty*, esp. 3 and 13–14 (where Singer analogizes donating money to an INGO to saving a child from an oncoming train).

[7] See Chapter 6 for full discussion of the idea that INGOs should allocate humanitarian aid "based on need alone."

[8] As discussed in Chapter 1, some INGOs started out doing rescue construed almost this narrowly. However, virtually all quickly broadened the scope of their activities. There are organizational and ethical reasons for this. See discussion of "ethics creep" in Chapter 1, footnote 54.

[9] Singer, "Famine, Affluence, and Morality"; Jeremy Waldron, "Who Is My Neighbor? Humanity and Proximity," *Monist* 86.3 (2003): 333–54.

[10] Oxfam, for example, spends 26.2% of its overall budget on "Life and Security" operations. See Oxfam International, "Annual Report 2012–2013," 71 <http://www.oxfam.org/sites/www.oxfam.org/files/oxfam-annual-report-2012-2013.pdf>. In 2013, CARE spent 24% of its budget on "emergency response and rehabilitation" (see <http://www.care.org>).

[11] In 2009 MSF classified only 22% of its interventions as emergency/short-term (Abu Sada, *In the Eyes of Others*, 5). See also Redfield, *Life in Crisis*, ch. 8.

[12] International Rescue Committee, "About the International Rescue Committee" <http://www.rescue.org/about>.

"carry out rescue operations,"[13] this is only a small part of what Oxfam and other large INGOs actually do, even within their "emergency" or "humanitarian" programs. As a result, there are broad swaths of INGOs' activities for which the social role of rescuer provides no guidance at all.[14]

Second, even when INGOs undertake rescue activities narrowly construed, the social role of rescuer is misapplied to them. According to the rescuer narrative, prototypical rescuers react immediately and reflexively to emergencies as they arise. By immediately springing into action, they acknowledge the moral urgency of the situation. (They avoid having—to use Bernard Williams' famous phrase—"one thought too many.") In contrast, humanitarian INGOs *deliberate, in advance, about how to allocate their limited resources* among countries, regions, issues, and types of activities, including tradeoffs between emergency aid and other activities.[15] Other kinds of rescue organizations, such as ambulance crews and fire departments, no doubt deliberate in this way as well. But because the rescue *narrative* does not recognize these kinds of decisions, it provides no guidance regarding how to make them.

Third, prototypical rescuers—even those that literally work in warzones, such as Red Cross medics—are generally seen as acting outside the realm of politics. But while many humanitarian INGOs strive to be apolitical, as I noted in Chapter 1, it is virtually impossible for them to avoid having political effects. Their resources are sometimes stolen by combatants and used to perpetuate conflict; their presence can increase the perceived legitimacy of a brutal regime; the services they provide can encourage domestic governments to be less accountable to their citizens.[16] Conceiving of INGOs as occupying the social role of rescuer not only *provides no leverage for addressing these political effects*; it also *actively obscures them*, by suggesting that INGOs can be apolitical.

Fourth, while prototypical rescue is short-term and small-scale, *humanitarian aid by INGOs is often long-term and large-scale*. Humanitarian INGOs collectively, and some INGOs individually, provide basic services to tens of millions of people for years or decades. Because the rescuer narrative implies that INGOs' activities are short-term and relatively small-scale, it offers few resources for addressing the ethical responsibilities INGOs might develop as

[13] Bernard Williams, "Is International Rescue a Moral Issue?" *Social Research* 62.1 (1995): 67–75 (74).

[14] Some authors, most notably David Rieff (in *A Bed for the Night: Humanitarianism in Crisis* (New York: Simon & Schuster, 2003)), argue that INGOs should, in effect, be something like rescuers. In contrast, the rescuer approach *assumes* that INGOs are rescuers and then asks (or assumes) what their responsibilities are as a result of occupying this role.

[15] See Chapter 6 for full discussion.

[16] See Tony Vaux, *The Selfish Altruist: Dilemmas of Relief Work in Famine and War* (London: Earthscan, 2002), Alexander De Waal, *Famine Crimes: Politics & the Disaster Relief Industry in Africa* (Bloomington: Indiana University Press, 1997), and full discussion in Chapter 3.

a result of providing basic services to large populations for long periods—for example responsibilities that might emerge as a result of aid recipients coming to rely on them, helping them, or developing relationships with them.

Fifth, the rescuer narrative suggests that there is only one, or at most a few, rescuers at the scene of any given rescue operation. That is, the standard problem for rescuers is too many victims and too few rescuers—not the other way around. But because humanitarian INGOs rely on donors for funds, they have a strong incentive to focus their efforts on high-profile emergencies that generate intense media interest, and hence, donations, such as Kosovo in the 1990s, Indonesia after the 2004 tsunami, Haiti after the 2010 earthquake, and Darfur in the 2000s.[17] As a result, *INGOs providing humanitarian aid sometimes operate in contexts where there are too many "rescuers."* This dynamic can result in what David Rieff, writing about Kosovo, called a "humanitarian circus": hundreds or thousands of INGOs and other humanitarian actors rush into a given context, banners flying, competing for "victims," engaging in redundant activities, and increasing the burden on domestic government and UN agencies charged with monitoring and fostering coordination among them.[18] As aid practitioner Simon Worrall described the situation in Al Fasher, Darfur (Sudan) in 2004: "[w]e can only access about a tenth of the population, so all the NGOs that are here with money falling out of their pockets are treading on each others' toes for territory, it's pathetic."[19] Because the rescuer narrative assumes too few rather than too many rescuers, it says nothing about the ethical predicaments or responsibilities associated with humanitarian circuses.

Sixth, prototypical rescuers respond to emergencies after they happen: the alarm bell rings and fire fighters dash to their trucks; an earthquake strikes and search and rescue teams rush in. In contrast, humanitarian INGOs *influence which situations get recognized as emergencies in the first place*—and which do not. By making what we might call "emergency claims" about some situations and not others, humanitarian INGOs help to shape not only which specific situations are recognized as emergencies, but also what general kinds of features lead specific situations to be socially recognized as emergencies.[20] Because it assumes that rescuers only *respond* to (objective) emergencies, the concept of rescuer does not provide any guidance for thinking about the ethical predicaments that INGOs might face as a result of their role in using emergency claims to (a) influence what specific situations are

---

[17] Toby Porter, "An Embarrassment of Riches," *Humanitarian Exchange Magazine* 21 (Humanitarian Practice Network (2002) <http://www.odihpn.org/humanitarian-exchange-magazine/issue-21/an-embarrassment-of-riches>.

[18] David Rieff, "Kosovo's Humanitarian Circus," *World Policy Journal* 17.3 (2000): 25–32.

[19] Personal communication (e-mail) from Simon Worrall, June 25, 2004.

[20] Rubenstein, "Emergency Claims and Democratic Action," *Social Philosophy and Policy* 32.1 (2015): 101–126.

recognized as emergencies or (b) help shape the discursive content of the concept of emergency more generally.

Finally, prototypical *rescuers rescue helpless victims*. At a conceptual level, rescuers need victims: while the concept of "victim" can exist without rescuers—conceptually, victims only need villains—there are no rescuers without victims. Yet the people INGOs try to assist are virtually never entirely helpless. Of course, people sometimes need significant outside assistance to continue living, regain their health, or escape from extreme poverty. But every person INGOs seek to assist is a complicated human being, and most have a far greater capacity to ameliorate their own situation than the image of them as victims suggests. Many INGOs recognize this, and have sought to break away from the victim/rescuer dynamic, with varying degrees of success. Viewing INGOs as rescuers fails to acknowledge these efforts and the valid reasoning behind them.

Some of these shortcomings of the rescuer role derive from what it leaves out, such as activities other than rescue. These shortcomings could potentially be ameliorated by complementing the rescuer conception with one or more other conceptions of INGOs. But other shortcomings of the rescuer conception derive from what it *does* include, for example the idea that INGOs' intended beneficiaries are helpless victims. These shortcomings are far more difficult to ameliorate by simply complementing the rescuer conception with others.

Despite these limitations, the idea that humanitarian INGOs are and should be rescuers captures a crucial insight: many issues that humanitarian INGOs address are of tremendous moral urgency. People's lives are at stake. The rescuer approach raises the question: How can an account of humanitarian INGO political ethics reflect this urgency, and the valuation of individual human lives that undergirds it, while avoiding the distortions that come from conceiving of INGOs as rescuers?

2.2 INGOs as Partners

> *"[E]verybody wants to be a partner with everyone else on everything, everywhere."*
>
> —Alan Fowler[21]

Unlike the conception of humanitarian INGOs as rescuers, which has been invoked primarily by moral philosophers in the context of humanitarian aid, the idea that these INGOs are and should be partners is ubiquitous

---

[21] Alan Fowler, "Beyond Partnership: Getting Real about NGO Relationships in the Aid System," *IDS Bulletin* 31.3 (2000): 1–13.

across the full range of activities that humanitarian INGOs undertake, including development aid and advocacy, and is endorsed by a wide array of aid practitioners, scholars, and activists with egalitarian sensibilities.[22] Indeed, among INGOs, partnership is "a popular, if not obligatory, strategy."[23]

Broadly speaking, partnership refers to "equality in ways of working and mutuality in respect for identity, position, and role."[24] In practical terms, it can take the form of an attitude or ethos that shapes interpersonal interactions between INGO employees and the employees of domestic organizations (e.g. domestic NGOs, community-based organizations [CBOs], or government agencies) based in the countries where INGOs work, or in guidelines for how INGOs and domestic organizations should work together. Such guidelines themselves vary greatly: one aid professional describes partnership as working together on the basis of trust and ongoing negotiation rather than formalized contracts; another aid organization refers to the domestic organizations with whom it enters into formalized contracts as its "partners."[25]

While the social role of rescuer is normatively attractive because it acknowledges the urgency of saving individual lives—that is, it reflects humanitarian norms—the concept of partnership is normatively attractive because it focuses on equality: partners have equal status and/or make decisions together on an equal basis. However, the *kind* of equality that is actually achieved within INGO partnerships is often quite superficial. While INGO and NGOs employees might treat each other as equal partners in everyday interactions, INGOs are typically the main source of funding for their domestic NGO partners.[26] Even when domestic NGOs receive funding from other sources, they tend to be more constrained than INGOs for other reasons; for example, they are more rooted in a single geographic location. NGOs therefore typically have a weak bargaining position vis-à-vis INGOs.[27] The partnership lens does not address

---

[22] Hugo Slim. "The Grammar of Aid," Introduction to *Collaboration in Crises: Lessons in Community Participation from Oxfam International's Tsunami Research* (Oxford: Oxfam International, 2009) <http://www.oxfam.org/sites/www.oxfam.org/files/collaboration-crises-lessons-tsunami.pdf>.

[23] Emma Crewe and Elizabeth Harrison, *Whose Development? An Ethnography of Aid* (London: Zed Books, 1998), 71.

[24] Alan F. Fowler, "Authentic NGDO Partnerships in the New Policy Agenda for International Aid: Dead End or Light Ahead?" *Development and Change* 29.1 (1998): 137–59 (141).

[25] Fowler, "Authentic NGDO Partnerships in the New Policy Agenda for International Aid." See Chapter 5 for discussion of Oxfam's "partnerships" with domestic Ghanaian NGOs.

[26] Crewe and Harrison, *Whose Development?*, ch. 4. In a recent survey of NGOs about their INGO partners, NGOs gave high marks to INGOs on how well INGO staff listened and responded to NGOs. INGOs received lower marks on things like giving NGOs financial autonomy, and including them in strategic planning. Keystone Accountability, *Keystone Performance Surveys NGO Partner Survey 2010* (London: Keystone Accountability, 2011).

[27] INGOs are typically on both ends of this dynamic simultaneously: just as domestic NGOs and CBOs are often in a disadvantaged bargaining position vis-à-vis INGOs, INGOs

these deeper inequalities. It therefore paints the relationship between INGOs and domestic NGOs and CBOs as more equal and less deeply imbued with unequal power relations than it is.[28]

Largely because the ideal of partnership papers over structural inequalities in this way, several commentators have concluded that, in the context of humanitarian and development INGOs, partnership is "a generally disappointing story."[29] Partnerships are often "more illusion than reality."[30] Indeed, on some accounts, calling relationships between INGOs and NGOs partnerships serves to "mask paternalistic practices on the part of [I]NGOs."[31]

The partnership lens also obscures another form of power that INGOs exercise. By publicizing their willingness to "partner with" (i.e. fund) some types of NGOs and CBOs but not others, INGOs can influence which NGOs and CBOs come into existence. For example, residents of a rural village deciding whether to form a farming cooperative or women's club, as well as poor country elites looking to start an NGO, are, quite understandably, likely to look first to see what kinds of organizations and projects INGOs are funding.[32] Even if INGOs could be entirely equal partners with already-existing domestic organizations, the partnership lens says nothing about what responsibilities, if any, they have as a result of their role in shaping which domestic organizations come into existence in the first place.

The discussion so far might seem to suggest that there is nothing wrong with partnership in theory. *Real* partnership—partnership that overturns structural inequalities and is attentive to the ethical implications of the incentives it creates—is still a worthwhile goal; it is just difficult to achieve in practice. Yet as Hoksbergen argues, even this sort of partnership "is in itself a concession to the reality of Northern power, for the larger share of decision making ought to be in the South, not the North."[33] Hoksbergen's comment implies that partnership as an ideal tends to rely on one particular

are often in a disadvantaged bargaining position vis-à-vis their own large-scale donors (e.g. bilateral government aid agencies such as USAID and foundations). Like the organizations they fund, INGOs also have a very strong economic and organizational incentive to abide by *their* donors' preferences—including, in some cases, preferences that INGOs work with local partners!

[28] Crewe and Harrison, *Whose Development?*, ch. 4, esp. 75.

[29] Fowler, "Authentic NGDO Partnerships in the New Policy Agenda for International Aid," 139.

[30] Fowler, "Authentic NGDO Partnerships in the New Policy Agenda for International Aid," 139.

[31] Deborah Eade and Ernst Ligteringen (eds.), *Debating Development: NGOs and the Future* (Herdon, VA: Stylus Publishing, 2001), 15.

[32] Ann Swidler and Susan Cotts Watkins, "'Teach a Man to Fish': The Sustainability Doctrine and Its Social Consequences," *World Development* 37.7 (2009): 1182–96.

[33] Roland Hoksbergen, "Building Civil Society through Partnership: Lessons from a Case Study of the Christian Reformed World Relief Committee," *Development in Practice* 15.1 (2005): 16–27 (20).

conception of equality, which I will call "participation equality": the idea that everyone who is able and willing to contribute to a shared goal should be allowed to participate in achieving that goal. Hoksbergen implies that another kind of equality is more salient in this context: equality understood as proportionality between how affected people are by a decision and how much say they (or their representatives) have in making it.[34] We might call this sort of equality "political equality."[35] If political equality is a more appropriate orienting ideal than participation equality in the context of INGO/NGO joint projects, then partnership is an inadequate ideal for humanitarian INGOs, because while it might promote participation equality, it does not promote political equality.[36]

A final drawback to holding up partnership as an ideal for INGOs to pursue is that it conflates equality with harmony, thereby obscuring the potentially positive role of dissension in relationships between INGOs and domestic organizations. Insofar as the valuation of harmony over dissension works in the interests of those who have more power, an emphasis on partnership (and therefore on harmony) might further empower INGOs at the expense of domestic organizations. In contrast, a more "agonistic" model of these relationships would direct attention to the constructive role that conflict can play in the context of INGOs' activities.[37]

Describing the results of a study of perceptions of humanitarian action, Jochum states that "[i]n a growing number of societies, critics see humanitarian action as a costly, archaic form of unilateral charity, weakening national states or civil society actors. They are urging us to be more associated, to be part of a relationship of equals."[38] The question that the partnership conception raises, but does not adequately address is: what does—or more accurately, what should—it mean for INGOs to be part of a relationship of equals? What, exactly, ought to be equalized?[39]

[34] Amartya Sen, "Equality of What?" In *The Tanner Lecture on Human Values, I*, ed. Sterling M. McMurrin (Cambridge: Cambridge University Press, 2011), 197–220; Robert E. Goodin, "Enfranchising All Affected Interests, and Its Alternatives," *Philosophy & Public Affairs* 35.1 (2007): 40–68.
[35] See Chapter 5 for full discussion.
[36] The difficulties with partnership are more severe if the pursuit of participation equality actively undermines political equality, rather than simply being a less normatively attractive goal.
[37] On agonism, see Chantal Mouffe, "Deliberative Democracy or Agonistic Pluralism?" *Social Research* 66.3 (1999): 745–58. Slim ("The Grammar of Aid") discusses the need for "a healthy struggle around the process." Oxfam's "partnership principles" (discussed in Chapter 5) also mention disagreement.
[38] Bruno Jochum, "Perception Project: A Remedy Against Complacency," in *In the Eyes of Others*, 104.
[39] Sen, "Equality of What?"

2.3 INGOs as Agents for their Donors

> *"An [INGO] is not merely an actor in its own right but is also an agent and trustee for its contributors ..."*
>
> —Thomas Pogge[40]

The claim that INGOs are agents for their donors can be interpreted in at least two ways: it can mean that INGOs discharge their donors' *moral responsibilities* on their donors' behalf, or that INGOs act consistently with their donors' *preferences*.[41] Some authors have assumed that these two interpretations converge in practice, that is, that donors prefer for INGOs to discharge donors' moral obligations on donors' behalf. For example, Thomas Pogge argues that "[a]n [INGO]...must...reflect...on its contributors' moral responsibilities, which these contributors entrust it with discharging."[42]

In practice, however, these two interpretations of what it means for INGOs to be agents for their donors often pull in different directions. For example, Pogge himself argues that people in wealthy countries have negative and intermediate duties to stop imposing an unjust global order on the rest of the world and provide compensation for having done so.[43] Yet donors to INGOs frequently donate for reasons other than to discharge these duties. For example, some corporate and governmental donors to INGOs donate in order to shore up their reputations, create demand for their products, or fight terrorism. Individuals often donate to help alleviate what they perceive as intense suffering, such as that endured by victims of the 2010 Haiti earthquake or the 2004 Indian Ocean tsunami. Because donors' preferences regarding how INGOs should use their donations often diverge from what many philosophers, at least, take to be donors' responsibilities, INGOs often cannot both act as agents for donors' preferences *and* discharge (what many philosophers take to be) donors' moral obligations simultaneously.

Yet choosing one or the other seems highly implausible: the idea that INGOs ought to promote their donors' preferences regardless of the content of those preferences makes little sense, ethically. Likewise, the idea that

---

[40] Thomas Pogge, "Moral Priorities for International Human Rights NGOs," in *Ethics in Action*, ed. Daniel A. Bell and Jean-Marc Coicaud (New York: Cambridge University Press, 2006), 218–56 (222).

[41] This is not quite the same as the more familiar distinction between "delegate" and "trustee" forms of representation, which involve promoting a constituency's preferences and (the representative's conception of their) interests, respectively, unless one thinks that it is in one's interest to have one's moral responsibilities discharged on one's behalf. Hanna Fenichel Pitkin, *The Concept of Representation* (Berkeley: University of California Press, 1967).

[42] Pogge, "Moral Priorities for International Human Rights NGOs," 222.

[43] Thomas W. Pogge, *Politics as Usual: What Lies Behind the Pro-Poor Rhetoric* (Malden, MA: Polity Press, 2010); Thomas W. Pogge, *World Poverty and Human Rights*, 2nd edn. (Malden, MA: Polity Press, 2008).

INGOs should discharge their donors' moral responsibilities even if doing so conflicts with donors' preferences is practically infeasible, because donors are unlikely to donate if they do not approve of how an INGO will use their money.

In addition to assuming that donors want INGOs to discharge donors' moral responsibilities on donors' behalf, Pogge also argues explicitly that donors' negative and intermediate duties and INGOs' own positive duties, which Pogge takes to be maximally alleviating morally important harm, will "largely coincide in content":[44]

> Insofar as we citizens of rich countries (through our governments) participate in, or profit from, the imposition of this unjust order, we are materially involved in a large majority of all the harm human beings are suffering worldwide. [INGOs] and their contributors therefore rarely face actual hard choices between morally less valuable harm reductions that we have *intermediate* moral reasons to achieve and morally more valuable harm reductions that we have only *positive* moral reasons to achieve.[45]

The problem with this argument is that it relies on our ignorance about causal chains within global networks: if we knew exactly which unjust aspects of the global order a donor—say, Wal-Mart—imposed, we would know what an INGO would have to do to discharge that donor's negative or intermediate duties on that donor's behalf. There is no reason to assume that this would match the INGO's positive duties to maximally alleviate morally important harm. For example, Wal-Mart's strongest negative and intermediate duties might be to workers in the South Asian countries where its suppliers are located, while its donations might do more to alleviate morally important harm among extremely poor people in sub-Saharan Africa.[46]

We have now identified three responsibilities for INGOs, the practical demands of which will often fail to align. Two of these—that INGOs should promote their donors' preferences and discharge their donors' moral responsibilities on their donors' behalf—are possible conceptions of what it might mean for INGOs to be agents for their donors. The third is Pogge's own account of INGOs' positive duties.[47] However, *any* account of INGOs' positive

---

[44] Pogge, "Moral Priorities for International Human Rights NGOs," 221.

[45] Pogge, "Moral Priorities for International Human Rights NGOs," 254. Pogge also says things that pull in the opposite direction (toward the idea that INGOs should follow his principle for them even if donors disapprove): "if clearly explained in the [NGO's] publications and Web site, [following Pogge's principle] would not violate any trusteeship duties" ("Moral Priorities for International Human Rights NGOs," 276).

[46] Jennifer C. Rubenstein, "Pluralism about Global Poverty," *British Journal of Political Science* 43.4 (2013): 775–97.

[47] I do not discuss this conception in this chapter because I discuss it at length in Chapter 6 and because Pogge suggests that it leaves INGOs with significant discretion, such that it does not amount to a replacement for an account of humanitarian INGO ethics.

duties might conflict with INGOs' responsibilities to their donors, whether these responsibilities are construed as discharging donors' moral responsibilities or acting according to their preferences.

A final reason to avoid conceptualizing INGOs as agents for their donors is that this conception suggests that donors only influence INGOs—not the other way around. Yet as I argue in Chapter 7, INGOs collectively, and some INGOs individually, play a significant role in shaping donors' (and potential donors') perceptions of issues of severe poverty and famine.

The idea that humanitarian INGOs are agents for their donors draws our attention to a crucial element of INGOs' ethical terrain: their responsibilities to their donors. But what are these responsibilities? Are they responsibilities to promote donors' preferences, discharge donors' moral obligations on donors' behalf, or something else? How should INGOs understand the relationships among their responsibilities to their donors, their responsibilities to current aid recipients and their responsibilities to potential recipients? These are questions that the idea of INGOs as agents for donors raises, but does not adequately answer.

2.4 INGOs as Agents for their Intended Beneficiaries

> "Most ordinary people have little or no idea of who we are and what we do. The range of misconceptions is amazingly broad: from MSF being a Chinese organization to a Muslim confessional charity to a subsidiary of Western States..."
>
> —MSF Official[48]

A fourth prominent interpretation of INGOs' social role is that they are, or should be, agents for their intended beneficiaries.[49] As I will interpret it here, this is the view that INGOs' *primary role* is to act consistently with, and promote, their intended beneficiaries' preferences, *to such an extent that there is no need for an(other) account of humanitarian INGO political ethics.*[50] In contrast, the idea that humanitarian INGOs should take the preferences of their intended beneficiaries very seriously and be responsive to them—which I wholly endorse—is not what is at issue here, because it does not purport to obviate the need for another account of humanitarian INGO political ethics.

From one perspective, the idea that INGOs should be agents for their intended beneficiaries can seem obviously true: if INGOs' aim is to help

---

[48] Abu-Sada, ed., *In the Eyes of Others*, 103.

[49] By "intended beneficiaries," I mean the individuals that a given INGO is actively seeking to assist, not everyone that it could assist given its mandate.

[50] Agency relationships can also involve acting according to or promoting interests, but for purposes of analytic clarity I will define agent-for-beneficiaries in terms of preferences, and discuss the issue of interests in the next sub-section.

people, why should they think of themselves as anything *other* than agents for those people? Wouldn't anything else be deeply paternalistic, undemocratic, inegalitarian, and perhaps even unjust? Yet there are several reasons why a conception of INGOs as agents for their intended beneficiaries cannot stand in for an account of humanitarian INGO political ethics.

First, this conception says nothing about decisions that INGOs make prior to entering into relationships with particular groups of "intended beneficiaries." These include decisions about in what regions or countries to work, and around what kinds of issues to try to galvanize constituencies. The "agent for intended beneficiaries" approach is only relevant when an INGO is already operating within a particular area or with a particular group.

When an INGO is already doing this, the idea that INGOs should be agents for their intended beneficiaries runs into several additional hurdles. One is the issue of majority preferences versus the rights or basic interests of minorities. The most natural interpretation of what it means for INGOs to act as agents for their intended beneficiaries is that they act as agents for *the majority* of their intended beneficiaries. Yet "beneficiaries have different and sometimes competing needs and aspirations."[51] For example, life-saving aid for a few people might generate a minor inconvenience for the majority, or the majority could hate a minority ethnic group, or everyone except those employed by an INGO might want it to leave. Democrats (by which I mean people committed to democratic norms, not members of a political party), often endorse individual rights and other constraints on majoritarianism to help prevent majorities from imposing their will on minorities in a way that violates the latter's rights or undermines their basic interests. Absent these constraints, construing INGOs as agents for their intended beneficiaries can conflict with basic requirements of justice.

The second issue is that the "agents for beneficiaries" framework, like Pogge's claim that INGOs should maximally alleviate morally important harm, seems to give INGOs too little leeway to act on their own judgments. Yet INGOs sometimes deeply disagree with their intended beneficiaries about what their priorities should be or how they should work. For example, Rony Brauman, a founder of MSF, describes working with the Karamajong in Eastern Uganda in the early 1980s:

> We very quickly observed that food was being taken away from the so-called target population of children under five and pregnant women to be given to the elders in these villages. For us, there is a very direct moral value attached to

[51] Paul Knox-Clarke and John Mitchell, "Reflections on the Accountability Revolution," *Humanitarian Exchange Magazine* 52 (Humanitarian Practice Network) (2005) <http://www.odihpn.org/humanitarian-exchange-magazine/issue-52/reflections-on-the-accountability-revolution>.

pregnant women and to children...but for the Karamajong...maintaining their elders was of supreme importance..."[52]

In these sorts of situations, it is reasonable to think that INGOs should deliberate, unhurriedly and in good faith, with a wide range of intended beneficiaries. The idea that INGOs should not raise a fuss, but instead simply enact their intended beneficiaries' existing preferences, underestimates the latter's capacity to engage with new ideas and change their minds. It also overlooks the fact that there are many people who want aid but are not receiving it. These considerations suggest that if an INGO cannot come to a workable compromise with a group of aid recipients after extensive good-faith deliberation, it should consider working elsewhere. Finally, the question of how much leeway or discretion INGOs should have simply on account of being (to some extent) non-governmental actors is a question that the agent for beneficiaries account raises but does not address.

A final "problem" with conceiving of INGOs as agents for their intended beneficiaries involves the issue of informed preferences. If INGOs acting consistently with their intended beneficiaries' preferences is intended in part to promote the latter's interests, but it is difficult for intended beneficiaries to get sufficiently comprehensive and accurate information about INGOs,[53] then this benefit of the agent for intended beneficiaries conception is reduced. However, I mention this issue primarily to suggest that it is unlikely to be decisive: rather than reject the agent for intended beneficiaries conception on these grounds, it would make more sense to demand more transparency and publicity on the part of INGOs. In addition, even if intended beneficiaries are not fully informed about what is in their best interest, they might be more informed than INGOs. Finally, INGOs acting consistently with their intended beneficiaries' preferences can do things other than promote the latter's interests narrowly construed: they can foster trust, show respect, and learn from local populations.

If the social role of rescuer captures the moral urgency of humanitarianism and the social role of partner captures the importance of equality, the idea that INGOs are agents for their intended beneficiaries (together with the concept of accountability, discussed below) primarily captures the relevance of democratic norms. But it does not offer an adequate specification

---

[52] Rony Brauman, quoted in Redfield, *Life in Crisis*, 174. Brauman explains that this redistribution was undertaken for reasons that would make sense even to Westerners. He also states that he no longer thinks that prioritizing women and children is necessarily moral: "Nobody was right; nobody was wrong."

[53] See also "Listening Exercise Report" from Tamil Nadu, Southern India (Oxfam and Listening Project, March 2012) and Antonio Donini, Larissa Fast, Greg Hansen, Simon Harris, Larry Minear, Tasneem Mowjee, and Andrew Wilder, "Humanitarian Agenda 2015: Final Report: The State of the Humanitarian Enterprise" (Feinstein International Center, 2008), 10.

of those norms. What does it look like for INGOs to be democratic in their relationships with their intended beneficiaries, in light of concerns about the rights and interests of minorities, disagreement between INGOs and their intended beneficiaries, and considerations of INGOs' own autonomy? In raising this question, the agent for intended beneficiaries approach—like the other approaches discussed above—broaches a critical issue, but does not address it adequately.

2.5 Accountability

Those who hoped that the 'accountability revolution' would be the silver bullet for the sector have been disappointed.
    —2013 Humanitarian Accountability Partnership Report[54]

Like "partnership," "accountability" is now a major buzzword among scholars and practitioners of humanitarian aid. Over the past fifteen years, INGOs have undertaken a range of reforms and initiatives under the banner of accountability, especially accountability to aid recipients. For example, the Humanitarian Accountability Partnership (HAP) was founded in 2003 with the express purpose of "making humanitarian action accountable to beneficiaries."[55]

While some progress has been made, it is clear that such efforts have not fully succeeded. As Donini et al. report:

> Despite the rhetoric of downward accountability to beneficiaries, mainstream humanitarians continue to talk principally to the like-minded, shunning different or dissenting voices. Much that is local and non-western in humanitarian action goes unrecognized: the coping mechanisms of communities, the parallel life-saving universe that includes *zakat*, migration and remittances.[56]

One possible explanation for the simultaneous widespread endorsement of the ideal of accountability and difficulty implementing it is that "accountability" can mean many different things. As one aid worker stated,

> accountability has now become part of our day-to-day jargon, but that's a disadvantage in many ways. Once you start asking staff from humanitarian agencies what they understand by accountability you quickly discover that comprehension varies a lot depending on who you are talking to.[57]

---

[54] Human Accountability Project, "2013 Humanitarian Accountability Report," June 2013, 9 <http://www.hapinternational.org/pool/files/2013-har.pdf>.
[55] Humanitarian Accountability Partnership, "What is Accountability?"
[56] Donini et al., "The State of the Humanitarian Enterprise," 4.
[57] Human Accountability Project, "2013 Humanitarian Accountability Report," 23. See also Knox-Clarke and Mitchell, "Reflections on the Accountability Revolution."

Thus, in order to determine whether "accountability to intended beneficiaries" might obviate the need for a new account of humanitarian INGO political ethics, we need to nail down what we are talking about a bit more precisely (while also remembering that the political effects of the concept of accountability in the world are in large measure a result of its ambiguity). On one prominent definition, accountability has three main components: (1) *standards* that an actor is supposed to meet, (2) an *account*, usually public, of whether the actor has met those standards, and if not, whether it has an adequate justification or excuse, and (3) meaningful *sanction* if the actor failed to meet the standards without adequate justification or excuse.[58] This definition offers some critical purchase on conceptions of accountability circulating in the humanitarian sector. For example, even though the HAP states that its purpose is to make humanitarian action accountable to beneficiaries, its definition of accountability says nothing about empowering intended beneficiaries (or other vulnerable groups) to sanction INGOs. Indeed, HAP emphasizes that it is not a "humanitarian claimants union."[59]

There are two main problems with taking the aspiration toward accountability, understood in this way, as a stand-in for an account of humanitarian INGO political ethics. First, it is one thing to define accountability; it is another to identify the content of the three components just described. "Filling in" those components involves answering many of the same questions that an account of humanitarian INGO political ethics must also answer; it covers much of the same ground.

The second issue is that, even if we did have a full account of the three components of accountability, the terrain of humanitarian INGO political ethics extends beyond issues of accountability. For instance, accountability focuses on the standards that actors are supposed to meet. Yet the language of accountability offers little leverage for dealing with situations in which actors cannot meet two relevant standards simultaneously; that is, it offers little leverage for dealing with possible conflicts among different responsibilities. In addition, the concept of accountability offers little leverage for thinking about the ethics of activities that are not responsibilities to an already-existing individual or group, for example galvanizing a constituency around an issue. Moreover, as HAP itself notes: "International organisations

[58] Jennifer C. Rubenstein, "Accountability in an Unequal World," *The Journal of Politics* 69.03 (2007): 616–32. See also Adam Branch, *Displacing Human Rights: War and Intervention in Northern Uganda* (New York: Oxford University Press, 2011), 113. On this definition, the main distinctions between accountability and the agent-for-intended beneficiaries approach are that the latter specifies one type of standard (consistency with intended beneficiaries' preferences) and says nothing about account-giving or sanctioning.

[59] Humanitarian Accountability Partnership, "What is Humanitarian Accountability?" But see also Human Accountability Project, "2013 Humanitarian Accountability Report."

and donors have no formal responsibility to respond in particular ways to a given situation. Even within a given crisis response, *organisations are generally accountable only for what they do, and how they do it; not for what they fail to do.*[60] In contrast, political ethics provides a language for addressing omissions.[61] Finally, a theory of humanitarian INGO accountability might direct our attention toward organizational capacities or virtues that have direct bearing on accountability, such as a capacity for public reason-giving. However, an account of political ethics can also attend to other capacities and virtues, such as equanimity or the ethics of resistance (discussed in Chapters 4 and 6, respectively).

In sum, the work of "filling in" the three components of the concept of accountability overlaps with the work of developing an account of humanitarian INGO political ethics, but political ethics extends beyond accountability to INGOs' intended beneficiaries.

2.6 Traditional Humanitarian Principles

"Aid priorities are calculated on the basis of need alone."
—The Code of Conduct for the International Red Cross and Red
Crescent Movement and NGOs in Disaster Relief

Yet another prominent, and in the view of some humanitarians very promising, basis for an account of humanitarian INGO political ethics are the traditional principles of classical humanitarianism developed by the International Committee of the Red Cross: "humanity," "impartiality," and "independence."[62] Virtually all of the major Western-based humanitarian INGOs have endorsed these principles. The Code of Conduct for the International Red Cross and Red Crescent Movement and NGOs in Disaster Relief, which includes these principles, has been signed by 492 INGOs and NGOs. (A fourth principle, "neutrality," is more controversial, but also widely accepted.)[63]

---

[60] Human Accountability Project, "2013 Humanitarian Accountability Report," 6. My italics. While the text is somewhat ambiguous, from the context this appears to be a descriptive rather than normative statement: it is a complaint that while INGOs should be held accountable for their omissions, they typically are not.

[61] Another perceived limitation of accountability that is often raised by practitioners is that it can be costly and time-consuming for everyone involved (not only INGOs, but also aid recipients, host governments, donors, and others). It is not clear that accountability is more costly and time-consuming than other equally effective ways of achieving the same ends.

[62] Jean Pictet, "The Fundamental Principles of the Red Cross: Commentary," International Committee for the Red Cross Resource Centre, January 1, 1979 <http://www.icrc.org/eng/resources/documents/misc/fundamental-principles-commentary-010179.htm>. These principles are more specific than what I call "humanitarian norms." See discussion in Chapter 1.

[63] David Rieff, "Afterword," in *Slaughterhouse: Bosnia and the Failure of the West* (New York: Touchstone, 1996), 253; Hugo Slim, "Claiming a Humanitarian Imperative: NGOs and the Cultivation of Humanitarian Duty," *Refugee Survey Quarterly* 21.3 (2002): 113–25.

One obvious limitation of these principles is that they are only meant to apply to humanitarian activities; they therefore provide little or no guidance regarding other activities that humanitarian INGOs regularly undertake, such as development aid, scientific research, or advocacy on non-humanitarian issues. Nor do these principles provide guidance regarding how resources should be allocated between humanitarian action and other activities.

But even within the domain of humanitarian action, these principles are of only limited help. For example, the ICRC Code states that "we recognize our obligation to provide humanitarian assistance wherever it is needed."[64] It also states that "[w]e shall endeavor not to act as instruments of government foreign policy." But the Code says nothing about situations—such as those in which combatants effectively control refugee settlements, or impose very high "taxes" on INGOs—in which "providing humanitarian assistance wherever it is needed" seems to *require* INGOs to act as instruments of government foreign (or domestic) policy. Likewise, the ICRC Code states that "[i]n our information, publicity and advertising activities, we shall recognize disaster victims as dignified humans, not hopeless objects," and also that signatories "will not allow external or internal demands for publicity to take precedence over the principle of maximizing overall relief assistance." However, the Code says nothing about what INGOs should do if it seems as if the only way for them to "maximize[e] overall relief assistance" is by portraying victims as hopeless objects (e.g. when using such images seems to be the only way to raise badly needed funds). Nor does it address conflicts between maximizing overall assistance and aid based on need alone. I do not mean to suggest that to be adequate, an account of humanitarian INGO political ethics must, or even can, offer determinate prescriptions for navigating these conflicts. But it should acknowledge and address them directly.

2.7 INGOs as Neo-Colonialists

I turn now to two approaches to humanitarian INGOs that threaten to obviate the need for an account of humanitarian INGO political ethics not by providing such an account, but rather by suggesting that INGOs are so fundamentally flawed that any account of INGO political ethics is beside the point, and indeed serves only to further legitimate organizations that should not exist.

One of these approaches—the more damning of the two allegations—accuses INGOs of being, in effect, colonialists in new uniforms. As Cohen,

---

[64] IFRC, "The Code of Conduct for the International Red Cross and Red Crescent Movement and NGOs in Disaster Relief" <http://www.ifrc.org/en/publications-and-reports/code-of-conduct/>. The other quotations in this paragraph are from this source.

Küpçü, and Khanna write: "Not so long ago, former colonial masters and superpower patrons propped...up [states 'teetering on the edge']. Today, however...private actors [including INGOs] have become the 'new colonialists' of the 21st century."[65] Although the rhetoric here is rather sweeping, there are striking parallels between INGOs and neo-colonial governments. For example, both INGOs and (some) colonial governments describe themselves as "helping" or "saving" distant populations. Yet like many colonial governments, some INGOs also dominate the populations they "help," create dependency,[66] weaken existing governance structures, and make people (in at least some respects) worse-off, all the while benefiting from their activities. INGOs can also abet other actors seen as neo-colonial (such as governments engaged in "humanitarian" military intervention). Finally, INGOs sometimes (intentionally or unintentionally) engage in the classic colonial tactic of rendering populations more "legible," and so easier to control, by gathering information about them, or encouraging them to live in particular areas or adopt particular practices.[67]

Yet in order to count as a reason against developing an account of humanitarian INGO political ethics, this analogy must do more than identify parallels between humanitarian INGOs and neo-colonialists. It must show that these parallels are so deep and pervasive, and involve such serious moral violations, that humanitarian INGOs should shut their doors immediately. However, most analogies between humanitarian INGOs (in general) and colonial governments do not go this far. This is because, while there are significant similarities, there are also significant differences between INGOs and colonial governments. Among other things, humanitarian INGOs do not murder or enslave people or steal their territory. Even the authors (cited above) who call INGOs the "new colonialists of the 21st century" do not say that they should disband; they simply say that INGOs should be more accountable.

[65] Michael A. Cohen, Maria Figueroa Küpçü, and Parag Khanna, "The New Colonialists." See also Craig Calhoun, The Idea of Emergency: Humanitarian Action and Global (Dis)Order," in Didier Fassin, and Mariella Pandolfi (eds.), Contemporary States of Emergency: The Politics of Military and Humanitarian Interventions (New York: Zone Books, 2010), 29–58; Mahmood Mamdani, Saviors and Survivors: Darfur, Politics, and the War on Terror (New York: Pantheon Books, 2009), 275; Issa G. Shivji, "Silences in NGO Discourse: The Role and Future of NGOs in Africa," African Development 31.4 (2006): 22–51. In A Cause for Our Times: Oxfam—The First Fifty Years (New York: Oxford University Press, 1992) Maggie Black notes that some of the first Oxfam employees were the children of British colonial administrators.

[66] Dependency is a complicated issue: it is not clear how widespread the attitudes and actions associated with "aid dependency" are. In addition, virtually everyone "depends" on the kind of public services that INGOs frequently provide, and INGOs depend on their donors. See Paul Harvey and Jeremy Lind, "Dependency and Humanitarian Relief: A Critical Analysis" (London: HPG Report 19, July 2005).

[67] James C. Scott, Seeing Like a State: How Certain Schemes to Improve the Human Condition Have Failed (New Haven: Yale University Press, 1998).

The neo-colonialism allegation directs our attention to very significant problems with INGOs. It also suggests one set of reasons why justice-based norms are relevant to humanitarian INGOs, despite some INGOs' claims to stay out of politics. However, on its own it does not obviate the need for an account of humanitarian INGO political ethics. To the contrary, it highlights important reasons why we need such an account.

2.8 INGOs as Multinational Corporations

The final conception of humanitarian INGOs that I will consider is that they are not significantly different from multinational corporations (MNCs). There are two main versions of this argument. One is highly critical of INGOs. For example, Cooley and Ron note that INGOs frequently "condemn their rivals' marketized or 'corporate' mentalities."[68] The other version, often emphasized by people in the business world and scholars who study business, suggests that the similarities between INGOs and MNCs are either good or normatively neutral.[69] I will address these in turn.

The critical version of the analogy often invokes a parallel between two tripartite relationships: INGOs are directly accountable to their donors and provide goods and services to aid recipients, while MNCs are directly accountable to their shareholders and boards of directors and provide goods and services to their customers.[70] That is, INGOs are like MNCs, donors are like shareholders, and aid recipients are like customers (see Fig. 2.1). This analogy is highly misleading. While aid recipients and customers both receive goods and services, they do so under drastically different conditions: customers can sanction MNCs by refusing to buy their products, but as was discussed above, it is currently very difficult for aid recipients to sanction INGOs. It is therefore not aid recipients but rather *donors* to INGOs that are analogous to an MNC's customers: just as customers use market forces to reward or sanction MNCs by buying their products or not, donors use market forces to reward or sanction INGOs by donating to them or not. Rather than being analogous to

---

[68] Alexander Cooley and James Ron, "The NGO Scramble: Organizational Insecurity and the Political Economy of Transnational Action," *International Security* 27.1 (2002): 5–39 (8). See also Susan Cotts Watkins, Ann Swidler, and Thomas Hannan, "Outsourcing Social Transformation: Development NGOs as Organizations," *Annual Review of Sociology* 38.1 (2012): 285–315 and Stephen Hopgood, "Saying 'No' to Wal-mart? Money and Morality in Professional Humanitarianism," in *Humanitarianism in Question: Politics, Power, Ethics*, ed. Michael Barnett and Thomas G. Weiss (Ithaca: Cornell University Press, 2008), 98–123. Hopgood's main focus is on the opposite question: whether MNCs can and should be humanitarian organizations.

[69] Nathalie Laidler-Kylander and Bernard Simonin, "How International Nonprofits Build Brand Equity," *International Journal of Nonprofit and Voluntary Sector Marketing* 14.1 (2009): 57–69.

[70] Rony Brauman, MSF and Anne Fouchard, MSF (interviews).

47

How the INGO/MNC analogy is often understood:

How the INGO/MNC analogy ought to be understood:

Figure 2.1. Two versions of the INGO/MNC analogy

customers, aid recipients are more like low-skilled workers working in a factory that supplies MNCs: just as low-skilled workers sometimes benefit from MNCs but often cannot effectively sanction them, aid recipients sometimes benefit from INGOs but often cannot effectively sanction them.[71]

If donors are analogous to customers and aid recipients are analogous to factory workers (who help to produce the "goods" that donors "buy"), then the relationship between donors and aid recipients is analogous to the relationship between customers and factory workers: just as it is difficult for a customer to discern how her purchase of a T-shirt affects the factory worker who made it, it is also difficult for donors to discern how their donations to INGOs affect aid recipients. In short, rather than an analogy between INGOs/donors/aid recipients and MNCs/shareholders/customers, the more apt analogy is between INGOs/donors/aid recipients and MNCs/customers/low-wage factory workers.

This latter specification of the analogy offers a way of viewing INGOs that can, I think, help to generate and clarify deep and important criticisms. In particular, it directs our attention to the ways in which INGOs "sell" emergency aid, advocacy, and other activities to their donors, and act as "wholesalers" between donors and activists from poor, marginalized, or oppressed groups (who "market" their cause to INGOs).[72] It also highlights that donors to INGOs are not merely charitable do-gooders, but also consumers of goods

---

[71] This analogy (like all analogies) has limited scope, and focuses primarily on power dynamics; I do not mean to suggest that the experience of working in a factory is substantively like receiving humanitarian aid.

[72] Clifford Bob, *The Marketing of Rebellion: Insurgents, Media, and International Activism* (New York: Cambridge University Press, 2005); Tim Large, "TIP SHEET: How to 'Sell' Forgotten

ranging from free return address labels and note cards to the opportunity to express sentiments of cosmopolitan solidarity.

However, to undermine the argument of this chapter, the MNC/INGO analogy needs to tell us that INGOs are so morally compromised by their similarities to MNCs that an account of humanitarian INGO political ethics is beside the point. But as with the analogy to colonialists, even critics who highlight INGOs' increasingly corporate, professionalized, bureaucratic, organizational culture and practices generally do not claim that this is in itself a reason for INGOs to close their doors.

We turn now to the claim that humanitarian INGOs' similarities to MNCs are either good or neutral. For this argument to count against the need to develop an account of humanitarian INGO political ethics, the similarities would have to be such that accounts of business ethics for MNCs would suffice for INGOs. But this is clearly not the case. Accounts of business ethics and stakeholder democracy offer some insights into INGOs, but they also have significant limitations.[73] Among other things, donors have different self-understandings and often much less direct interaction with what they are "buying" than customers often do. Aid recipients face different challenges, and have different experiences, than factory workers. INGOs also operate in contexts of severe conflict and instability that MNCs generally seek to avoid (unless their role is to provide security or logistical support in conflict settings), and have sources of moral authority that virtually all MNCs lack. The positive or neutral version of the analogy to MNCs therefore does not obviate the need for an account of humanitarian INGO political ethics, any more than the critical version does.

2.9 Conclusion

The eight extant approaches to conceptualizing and/or normatively evaluating humanitarian INGOs examined in this chapter have significant

Emergencies," *Thomson Reuters Foundation*, October 5, 2005 <http://www.trust.org/item/2005 1005114500-7oiru/>.

[73] For stakeholder theories of business ethics and democracy, see: Jem Bendell, "In Whose Name? The Accountability of Corporate Social Responsibility," *Development in Practice* 15.3–4 (2005): 362–74; Andrew Crane, Dirk Matten, and Jeremy Moon, "Stakeholders as Citizens? Rethinking Rights, Participation, and Democracy," *Journal of Business Ethics* 53.1–2 (2004): 107–22; Terry Macdonald, *Global Stakeholder Democracy: Power and Representation Beyond Liberal States* (New York: Oxford University Press, 2008); Dirk Matten and Andrew Crane, "What is Stakeholder Democracy? Perspectives and Issues," *Business Ethics: A European Review* 14.1 (2005): 6–13; Brendan O'Dwyer, "Stakeholder Democracy: Challenges and Contributions from Social Accounting," *Business Ethics: A European Review* 14.1 (2005): 28–41; Robert R. Phillips, Edward Freeman, and Andrew C. Wicks, "What Stakeholder Theory is Not," *Business Ethics Quarterly* 13.4 (2003): 479–502.

insufficiencies. Because, in addition to being insufficient, they also actively *mis*-describe humanitarian INGOs' activities, relationships, capacities, and/ or effects, layering these different "maps" on top of each other does not provide an adequate account of humanitarian INGO political ethics.

We therefore need a new map—but not one drawn entirely from scratch. Each of the approaches discussed above offered us something—an insight, a way of seeing, a question—that ought to inform our new map. In particular, this new map should reflect the relevance of humanitarian norms to INGOs' activities as captured by the social role of rescuer, the importance of egalitarian norms as suggested by the social role of partner, the relevance of democratic norms as suggested by the ideas that INGOs are agents for their intended beneficiaries and should be accountable to their intended beneficiaries, and the relevance of justice-based norms, as suggested by the colonialism analogy. Our new map should also acknowledge that INGOs have responsibilities to their donors, as suggested by the idea that INGOs are agents for their donors. It should attend to the traditional principles of classical humanitarianism, and it must incorporate awareness of the parallels between INGOs and MNCs.

I turn now to sketching this new map. My aim is to transcend the limitations of the eight approaches described in this chapter, while retaining their insights and responding to their provocations. It is striking that, of the eight approaches to INGOs discussed in in this chapter, only one—the neo-colonialism analogy—invokes the notion that INGOs are in any way governmental. In our new map, in contrast, the idea that humanitarian non-governmental organizations govern takes center stage.

3

A Map of Humanitarian INGO
Political Ethics

[B]efore MSF opened its hospital in Marere in July 2003, the region had very few young people, because so many were dying from preventable diseases. Now, if you take a simple walk around the town, you will see many youngsters who maybe wouldn't be here today if we hadn't given them immunizations and medical treatment. People jokingly call any child under the age of 11 "the MSF generation."

—Hussein Sheikh Qassim, MSF medical activities
manager in southern Somalia, July 2011[1]

On January 12, 2010 at 4:53 p.m., Haiti was struck by a 7.0 magnitude earthquake. At the time, the tiny Caribbean country was already reeling from numerous ongoing challenges: an average GDP of less than $2 a day, an average life expectancy of 62 years, illiteracy rates hovering near 50%, and extremely high rates of HIV/AIDS.[2] While Haiti had recently achieved some political stability after decades of turmoil, its political institutions remained fragile.[3] The combined effects of the earthquake and Haiti's pre-existing economic, social, and political difficulties proved catastrophic. Hundreds of thousands of people were killed: crushed beneath poorly constructed buildings, dead from wounds that could have been treated with adequate medical care, or felled by preventable diseases. Millions more were injured or left homeless. A few months into the massive relief and reconstruction effort, an

---

[1] MSF-Canada. "We Are Seeing Sick Patients Who, on Top of Being Sick, Are Actually Starving." August 19, 2011 <http://sites.msf.ca/news-media/news/2011/08/we-are-seeing-sick-patients-who-on-top-of-being-sick-are-actually-starving/>.

[2] Central Intelligence Agency. "Haiti," in *The World Factbook*. Washington, DC: Central Intelligence Agency. Page last updated on March 27, 2014 <https://www.cia.gov/library/publications/the-world-factbook/geos/ha.html>; United Nations Development Programme. "Human Development Indicators, Haiti." Human Development Reports <http://hdr.undp.org/en/countries/profiles/HTI>.

[3] US Department of State. "U.S. Relations With Haiti." Bureau of Western Hemisphere Affairs. Fact Sheet, February 11, 2013 <http://www.state.gov/r/pa/ei/bgn/1982.htm>.

aid worker commented that, "[n]o one has bothered to explain the humanitarian system to the Haitians and this is their government, effectively. They are doing everything a state would be doing—providing services, security and managing the country."[4]

The situation in Haiti after the 2010 earthquake was extreme, but not unique. It highlights three features of humanitarian INGOs that fundamentally shape their political ethics—or so I shall argue in this chapter.[5] First, these INGOs regularly engage in governance functions. They tend not to do so to the same "degree," so to speak, as some other types of actors, such as domestic governments or entrenched global governance institutions. Nor do they engage in governance all the time. Rather, they are *sometimes somewhat governmental*.

While the term "governance" can be used in many ways, I argue that humanitarian INGOs are governmental in two very specific ways (without denying that they might also be governmental in other ways). First, humanitarian INGOs regularly serve conventional governance functions—that is, they serve functions similar or identical to those often served by conventional (domestic) governments. For example, even before the 2010 earthquake, 80% of basic services in Haiti were provided by international or domestic NGOs.[6] Second, humanitarian INGOs engage in global governance. That is, they help to shape or constitute international institutions, both formal and informal. For example, the UN often uses the "Cluster Approach" to organize aid provision.[7] This approach, which has been widely criticized, involves organizing INGOs, domestic NGOs, UN agencies, and host government ministries into "clusters" that address particular issues, such as water or housing. In Haiti, critics argued that while the Cluster Approach facilitated better communication between UN agencies and INGOs, it excluded Haitian organizations and individuals, largely because cluster meetings took place at a hard-to-reach location and were conducted in English.[8] The INGOs

---

[4] Maura R. O'Connor, "Does International Aid Keep Haiti Poor?" *Slate*, January 7, 2011. For more recent background information on the aftermath of the earthquake, see Vijaya Ramachandran, "Is Haiti Doomed to Be the Republic of NGOs?" *Huffington Post*, January 12, 2012 <http://www.huffingtonpost.com/vijaya-ramachandran/haiti-relief-ngos_b_1194923.html>.

[5] As in the rest of this book, unless otherwise stated, by "humanitarian INGOs" I mean large-scale, mainstream, donor-funded INGOs that are based in wealthy Western countries and that do humanitarian aid in addition to whatever else they do.

[6] Kevin Edmonds, "Beyond Good Intentions: The Structural Limitations of NGOs in Haiti," *Critical Sociology* 39.3: 439–52.

[7] United Nations Office for the Coordination of Humanitarian Affairs, "Cluster Coordination" <http://www.unocha.org/what-we-do/coordination-tools/cluster-coordination>.

[8] Andrea Binder and François Grünewald, "Cluster Approach Evaluation, 2nd Phase: Haiti" (Berlin: Global Public Policy Institute, 2010) <http://www.urd.org/IMG/pdf/GPPi-URD_Haiti_EN.pdf>; Haiti Grassroots Watch, "The 'Cluster' System in Haiti." *Ayiti Kale Je—Haiti Grassroots Watch*, Dossier 1, Story 4, October 12, 2010 <http://haitigrassrootswatch.squarespace.com/dossier1story4/>; O'Connor, "Does International Aid Keep Haiti Poor?"

that participated in this system without criticizing it enhanced its power and perceived legitimacy. They thereby helped to further entrench and solidify a global governance institution, active not only in Haiti but also in many other countries, that seems to fall short when measured against democratic norms.

Second, humanitarian INGOs are *highly political*. Again, I mean this term in two specific ways, although I do not deny that INGOs can be political in other ways as well. First, humanitarian INGOs are political in that they have effects—often unintended, negative effects—that have political content; for example, they involve power relations among groups, or occur as a result of political processes or dynamics. Humanitarian INGOs are also political in that they exercise discursive power; that is, they help to shape widely shared meanings. For example, more than half of the US population donated money to INGOs and the Red Cross to help the victims of the Haiti earthquake.[9] The fact that so many people in the US found donating, often by text message, to be an appropriate response to the earthquake—rather than, say, ignoring it, condemning the Haitian people for their sins, or taking up arms on their behalf[10]—was due at least in part to INGOs' role in shaping perceptions of the earthquake's meaning.[11]

In addition to being sometimes somewhat governmental and highly political, humanitarian INGOs are *often second-best* actors. This is so with regard to a range of activities, including governance activities: INGOs not only govern *less* than conventional governments and other governmental actors as a descriptive matter, they also often govern *less well* as a normative matter.[12] By "less well" I mean less effectively, and in ways that are less consistent with democratic, egalitarian, humanitarian, and justice-based norms.[13] As Paul Farmer writes with regard to post-earthquake Haiti:

> The international community doesn't know best. Local people do. [INGOs] ... cannot replace the state—nor can the United Nations or anyone else. We don't have the expertise, and we won't stay forever. We don't have the same stake in building a community that the locals themselves have.[14]

[9] This figure is based on self-reports. See Kristen Purcell and Michael Dimock, "Americans Under Age 40 are as Likely to Donate to Japan Disaster Relief through Electronic Means as Traditional Means," *Pew Research Center's Internet & American Life Project*, March 23, 2011 <http://www.pewinternet.org/2011/03/23/americans-under-age-40-are-as-likely-to-donate-to-japan-disaster-relief-through-electronic-means-as-traditional-means/>.

[10] As some Americans did to fight Franco in the Spanish Civil War.

[11] See Didier Fassin, *Humanitarian Reason: A Moral History of the Present* (Berkeley: University of California Press, 2012), 226. This claim is difficult to prove, but it seems more likely than the alternative (that INGOs played little or no role in generating this perception).

[12] By distinguishing between quantity and quality of governance, I leave open the conceptual possibility that governance by a "less governmental" actor is normatively better than governance by a "more governmental" actor.

[13] See Chapter 1 for a discussion of these norms.

[14] Paul Farmer, "Five Lessons From Haiti's Disaster," *Foreign Policy*, November 29, 2010 <http://www.foreignpolicy.com/articles/2010/11/29/5_lessons_from_haitis_disaster>.

In addition to being second-best at governance activities, humanitarian INGOs are also sometimes second-best at a range of other activities, and compared to a range of other actors (not only governmental actors). They can also be second-best compared to an institutional structure or state of affairs. That is, in some cases what is first-best compared to an INGO is not another actor, such as a government or domestic NGO, but rather an entirely different configuration of actors and institutions.

This chapter "maps" the three features of humanitarian INGOs' ethical and political terrain just described: that they are sometimes somewhat governmental (with regard to conventional governance and global governance), highly political (in that they have unintended political effects and exercise discursive power), and often second-best (although sometimes actors of last resort). I will argue that this map is not only more descriptively accurate than the eight approaches to conceptualizing and normatively evaluating humanitarian INGOs discussed in the previous chapter, it also directs our attention in more productive ways: toward the activities, relationships, capacities, and effects that generate significant political and ethical responsibilities on the part of humanitarian INGOs, toward the most important ways in which these responsibilities regularly come into practical conflict with each other, toward the ethical predicaments that arise as a result of these conflicts, and—though more tentatively—toward what routes humanitarian INGOs might take to navigate these predicaments in ways that are consistent, or as consistent as possible, with democratic, egalitarian, humanitarian, and/or justice-based norms.

Alas, the map of humanitarian INGO political ethics sketched in this chapter does not reveal many direct or easy paths. Instead, it shows that INGOs regularly face conflicts among and between their ethical, political, and practical responsibilities and commitments. That is, there is often no way for INGOs to act—that is, to provide humanitarian aid in a particular location, engage in advocacy on a particular issue, etc.—and sometimes no way for INGOs to stop acting, without significant moral compromise or sacrifice.

In addition to showing that this is the case, an account of humanitarian INGO political ethics can also suggest that some moral compromises are more acceptable than others. However, an account of humanitarian political ethics that does not do this does not for this reason fail, any more than a map that does not suggest that there is one clearly best route across a particular terrain fails: there simply might not *be* one clearly best route, or even any particularly good ones. But even if this is the case, it is still important to try to identify the least-bad options, and discern both how bad they are, and why they are less bad than the alternatives.

In later chapters, I will argue that this sort of analysis is not only important for individual INGOs deciding what to do in particular contexts; it is also essential for an overall assessment of humanitarian INGOs as actors, and for our understanding of the ethical and political position of donors. In particular, if one result of INGOs being sometimes somewhat governmental, highly political, and often second-best is that they regularly face tragic ethical conflicts in which all available courses of action or inaction involve serious moral compromise, then it is not only INGOs themselves that must make moral compromises; anyone who empowers INGOs or entrusts INGOs to act on their behalf is party to those compromises, as well. More fundamentally, the very fact that INGOs persistently face severe ethical conflicts matters, *regardless of how they choose to navigate those conflicts*, because it raises the question of whether there might be other, better, ways to address the issues that humanitarian INGOs address.

The next three sections discuss each of the three main features of our map in turn: that humanitarian INGOs are sometimes somewhat governmental (3.1), highly political (3.2), and often second-best (3.3). Section 3.4 briefly discusses the moral permissions or freedoms (as opposed to the responsibilities) generated by these features. Section 3.5 shows how this map provides a basis for conceptualizing four ethical predicaments that humanitarian INGOs regularly face.

3.1 Humanitarian INGOs are Sometimes Somewhat Governmental

Humanitarian INGOs sometimes engage in two forms of governance, albeit usually to a limited degree: conventional governance and global governance. Before discussing these, though, I want to briefly explain the order of exposition of what follows. My claim is that humanitarian INGOs are *sometimes somewhat* governmental—not that they are exactly like, or even very similar to, conventional governments. Indeed, while humanitarian INGOs engage in activities, develop relationships and capacities, and have effects that are in some ways like those of conventional governments, in many respects they are dramatically different from conventional governments. For example, unlike many conventional governments, humanitarian INGOs are not elected. They rely on voluntary donations rather than mandatory taxes for funding, do not have a monopoly on the legitimate use of force, and are perceived as outsiders by their "constituents." However, because many of the ways in which INGOs differ from conventional governments also make them normatively worse at governing (or so I shall argue), my discussion of these differences unfolds later in the chapter, in the section on humanitarian INGOs as second-best actors. In order to understand the ethical predicaments that humanitarian INGOs face, we must look at how their similarities to conventional governments generate one set of responsibilities (described in this section), while their differences from and inferiority to conventional governments and other governmental actors generate another, often conflicting, set of responsibilities (described in later sections). It is only once we have all of these responsibilities before us that we will be able to understand the ethical predicaments that INGOs face as a result of conflicts among these responsibilities.

3.1.1. *Conventional Governance*

By "conventional governance" I mean the activities, relationships, capacities, and effects that are widely seen as the bailiwick of conventional governments. When scholars use the term "governance" in reference to humanitarian INGOs, they often mean global governance—or, in some cases, Foucauldian governance or discursive power—not conventional governance.[15] But humanitarian INGOs *do* sometimes engage in conventional governance, although to a lesser degree than well-functioning conventional governments. This is worth noticing because political theorists and philosophers have said a great deal about the responsibilities that conventional governments have as a result of engaging in conventional governance. These accounts—even though they are quite diverse—tend to be much more well developed than accounts of the responsibilities associated with global governance. So while it is perhaps more difficult to show empirically that INGOs engage in conventional governance than it is to show that they engage in global governance or exercise discursive power, insofar as we *are* able to show this, the normative leverage provided by the comparison is much greater.

This means that, in comparing INGOs to conventional governments, we are not interested in just any similarities between them, nor are we only interested in the extent to which INGOs share the core, constitutive, or definitional features of conventional governments (whatever one takes those to be). Rather, our interest is in how much humanitarian INGOs resemble

---

[15] See Catherine Lu, "World Government," in *The Stanford Encyclopedia of Philosophy* (Fall 2012 edition), ed. Edward N. Zalta <http://plato.stanford.edu/archives/fall2012/entries/world-government/>; Fassin, *Humanitarian Reason*; and Michael N. Barnett, "Humanitarian Governance," *Annual Review of Political Science* 16.1 (2013): 379–98. As I discuss further below, an important exception is critics of INGOs, such as De Waal (Alexander De Waal, *Famine Crimes: Politics & the Disaster Relief Industry in Africa* (Bloomington: Indiana University Press, 1997)), and Cohen, Küpçü, and Khanna (Michael A. Cohen, Maria Figueroa Küpçü, and Parag Khanna, "The New Colonialists," who argue that by serving domestic governance functions, INGOs are displacing conventional domestic governments in countries such as Afghanistan and Haiti. These critics focus more on the negative effects of INGOs engaging in governance than on the responsibilities that they might develop as a result of these activities. In contrast, I suggest that we need to keep both in view, and indeed that the presence of both of these dynamics is a major source of the ethical predicaments that INGOs face.

conventional governments, specifically with regard to the activities, relationships, capacities, and effects that lead conventional governments to have particular ethical responsibilities.[16]

Although, as just noted, discussions of humanitarian INGO *governance* usually focus on global governance or discursive power rather than conventional domestic governance, commentators and analysts do sometimes analogize humanitarian INGOs to conventional governments. However, they usually analogize INGOs to the *foreign* policies and practices of *donor* governments. For example, Development Initiatives observes that "if [Médecins Sans Frontières] were a country [in 2010], [it] would have been the second largest humanitarian donor after the United States and ahead of the United Kingdom."[17] This type of comparison is helpful for understanding the relative scale of INGOs' spending compared to humanitarian aid spending by donor governments. But for the reasons just elucidated, we want to compare INGOs to conventional *domestic* governments. Moreover, we want to compare INGOs to our *ideas* about the ethical and political responsibilities of conventional governments—not what these governments actually do (that will come later, and serve another purpose). This means that we are not ultimately concerned with how much money INGOs spend—even how much they spend compared to domestic governments. Rather, we are concerned with what their spending tells us about the substance of INGOs' activities, relationships, capacities, and effects, and how these compare to the responsibility-generating activities, relationships, capacities, and effects of conventional governments.

Humanitarian INGOs regularly engage in at least three kinds of conventional governance activities: they provide basic services, such as food, water, and medical care to large populations for extended periods; they influence the coercive policies and practices of conventional governments; and they make large-scale decisions about resource use that have public effects. There are no precise formulas or cut-off points for identifying when a humanitarian INGO's activities function as a form of conventional governance, but ethical and political judgments are rarely precise in this way. Rather, what

---

[16] This strategy is similar to that used by some cosmopolitan theorists to show that individuals have demanding moral duties across borders: Cosmopolitans argue that relationships among individuals in different countries are relevantly like relationships among fellow-citizens, and global institutional structures are relevantly like domestic institutional structures, such that individuals' responsibilities to foreigners are similar to their responsibilities to co-nationals. See Charles R. Beitz, *Political Theory and International Relations* (Princeton, NJ: Princeton University Press, 1999); Thomas W. Pogge, *World Poverty and Human Rights*, 2nd edn. (Malden, MA: Polity Press, 2008); Thomas Nagel, "The Problem of Global Justice," *Philosophy & Public Affairs* 33.2 (2005): 113–47; Peter Singer, *The Life You Can Save: Acting Now to End World Poverty*.

[17] Velina Stoianova, *Private Funding: An Emerging Trend in Humanitarian Donorship* (Wells, UK: Global Humanitarian Assistance, 2012), 6.

the conventional governance framework provides is an interpretive lens that helps us to see possible ethical or political implications of INGOs' activities (and capacities, relationships, and effects) that we would otherwise have overlooked or misconstrued.

3.1.1.1 BASIC SERVICE PROVISION

Humanitarian INGOs regularly provide basic services, including access to food, shelter, clean water, medical care, education, sanitation facilities, and information, to large populations—sometimes hundreds of thousands of people in a contiguous geographic area—for extended periods, sometimes years or decades. For example, as one MSF employee working in South Somalia stated in 2011:

> MSF is saving a lot of people—children and adults—who might otherwise have died, from malnutrition or from preventable causes. There are no other agencies anywhere near here, and we are the only organization providing assistance—in terms of both health care and food—in this region. We have been doing this for years.[18]

This sort of service provision, I want to argue, often functions as a form of conventional governance. Basic service provision by INGOs is more conventionally governmental the more that it is large-scale, formal, long-term, and under the INGO's own control (rather than that of host governments, occupying forces, or institutional donors). Basic service provision is even more governmental if, because of the features just mentioned, aid recipients reasonably come to rely on these services and/or other actors do not provide these services. Yet another common effect of this kind of service provision—one that does not necessarily make it more governmental, but that is the result of other characteristics that make it governmental—is that INGOs benefit from providing these services.

Basic service provision is not always governmental: when the Good Samaritan of the biblical parable provides food and lodging to the Levite he finds lying beaten and robbed by the side of the road, his actions are paradigmatically private and charitable, not governmental. So how often do INGOs, individually and/or collectively, provide basic services in ways that are (somewhat) governmental? Because we have not established firm boundaries between what is governmental and what is not, we cannot answer this question precisely. But all we need to establish is that INGOs engage in conventional governance often enough that an account of humanitarian INGO political ethics should address it. And indeed, somewhat governmental basic

---

[18] MSF-Canada, "We Are Seeing Sick Patients Who, on Top of Being Sick, Are Actually Starving."

service provision by INGOs appears to be widespread. As in Haiti before the earthquake, in 2008, 80% of all public services in Afghanistan, including health care and education, were delivered by international and local NGOs.[19] More generally, anthropologists Bornstein and Redfield note that in "white jeep states," "international agencies and NGOs play a significant role in providing what welfare services exist."[20] Writing about "unusable Africa," James Ferguson describes "a kind of government by NGO, often in a humanitarian mode, with a hodgepodge of transnational private voluntary organizations carrying out the day-to-day work of providing rudimentary governmental and social services, especially in areas of crisis and conflict."[21]

We can also get a sense of the scale of conventional governance by INGOs by looking at the activities of individual INGOs. CARE reports that in 2012, it "reach[ed] more than 83 million people."[22] The same year, Save the Children "helped 125 million girls and boys."[23] Oxfam UK "supported more than 13.5 million people in 2012–13."[24] In 2012, MSF medical teams carried out more than 8.3 million outpatient consultations and treated over 1.6 million cases of malaria.[25] Not all these individuals received basic services from INGOs; some were "helped" or "reached" by development projects or other activities. Of those who did receive basic services, some received services from more than one INGO. Even accounting for all of this, it seems likely that several million people received aid in a somewhat governmental way in 2012—and that is just taking into account four INGOs.

Yet another way to understand the extent to which service provision by INGOs is governmental is to examine countries in which humanitarian INGOs clearly serve(d) a conventional governance role, such as Haiti and Afghanistan, and notice that these cases alone involve millions of people. To return to the Haiti example, even before the 2010 earthquake, INGOs in Haiti often had "greater capacity and more funding than the Haitian government."[26] Haiti was often referred to as a "Republic of NGOs" because INGOs played such a crucial role in providing basic services, often with little effective

---

[19] Cohen, Küpçü, and Khanna, "New Colonialists".

[20] Erica Bornstein and Peter Redfield, *Forces of Compassion: Humanitarianism Between Ethics and Politics* (Santa Fe, NM: School for Advanced Research Press, 2011), 20–2.

[21] James Ferguson, "Seeing Like an Oil Company: Space, Security, and Global Capital in Neoliberal Africa," *American Anthropologist* 107.3 (2005): 377–82 (380).

[22] CARE, "About Us" <http://www.care.org/about>.

[23] Save the Children, "Interactive Map" <http://www.savethechildren.org/site/c.8r KLIXMGIpI4E/b.7801347/k.981A/Interactive_Map.htm>.

[24] Oxfam UK, "Countries We Work In" <http://www.oxfam.org.uk/what-we-do/countries-we-work-in>.

[25] MSF, "International Activity Report 2012," July 16, 2013 <http://www.msf.org/sites/msf.org/files/msf_activity_report_2012_interactive_final.pd>.

[26] Madeleine Kristoff and Liz Panarelli, "Haiti: A Republic of NGOs?" (Washington, DC: The United States Institute of Peace, 2010).

oversight by the Haitian government.[27] As noted above, the same can be said for some regions of Afghanistan in the late 2000s. Likewise, in 2012, 463,000 Somalis lived in the Dadaab refugee camp in northeast Kenya; ten thousand of them were born in the camp to refugee parents who were also born in the camp.[28] While the camp was officially overseen by the UNHCR and the Kenyan government, the INGO CARE was the main provider of food, water, sanitation, and hygiene services to residents of the camp for many years.[29] Based on these considerations, rough as they are, I conclude that humanitarian INGOs engage in somewhat governmental basic service provision often enough that it comprises a significant feature of their political and ethical landscape.

What responsibilities do humanitarian INGOs have as a result of engaging in somewhat governmental basic service provision? What would it look like, and is it even possible, for these INGOs to provide somewhat governmental services in ways that are consistent with democratic, egalitarian, justice-based, and humanitarian norms? One answer to this question is offered by the English utilitarian philosopher John Stuart Mill. Mill, who lived in the mid-nineteenth century and was a keen critical observer of the humanitarian and social reform efforts of his time, wrote that,

> When a person, either by express promise or by conduct has encouraged another to rely upon his continuing to act in a certain way—to build expectations and calculations, and stake any part of his plan of life upon that supposition—a new series of moral obligations arises on his part toward that person, which may possibly be overruled, but cannot be ignored.[30]

In this passage Mill is discussing individuals. Contemporary philosopher John Simmons explains why it is especially important for actors that make "institutional rules," such as governments, to acknowledge the moral obligations that Mill describes. The crucial issue here is "rug-pulling":

> [I]n changing even unjust institutional rules, we are generally sensitive to the moral dangers of "rug-pulling"...that is, cases where people base life plans or important activities on the reasonable expectation that the rules will remain

---

[27] Kristoff and Panarelli, "Haiti: A Republic of NGOs?"

[28] UNHCR, "Dadaab—World's Biggest Refugee Camp 20 Years Old" <http://www.unhcr.org/4f439dbb9.html>.

[29] CARE, "Ongoing Crisis in the Horn of Africa" <http://www.care.org/emergencies/horn-of-africa-hunger-crisis>. While it is difficult to say for certain how much autonomy CARE exercised in its day-to-day operations, it is likely that this autonomy was significant. The more significant it was, the more governmental CARE's role.

[30] John Stuart Mill, "On Liberty," in *On Liberty and Other Writings*, ed. Stephan Collini (Cambridge: Cambridge University Press, 1989), 103–4. Mill also observed that "Charity almost always does too much or too little: it lavishes its bounty in one place, and leaves people to starve in another." Cited in James W. Nickel, *Making Sense of Human Rights* (Malden, MA: Blackwell, 2007), 147–8.

unchanged (or, worse, where they are simply *required* to structure their activities around existing rules) and then have the rug pulled from beneath them by sudden institutional change.[31]

Simmons is not saying that governments have responsibilities to avoid abrupt and disruptive changes because they are governments. Rather, his claim is that *any* actor that lays down a rug (so to speak) has a responsibility to avoid, as much as possible, pulling that rug out from under the people who are on it. One might think that rug-pulling in a refugee camp, IDP settlement, or other context where people's lives are already significantly disrupted would be less objectionable than rug-pulling in a more stable context. I would contend that if anything, the opposite is true. In the first place, as noted above, people often live in refugee camps for years, decades, or even their entire lives. In addition, stability and predictability are not the sorts of things that only matter once one has them to a certain degree; every little bit helps. Indeed, when people are just scraping by, any change in the structures or resources that they rely on can lead to an avalanche of ill effects.

While Mill and Simmons are both liberals, albeit of different stripes, this is not a distinctively liberal insight. Even though it emphasizes the importance of individuals being able to pursue their own plans of life, which is an important liberal value, the point about rug-pulling also acknowledges a fact that liberals are often accused of forgetting: individuals are deeply imbricated in each other's lives, and institutions and structures are also imbricated in individuals' lives, such that my decisions are likely to affect your options, and vice versa. It is very difficult—indeed, it is sometimes impossible—for us to simply leave each other alone. All of this suggests that the more basic service provision by INGOs resembles basic service provision by a conventional government—which is to say, the more it functions like a rug—the greater INGOs' responsibilities to continue providing those services or ensure that they are provided by others. As Mill notes, these responsibilities might be overruled by other factors, but they cannot be ignored.

This responsibility does not arise from "helping" itself—I am not suggesting that helping engenders a responsibility to continue helping.[32] Rather, these additional responsibilities arise because it is impossible for INGOs to help without also doing other responsibility-generating things simultaneously, such as creating the "rug" on which aid recipients stand, displacing other service providers, developing relationships with the aid recipients, and benefiting from those relationships. It is these other things (or, one might

---

[31] A. John Simmons, "Ideal and Nonideal Theory," *Philosophy & Public Affairs* 38.1 (2010): 5–36 (20). I thank Colin Kielty for bringing this passage to my attention.

[32] This might be the case in other contexts, such as medical professionals' responsibility to continue providing certain kinds of care once they have started.

say, these additional dimensions of INGOs' helping activities) that are the source of the responsibilities discussed above, rather than "helping" narrowly construed.

As will become clear in the next chapter, a crucial feature of this argument about rug-pulling is that it provides a basis for defending an INGO's decision to continue providing aid even when in so doing that INGO has some negative effects. It does this by offering a sophisticated account of the *consequences* of withdrawing. In contrast, INGOs sometimes defend decisions to continue providing aid in these circumstances on the basis of a *duty* to provide aid, or the "humanitarian imperative."[33] Duty-based arguments and arguments that aid is intrinsically valuable are dangerous in these contexts because, by justifying the provision of aid on grounds other than its likely effects, they can end up undermining the interests of the very people INGOs claim to serve. However, such arguments have sometimes seemed like the only way to capture the intuition—shared, in some cases, by expatriate aid workers on the ground, locally hired aid workers, and aid recipients—that despite their negative effects, INGOs really should stay and continue to provide aid. The rug-pulling argument provides an alternative to duty-based arguments by highlighting consequences that are difficult to see from the perspective of a cost-benefit analysis that does not recognize INGOs' conventional governance role. It also provides an alternative to arguments based on "special obligations" or obligations that INGOs have only in virtue of having an established relationship with a particular group. While such relationships have normative significance, putting too much weight on them can unfairly disadvantage people who need and want aid, but have thus far been passed over.[34]

When conventional governments provide basic services, there is an expectation that they will not only continue to do so (or provide significant advanced warning that they are planning to stop), but also that they will do so in a way that is non-arbitrary, respectful, and responsive to people's preferences and interests. There is also an expectation that they will explain the reasons for their actions publicly. Governments do not have these responsibilities only because they are formally elected. They also have these responsibilities because they are official actors with moral authority that serve governance functions. Insofar as INGOs share these features, their responsibilities resemble those of conventional governments.

---

[33] Hugo Slim, "Claiming a Humanitarian Imperative: NGOs and the Cultivation of Humanitarian Duty," *Refugee Survey Quarterly* 21.3 (2002): 113–25.

[34] Lisa Fuller, "Justified Commitments? Considering Resource Allocation and Fairness in Médecins Sans Frontières-Holland," *Developing World Bioethics* 6.2 (2006): 59–70.

3.1.1.2 INFLUENCING COERCIVE GOVERNMENT POLICIES AND PRACTICES

A second conventional governance activity that humanitarian INGOs regularly undertake is intentionally influencing the coercive policies and practices of domestic governments.[35] Many large humanitarian INGOs engage in advocacy on issues such as fair trade, access to essential medicines, banning land mines, and reducing the use of US agricultural surplus in aid programs.[36] While precise figures are difficult to find because of how INGOs report their spending, Oxfam UK spent $30 million (7% of its total spending) on advocacy in 2012–13.[37] In 2011–12, Doctors Without Borders (US) spent $8.9 million on "direct program support, advocacy on behalf of our patients and programs, and public education and communications."[38]

Discussions of policymaking often distinguish between government officials who govern, and advocates who seek to influence government officials. This distinction is, however, blurry in practice, especially when governments are under-resourced or the issue in question has low salience with the general public. Under these conditions, advocates sometimes go beyond simply educating or deliberating with government officials, to actually engage in policymaking themselves.[39] Humanitarian INGOs' advocacy is sometimes governmental in this way.

What responsibilities do INGOs have as a result of engaging in this type of conventional governance? A widely accepted tenet of democratic theory is that, in shaping domestic policy, legislators should promote the preferences and interests of the people likely to be significantly affected by their

---

[35] Advocacy efforts in conventional governance and global governance contexts are often closely connected empirically. I distinguish them conceptually for the methodological reason described above: we have much more well-developed accounts of the responsibilities associated with the former than the latter.

[36] See, for example, Oxfam International, "Trade Campaign" <http://www.oxfam.org/en/campaigns/trade>; MSF Access Campaign, "About Us" <http://www.msfaccess.org/the-access-campaign>; International Campaign to Ban Landmines, "National Campaigns" <https://www.icbl.org/index.php/icbl/Campaigns>; CARE, "Support Food Aid Reform" <http://www.care.org/work/advocacy/food-aid>; Eben Harrell, "CARE Turns Down U.S. Food Aid," *Time*, August 15, 2007 <http://content.time.com/time/nation/article/0,8599,1653360,00.html>.

[37] Oxfam, "Oxfam Annual Report and Accounts 2012–2013," 5 <http://www.oxfam.org/sites/www.oxfam.org/files/oxfam-annual-report-2012-2013.pdf>.

[38] MSF-USA, "US Annual Report 2012," 62 <http://www.doctorswithoutborders.org/sites/usa/files/attachments/msf_usa_annual_report_2012.pdf>.

[39] Describing the "cosy" relationship between Oxfam and the Blair government, Katherine Quarmby writes: "Part of the closeness is in the exchange of personnel. This is not new. Frank Judd, a former director of Oxfam, became a Labour peer and spoke for the party on international development in the Lords in the 1990s. But the links have become more intimate under this government. Shriti Vadera, who advises Brown on international development, is an Oxfam trustee. Justin Forsyth was director of policy and campaigns at Oxfam before joining the Downing Street Policy Unit to advise Blair on the issue. When Oxfam recently advertised for Forsyth's successor, two of the four candidates called for vetting were either current or former special advisers." Catherine Quarmby, "Why Oxfam Is Failing Africa," *The New Statesman*, May 30, 2005 <http://www.newstatesman.com/node/150728>.

decisions (a group that is, rightly or wrongly, usually assumed to be comprised of their constituents or the citizens of their country).[40] One might think that legislators have this responsibility because they are elected, and that, because INGOs are not elected, they do not have this responsibility. But as with basic service provision, this gets things partially backwards: while legislators have a duty to respond to the interests and preferences of their constituents because they are elected, they are also elected because it is normatively important for coercive policies and practices to track the interests and preferences of their constituents (who are, again, assumed to be the same as those whom legislative policies significantly affect). Thus, the more that INGO advocacy influences domestic government policies, the greater INGOs' responsibility to promote the preferences and interests of the poor and marginalized people likely to be significantly affected by those policies—that is, the greater their responsibility to be good democratic representatives of these groups.

3.1.1.3 LARGE-SCALE DECISIONS ABOUT RESOURCE USE

A third conventional governance activity that INGOs regularly undertake is making large-scale decisions about resource use. These decisions are typically major budgetary decisions about how to allocate resources among particular activities, issues, initiatives, and countries, including the activities of basic service provision and advocacy just described. Of course, governments are not the only types of actors that make large-scale decisions about resource use; multinational corporations, religious orders, and foundations do as well. So why should we think that in making these decisions, INGOs' activities, and hence responsibilities, resemble those of conventional governments? The reason is that, like governments (but to a lesser degree), INGOs' large-scale decisions about resource use are decisions about governmental activities: activities that have large-scale and sometimes coercive effects. These decisions have implications not only for the private interests of many people, but also for their shared, collective interests.[41] In other words, INGOs' decisions about resource use are governmental insofar as they are not only large-scale, but also have public effects.

These decisions are more governmental the more resources they involve, the more people they affect, the more profound these effects are, and the more they relate to matters of public concern. INGOs' large-scale decisions about resource use are also more governmental the more discretion INGOs have

---

[40] Robert E. Goodin, "Enfranchising All Affected Interests, and Its Alternatives."

[41] Insofar as multinational corporations and other types of actors also engage in large-scale decisions about resource use that are governmental, their responsibilities might resemble those of governments, too.

in making these decisions, rather than being constrained by the demands of donors or host governments.

One might object to this analogy between INGOs and conventional governments by noting that while normative insights about how governments should allocate resources are most settled—or at least, the lines of debate surrounding them are clearest—with regard to *domestic* allocative decisions, INGOs' large-scale decisions about resource use regularly allocate resources *internationally*, among dozens of different countries. This difference is, however, less significant than it might initially appear to be: just as governments have a *prima facie* responsibility to treat all of their citizens equally, INGOs have a *prima facie* responsibility to treat all individuals equally. In both cases there are profound questions about what "equal treatment" should mean, especially given that different citizens/individuals have different histories, preferences, capabilities, etc. But neither domestic governments nor INGOs are supposed to grant any one group special, preferred status.

Having established that INGOs sometimes act analogously to conventional governments in their large-scale decisions about resource use, we now want to draw on what we know about domestic governments to elucidate INGOs' responsibilities in making these decisions. In particular, how should governments make large-scale decisions about resource use in the face of repeated emergencies that are interspersed with non-emergency situations that are also quite dire? Unfortunately, as far as I have been able to discern, very little political theoretical work addresses this question. Instead, there is, on the one hand, work about distributive justice under "normal" conditions, for example by John Rawls and his interlocutors. These authors view large-scale emergencies as "non-ideal" complications to address later, after ideal theory has been mostly worked out.[42] On the other hand, there is work about decision-making within acute emergencies, for example the literature on the ethics of triage.[43]

While neither of these literatures directly addresses our question, they converge on the idea that, when people's very survival is at stake and resources are scarce, governments should put significant weight on avoiding as much morally important harm and suffering as possible—as opposed to, say, strictly

---

[42] John Rawls, *A Theory of Justice*, revised edn. (Cambridge, MA: Harvard University Press, 1999); Simmons, "Ideal and Non-Ideal Theory."

[43] John C. Moskop and Kenneth V. Iserson, "Triage in Medicine, Part II: Underlying Values and Principles," *Annals of Emergency Medicine* 49.3 (2007): 282–87. While theorists such as Nomi Claire Lazar (*States of Emergency in Liberal Democracies* (Cambridge and New York: Cambridge University Press, 2009)) and Bonnie Honig (*Emergency Politics: Paradox, Law, Democracy* (Princeton, NJ: Princeton University Press, 2009)) have pushed back against the tendency to think in terms of norms and exceptions (as embodied in the work of Carl Schmitt and his interlocutors), they have not elucidated the implications of their views for resource distribution.

prioritizing civil and political liberties over economic and social well-being, or ensuring that economic inequalities benefit the worst-off.[44] Thus, if we want to know how INGOs should make large-scale decisions about resource use in situations involving intermittent and ongoing emergencies and serious non-emergencies, the literature on resource allocation suggests that a central guiding principle should be to maximally alleviate morally important harm.

To summarize, INGOs engage in at least three types of conventional governance—or more precisely, three activities for which normative arguments about conventional domestic governments seem to offer some leverage: basic resource provision, helping to shape coercive government policies, and making large-scale decisions about resource use that have public effects. With regard to basic resource provision, the comparison to governments suggests that the more governmental INGOs' role, the more reason they have to continue providing aid, even when doing so involves moral compromise. With regard to advocacy and other activities that influence the coercive policies of domestic governments, the comparison to governments suggests that INGOs should seek to be good representatives of poor and marginalized people. Finally, in the context of large-scale decisions about resource use, the comparison to governments suggests that INGOs should place significant weight on maximally alleviating morally important harm.

These, then, are the routes that look most plausible when we consider *only some* features of humanitarian INGOs' political ethical terrain: those that involve conventional governance activities and relationships. We turn next to identifying additional features on our map—features that call these initially plausible routes into question.

3.1.2. *Global Governance*

By "global governance" I mean helping to shape the rules and practices of international and supranational institutions, both formal and informal—that is, helping to shape coercive institutions that operate above the level of the nation-state.[45] It is widely accepted that humanitarian INGOs sometimes

---

[44] Moskop and Iserson ("Triage in Medicine, Part II") suggest that while other approaches are sometimes used, utilitarianism is most widely accepted by emergency professionals for dealing with triage situations. Rawls (*Theory of Justice*, rev. ed) argues that allocation of commodities to needy individuals does not fall within his theory (56) and that poorer societies sometimes have good reason to prioritize economic development over preservation of political liberty in order to eventually secure political liberty (Section 26).

[45] Allen Buchanan and Robert O. Keohane, "The Legitimacy of Global Governance Institutions," *Ethics & International Affairs* 20.4 (2006): 405–37; Thomas Risse, "Global Governance and Communicative Action," *Government and Opposition* 39.2 (2004): 288–313; Thomas Risse (ed.), *Governance Without a State? Policies and Politics in Areas of Limited Statehood* (New York: Columbia University Press, 2013), 2; Anne-Marie Slaughter, *A New World Order* (Princeton, NJ: Princeton University Press, 2005), especially ch. 4; David Held, Anthony McGrew, David Goldblatt,

engage in global governance, so defined. They do not do so to the same extent as formal global governance institutions themselves, such as the World Bank, or powerful states such as the US (via its participation in, or pressuring of, global governance institutions). However, humanitarian INGOs do engage in global governance somewhat, in two main ways. Through their advocacy and public campaigns, they *causally influence* the rules and practices of coercive global institutions, such as the World Bank and the World Trade Organization.[46] They also help to *constitute*—that is, they are themselves part of—what Michael Barnett calls the "international humanitarian order."[47] Barnett argues that this order engages in "the global governance of humanity" or what he calls "humanitarian governance" because its activities are large-scale, formalized, and "increasingly legitimated and organized in and around international institutions, norms, and laws."[48]

What ethical responsibilities do humanitarian INGOs have as a result of engaging in global governance? The approach I have taken so far has been to say that the more humanitarian INGOs engage in governance, the more they develop ethical responsibilities that resemble those of other actors that engage in governance. This approach bears less fruit in the context of global governance than it does in the context of conventional governance, because while there has been a great deal of scholarly work on global governance— describing it empirically, speculating about how democratic global governance institutions might be, and identifying mechanisms for constraining them—there is surprisingly little work elucidating the ethical responsibilities that actors develop as a result of engaging in global governance.[49]

Nonetheless, we know that global governance institutions draw citizens of different countries into thicker, and often more formalized, relationships

---

and Jonathan Perraton (eds.), *Global Transformations: Politics, Economics and Culture* (Stanford, CA: Stanford University Press, 1999).

[46] Cf. Buchanan and Keohane, "The Legitimacy of Global Governance Institutions."

[47] For aid workers who regularly deal with, and feel powerless in the face of, global governance institutions, the idea that INGOs engage in global governance might seem to attribute entirely too much power to INGOs. I do not deny that feelings of powerlessness are likely to be the primary register in which many individual aid workers experience global governance institutions, especially formal institutions. Nor do I deny that these feelings are based on accurate perceptions of their own personal power, or even the power of the INGO for which they work, vis-à-vis these institutions in a given instance. But these experiences of individuals do not disprove the claim that INGOs collectively, and sometimes INGOs individually, engage in global governance to a limited degree.

[48] Barnett, "Humanitarian Governance," 380.

[49] For example, David Held notes in passing that "the tentative acceptance of the equal worth of all human beings finds reinforcement in…the development of new codes of conduct for IGOs and INGOs" ("From Executive to Cosmopolitan Multilateralism," in *Taming Globalization: Frontiers of Governance*, ed. David Held and Mathias Koenig-Archibugi (Malden, MA: Polity Press, 2003), 160–86 (171–2)). But rather than saying more about these codes and what they might include, he focuses instead on what the institutional structure of a global cosmopolitan polity might look like (173–83).

with each other. These institutions therefore create possibilities for violating democratic, egalitarian, humanitarian, and, especially, justice-based norms that did not exist previously. And *this* suggests that when humanitarian INGOs help to causally influence or constitute global governance institutions, they have a responsibility to try to ensure that those institutions will act consistently with democratic, egalitarian, and justice-based norms. In other words, because (or insofar as) humanitarian INGOs help to constitute the international humanitarian order, they cannot ethically say, "we are not in the justice business or the institution-building business; we merely save lives." They are *already* helping to shape a global governance institution called the international humanitarian order.[50]

For example, the "Sphere Project" includes both technical standards and more general ethical guidelines for humanitarian aid provision in disasters.[51] Many INGOs use these standards and guidelines to guide their own practice; they are also used by funding and UN agencies to evaluate INGOs, and by INGOs to evaluate each other. As such, these standards are a constitutive aspect of the international humanitarian order. Several of the large humanitarian INGOs have played a crucial role in developing the Sphere standards, promoting their use, and enhancing their legitimacy. Yet these standards have been criticized on several grounds, including their inapplicability to extreme situations and their potential to sideline domestic NGOs based in disaster-affected countries that lack the technical capacity of INGOs.[52] If we conceptualize the Sphere standards as an aspect of global humanitarian governance, and the humanitarian INGOs that participate in the standards as participating in shaping a global governance institution, then it appears that humanitarian INGOs have a responsibility to help ensure that the Sphere standards are consistent not only with humanitarian norms, but also with justice-based (and egalitarian and democratic) norms.[53]

The responsibilities that INGOs have as a result of engaging in global governance intersect with the responsibilities they have as a result of

---

[50] Cf. Epigraph to Chapter 8. While thinkers such as Rawls have suggested that there is a "natural duty" to help create and sustain just institutions, the responsibility here is closer to being an intermediate duty because INGOs are already involved in the institutions. See Rawls, *A Theory of Justice*, rev ed., 293. In arguing that INGOs help to constitute a global institutional order, I am trying to persuade "institutionalist" scholars—those who believe that judgments of justice and injustice apply primarily to institutions rather than individuals or organizations—that INGOs raise issues of justice, even by institutionalists' own lights. See Jennifer C. Rubenstein, "Humanitarian NGOs' Duties of Justice."

[51] The Sphere Project, *Humanitarian Charter and Minimum Standards in Humanitarian Response* <http://www.spherehandbook.org/>.

[52] MSF, "US Annual Report 2012."

[53] Much of the Rawls-inspired literature on duties surrounding institutions involves responsibilities to make those institutions more just. But democratic and egalitarian norms are often part of what is meant by justice in this context.

engaging in conventional governance in several different ways. Most notably, insofar as INGOs' responsibilities as global governance actors involve pressuring other actors and helping to build or reform institutions, while their responsibilities as conventional governance actors involve more direct responsibilities to particular populations, these two sets of responsibilities are likely to come into practical conflict, at least to some degree. I return to this point below.

3.2 Humanitarian INGOs are Highly Political

In addition to being sometimes somewhat governmental, humanitarian INGOs are also highly political. This is, of course, a very vague idea: the term "political" can be used to describe a wide range of phenomena involving the exercise of power and/or large numbers of people. This vagueness is helpful in that it creates a sort of residual category: we can acknowledge that INGOs are different from individual good Samaritans for a host of reasons involving how INGOs exercise power over, and relate to, large numbers of people, without attempting to specify all of these in advance. However, humanitarian INGOs are often political in two very specific ways that have implications for their political ethics: they frequently have unintended negative effects that are political themselves or occur as a result of political processes, and they frequently exercise discursive power.

3.2.1. *Unintended Negative Political Effects*

It is obvious that INGOs act politically at least some of the time, for example when they engage in advocacy campaigns of any sort, or when they undertake the governance functions described above.[54] But what about when activities such as basic service provision or large-scale decisions about resource use are *not* sufficiently large-scale, formalized, or long-term to be governmental? Are these activities still political? How, if at all, are governmental versions of these activities political in ways not captured by describing them as governmental? One answer to this question is that humanitarian INGOs operate in political contexts, including contexts of ongoing or intermittent violent group conflict. However much they try to wall themselves off from these contexts, for example by demanding "humanitarian space," it is virtually impossible for them to do so.[55] As a result, they often end up having unintended negative effects that are political in their content, or result from political dynamics.

---

[54] I discuss the unintended negative effects of INGOs' *governmental* activities, such as displacing "first-best" actors or enabling them to shirk, in a later section.

[55] The term "humanitarian space" refers to minimal conditions that some INGOs argue are necessary to provide humanitarian aid in a way that conforms to traditional humanitarian

Humanitarian INGOs have unintended negative political effects when they bring large quantities of resources into resource-poor environments, and those resources are used in ways that exacerbate conflict or tension among groups, or give everyone an incentive to keep fighting. This dynamic is most obvious in contexts of violent group conflict such as the Rwandan refugee camps in Zaire after the Rwandan genocide, mentioned in Chapter 1 and discussed in the next chapter.[56] However, it arises in more peaceful contexts as well.[57] INGOs also have political effects—effects that are sometimes but not always negative—when they provide "humanitarian alibis" to governments looking to avoid engaging in "humanitarian" military intervention.[58] INGOs have unintended negative political effects when they provide witting or unwitting support for the "War on Terror," for example, by leading populations to have a more positive opinion of the United States than they would otherwise.[59] Finally, as I noted above, humanitarian INGOs can exacerbate local political tensions by only hiring members of one ethnic group or paying highly disparate salaries to different categories of employees.[60]

What responsibilities do INGOs have as a result of these, and other, unintended, but often not unanticipated, negative political effects? It seems apparent that INGOs have a responsibility to minimize these effects when they can do so without reducing the quantity or quality of aid. When there appears to be a tradeoff between providing aid and avoiding negative effects, INGOs must decide how much and what kinds of negative effects to accept in order to continue providing aid—or whether to reduce or end aid in order to avoid negative effects. I will say more about the difficulties of making these decisions in ways that are responsive to democratic,

principles. These conditions include things like unfettered access to civilians on both sides of the conflict and being allowed to directly monitor aid provision. Unfortunately, the term "humanitarian space" is highly misleading, in that it implies that INGOs can create and operate in a politics-free zone.

[56] The quantity of humanitarian aid provided by INGOs in some contexts is so dwarfed by other sources of income for combatants that it probably does not significantly affect conflict dynamics. But in other contexts—such as the case of the Rwandan refugee camps in Zaire— aid seems to have played a central role in enabling conflict and oppression to continue (Fiona Terry, *Condemned to Repeat? The Paradox of Humanitarian Action* (Ithaca, NY and London: Cornell University Press, 2002), ch. 5).

[57] James Ferguson, *The Anti-Politics Machine: 'Development,' Depoliticization, and Bureaucratic Power in Lesotho* (Minneapolis: University of Minnesota Press, 1994).

[58] The 1994 Rwandan genocide is a case in which humanitarian military intervention was almost certainly justified.

[59] Thus, Colin Powell called US-based INGOs a "force multiplier" for the US military. Bruce Falconer, "Armed and Humanitarian," *Mother Jones*, May 19, 2008 <http://www.motherjones.com/politics/2008/05/armed-and-humanitarian>.

[60] Till Bruckner, "Secret NGO Budgets: Publish What You Spend," *AID WATCH*, May 24, 2010 <http://aidwatchers.com/2010/05/secret-ngo-budgets-publish-what-you-spend/>. This is a fascinating issue that deserves more attention than I am able to devote to it here. See especially the debate in the comments responding to this blog post.

egalitarian, humanitarian, and justice-based norms in the next chapter. The important point for now is that the outlines of some of the ethical predicaments that INGOs face are beginning to come into view: the more that humanitarian INGOs fill a conventionally governmental role, the more reason they have to act like governments in the specific senses of not pulling the rug out from under people, representing well, and maximally alleviating morally important harm. Yet because they cannot wall themselves off from politics, INGOs often have unintended negative political effects, which in turn give them good reasons to reduce their presence, or even withdraw.

3.2.2. *Discursive Power*

In addition to having unintended negative political effects, humanitarian INGOs are also highly political in a second way: they exercise what I call "discursive power," by which I mean the power to shape widely shared meanings.[61] As Dryzek and Niemeyer write, expanding on this idea:

> A discourse can be understood as a set of categories and concepts embodying specific assumptions, judgments, contentions, dispositions, and capabilities. It enables the mind to process sensory inputs into coherent accounts, which can then be shared in intersubjectively meaningful fashion...Discourses enable as well as constrain thought, speech, and action. Any discourse embodies some conception of common sense and acceptable knowledge; it may embody power by recognizing some interests as valid while repressing others. However, discourses are not just a surface manifestation of interests, because discourses help constitute identities and their associated interests.[62]

INGOs exercise discursive power when they use terms, images, and concepts, such as "humanity," "suffering," and "emergency," in ways that help to structure people's perceptions and influence their assumptions about what is normal and natural. Discursive power understood in this way is not necessarily

---

[61] While several authors have explored humanitarianism through a Foucauldian lens, I use the broader and less normatively laden category of *discursive power* in order to sidestep interpretive controversies about Foucault and avoid the suggestion that we should always be deeply suspicious of INGO power. See also Didier Fassin, "Moral Commitments and Ethical Dilemmas of Humanitarianism," in *In the Name of Humanity: The Government of Threat and Care*, ed. Ilana Feldman and Miriam Iris Ticktin (Durham, NC: Duke University Press, 2010), 238–55 (263); Risse, "Global Governance and Communicative Action" and citations therein; Fassin, *Humanitarian Reason*, 1; Ilana Feldman and Miriam Iris Ticktin, "Government and Humanity," in *In the Name of Humanity*, ed. Feldman and Ticktin, 5 and 13 for discussions of humanitarian governance as Foucauldian governance.

[62] John S. Dryzek and Simon Niemeyer, "Discursive Representation," *American Political Science Review* 102.04 (2008): 481–93 (482).

fully intentional. It is also not necessarily normatively bad (or good); it could turn out to be either, both, or neither, in a given instance.

Humanitarian INGOs sometimes exercise discursive power in the context of their conventional or global governance activities. For example, when making and publicly defending large-scale decisions about resource use, INGOs often deploy the concept of "emergency" in ways that help to shape widely shared perceptions of what counts as a basic human need. In so doing, they exercise discursive power. More generally, as Feldman and Ticktin write,

> humanitarian organizations often find themselves in the position of governing— managing, servicing—the populations they seek to aid. Even as practitioners express considerable discomfort in this position, human rights and humanitarianism have been crucially important forms of action in helping to constitute humanity as a 'real' category of central importance to governance.[63]

In other words, by engaging in conventional governance ("managing, servicing" populations), humanitarian INGOs exercise discursive power, in the sense of helping to create a world in which, for example, "serving humanity" functions as a justification for a variety of projects that, in Dryzek and Niemeyer's terms, "constrain thought, speech and action." Humanitarian INGOs also exercise discursive power in the context of activities that are not (or at least, not in any obvious way) conventional or global governance activities. For example, as I discuss in Chapter 7, they exercise discursive power when they portray severe poverty and famine to audiences in donor countries and facilitate photojournalists in doing so.

There are fewer settled debates, and even fewer shared conclusions, about what responsibilities governments (or other actors) have as a result of exercising discursive power than there are about what responsibilities they have as a result of engaging in conventional or even global governance. For example, we have a fairly good idea of what is required for a government to allocate resources justly during an emergency—at least, we understand the main lines of debate about this question. But apart from constraints on manipulating others, we do not have a good idea of what it means for a government— or any other actor—to be just or unjust in helping to shape perceptions of what *counts* as an emergency in the first place. Yet the latter is, if anything, a deeper and more far-reaching form of power than the former.[64]

---

[63] Feldman and Ticktin, "Government and Humanity," 13–14.

[64] On manipulation, see Simone Chambers, "Rhetoric and the Public Sphere: Has Deliberative Democracy Abandoned Mass Democracy?" *Political Theory* 37.3 (2009): 323–50 and Jane Mansbridge, "Rethinking Representation," *American Political Science Review* 97.4 (2003): 515–28. But cf. Lisa Disch, "Toward a Mobilization Conception of Democratic Representation," *American Political Science Review* 105.1 (2011): 100–14. Corey Lang Brettschneider (*When the State Speaks, What Should It Say? How Democracies Can Protect Expression and Promote Equality* (Princeton,

So without relying on analogies to governments or other actors, we must ask the question directly: what responsibilities do INGOs have as a result of exercising discursive power? What does it look like for INGOs to exercise discursive power in ways that are consistent with democratic, egalitarian, humanitarian, and justice-based norms? This question is especially vexing with regard to humanitarian norms, because humanitarian INGOs often exercise discursive power *through* invocations of humanitarian norms, as the foregoing quotation from Feldman and Ticktin suggests. Moreover, any given instance of the exercise of discursive power can have a range of effects. As Feldman and Ticktin also note, "as an object of government, humanity does make new forms of global connection possible, but these connections can be debilitating as well as liberating, threatening as well as a source of protection."[65] For example, as I discuss in Chapter 7, the images in humanitarian INGO fundraising materials can prompt viewers in donor countries to open their eyes to things happening in the world that they had not previously been willing (or able) to see. But these same images can also lead these audiences to develop inaccurate perceptions of aid recipients, for example perceptions of them as incapacitated victims.

It is neither possible nor normatively desirable for INGOs to have *no* role in shaping other people's perceptions and assumptions: we inhabit this world together; no one's perceptions are, or should be, entirely of their own making. Nonetheless, one concrete way that discursive power can cause real harm is by limiting people's capacity for critical reflection.[66] It appears, therefore, that by exercising discursive power, INGOs develop the responsibility to avoid exercising that power in ways that make it more difficult for others to critically examine and—if they so choose—revise their own perceptions and assumptions. Of course, there is likely to be disagreement about when the exercise of discursive power constrains critical reflection and when it enhances it. For example, when is the language of human rights emancipatory, when does it foreclose or displace other valuable modes of political action, and when does it do more than one of these things simultaneously? I doubt that it is possible to answer this question in the abstract. But an adequate account of humanitarian INGO political ethics must direct attention to the ethics of INGOs' exercise of discursive power, rather than either failing to recognize it or seeking to eliminate it entirely.

NJ: Princeton University Press, 2012)) focuses largely on explicit talk by the state, rather than how the state shapes underlying shared meanings.

[65] Feldman and Ticktin, "Government and Humanity," 13.

[66] This is not uncontroversial. There are ways of life, including those practiced by large numbers of people in the contemporary US, that appear to value obedience more than critical reflection, but are nonetheless deeply valued by their adherents. I am suggesting that, while INGOs might have a duty to respect these ways of life in some respects, they do not have a duty to treat forms of discursive power that support critical reflection as morally equivalent to forms of discursive power that undermine it, just because some ways of life oppose such reflection.

3.3 Humanitarian INGOs are Often Second-Best Actors

Humanitarian INGOs are often second-best actors.[67] That is, in any given situation, it is likely that whatever they are doing could be done more effectively, and/or in a way that was more consistent with democratic, egalitarian, justice-based, and/or humanitarian norms, by some other type of actor, such as a government agency, domestic NGO, civil society organization, social movement, or UN agency. In some cases, humanitarian INGOs are second-best compared not to another actor, but rather to an institutional structure or state of affairs. For example, I argue in Chapter 7 that when it comes to portraying famine and severe poverty, there is no one first-best actor; rather, there is a first-best state of affairs in which a large number of portrayals are created and circulated by a wide range of differently situated actors.

In some cases, however, INGOs are not second-best actors; they are instead actors of last resort: however poor their performance in absolute terms, there is no one (even potentially) on the sidelines, willing and able to step in to replace them. As the next chapter illustrates, these situations are by no means ethically easier than situations in which INGOs are second-best actors, but they are different. As I shall now explain, the intuitive notion that INGOs are often second-best actors is not only more complicated than it initially appears to be, it is a crucial feature of the ethical and political terrain that INGOs occupy, shaping the ethical predicaments they must navigate in important ways.

When INGOs are clearly second-best actors in the present, they should withdraw. Such situations, although perhaps difficult from an organizational or practical perspective, are not difficult from an ethical perspective. The more ethically challenging situations are those in which INGOs are first-best in the present, at least along some important dimensions, but second-best compared to other types of actors with regard to their *potential* capacities. An INGO is second-best in this sense (which is the sense I will use in the rest of this book), if it can perform a given function better than some other actor at T_1, but (there is some reason to hope that) the other actor, if supported, or at least not stymied or enabled to shirk, could perform this function better at T_2. A given INGO can therefore be second-best compared to one actor but not another, with regard to one activity but not another, or at one time-scale but not another.

---

[67] As I noted in Chapter 1, by "second-best" I mean something less than first-best—not second-best as opposed to, say, third- or seventh-best.

A resident of Kyrgyzstan, interviewed about his perceptions of humanitarian aid, expressed the ambivalence that is often generated by INGOs acting as second-best actors:

> [i]f international organizations can help Kyrgyzstan and its people, why not accept that help, especially as the Kyrgyz government is unable to deal with the problems existing in society. But ideally it should be the government that resolves health problems. What difference does it make where the help comes from? The most important thing is that it can be provided.[68]

Judgments about whether a given INGO in a given situation is second-best are, then, judgments about future rather than present capacity. They are also comparative rather than absolute. If there is no significant possibility that another actor will perform a given activity better than a given INGO at T_2, then that INGO is not second-best, however poor its performance in absolute terms. Likewise, if another actor will clearly perform a given activity better than an INGO at T_2, then the INGO is a second-best actor, even if it can perform the activity well in absolute terms. The poor performance of INGOs always raises ethical issues. However, these issues are very different, depending on whether an INGO is a second-best actor, in which case the worry is about it displacing first-best actors, or whether it is an actor of last resort (i.e. first-best but still poor in absolute terms), in which case there is a much deeper question about why this is the case, and whether INGOs have contributed to the creation or perpetuation of this state of affairs (see the discussion of the 2014 Ebola epidemic in the postscript at the end of Chapter 8).

Determining whether a given INGO is a first- or second-best actor involves complex normative and empirical judgments. Yet regardless of whether INGOs make these judgments explicitly, their actions always imply a judgment about whether they are first- or second-best actors. They cannot remain neutral on this question.

3.3.1. INGOs as Second-Best Actors and Conventional Governance

The idea that humanitarian INGOs are often second-best actors is easiest to grasp in the context of their conventional governance activities, especially insofar as we assume that governments are first-best actors for undertaking these activities. But even here, a complication immediately arises: the question of whether non-governmental actors are better or worse than conventional governments at undertaking putatively governmental activities under even (so-called) normal conditions is a central point of contention among

---

[68] Caroline Abu-Sada (ed.), *In the Eyes of Others*, 26.

anarchists, libertarians, liberals, social democrats, socialists, and communists (among others). For example, some commentators on the left as well as the right do not think that domestic governments are necessarily first-best providers of basic services. As Patience Kabamba writes

> Today there is a sort of obsession with the state and with state functions among academics. This obsession is partly due to Western guilt or frustration at the high levels of inequality in the world. In order to relieve their guilt at so much wealth stolen from the rest of the world, they want to bring the rest of the world closer to their level, and the main way they want to do this is through the actions of the state, or they think it cannot be done without the state. In contrast to this, and from my ethnographic experience as native of the Congo, I think that the arguments should stress on "mediating institutions" (or middle level ones), like the family, ethnic groups or kinship communities.[69]

Given widespread disagreement about the relative merits of the state and other actors in serving (putative) governance functions, as well as, in some cases, disagreement about whether *anyone* should perform those functions, it is an important feature of my account that it does not require resolving these disputes. Rather, the concept of the second-best as I develop it here provides a language for people who hold these different views about the role of the state to understand how their views might affect their conception of INGO political ethics.

In order to show this to be the case, I turn now to explaining, from a broadly liberal or social democratic perspective, why INGOs are often second-best actors compared to conventional governments when it comes to conventional governance activities. Unlike democratically elected governments, INGOs are not authorized by the vulnerable groups they significantly affect, nor are these groups generally able to effectively hold INGOs accountable (in the sense of sanctioning them).[70] This suggests that INGOs are less likely to be responsive to those they serve than democratically elected governments. Also unlike conventional governments, INGOs depend on voluntary contributions rather than taxes to fund their activities. This means that, not only is their funding uncertain, but they must attract and retain donors who might have very different priorities than, or little understanding of, INGOs' intended beneficiaries. While INGOs sometimes rely on armed guards, they do not have a monopoly on the legitimate use of force in the places where they work. This makes them very vulnerable to being used by others as tools for ends that undermine their objectives, as I discuss in Chapter 4. Unlike conventional governments, domestic NGOs, and civil society organizations

---

[69] Patience Kabamba, "The Real Problems of the Congo: From Africanist Perspectives to African Prospectives," *African Affairs* 111.443 (2012): 202–22.

[70] See Chapter 2 for a discussion of accountability.

based in aid-recipient countries, INGOs are based in wealthy Western countries and their upper-level managers are mostly from those countries. As a result, their decisions and actions often reflect a limited understanding of the social, political, religious, economic, and cultural dynamics of the places where they work. In addition, because most of these upper-level managers are white, INGOs tend to evoke patterns of colonial and imperial domination at a symbolic (and sometimes political and material) level, despite the sincere good intentions of the individuals involved.[71]

These are just a few reasons why INGOs are often second-best actors when it comes to conventional governance activities (from, again, a liberal democratic or social democratic perspective). Of course, judging whether a given INGO is first-best or second-best in a specific case requires taking many more factors into account. In particular, one must consider not only the intentions and capacities of INGOs and possible first-best actors, but also what is required to engage in a particular activity well. For example, when it comes to designing and managing a public health program, the question is not only, Is an INGO more stable than a government agency?, but also, How important is stability? and What does stability involve?

Finally, judgments about which actors are first- versus second-best can vary dramatically based on the time horizon one adopts. For example—and to continue with the example of public health and "stability"—one MSF official argued that,

> ideologically, when we talk about the Ministry of Health, we think "stable," and when we talk about private structures, including MSF, we think "unstable." However in many situations, we are actually more stable, in that environment, in terms of service delivery, than the public institutions.[72]

This judgment, however, seems to assume a relatively short time horizon, one measured in years rather than decades. Someone who adopted a longer time horizon might have a different assessment.[73]

---

[71] These relationships are never simple, however. As Donini et al. write: "Foreigners in big white vehicles are outsiders *par excellence*. But a national NGO worker arriving in a village on a bedraggled motorbike may also be seen as an outsider. Moreover, being national, or even local, is not a guarantee of acceptability. Often, foreigners are seen as more neutral and impartial, less corrupt, and therefore more acceptable than locals" (Antonio Donini, Larissa Fast, Greg Hansen, Simon Harris, Larry Minear, Tasneem Mowjee, and Andrew Wilder, "Humanitarian Agenda 2015: Final Report: The State of the Humanitarian Enterprise" (Feinstein International Center, 2008), 7).

[72] Abu-Sada, *In the Eyes of Others*, 78.

[73] For example, Peter Leeson ("Better Off Stateless: Somalia before and after Government Collapse," *Journal of Comparative Economics* 35.4 (2007): 689–710) argues that Somalia is "better off stateless" because whatever state that emerged would, in his view, be worse than the status quo ante. However, if one adopted a longer time horizon than that which Leeson implicitly adopts, one might well come to a different conclusion. (Leeson compares indicators in a stateless Somalia to those in an *earlier* period when there was a state and concludes that the former was preferable to the latter. However, he acknowledges that further gains might require a state.)

For all of the reasons just described—uncertainty about INGOs' and other actors' capacities and incentives, philosophical and practical disagreement about what makes an actor first- versus second-best, and divergent views about the relevant time horizon—INGOs' status as a first- or second-best actor can be difficult to assess, and a source of disagreement. These difficulties and disagreements do not, however, mean that we should just give up on trying to make these assessments.

Indeed, even though they do not use the terms presented here, INGOs, their critics and interlocutors make judgments of second-bestness frequently; they cannot be neutral on this question. For example, one commentator noted that there is, in Haiti, a "permanent debate between those who favour parallel solutions (such as creation of public services outside the formal political system, even with the danger that they become permanent), and those who emphasise institutional reforms from within the formal system."[74] The concept of the second-best therefore does not introduce a radically novel way of thinking about INGOs. Rather, it is a reconstruction, and I hope clarification, of a relatively well-known idea.

What responsibilities do INGOs have as a result of being second-best actors? I argued above that insofar as INGOs' activities, relationships, capacities, and effects resemble those of conventional and global governance actors, INGOs have reason to engage in conventional and global governance activities as well as possible. But insofar as INGOs are second-best actors, they have reason to *not* do this, but to instead step back and support or pressure first-best actors to undertake the activity in question. For example, I argued above that insofar as INGOs engage in the conventional governance activity of shaping coercive government policies, they should represent poor and marginalized groups as well as possible. But insofar as INGO advocates are second-best representatives, they have a responsibility to *not* do this, but instead to step back and support first-best representatives in undertaking these activities.[75] As Monique Deveaux writes, a "more calibrated set of responsibilities on the part of institutions and individuals in the global North," might include "agents in affluent countries step[ping] out of the way and refrain[ing] from blocking the efforts of poor movements to mobilize on behalf of their own interests."[76]

---

[74] Capacity.org, "Parallel Service Delivery in a Fragile State" <http://www.capacity.org/capacity/opencms/en/topics/fragile-environments/parallel-service-delivery-in-a-fragile-state.html>.

[75] Cf. Onora O'Neill, "Global Justice: Whose Obligations?" in *The Ethics of Assistance: Morality and the Distant Needy*, ed. Deen K. Chatterjee (Cambridge: Cambridge University Press, 2004), 242–59 (252–3), who suggests that non-governmental actors that undertake government functions should seek to do exactly what a (competent and democratic) conventional government would have done. She therefore seems to view the total absence of the state as the paradigm case for situations of political instability or severe poverty.

[76] Monique Deveaux, "The Global Poor as Agents of Justice," *Journal of Moral Philosophy* (forthcoming). See also Suzanne Dovi, "In Praise of Exclusion," *The Journal of Politics* 71.3 (2009): 1172–86.

As I explain more fully in Chapters 5 and 6, what Deveaux describes as a re-calibration, I see as a fundamental (re)orientation, for INGOs, away from a whole-hearted commitment to undertaking a given activity or achieving a certain objective as well as possible themselves, and toward a much more cautious, chary, high-wire act of provisionally trying to undertake particular activities or achieve particular objectives, while also not displacing first-best actors, and remaining open to revising their activities and objectives.

These responsibilities differ dramatically from those generated by INGOs' conventional and global governance activities and their exercise of discursive power. They are more aligned with the responsibilities INGOs have as a result of having unintended negative political effects. But while being second-best is a moral hazard that makes INGOs more likely to have certain kinds of unintended negative effects, such as displacing others, second-bestness is not in itself an unintended negative effect.

To better understand the responsibilities that INGOs have as a result of often being second-best actors, it is useful to consider four ideal-type cases, two in which INGOs are second-best actors and two in which they are not. In *low capacity* cases, first-best actors such as domestic governments or domestic NGOs have basically good intentions, but their current capacity to undertake a given activity (e.g. provide basic services) is limited.[77] This means that INGOs are second-best actors. They have a negative duty to *avoid displacing* first-best actors, and perhaps a positive or compensatory duty to help them develop their capacities. (The duty would be compensatory if INGOs had in the past caused or contributed to their capacities being limited.)[78] Kristoff and Panarelli describe this dynamic as it unfolded in Haiti:

> NGOs often have greater capacity and more funding than the Haitian government...For example, in FY 2007–2008, USAID spent $300 million in Haiti, all of which was implemented through foreign NGOs. These projects often had more money than the entire Haitian Ministry of Planning. As a result, the Haitian government had little chance to develop the human or institutional capacity to deliver services. The Haitian people have learned to look to NGOs, rather than the government, for provision of essential services. Funneling aid through NGOs perpetuated a cycle of low capacity, corruption and [un]accountability among Haitian government institutions.[79]

In *indifferent intentions* cases, first-best actors have sufficient capacity, but indifferent or (from INGOs' perspective) moderately bad intentions. These cases arise most often in the context of basic service provision and decisions

---

[77] They have low capacity, that is, from the perspective of the INGO making this assessment.
[78] I explain in Chapter 4 why we should generally see these compensatory duties as overridden by other considerations.
[79] Kristoff and Panarelli, "Haiti: A Republic of NGOs?" 1.

about resource use, rather than advocacy. In these cases, INGOs have a responsibility to *avoid enabling conventional governments (or other first-best actors) to shirk* their responsibilities. It can be difficult to tell whether, in a given case, INGOs are dealing with first-best actors that have low capacity, indifferent intentions, or both.

In *hostile* cases (which usually involve governments as first-best actors, so I will focus on governments in what follows), governments are not merely indifferent; they are actively hostile toward their citizens or denizens—the very people INGOs wish to assist. There is therefore virtually no chance that these governments will use their capacities to protect or assist these groups in the short or medium term. In these cases, unlike the first two types of cases, INGOs are not second-best actors. Their main worry is not that they are displacing first-best actors or enabling them to shirk. Rather, the worry is that, in substituting for or cooperating with a hostile regime, they will facilitate the regime's unjust or oppressive activities.[80] Adam Branch argued that this is what happened in Northern Uganda in the 1990s:

> humanitarianism served not only to enable the Ugandan government's militarization and violent repression of dissent, but also to depoliticize the population and thus prolong and intensify war and violence, with devastating consequences. State violence and humanitarianism each depended on the other for its own viability, as the regime of state violence against the Acholi in the camps was *only* possible because of the intervention of the aid agencies, and the aid agencies' administrative management strategy was *only* possible because of their direct and indirect reliance on state violence.[81]

On this account, there is no first-best and second-best; humanitarian INGOs are instead directly dependent on state violence, and vice versa.

Finally, in cases of *non-existent first-best actors*, humanitarian INGOs are, again, not second-best actors. Because there is no first-best actor, there is no meaningful chance that such an actor will effectively undertake the activity in question.[82] In these cases, INGOs again do not have responsibilities to avoid displacing first-best actors, or to pressure or support them to take on particular functions, because there is no first-best actor to displace, pressure, or support. Situations that are sometimes said to approximate this scenario include "failed states," such as Somalia in the 1990s and Congo in the early 2000s. In Congo, for example, MSF employees did not fear undermining

---

[80] Mary B. Anderson, *Do No Harm: How Aid Can Support Peace—or War* (Boulder, CO: Lynne Rienner Publishers, 1999).

[81] Adam Branch, *Displacing Human Rights: War and Intervention in Northern Uganda* (New York: Oxford University Press, 2011), 91 (my italics).

[82] Peter Redfield, "Bioexpectations: Life Technologies as Humanitarian Goods," *Public Culture* 24.1 (2012): 157–84.

local capacities because in their estimation, as one aid worker put it, "they [the Congolese] could do nothing without us..."[83] Likewise, the "permanent" debate about Haiti mentioned above is, in effect, about whether or not Haiti is a failed state.

Yet even in contexts that are labeled as failed states for other purposes,[84] there is often *some* domestic governance capacity that INGOs could support. So while we want to leave conceptual space for the possibility that a first-best actor is simply absent, we should also acknowledge that (a) such cases are likely to be rare, especially when governments are first-best actors, and (b) there is not a bright line between supporting a nascent first-best actor and helping to bring a non-existent first-best actor into existence. Even in a case where a first-best actor is non-existent, an INGO could have a responsibility, however minimal, to not undermine, or even help create, conditions suitable for the emergence of such a first-best actor.

3.3.2. INGOs as Second-Best Actors, Global Governance, and Discursive Power

I have been discussing the ethical and political implications of INGOs being second-best actors in the context of their conventional governance activities. We turn next to the questions of whether INGOs can be second-best actors in the context of global governance and discursive power, and if they can be, how this influences their ethical and political responsibilities. I suggested above that by engaging in global governance, INGOs develop a responsibility to push the global governance institutions in which they participate to act consistently with relevant ethical norms. I also argued that INGOs have a responsibility to avoid exercising discursive power in ways that make it more difficult for other people to reflect critically on their own perceptions and assumptions.

These normative standards, rough as they are, provide a basis for evaluating how well INGOs engage in global governance and exercise discursive power compared to other actors. They therefore suggest how INGOs might be second-best actors when it comes to these activities. However, the ethical responsibilities that INGOs have as a result of being second-best actors in these contexts differ from the ethical responsibilities that they have as a result of being second-best actors in the context of conventional governance. This is because, in the context of global governance and (especially) discursive power, the exercise of power is much less likely to be zero-sum than it is in the context of conventional governance activities. Displacement of first-best actors is,

---

[83] Peter Redfield, *Life in Crisis: The Ethical Journey of Doctors Without Borders* (Berkeley: University of California Press, 2013), 186.

[84] For example, Leeson, "Better Off Stateless."

therefore, a less salient concern; there is more room for INGOs to continue to play a role, even as first-best actors take a more dominant position. For example, I argue in Chapter 7 that, when it comes to the exercise of discursive power through the use of images of famine and severe poverty, a first-best scenario is one in which INGOs and many other differently situated actors exercise this power, not that INGOs play no role.

3.4 Moral Permissions

I have been discussing the political and ethical responsibilities that humanitarian INGOs have as a result of their activities, relationships, capacities, and effects. The flip-side of this question is whether INGOs have special moral *permissions* (i.e. moral freedoms to do things that would otherwise be blameworthy), because of these activities, relationships, capacities, and effects. This question matters because, generally speaking, the more political or ethical responsibilities INGOs have, the more, and more challenging, the ethical conflicts they are likely to face; conversely, the more moral permissions they have, the fewer, and less wrenching, the ethical conflicts they are likely to face.[85]

Onora O'Neill suggests that INGOs that take on governance "tasks" have significant moral permissions, or what she calls "exemptions," as a result. "[E]ntitlement to exemptions," she writes, "is related to task, not to status."[86] For example, O'Neill argues, non-state actors that provide humanitarian aid in famine situations have a moral permission to "hoard" food, because doing so enables them to provide that aid.[87] However, if we look at governance activities more broadly, we see that, at least from a liberal democratic perspective, many important moral permissions associated with governance, especially those that involve coercion, derive from, or at least require, a formal status that INGOs lack. For example, even when INGOs provide schooling or vaccinations, they cannot, morally speaking, coerce people to send their children to school or have them vaccinated; in contrast, the state (arguably) can. We should therefore not expect any sort of equivalence between the responsibilities generated by INGOs being somewhat governmental, and in particular providing governmental services, and the moral permissions generated by INGOs being somewhat governmental.

Does being a second-best actor generate moral permissions for INGOs? One might think that it does. Substitute teachers, theatrical understudies, and the neighbor who watches a child whose parent unexpectedly has to work late

---

[85] This might not always be true. For example, a moral permission could give INGOs a reason to engage in some activity that then generated a new responsibility.

[86] O'Neill, "Global Justice," 255.   [87] O'Neill, "Global Justice."

all appear to have a moral permission to diverge from the high standards (of teaching, performance, and child care, respectively) that we expect from the "first-best" teacher, actor, or parent. But upon further inspection, these lower standards do not derive from the substitute, understudy, or neighbor merely being relatively less adept at the relevant tasks—that is, they do not derive from them being second-best. Rather, they derive from other aspects of these situations.

For example, we hold the substitute teacher to a lower standard of teaching *in any given classroom,* but this is because he is willing and able to fill in for a wide range of teachers on short notice. The same holds for the understudy. We do hold the neighbor to a lower standard, but this is because she is only watching the child for a short period and is doing the parent a favor. So long as she does not endanger the child, what she does—say, allowing the child to stay up late and eat cookies for dinner—matters less than what the parent does, because she is only watching the child for a short period. It thus appears that in some cases, such as that of the substitute teacher or understudy, second-best actors do not have special moral permissions—the standards that apply to them are different, but not lower, than the standards that apply to first-best actors—or they only apply to second-best actors who are on the scene for a short period and are clearly operating in a supererogatory fashion. INGOs do not meet these criteria, at least most of the time.

Moreover, in the context of humanitarian INGOs, the very boundary between responsibilities and permissions sometimes blurs. For example, in the next chapter I argue that INGOs that provide basic services should sometimes continue providing those services, even when doing so contributes to injustices perpetrated primarily by others. This sounds at first like a claim about moral permissions: INGOs are not blameworthy if they do something—knowingly contribute to injustice—that would be normally be prohibited. But insofar as INGOs do not want to contribute to injustice, the assertion that they should stay and continue to provide aid functions more like a responsibility than a permission. Indeed, I will argue that INGOs *should* experience providing aid that contributes to injustice as a responsibility rather than a permission: if an INGO's attitude is, "hooray, our services are sufficiently governmental that we can now stay and contribute to injustice," something has indeed gone wrong.

3.5 Conclusion: Four Ethical Predicaments

I have argued that humanitarian INGOs are sometimes somewhat governmental, highly political, and often second-best (see Fig. 3.1). They are sometimes somewhat governmental in that they engage in conventional governance and global governance. Moreover, they engage in at least three kinds of conventional governance: providing basic services, helping shape the coercive policies of domestic governments, and making large-scale decisions about resource use that have public effects. They are highly political in ways that lead them to regularly have unintended negative effects; they also exercise discursive power. Finally, humanitarian INGOs are often second-best actors. While engaging in governance and being second-best are not in themselves negative effects, they put INGOs at high *risk* of having several additional kinds of unintended negative effects, most prominently, displacing first-best governmental actors.

In what configurations do these features of INGOs' political-ethical terrain usually appear? How must INGOs navigate among the responsibilities they produce? I will argue that these features constellate in such a way that humanitarian INGOs regularly face four ethical predicaments: the problem of spattered hands, the quandary of the second-best, the cost-effectiveness conundrum, and the moral motivation tradeoff.

SH When humanitarian INGOs provide basic services in conflict settings, they—unlike individual good Samaritans—sometimes take on a somewhat governmental role or function. In these cases, withdrawing aid can amount to "pulling the rug out" from beneath the feet of vulnerable people. The effects of rug-pulling are especially severe when INGOs are *not* second-best actors, such that there is no other entity willing or able to take their place if they withdraw. However, because humanitarian INGOs are highly political, they generally cannot avoid having some unintended negative effects. In conflict settings, these negative effects often take the form of INGOs contributing knowingly but unintentionally to injustices perpetrated

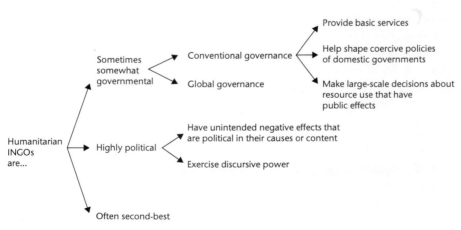

Figure 3.1. Features of a map of humanitarian INGO political ethics

primarily by others. Yet INGOs, like everyone else, have a *prima facie* negative duty to avoid contributing to injustices (including those perpetrated primarily by others). So should INGOs continue to provide aid under these circumstances, on both humanitarian and justice-based grounds, so as to avoid pulling the rug out from under people, or should they withdraw, so as to avoid contributing to injustices perpetrated primarily by others? I call this predicament the *problem of spattered hands.*

In spattered hands ethical predicaments, humanitarian INGOs are typically not second-best actors. In many situations, however, humanitarian INGOs *are* second-best actors, for example when they undertake advocacy campaigns on domestic or global issues. Insofar as INGO advocacy serves a conventional governance function, INGOs have a responsibility, rooted in democratic norms, to represent the interests and preferences of the poor and marginalized people likely to be significantly affected by the issues about which they are advocating. But if they are second-best—say, compared to domestic NGOs, social movements, or other actors—INGOs also have a responsibility, rooted in democratic and egalitarian norms, to avoid displacing these first-best actors, by not engaging in representation themselves, but instead stepping back. To what extent should INGOs forge ahead, trying to represent poor and marginalized groups as well as possible in their advocacy efforts, and to what extent should they explicitly step back and promote advocacy by other, potentially superior representatives? I call this the *quandary of the second-best.*

Like INGOs' advocacy efforts, their large-scale decisions about resource use also often serve a conventional governance function. Insofar as this is the case, INGOs have a responsibility, rooted in justice-based norms, to make these decisions in a way that puts significant weight on maximally alleviating morally important harm. Under conditions of limited resources, this means that they have a responsibility to be cost-effective. But INGOs' large-scale decisions about resource use are not only instances of conventional governance; they are also enactments of global governance by second-best actors that have discursive effects. As a result, INGOs have good justice- and democracy-based reasons to pursue more political, symbolic, and expressive forms of political action—even though such action often cannot be shown to be cost-effective. How much weight should INGOs put on considerations of cost-effectiveness in their large-scale decisions about resource use? I call this the *cost-effectiveness conundrum.*

Finally, the same logic that tells us that humanitarian INGOs should be as cost-effective as possible also suggests that they should try to raise as much money as they can use effectively (so long as that money is not being diverted from other, more worthwhile uses). But in raising funds, and especially in using visual images to raise funds, INGOs also exercise discursive power.

As I argued above, they have a responsibility, based largely in democratic, egalitarian, and justice-based norms, to avoid exercising this power in ways that undermine critical reflection. Yet social psychologists have found that the types of images that are most effective at raising funds for INGOs tend to be photographs of a single child (or woman) looking helpless and miserable. These images appear to undermine critical reflection, and have other negative effects as well. Should INGOs try to raise as much money as possible, or should they seek to avoid these negative effects? I call this the *moral motivation tradeoff.*

MMT

I have argued that interpreting humanitarian INGOs as sometimes somewhat governmental, highly political, and often second-best helps us to see that they regularly face four distinctive ethical predicaments. I have described these predicaments in a very schematic, preliminary way. That is, I have sketched a very high altitude map.[88] It is time, now, to zoom in: to describe these ethical predicaments in more detail, examine specific examples of them, ask whether there are better and worse routes for INGOs to take in navigating them, and consider whether these routes broaden our understanding of what it means to act consistently with—or undermine—democratic, egalitarian, humanitarian, and justice-based norms in the contemporary world.

---

[88] I therefore wait until Chapter 8 to show that this map addresses the questions raised by the approaches discussed in Chapter 2, while avoiding the shortcomings of those approaches.

4

The Problem of Spattered Hands

Forget the dream of a harm-free intervention.

—Médecins Sans Frontières employee[1]

In June 1994, about a hundred days after it began, the Rwandan genocide finally ended when the Tutsi-dominated Rwandan Patriotic Front
(RPF) routed the Hutu-dominated Rwandan Armed Forces (Forces Armées
Rwandaises or FAR). FAR members fled to Tanzania, Burundi, and what was
then Zaire, accompanied by about 2 million Hutu civilians. These civilians
included "bona fide refugees," as well as "Rwandans who had been ordered to
flee, and people evading revenge or prosecution for crimes they committed
during the genocide."[2] In Zaire, soldiers, innocent civilians, and perpetrators
of genocide streamed together into makeshift camps, which quickly became
highly militarized. The now "ex"-FAR members, seeking to regroup militar-
ily, siphoned off vast quantities of aid intended for civilians. They also used
the civilian presence in the camps to generate international sympathy, and
the civilians themselves as human shields. Indeed, the "ex"-FAR found the
civilian presence in the camps so beneficial that they conducted elaborate
propaganda and surveillance campaigns to deter civilians from returning to
Rwanda.

---

[1] MSF-Holland, "Justice and MSF Operational Choices." Report of a discussion held in
Soesterberg, Netherlands, June 2001.
[2] Fiona Terry, *Condemned to Repeat? The Paradox of Humanitarian Action* (Ithaca and London:
Cornell University Press, 2002), 173. The rest of my account of the camps in Zaire draws on
Condemned to Repeat?, ch. 5. See also Chiara Lepora and Robert E. Goodin, "Grading Complicity
in Rwandan Refugee Camps," *Journal of Applied Philosophy* 28.3 (2011): 259–76, also in Chiara
Lepora and Robert E. Goodin, *On Complicity and Compromise* (New York: Oxford University Press,
2013); Larry May, *Genocide: A Normative Account* (New York: Cambridge University Press, 2010);
and Linda Polman, *The Crisis Caravan: What's Wrong With Humanitarian Aid?* trans. Liz Waters
(New York: Metropolitan Books, 2010). Perpetrators of genocide are not entitled to asylum under
international law, but after the Rwandan genocide there was no system in place to identify suspects and give them a fair trial. For criticism of the initial decision to not separate soldiers and
civilians, see Lepora and Goodin, "Grading Complicity in Rwandan Refugee Camps."

The INGOs providing food, water, health care, and other services in the camps included Oxfam, CARE, the International Rescue Committee, and World Vision. These INGOs knew that the "ex"-FAR were diverting aid from civilians and using the camps as a military staging ground. They had also heard Rwandan president Paul Kagame's warnings that the Rwandan government would at some point cross the border and close the camps by force (which it eventually did, in a chaotic process that resulted in the deaths of thousands of people).[3] These INGOs therefore faced a wrenching decision: should they stay and continue providing aid, knowing that in so doing they were feeding perpetrators of genocide, helping the "ex"-FAR to regroup, and encouraging Hutu civilians to stay in an insecure environment, or should they leave the camps, thereby denying life-saving goods, services, and moral support to innocent people?[4] As Fiona Terry—an aid worker for MSF-France who was present in the camps—wrote, "aid agencies could only choose between remaining or withdrawing."[5] Most INGOs, UN agencies, and other organizations chose to stay. A few, including MSF-France and the International Rescue Committee, chose to leave.

This situation is just one example of an extremely difficult type of ethical predicament that humanitarian organizations regularly face, and have faced repeatedly over the last forty years: how should they respond when their well-intended and in some ways beneficial actions, such as providing food, water, and shelter to displaced people, are partially redeployed by third parties for what they see as unjust purposes?[6] While this predicament can arise in a variety of contexts, it is most well-documented in cases where INGOs provide basic services in conflict or post-conflict settings; such situations will therefore be the main focus of this chapter.

This type of ethical predicament raises at least three questions. First, under what conditions should INGOs facing these predicaments continue to provide aid, and under what conditions should they withdraw? That is, under

---

[3] According to Terry, over 200,000 Rwandan Hutus never made it back to Rwanda. Several thousand of them are known to have been killed; what happened to the rest remains unclear. See Terry, *Condemned to Repeat?*, 230.

[4] It is not clear whether, how quickly, and how well other organizations stepped in to provide the services that had been provided by the INGOs that left. However, the best case scenario appears to have been that the INGOs that left were only replaced after a significant delay, and by INGOs with less expertise (Terry, *Condemned to Repeat?*, 202).

[5] Terry, *Condemned to Repeat?*, 206. As Terry also notes, at one point fifteen INGOs banded together to demand better conditions for aid provision, some of which they received, but this seems to have not changed the overall situation significantly (*Condemned to Repeat?*, 177, 189).

[6] For other cases, see Polman, *The Crisis Caravan*; Tony Vaux, *The Selfish Altruist: Dilemmas of Relief Work in Famine and War* (London: Earthscan, 2002); Jonathan Moore, *Hard Choices: Moral Dilemmas in Humanitarian Intervention*(Lanham, MD: Rowman & Littlefield, 1998); Alexander De Waal, *Famine Crimes: Politics & the Disaster Relief Industry in Africa* (Bloomington: Indiana University Press, 1997). But cf. Charles Kenny, "Belief in Relief," *The Washington Monthly*, December 2010 <http://www.washingtonmonthly.com/features/2010/1011.kenny.html>.

what conditions is staying and providing aid (but also having negative effects, including contributing to injustices perpetrated by third parties) or withdrawing (and so avoiding negative effects, but also not providing basic services) more consistent with democratic, humanitarian, and/or justice-based norms?[7] I call this the "stay or go" question.[8]

Humanitarian INGOs that provide basic services in conflict settings face the stay or go question repeatedly. This raises a second question, or more precisely, set of questions, about their more temporally extended responsibilities: what responsibilities, if any, do INGOs have to cultivate, in advance, the capacity to exercise good practical judgment in the face of stay or go questions, such that they are prepared for these questions when they arise? What responsibilities, if any, do INGOs have to offer explanation, apology, and/or compensation for how they handle these questions after the fact? What responsibility do they have to help prevent stay or go questions from arising in the future?

A third question arises because of how these ethical predicaments shape the contours of INGOs' agency. Sharon Krause defines "distributed agency" as agency that is "an emergent property of interactions among bodies."[9] Distributed agency typically involves actors that are indifferent to each other, such as individual drivers who do not know each other contributing jointly to global warming, or even actors and material substances jointly contributing to some outcome. But INGOs' agency is distributed between themselves and other actors whom they actively deplore, actors whose intentions are diametrically opposed to their own, such as, in the case of the INGOs in the Rwandan camps, the "ex"-FAR. I call this sort of distributed agency *dramatically distributed agency*, where what is dramatic is the range of intentions and objectives of the actors whose agency has joint effects.

---

[7] Egalitarian norms do not seem to provide much leverage here over and above what is implied by the other norms, so I exclude them.

[8] I do not assume that the answer to this question is the same for all INGOs in a given context. In some cases, the main value of withdrawing (or threatening to withdraw) is to pressure a regime to alter its behavior; such a threat might only be effective if INGOs are able to coordinate with each other to present a united front. In such a case, it might only be justifiable for an INGO—especially a very competent INGO—to withdraw if other INGOs are withdrawing. Conversely, it might only be justifiable for an INGO to withdraw if other INGOs are going to stay and continue to provide services or serve as witnesses for the population. That is a division of moral labor, with some INGOs continuing to provide aid while others withdraw in protest, might yield the best outcome. (Garrett Cullity, "Compromised Humanitarianism." Individual INGOs also face questions about whether to stay or go for other reasons, such as security concerns. While these are sometimes of paramount importance, I am not able to address them here.

[9] Sharon R. Krause, "Bodies in Action: Corporeal Agency and Democratic Politics," *Political Theory* 39.3 (2011): 299–324. Krause is mainly interested in agency distributed between humans and the material world.

While some types of actors with dramatically distributed agency, such as slaves, do not have significant power over others, INGOs with dramatically distributed agency often exercise significant power over their intended beneficiaries.[10] Thus, the third question raised by the ethical predicaments examined in this chapter is: what does it look like for INGOs to act consistently with democratic, humanitarian, and justice-based norms, when their agency is dramatically distributed but they also have significant power over others?

The first part of this chapter examines several possible approaches to analyzing these three questions: the principle of *do no harm*, which is well known to aid practitioners; the concept of *complicity*, which has been utilized recently by political philosophers studying the case of the humanitarian INGOs in the Rwandan camps; the *doctrine of double effect* (DDE), which has not been applied extensively to humanitarian INGOs but is likely to strike some readers as relevant; and finally the theory of *dirty hands*, which has been applied to humanitarian INGOs only in passing yet is also likely to strike some readers as relevant. I focus primarily on the stay or go question, about which most of these approaches have more to say. I argue that of these four approaches, dirty hands is the most helpful, but all have serious limitations.

The next part of the chapter therefore proposes what I will argue is a superior approach: we should characterize ethical predicaments such as those faced by the INGOs in the Rwandan refugee camps in Zaire as *spattered hands problems*. This interpretation or "map" of these predicaments is more helpful than the four approaches just mentioned for addressing the three questions described above. One upshot of the spattered hands framework is that the more that INGOs' provision of basic services resembles that of a conventional government, the greater their responsibility to *allow their hands to be spattered*—that is, to continue providing aid even though in so doing they contribute to injustices perpetrated primarily by others.

In the next section I specify more precisely the features of situations in which INGOs face spattered hands problems and explain what makes these situations distinctive and challenging. Section 4.2 explains why do no harm, complicity, DDE, and dirty hands are inadequate bases for analyzing these situations (even though dirty hands is most helpful). Section 4.3 introduces the spattered hands approach and explains why it is superior for addressing the three questions outlined above.

---

[10] Cf. Patchen Markell, "The Insufficiency of Non-Domination," *Political Theory* 36.1 (2008): 9–36. (Even if some slaves did sometimes have significant power over others, for example other slaves, the example should still help to clarify the concept of dramatically distributed agency.)

4.1 The Distinctiveness of Spattered Hands Ethical Predicaments

The provision of basic services by humanitarian INGOs in conflict settings can have a host of unintended negative effects. This chapter examines the implications of one especially challenging kind of unintended negative effect: INGOs contributing knowingly but unintentionally to active injustices perpetrated primarily by others. These unintended negative effects are not necessarily more grievous than other kinds of unintended negative effects, but they have political, ethical, psychological, and philosophical dimensions that make them especially challenging subjects for normative analysis.

INGOs contribute to active injustice perpetrated primarily by others in several ways. Combatants sometimes steal or extort some of the goods and services provided by INGOs and use them to perpetuate conflict. Reporting on the findings of a large, multi-country study, Mary Anderson writes that "[a]id resources are often stolen by warriors and used to support armies and buy weapons."[11] Likewise, by providing aid, INGOs can make it possible or easier for armed groups to coercively relocate civilians. For example, in Ethiopia in the mid-1980s, government forces rounded up patients at feeding centers run by INGOs and forcibly relocated them.[12] INGO aid can also make it more lucrative for combatants to violently steal from or directly attack civilians. For example, Terry reports that "in Liberia and Somalia, combatants forcibly seized relief items from civilians after distribution; in the Democratic Republic of Congo, rebel forces followed aid vehicles at a distance and slaughtered refugees who emerged from hiding to receive aid."[13] In yet other cases, oppressive regimes use the presence of INGOs to make themselves appear more legitimate to outside observers, or use the information that INGOs gather in the course of their activities to monitor and control populations.[14]

While contributing to active injustices perpetrated primarily by others is the main distinguishing feature of spattered hands ethical predicaments,

---

[11] Mary B. Anderson, *Do No Harm: How Aid Can Support Peace—or War* (Boulder, CO: Lynne Rienner Publishers, 1999), 39. See also Polman, *The Crisis Caravan*; Adam Branch, "Against Humanitarian Impunity: Rethinking Responsibility for Displacement and Disaster in Northern Uganda," *Journal of Intervention and Statebuilding* 2.2 (2008): 151–73. Kenny ("Belief in Relief") argues that the Rwanda case is very extreme.

[12] Rony Brauman, "Refugee Camps, Population Transfers, and NGOs," in *Hard Choices: Moral Dilemmas in Humanitarian Intervention*, ed. Jonathan Moore (Lanham, MD: Rowman & Littlefield, 1998), 177–94. See also Hugo Slim, "Doing the Right Thing: Relief Agencies, Moral Dilemmas and Moral Responsibility in Political Emergencies and War," *Disasters* 21.3 (1997): 244–57.

[13] Terry, *Condemned to Repeat?*, 52.

[14] François Jean gives the example of North Korea (François Jean and Médecins Sans Frontières (eds.), *Populations in Danger 1995: A Médecins Sans Frontières Report* (Rushcutters Bay, NSW: Halstead Press, 1995)); Vaux (*The Selfish Altruist*) gives the example of the Taliban in Afghanistan.

two other features are also important. First, from the perspective of whoever is evaluating an INGO, that INGO must have mostly good intentions. If one thinks that an INGO has evil intentions, or is, say, only a scheme to enrich its managers, then the immediate question at hand is how to stop the INGO from acting on its evil or selfish intentions, not whether it should contribute to injustices perpetrated primarily by others. Likewise, if an INGO has good intentions but is not having any good effects, then there is no reason for it to continue providing aid—and so, again, wrenching questions about whether it should continue to provide aid, such as those faced by the humanitarian INGOs in the camps in Zaire, do not arise.[15] Our main interest here, then, is situations in which INGOs have (1) mostly good intentions and (2) at least some good effects, yet (3) contribute knowingly but unintentionally to active injustices perpetrated primarily by others.

4.1.1. *Sins of Commission and Sins of Omission*

In navigating these situations, INGOs can commit what we might call "sins of commission" (staying when they should go) or "sins of omission" (going when they should stay).[16] In order to determine whether an INGO has committed one of these sins, we need, among other things, an account of the kinds of considerations that *should* inform INGOs' responses to stay or go questions. Also necessary, however—and somewhat easier to come by—is an account of relevant sources of bias, that is, factors that should *not* inform these decisions, or should play at most only a very small role in them. I turn now to explicating several of these factors.

There are at least three sources of bias likely to push INGOs toward sins of commission. First, INGOs have very strong institutional incentives to stay and continue providing aid in high-profile situations that generate publicity and donations. Publicity and donations are not necessarily morally objectionable—among other things, they can help INGOs to fund "unsexy" projects elsewhere—but they are unlikely to justify INGOs continuing to provide aid when there are valid reasons on the other side, such as that they are having significant negative effects.[17] Along the same lines, if an INGO's publicly declared *raison d'être* is to save lives and alleviate suffering by providing humanitarian aid, the damage to its image and fundraising efforts that might result from withdrawing can create an incentive to stay

---

[15] Branch argues that this was the case in Northern Uganda in the mid-1990s. See Adam Branch, *Displacing Human Rights: War and Intervention in Northern Uganda* (Oxford: Oxford University Press, 2011), esp. 91–2, and Branch, "Against Humanitarian Impunity."

[16] I use these terms colloquially; as I shall argue, "sin" is usually a significant over-statement.

[17] Peter Redfield, *Life in Crisis: The Ethical Journey of Doctors Without Borders* (Berkeley: University of California Press, 2013), ch. 6.

(although as the case of MSF discussed later in this chapter suggests, this is not always the case).

In addition to institutional incentives, expatriate aid workers also have strong psychological sources of bias toward staying (locally hired aid workers, of course, typically have no choice but to stay).[18] Once aid workers have developed relationships with members of a community where they are working, the prospect of "abandoning" that community can be horrifying. This horror expresses a valid moral insight. But interpersonal relationships have so much psychological force that they can "stack the deck" against withdrawing, when equally serious reasons to withdraw are not based on such relationships.

A third possible driver of sins of commission are philosophical concepts and ideas from within the tradition of humanitarianism that can be interpreted as offering strong support for staying regardless of the consequences, in particular the "duty to intervene," the "right to intervene," and the "humanitarian imperative."[19] The first two of these concepts were defended by Bernard Kouchner and other humanitarian thinkers in the 1970s and 1980s; the latter can be found in more recent documents, such as the Sphere standards.[20] Regardless of the "true" or best interpretation of these terms (which have been the subject of some debate), the important point for our purposes is that they have sometimes been interpreted to mean that INGOs have a duty to provide aid almost regardless of the consequences. As Hugo Slim writes,

> It is fairly obvious how international NGOs who have signed up to these three documents [the ICRC Code, the Sphere standards, and the Humanitarian Charter] understand humanitarian values today. They claim clearly that being humanitarian is a categorical imperative. It is an end in itself. It is an unconditioned ought and must never be subject to conditions. There are no "ifs" in the humanitarian imperative.[21]

I argue throughout this book that while a narrow focus on maximizing measurable good outcomes can be counter-productive, the idea that there is a "humanitarian duty" disconnected from consequences is extremely

---

[18] Didier Fassin, *Humanitarian Reason: A Moral History of the Present* (Berkeley: University of California Press, 2012), ch. 9.

[19] Gareth Evans, *The Responsibility to Protect: Ending Mass Atrocity Crimes Once and For All* (Washington, DC: Brookings Institution, 2008). 32–3. See also Hugo Slim, "Claiming a Humanitarian Imperative: NGOs and the Cultivation of Humanitarian Duty."

[20] David Rieff, "The Kouchner Conversion," *Project Syndicate*, August 1, 2007 <http://www.project-syndicate.org/commentary/the-kouchner-conversion/english>.

[21] Slim, "Claiming a Humanitarian Imperative." Slim argues that the writers of these documents did not have this sort of "fundamentalist" view, and he goes on to try to defend a duty-based humanitarianism that is "careful" without being consequentialist. However, he seems to suggest that some INGOs interpret the idea of humanitarian duty in this way.

dangerous. Insofar as the duty to protect and the humanitarian imperative are (mis)understood to mean that INGOs can ignore the effects of their actions, they are likely to contribute to sins of commission.

We turn now to the other side of the coin: possible drivers of sins of omission. In order to negotiate access to civilian populations in the context of violent group conflict, aid workers sometimes have to negotiate with local leaders of armed groups. Personally interacting with these individuals can make aid practitioners *feel* morally dirty.[22] While such feelings of moral contamination are entirely understandable, they can also help lead to sins of omission if they draw INGOs into a symbolic politics that is more about aid practitioners preserving their moral purity than the actual experiences, interests, and preferences of their intended beneficiaries.

A second factor that can contribute to sins of omission is excessively high expectations about what INGOs can accomplish on the part of INGOs and donors, in particular the assumption that INGOs can do significant good while avoiding all negative effects. These expectations often derive from the assumption that INGOs are entirely apolitical rescuers or good Samaritans.[23] The realization that this is *not* the case, that INGOs are embedded in political dynamics beyond their control and that as a result they regularly have unintended negative effects—can lead to what we might call "moral whiplash." Individuals get moral whiplash when they lurch from an (inaccurate) view of INGOs as heroes, good Samaritans, or do-gooding machines to an equally inaccurate view of them as inept devils with only selfish and/or malign intentions. Anyone, including aid recipients, can get moral whiplash. However, when INGO decision-makers or donors get moral whiplash, the result can be cynicism, a disparaging attitude toward aid-recipient societies, and/or a desire to disengage.

To summarize, institutional incentives, expatriate aid workers' psychological attachments, and (misreading of) philosophical resources such as the humanitarian imperative can push INGOs toward sins of commission. Feelings of moral contamination and moral whiplash can press them toward sins of omission. To resist these sources of bias, we need a positive account of how INGOs might conceptualize and navigate stay or go questions.

---

[22] Anderson, *Do No Harm.*

[23] James Orbinski, former president of MSF-International, describes himself as having these expectations based on this assumption (*An Imperfect Offering: Humanitarian Action for the Twenty-First Century* (New York: Bloomsbury Publishing, 2010)). Aid recipients also frequently have excessively high expectations of what INGOs can do, which can not only lead to cynicism when those expectations are not met, but also be deadly when they include the assumptions that INGOs will protect them from armed groups.

4.2 Do No Harm, Complicity, Doctrine of Double Effect, Dirty Hands

I turn now to examining several possible approaches to analyzing situations such as those faced by the INGOs in the Rwandan camps in Zaire. I discuss the specific ways in which each falls short, and then briefly discuss some additional limitations that they all share.

4.2.1 Do No Harm

Beginning in the early 1990s, aid scholar Mary B. Anderson and her Center for Development Alternatives promulgated what became an influential series of books, articles, handbooks, and workshops arguing that humanitarian INGOs should "do no harm."[24] Do no harm is now widely recognized by aid practitioners as an important "principle," "approach," or "framework" for managing and responding to aid's negative effects in conflict zones. For example, funding guidelines from the European Commission for Humanitarian Aid (ECHO) state that the "do no harm principle" which "seeks to ensure that assistance does not have unintended negative consequences" is "[a] minimum requirement for humanitarian interventions in all sectors."[25]

Taken literally, do no harm allows for *no* tradeoffs between providing aid and avoiding harm; the latter takes full priority over the former. By suggesting that it is more important for INGOs to avoid causing even minimal harm than it is for them to provide significant aid, this approach seems to prioritize the moral purity of INGOs and (typically expatriate) aid practitioners over the well-being of poor and disaster-affected people. The literal version of the do no harm principle therefore seems to urge, or indeed require, serious sins of omission.

One seemingly plausible way around this problem is to raise the bar for what counts as "harm." But if we do this, then the question shifts from whether INGOs should cause harm to whether a certain effect should count as a harm. Yet this re-conceptualization does not seem to offer much additional leverage on the problem. Moreover, by focusing narrowly on the undifferentiated category of "harm," the do no harm principle might lead INGOs or their interlocutors to "round up" negative effects to harms, and in so doing also contribute to sins of omission.

---

[24] Anderson, *Do No Harm*.
[25] European Commission Directorate-General for Humanitarian Aid, "Humanitarian Protection: DG ECHO's Funding Guidelines," Brussels, April 21, 2009 <http://ec.europa.eu/echo/files/policies/sectoral/Prot_Funding_Guidelines.pdf>.

A second seemingly promising way to make the do no harm principle more plausible is to take it less literally. Even though the uncompromising quality of the phrase invites a literal reading, aid scholars who endorse the do no harm principle often seem to use it to mean that INGOs should have few significant negative effects, not that they should do *no* harm. Anderson herself describes her approach not as a rigid prohibition, but rather as a "descriptive tool" that "identifies the categories of information that have been found through experience to be important for understanding how assistance affects conflict."[26] Likewise, UNICEF's version of the do no harm principle states (in part):

> Do no/less harm: Although aid can become part of the dynamics of the conflict and may even prolong it, humanitarian organizations must strive to "do no harm" or to minimize the harm they may be inadvertently doing simply by being present and providing assistance...[27]

However, if we interpret do no harm loosely, it shifts from being a too-rigid prohibition against doing any harm to either (a) erring too far in the other direction or (b) providing no guidance at all. An example of the principle providing no guidance is UNICEF's version quoted above, which goes on to direct humanitarian actors to avoid having negative effects "when such effects are not necessary to provide aid." This is good advice, as far as it goes. But what about when negative effects *are* necessary to provide aid? The principle says nothing about such cases. It therefore does not offer the wrong—or right— answer to the question of what the humanitarian INGOs in the Rwandan camps in Zaire should have done; it does not address their predicament at all.

An example of the do no harm principle being too permissive can be found in the Humanitarian Charter (mentioned above). The Charter endorses the "humanitarian imperative," which it defines as "the belief that all possible steps should be taken to prevent or alleviate human suffering arising out of conflict or calamity, and that civilians so affected have a right to protection and assistance."[28] A few paragraphs later, the Charter states that its

---

[26] Center for Development Alternatives, "The 'Do No Harm' Framework for Analyzing the Impact of Assistance on Conflict: A Handbook," Do No Harm Project (Local Capacities for Peace Project), a project of the Collaborative for Development Action, Inc. and CDA Collaborative Learning Projects, April 2004. (It is interesting to reflect on the conditions of possibility for, and the rhetorical work that is done by, the significant disconnect between the title "Do No Harm" and the substantive content of the books and workshops to which this title refers.)

[27] UNICEF, "UNICEF's Humanitarian Principles." PATH Training Programme, Participant Manual, July 2003 <http://www.unicef.org/pathtraining/Documents/Session%204%20 Humanitarian%20Principles/Participant%20Manual/4.2%20UNICEF%20Humanitarian%20 Principles.doc>. Another more recent document, UNICEF's "Core Commitments for Children in Humanitarian Action" also includes the do no harm principle, and its interpretation also does not provide useful guidance in dealing with the tradeoffs discussed here.

[28] The Sphere Project, *Humanitarian Charter and Minimum Standards in Humanitarian Response* <http://www.spherehandbook.org/>.

signatories "are committed to minimising any such adverse effects of our interventions [such as perpetuating conflict] *in so far as this is consistent with the obligations outlined above,*"[29] that is, insofar as it is consistent with the humanitarian imperative to provide aid. So the Charter directs INGOs to minimize adverse effects only insofar as this can be done while also complying with the humanitarian imperative to provide aid. When minimizing adverse effects would require diverging from the humanitarian imperative, for example by drastically reducing aid, the Charter seems to suggest that the humanitarian imperative—that is, providing aid—should take full priority. However, this position is just as extreme as, and no more justifiable than, the opposite claim that not doing harm should always take full priority over providing aid. Both extremes unjustifiably discount the effects of INGOs' actions and omissions on aid recipients and potential recipients.

4.2.2 Complicity

Several scholars and aid practitioners, most notably Robert Goodin and Chiara Lepora, have drawn on the concept of complicity to discuss the situation faced by the INGOs in the Rwandan refugee camps in Zaire. They have good reason for doing so: the concept of complicity is more nuanced than the principle of do no harm; in particular, it provides a language for recognizing when INGOs *contribute to* harm (or injustice) to a greater or lesser degree, rather than simply doing or not doing harm. Thus, Lepora and Millum argue that when a "principal actor...carries out a wrongful act" and "an accessory who does not actually perform the wrongful act" is nonetheless "in some way involved in it," that accessory is complicit.[30] Drawing on this conception of complicity, Goodin and Lepora offer a very helpful framework for "grading" the complicity of the humanitarian actors in the Rwandan refugee camps in Zaire.[31]

Yet the complicity approach also has several limitations that make it an insufficient guide for addressing the three questions articulated at the outset of this chapter. A first and more minor difficulty is that scholars such as Lepora and Goodin include, in their definition of complicity, cases in which actors know, or can reasonably be expected to know, that they are

---

[29] My italics.

[30] Chiara Lepora and Joseph Millum, "The Tortured Patient," *Hastings Center Report* 41.3 (2011): 38–47 (40). Larry May defines complicity as "responsibility for the commissions and omissions that allow harm to occur but are not necessarily causally efficacious in a straightforward way" (May, *Genocide*, 267). For another account of complicity that is very helpful but does not address the Rwanda case directly (and with which Lepora and Goodin in some respects disagree), see Christopher Kutz, *Complicity: Ethics and Law for a Collective Age* (Cambridge: Cambridge University Press, 2007).

[31] Lepora and Goodin, "Grading Complicity in Rwandan Refugee Camps."

contributing to injustice. On this definition, INGOs are complicit in the injustices to which they knowingly contribute, even if they are furiously opposed to those injustices. In ordinary usage, however, a complicit actor is not only involved in a wrongful act; it shares the principal perpetrator's (bad) intentions, at least to some degree. Applying the term "complicit" to INGOs can therefore seem to characterize INGOs' intentions as worse than they are, and could thereby lead third parties to pressure INGOs to commit sins of omission. It could also lead to unhelpful defensiveness on the part of aid practitioners who feel that their intentions are being unfairly maligned. Lepora and Goodin endorse this broad conception of complicity because they do not think that intentions matter much for the moral evaluation of actors, like INGOs, that are "plan-takers" rather than "plan-makers," that is, the main instigators of injustice.[32] But while Lepora and Goodin emphasize that INGOs' good intentions do not absolve them of responsibility for the effects of their actions, they say less about how to think about the fact that INGOs actively deplore the views and objectives of the actors with whom they are (ostensibly) complicit. As I noted above, this antipathy makes the situation faced by the INGOs in the Rwandan camps in Zaire, and other similar situations, cases of dramatically distributed agency. By assimilating all cases in which actors knowingly contribute to harm perpetrated primarily by others to the concept of complicity, the complicity framework does not help us to think through the implications of dramatically distributed agency.

A second, more serious, limitation of the complicity framework is that it provides no basis for measuring or conceptualizing the good that INGOs do. As noted above, Lepora and Goodin offer an extremely helpful framework for distinguishing among degrees of complicity among actors working in the Rwandan camps in Zaire. But when it comes to the question of what the INGOs in these camps should have done all things considered—that is, when it comes to the stay or go question—they acknowledge that complicity is only one part of the equation. As Lepora and Goodin write:

> Some levels of complicity should sometimes be deemed morally acceptable, because the benefit of an intervention outweighs the wrongness of contributing to wrongdoing.... In other cases, humanitarian organizations should refuse to intervene where the bad done by their complicity with wrongdoing would overwhelm the benefit of their direct aid intervention. Careful evaluation is required to tell which is which.[33]

---

[32] In their view, "people and their actions should be judged in terms of what those people do, not their intentions" (Lepora and Goodin, "Grading Complicity in Rwandan Refugee Camps," 271).

[33] Lepora and Goodin, "Grading Complicity in Rwandan Refugee Camps," 272.

We should not expect a map of the ethical predicaments that humanitarian INGOs face to replace this "careful evaluation" of specific cases. However, it would help to have a framework that could provide *some* insight or guidance regarding how to approach these benefits, analogous to what Goodin and Lepora's conception of complicity provides for negative effects.

4.2.3 *The Doctrine of Double Effect (DDE)*

The doctrine of double effect (DDE) comes much closer to providing this guidance than the concept of complicity. The DDE also focuses squarely on actors with mostly good intentions. In these respects, the DDE is more helpful for our purposes than either the principle of do no harm or the concept of complicity.

A central insight of the DDE is that "sometimes it is permissible to bring about as a merely foreseen side effect a harmful event that it would be impermissible to bring about intentionally."[34] According to the DDE, for a harm to be morally justified, it is necessary (though not sufficient) that it be an unintended side effect of achieving a good outcome, rather than a means to the end of achieving a good outcome. For example, killing civilians as a side effect of bombing a military installation is potentially morally justified, according to the DDE, whereas killing civilians so that survivors will oppose the war is not.

A full analysis of the DDE is beyond the scope of this book. The important point for our purposes is that even if this distinction is useful for analyzing military action, it is not very helpful for making judgments about whether INGOs working in conflict situations should stay or go. This is because, in these latter situations, INGOs' contributions to harm or injustice are almost always unintended side effects of efforts to achieve a good outcome, rather than means to an end of achieving a good outcome.[35] They therefore almost always fall on the "possibly morally permitted" side of the DDE's main distinction.

So this central aspect of the DDE does not offer much leverage on the cases before us. However, the DDE offers a further standard for determining which of these possibly morally permitted actions are indeed morally permitted: the beneficial effects of these actions must be "proportional" to (i.e. outweigh) their negative effects. That is, "there must be a proportionately grave reason for permitting the evil effect."[36] As basic as it is, this is a crucial

---

[34] Alison McIntyre, "Doctrine of Double Effect," in *The Stanford Encyclopedia of Philosophy* (Spring 2014 edition), ed. Edward N. Zalta <http://plato.stanford.edu/entries/double-effect/>.

[35] There are certainly exceptions. For example, INGOs sometimes contemplate withdrawing aid, for example to encourage refugees to return home. This might be seen as inflicting harm as a means to the end of achieving a good outcome, and so prohibited by the DDE.

[36] Cited in McIntyre, "Doctrine of Double Effect."

insight: I will argue below that proportionality should play a central role in practical judgments by INGOs and their observers about stay or go questions. But the DDE does not offer much more than this. It also does not offer much insight into how to apply the concept of proportionality to INGOs. The substantive cases most discussed in the DDE literature involve either heads of state or military leaders who directly violate moral rules or cause significant harm, or doctors in clinical settings making tradeoffs involving one person or a person and a fetus.[37] That is, they tend to involve fully governmental or fully non-governmental actors, not somewhat governmental actors. In addition, in both of these types of cases, the issue is usually about the justifiability of direct but unintended harm, not actors contributing knowingly but unintentionally to harms or injustices perpetrated primarily by others. So while the DDE can tell us *that* proportionality matters, it offers little guidance, in the form of accreted cases and commentary on those cases, regarding how to apply the principle of proportionality to the context of humanitarian INGOs.

The DDE also has two other shortcomings. One is that, while it is intended to help us determine what actors should do when faced with seeming moral conflicts, it does not provide any sort of account of the felt experience of those conflicts. The other is that the DDE offers little insight into INGOs' more temporally extended responsibilities; it is primarily about what actors should do in the moment, not about their responsibilities beforehand or after the fact.

4.2.4 *Dirty Hands*

While it is well known to political theorists and philosophers, the theory of dirty hands has thus far been mentioned only in passing in the literature on humanitarian action.[38] Compared to the approaches surveyed so far, it is in many respects a superior basis for grappling with situations like those faced by the INGOs working in the Rwandan refugee camps in Zaire. But it, too, falls short.

According to Michael Walzer's seminal account, politicians, especially political rulers, get their hands dirty when they undertake "a particular act of government" that "may be exactly the right thing to do in utilitarian terms,

---

[37] For example, McIntyre, "Doctrine of Double Effect"; David R. Mapel, "Revising the Doctrine of Double Effect," *Journal of Applied Philosophy* 18.3 (2001): 257–72; Georg Spielthenner, "The Principle of Double Effect as a Guide for Medical Decision-Making," *Medicine, Health Care and Philosophy* 11.4 (2008): 465–73.

[38] The only examples I have found in the humanitarianism literature are passing references in Slim, "Doing the Right Thing," Branch, "Against Humanitarian Impunity," Barnett, *Empire of Humanity*, and Lepora and Goodin, *Complicity and Compromise*, 170.

and yet leave the man who does it guilty of a moral wrong."[39] Walzer's main example is of a political ruler who must decide whether to order the torture of a rebel leader who knows the location of several ticking bombs that, if left to explode, will kill many people.[40] Walzer argues that it is right for the ruler to order the torture, because doing so will save the lives of many innocent people, to whom, as their ruler, he has particular responsibilities.[41] But ordering torture is also morally wrong. The ruler has dirty hands, Walzer argues, if he orders the torture, but does so grudgingly, and later publicly affirms that torture is wrong.[42]

At first glance, the dirty hands framework might seem to characterize precisely the situation of the INGOs in the Rwandan camps in Zaire: just as Walzer's politician could only do what was right in utilitarian terms (prevent the bomb from exploding) by engaging in a moral wrong (committing torture), INGOs could only do what was right in utilitarian terms (continue to provide aid), by engaging in a moral wrong (contribute to injustice perpetrated by others). Moreover, the dirty hands framework appears to have numerous other strengths compared to the other approaches surveyed above: unlike do no harm, dirty hands does not prioritize INGOs' moral purity over aid recipients' well-being. Unlike complicity, dirty hands incorporates not only reasons against but also reasons for contributing to injustice. Unlike the DDE, dirty hands captures the felt experience of moral conflict and offers insights into INGOs' more temporally extended responsibilities. Yet applying the framework of dirty hands to situations like that faced by the INGOs in the Rwandan camps in Zaire exaggerates, distorts, and/or overlooks several important features of these situations. As a result, applying the dirty hands framework to these situations is likely to not only misdescribe them, but also push INGOs toward sins of omission—that is, toward going when they should stay. (This is ironic, in that Walzer is often accused of being too accommodating of moral violations such as torture.)[43]

---

[39] Michael Walzer, "Political Action: The Problem of Dirty Hands," *Philosophy & Public Affairs* 2.2 (Winter, 1973): 160–80. For a recent overview, see C. A. J. Coady, "The Problem of Dirty Hands," in *The Stanford Encyclopedia of Philosophy* (Spring 2014 edition), ed. Edward N. Zalta <http://plato.stanford.edu/entries/dirty-hands/>

[40] On why this example is dangerously unrealistic, see Henry Shue, "Torture in Dreamland: Disposing of the Ticking Bomb," *Case Western Reserve Journal of International Law* 37.2/3 (2006): 231–9.

[41] As Coady ("The Problem of Dirty Hands") notes, theorists such as Michael Stocker think that dirty hands predicaments are not specific to politics; they can arise for anyone in any context. But while anyone can face a moral conflict, politicians have an especially strong reason to put more weight on outcomes, because they have responsibilities to their constituents.

[42] On Walzer's account, having dirty hands is, while not exactly fully justified, also not the same as merely being guilty, so one cannot wrongly choose to get one's hands dirty.

[43] Shue, "Torture in Dreamland."

First, because INGOs are unarmed, their negative effects are typically less violent and severe than those contemplated by politicians. At the same time, humanitarian INGOs can typically do less good than formal political actors. In other words, humanitarian INGOs cannot order torture or fire-bomb cities—but nor can they locate ticking bombs or end wars. While this appears to be a "mere" difference of degree, it amounts to a difference in kind, because in the INGO case (but not the torturing or bombing politician case), there is a distinctive challenge regarding how to make practical judgments about relatively minor contributions to gross injustices. As Hugo Slim writes, it would be

> morally negligent if excessive agonizing by or about relief agencies (the groaning of the white man and his burden) shouted out the accusations of blame which should be put squarely where they are most obviously due: with the killers, the rapists, the dispossessors and their political leaders who initiate and sustain the policies of excessive and unjust violence in today's wars and genocides.[44]

To say that humanitarian INGOs have dirty hands is, then, melodramatic, and unhelpfully so. The dirty-handed politician's sober sense of his own importance, his hand-wringing and public self-flagellation, are not appropriate for humanitarian INGOs, who, as Slim suggests, get something substantively wrong if they make themselves the center of the story.

Second, as just noted, while politicians facing dirty hands problems must decide whether to commit grave moral wrongs, INGOs typically must decide whether to contribute to injustices perpetrated primarily by others. So in addition to being less severe, situations such as that faced by the INGOs in the Rwandan refugee camps in Zaire are also less direct than dirty hands situations. This raises another important question: what are the ethical implications of indirectness? This question is obscured if one interprets the INGO case as a dirty hands problem.

Third, while political rulers can be manipulated, and while the political ruler who must choose between engaging in torture and allowing many people to be killed is certainly constrained, the experience of dramatically distributed agency—of having one's agency re-deployed for purposes opposite one's own, while one looks on helplessly—does not play a major role in Walzer's account of dirty hands; the political rulers with dirty hands is too powerful. Yet for INGOs, a significant part of the question they face is what to make of the fact that they are not merely contributing jointly with others to a bad outcome; instead, their resources are being intentionally and actively redeployed, often in an ongoing way, for purposes they deplore.

---

[44] Slim, "Doing the Right Thing," 247.

Fourth, Walzer characterizes dirty hands problems as conflicts between doing what is best in utilitarian terms and violating moral principles, that is, between doing what is prescribed by a more consequentialist versus a more rule-based approach to morality (the idea being that the wrongness of torture is not limited to its consequences). However, both horns of the conflicts that INGOs face can be described in more consequentialist terms. That is, they can be seen as conflicts between two sets of outcomes: one in which INGOs stay, so people receive aid that benefits them but (for example) violence is perpetuated, and one in which INGOs withdraw, so violence is perpetuated less than it would have been otherwise, but people also do not receive aid. Thus, while Walzer wants to say that the politician who ordered the torture is both right and wrong simultaneously, we can say something rather less paradoxical about the INGO that chooses to stay when the overall benefits of its actions outweigh the costs: it did the best thing under the circumstances, but there is still a moral remainder or sacrifice associated with its decision.

4.2.5 *Other Limitations*

While they are in some respects very different, the four approaches just described all operate almost exclusively in the registers of humanitarianism (in the case of do no harm) or morality and justice (in the case of complicity, doctrine of double effect, DDE, dirty hands)—not democratic norms. Yet given that stay or go questions have life-or-death significance for many people, and that democratic norms suggest that people should have a say in decisions that significantly affect them, democratic norms appear to be highly relevant to stay or go questions. I return to this issue below.

4.3 Spattered Hands

In light of these limitations, I turn now to outlining an alternative approach—an alternative "map"—that I will argue is superior to the four approaches discussed above. We should conceptualize situations such as those faced by the INGOs in the Rwandan refugee camps in Zaire, situations in which INGOs have mostly good intentions and some good effects, and contribute knowingly but unintentionally to injustices perpetrated primarily by others, as spattered hands problems. In navigating these predicaments, INGOs sometimes have a responsibility to *allow their hands to be spattered*—that is, they sometimes have a responsibility to grudgingly accept contributing to injustices perpetrated primarily by others.[45]

---

[45] In spattered hands ethical predicaments, every choice available—to stay and continue to provide aid, or to withdraw—involves moral sacrifice. So why does staying get the "spattered

The term "spattered" avoids the melodramatic overstatement of calling situations such as that faced by the INGOs in the Rwandan camps in Zaire cases of dirty hands, and the sins of omission that might follow. It conveys that INGOs' hands are not only less dirty than those of Walzer's conventional political leaders, but also dirty through more indirect means; they are spattered by dirt created primarily by others. Nonetheless, moral dirt still clings to them: INGOs' good intentions do not shield them from moral responsibility for the predictable effects of their actions, even if those effects are indirect. The spattered hands framework thus emphasizes that humanitarian INGOs are neither individual good Samaritans whose hands never touch moral dirt, nor government officials who get their hands fully dirty. It therefore provides a starting place for normative analysis that avoids distorting the ethically and politically significant features of these situations.

With this initial sketch of spattered hands before us, I turn next to the implications of the spattered hands framework for the three questions elucidated at the outset of this chapter.

4.3.1 *Spattered Hands and Stay or Go Questions*

Recall the stay or go question: should INGOs continue providing aid, even though in so doing they contribute to injustices perpetrated primarily by others, or should they withdraw? The spattered hands framework suggests, first, that in addressing this question, INGOs should focus primarily on the likely consequences of their actions. Rather than simply "doing no harm," they should, as the DDE suggests, seek to implement a principle of "proportionality." But in so doing, they should take into account how INGOs' conventional governance role influences its reasons to stay. In particular, when INGOs that engage in somewhat governmental service provision withdraw, they do not simply allow a situation to revert to the status quo ante; instead, their withdrawal is more akin to pulling the rug out from under people's feet.[46] The more governmental an INGO's service-provision role, the more apt the rug-pulling analogy is. When the analogy is apt, INGOs have a *prima facie* responsibility to continue providing aid. This responsibility is all the more pressing for INGOs that are *not* second-best actors, that is, for INGOs that have no other actors waiting in the wings, willing and able to step in and replace them.

---

hands" label? The logic here tracks the logic of the dirty hands argument: acting (ordering torture, continuing to provide aid) involves (contributing to) an active injustice, and so moral dirt of some kind, whereas the alternative (not torturing, ceasing to provide aid) is an omission, and so does not.

[46] See Chapter 3 for a full discussion.

If the negative effects of staying outweigh the benefits, INGOs have a duty to withdraw: no mandate or good intentions, no "duty to intervene" or "humanitarian imperative," generates a moral permission—much less a moral duty—for INGOs to continue providing aid when in so doing they do more harm than good. In contrast, and more controversially, when the benefits of aid outweigh its negative effects, humanitarian INGOs do not merely have a moral permission to stay and continue providing aid; they sometimes have a *duty* to do so—that is, a duty to grudgingly allow their hands to be spattered—even if their negative effects are still significant in absolute terms.[47] On this view, INGOs cannot simply walk away in order to "keep their hands clean" or avoid moral compromise. Just as a conventional government cannot walk away from its citizens, insofar as INGOs function as governments, they cannot walk away from the people they serve, if their presence is doing more good than harm.

This argument might at first seem to incentivize INGOs against serving a conventional governance function. Indeed, in interviews, MSF employees often spoke about not wanting to get dragged into a governance role, for just this reason.[48] If indeed the argument does create this incentive, that seems like a good thing: because of INGOs' limitations as actors, we should *want* them to look first for ways to pressure or support other, first-best actors, rather than engaging in governance themselves. That said, the sources of bias in favor of sins of commission described above are likely to create a much stronger incentive in the other direction, as are straightforward humanitarian arguments against passing over people in serious need.

I have suggested that in order to properly evaluate the overall consequences of staying or going, and therefore to answer the stay or go question in particular situations, INGOs must ask to what extent their provision of basic services functions as a form of conventional governance. While I cannot fully discuss them here, I want to briefly mention a few other considerations that might inform INGOs' judgments of proportionality.

First, in evaluating the benefits of aid, which benefits count? Presumably, the prevention of imminent death or severe suffering among aid recipients counts, while fun and exciting careers for expatriates do not count. But what about benefits to locally hired workers (who are sometimes also aid recipients themselves)? What about benefits to recipients who use aid for purposes

---

[47] Discussing the situation of the INGOs in the Rwandan camps, Terry writes, "[t]here has to be a point at which aid organizations acknowledge that by choosing to intervene and professing to alleviate suffering they undertake certain responsibilities to the people whose expectations they raise" (*Condemned to Repeat?*, 208). Terry means that the INGOs should have withdrawn to avoid conveying to civilians that the camps were safe when they were not. But this argument also cuts the other way: it can suggest that INGOs have a responsibility to stay.

[48] Kenny Gluck, interview, 2002.

other than what INGOs intend (e.g. they sell food and use the proceeds to buy materials for religious observance)?

Likewise, which costs count? In particular, do "opportunity costs" count? That is, in seeking to measure the negative effects of providing aid in a particular location, should INGOs include consideration of what else they could have done with those resources? Opportunity costs will be lower, and so will matter relatively less, if an INGO's funding is "tied" to a specific issue; these costs will be higher and so matter more if resources used in one context can be transferred somewhere else. In general, incorporating opportunity costs into the analysis is likely to give INGOs more reason to withdraw: "we have to stay because leaving would amount to unjustly pulling the rug out from under people" will often conflict with "we should go, because we can do so much more good elsewhere." While it is uncontroversial that INGOs should go when they are doing more harm than good, and plausible that they should stay when they are doing more good than harm (even if they are doing considerable harm in absolute terms), the idea that they should withdraw because they can do more good elsewhere is a bit more difficult to stomach. Indeed, it might seem to somehow disrespect current aid recipients. But while special obligations to current aid recipients or other factors might *outweigh* opportunity costs, there seems to be no reason for *excluding* such costs. Incorporating them would seem only to put people who have not yet received aid on more equal footing with current recipients.

A final consideration that must inform judgments of proportionality regarding stay or go decisions is: what time horizon should INGOs use in making these decisions? As I discuss below, a short time horizon is likely to shift INGOs' responses to stay or go questions in the direction of staying, because many of the negative effects of withdrawing basic services will be immediate, while a longer time horizon is likely to shift their responses in the direction of withdrawing, because the negative effects of contributing to injustice are likely to take longer to materialize (or to become visible).

4.3.1.1 SPATTERED HANDS IN THE RWANDAN REFUGEE CAMPS IN ZAIRE

Did any of the INGOs in the Rwandan refugee camps in Zaire adopt the spattered hands framework in deciding whether to stay or go? It is important to emphasize that adopting the spattered hands framework is not the same as allowing one's hands to be spattered. The former is a way of approaching the question; the latter is a justified decision to stay from the perspective of this approach. Based on the limited evidence available, it appears that both MSF-France and Oxfam adopted something like the spattered hands approach, while Oxfam, but not MSF-France, allowed its hands to be spattered.

Defending its decision to leave the Rwandan camps in Zaire, MSF argued that because the negative effects of aid exceeded the benefits, it had a duty to withdraw. In a letter to its contributors, it stated that, "[f]ar from participating in the resolution of the conflict, international aid perpetuates the situation and, worse still, prepares the crisis of tomorrow..."[49] This argument is entirely consistent with the spattered hands framework, which says that if negative effects outweigh the benefits, INGOs should withdraw. Likewise, Nicholas Stockton, then of Oxfam-UK, invoked the same consequentialist logic, but used it to defend the opposite decision: Oxfam should stay and continue providing aid, Stockton argued, because "the removal of water distribution services from the camps was more certain to provoke a large loss of life than the future of the refugee camps per se."[50] In order for an INGO that decides to stay to have spattered hands, and not merely be guilty of contributing to injustice, the benefits of it continuing to provide aid must not only outweigh the negative effects; the INGO must contribute to injustice only grudgingly.[51] That is, it must experience and describe such contributions as moral burdens, rather than as moral permissions or freedoms. If Stockton's argument is any indication, it appears that Oxfam exhibited this grudgingness.

MSF and Stockton/Oxfam thus agreed that the consequences of staying or going were the central considerations, but they came to different substantive conclusions about these consequences. What explains their disagreement? In addition to factors such as organizational culture and the kinds of services each organization provided, another explanation appears to be that they utilized different time horizons. MSF took (or at least, justified its decision by invoking) the long view, emphasizing INGOs' negative political effects on the "crises of tomorrow." In contrast, Stockton focused more on Oxfam's conventional governance function in the immediate future, in providing water in the camps. Neither organization publicly mentioned the opportunity costs of staying, although whether this was because such costs were low, they chose not to consider them, or they thought it disrespectful to mention them publicly, is not clear.

While Stockton defended Oxfam's decision to stay in the camps on consequentialist grounds roughly consistent with the spattered hands framework, the executive director of CARE UK, Charles Tapp, defended CARE's

---

[49] Cited in Terry, *Condemned to Repeat?*, 196. Even if, as some have alleged, MSF made this decision on internal organizational grounds and only publicly justified it in terms of its effects in the camps and on future conflicts, it is still instructive to consider why they chose this defense of their decision to withdraw, rather than some other one.

[50] Terry, *Condemned to Repeat?*, 201 (this is a direct quote of Terry paraphrasing Nick Stockton).

[51] Cf. Walzer ("The Problem of Dirty Hands," 171) who writes that the dirty-handed politician "will never be in a hurry to override the rules, but will wait until there is no choice, acting only to avoid consequences that are both imminent and almost certainly disastrous."

decision to stay in a very different way. He argued that "Care's remit is to provide humanitarian assistance. That is what we have to do."[52] That is, Tapp defended CARE's decision to stay in the camps on duty-based grounds, rather than with reference to consequences. In so doing, Tapp drew implicitly on the humanitarian imperative, discussed above.[53] The spattered hands framework rejects these sorts of arguments: treating aid recipients justly means putting consequences, not abstract notions of duty or rigid notions of role-based responsibilities, at the center of one's analysis of stay or go questions.

4.3.1.2 STAY OR GO QUESTIONS AND DEMOCRATIC NORMS

I argued above that while the do no harm, complicity, DDE, and dirty hands approaches operate primarily in humanitarian, egalitarian, or justice-based registers, democratic norms also appear relevant to situations such as those faced by INGOs in the Rwandan camps. What does the spattered hands framework tells us about the role of democratic norms in navigating these situations?

By conceptualizing INGOs as political and sometimes somewhat governmental, the spattered hands framework suggests that democratic norms are relevant to INGOs. In addition, by acknowledging but not exaggerating INGOs' negative effects, it lessens the aura of crisis around them, and thereby opens up space for discussion and deliberation. By focusing on consequences, the spattered hands framework emphasizes a particular kind of deliberation and discussion: deliberation and discussion about the likely effects of INGOs' continued presence or withdrawal. Democratic norms thus suggest that humanitarian INGOs should enact norms of transparency, deliberation, and reason-giving, discussing whether they should stay or go with a wide range of aid recipients and non-recipients.[54] However, in order to be more significantly democratic, INGOs must at least be open to debate and contestation regarding this emphasis on overall consequences itself.

In contrast, majoritarian decision-making procedures, such as binding referenda, are unlikely to be effective instantiations of democratic norms for addressing stay or go questions. As I noted at the outset, the civilians in the Rwandan refugee camps in Zaire were subject to an elaborate propaganda campaign by the "ex"-FAR; they did not have accurate information about security in the camps or their other options, let alone possibilities for

---

[52] Cited in Terry, *Condemned to Repeat?*, 197.

[53] Slim, "Claiming a Humanitarian Imperative," argues that arguments such as Tapp's profoundly misunderstand the humanitarian imperative.

[54] Even if INGOs cannot be fully transparent, in advance, about the conditions under which they will withdraw (in order to avoid being manipulated by actors who want them to leave), they ought to be as transparent as possible after the fact about their reasons for withdrawing or staying.

deliberating openly. These and other logistical factors are likely to render majoritarian decision procedures insufficiently democratic.

What if INGOs were able to overcome these hurdles, and put the question of whether they should stay or go to an at least minimally democratically legitimate vote? Would they then have a duty to implement this procedure and then abide by the outcome? It seems to me that if the vote were for them to leave, INGOs would have strong democratically based moral reasons to do so. If the vote were for them to stay, however, the issue is more complicated. Instituted broadly, the requirement that an INGO must stay in these circumstances appears very unjust: it would tip the scales heavily toward current aid recipients and against groups that were not receiving aid. It would also leave INGOs with virtually no autonomy.

4.3.2 Spattered Hands and INGOs' Temporally Extended Responsibilities

Perhaps because stay or go questions are so dramatic, they have been the central focus of aid practitioners and scholars interested in (what I am calling) spattered hands problems. But because these questions arise repeatedly, it makes little sense to treat them as rapidly arising one-off events. We must also examine the responsibilities that INGOs have both before and after they make these decisions. I will argue that democratic norms can play a more significant role here than in the context of immediate decisions about whether to stay or go; the spattered hands framework shows how this is so.

What might it look like for INGOs to cultivate a capacity to address stay or go questions in advance? They might study past cases in which INGOs have had to address stay or go questions and evaluate their responses with the benefit of hindsight.[55] They might develop protocols for establishing good relationships and open lines of communication with aid recipients, so as to be able to discuss stay or go questions with them when, or before, they arise. INGOs might also develop protocols for ensuring that decision-making about stay or go questions involves managers at headquarters, aid practitioners in the field, and a diverse array of aid recipients (and non-recipients) to reduce the effects of biases associated with each of these positions. Some INGOs do all of these things already.

Beyond this, however, I think that there is something else INGOs can do: they can cultivate an institutional ethos of equanimity, or evenness of mind. This ethos (one could also see it as an organizational virtue) is consistent

---

[55] Magone et al. is an example of precisely this sort of effort (Claire Magone, Michael Neuman, Fabrice Weissman, and Médecins Sans Frontières (eds.), *Humanitarian Negotiations Revealed: The MSF Experience* (London: Hurst & Co., 2011)). See also www.speakingout.msf.org.

with a wide range of affective styles, such as political outrage, dispassionate policy analysis, and compassionate concern and care. It emerges from an understanding that humanitarian INGOs are highly political actors that regularly face spattered hands ethical predicaments. Equanimity is helpful because it helps to reduce moral whiplash and the sins of omission to which it gives rise. Because equanimity is not quiescence, it does not draw INGOs into sins of commission.

As an institutional or organizational virtue, equanimity does not have to be embodied in the outlook of every aid worker: it leaves room for diversity among aid workers, for the visionary idealist to rub shoulders with the world-weary pragmatist. Equanimity can be the result of these interactions, or it can be instantiated in decision-making procedures within an organization, such as the practice, mentioned above, of dividing up responsibility for decision-making among differently situated actors. Wherever it is located, an institutional virtue of equanimity can help INGOs to resist being swayed by the sources of bias toward sins of omission and sins of commission mentioned at the outset of this chapter.

We might also imagine equanimity as a virtue not of individual INGOs, but rather of the INGO sector as a whole. More specifically, even though there are sometimes reasons for INGOs to coordinate with each other, for example to present a "united front" to a host government, INGOs are more likely to recognize and publicize other INGOs' unintended negative effects if they themselves have not played a role in causing them.[56] That is, perhaps we need a "division of moral labor" in the humanitarian INGO sector, or the humanitarian sector more generally, in which some INGOs (or other actors) act as "moral absolutists" that refuse to contribute to injustice themselves, and are therefore willing to point out when other actors have done so.[57]

The issue of INGOs being called to account for how they respond to stay or go questions brings us to the question of INGOs' responsibilities for how they address stay or go questions after the fact. It is here that the democratic strains in Walzer's account of dirty hands are suggestive, and can inform our understanding of spattered hands. Walzer argues that in order to have dirty hands, a politician who violates a moral rule must resign or apologize so as to publicly acknowledge that what he did was wrong (even though it was also right), and publicly reassert the value of the moral principle(s) that he violated. While Walzer focuses more on justice, guilt, and public order, this

---

[56] MSF is a notable exception. See Magone et al., *Humanitarian Negotiations Revealed*.

[57] Suzanne Dovi ("Guilt and the Problem of Dirty Hands," *Constellations* 12.1 (2005): 128–46) discusses moral absolutists in domestic politics. But Cf. Chapter 7, where I argue that a division of moral labor can be dangerous if it gives actors an "out" to act irresponsibly by claiming that others will compensate for their activities.

sort of public apology can also be read as embodying democratic norms, in the form of a (delayed) gesture of transparency and an openness to being held accountable through the imposition of a formal or informal sanction.

Unlike the politician with dirty hands, the INGO with spattered hands has not acted wrongly, and so does not need to publicly repent. However, it has made a moral sacrifice in the form of a contribution to injustice, and it has a corresponding duty to publicly reassert the value of that which it sacrificed. This reassertion might take the form of a public explanation and justification: the wrongness of contributing to injustice would be publicly acknowledged and reinforced by an explanation of the conditions that made a particular contribution to injustice a justifiable moral compromise. This sort of public explanation—if it was indeed sufficiently public—would open INGOs to evaluation and informal sanction by donors, INGOs, journalists, activists, and even aid recipients themselves.[58]

The judgments of these interlocutors would not necessarily be better (or worse) than those of INGOs themselves. However, they would be based on different incentives, experiences, identities, and commitments. In the short term, making explanations for decisions to stay or go a regular feature of INGOs' public communications might turn off some donors: if an INGO's hands are spattered, can its donors' hands be entirely clean? Over time, however, such an ongoing process of public reason-giving might help to reduce moral whiplash and deepen awareness, in the public cultures of both donor and aid-recipient countries, of INGOs' capacities and limitations.

Even if INGOs do not have a duty to apologize for allowing their hands to be spattered, they might still have a duty to compensate people who are harmed by the injustices to which they contribute.[59] But specifying and discharging these duties poses serious conceptual and logistical challenges: to whom, exactly, are these duties owed? What do they consist of? (Recall that we are talking about INGOs providing compensation for their contributions to injustices perpetrated primarily by others.) Perhaps most importantly, the costs of INGOs discharging duties of compensation to those they negatively affect would likely be borne in significant part by people in need of aid, both because resources that would have been used to provide aid would instead be used for compensation, and because, unless a major shift in donor attitudes were to occur, donations to INGOs that provided such compensation (and perhaps donations to all humanitarian INGOs) would likely be reduced.

---

[58] While there are equity-based difficulties with allowing aid recipients to sanction INGOs for withdrawing, there is much more justification for creating a system in which aid recipients could sanction INGOs for poor performance, via anything from a Yelp-type online rating system, to the use of a country's judicial system for more serious infractions (although the former could create an incentive for INGOs to work only in "easy" contexts).

[59] Here I only consider the possible need to compensate people who suffer from the active harms to which INGOs contribute, not people who suffer because INGOs chose to withdraw.

In light of these difficulties, a perhaps more promising way to conceptualize INGOs' duties to compensate for their contributions to injustice and other negative effects is to think of these duties as usually overridden by INGOs' duties to provide aid effectively and at least somewhat cost-effectively to people who are badly off. That is, duties of compensation exist, but are usually outweighed by other considerations. This leaves intact the idea that if INGOs engage in severely damaging sins of commission, they might have non-overridden duties of compensation. It is also a way to acknowledge the seriousness of the moral compromises that INGOs make, and thereby encourage them to make them carefully.

Over the long term, INGOs that find themselves repeatedly making significant moral compromises in the course of fulfilling their professional role or organizational responsibilities have a further responsibility to try to alter the conditions that make these compromises necessary. The primary way that INGOs have done this thus far is by demanding "humanitarian space," that is, demanding that particular preconditions for the provision of humanitarian aid (e.g. access to civilians in need on all sides of the conflict, freedom to monitor aid provision directly) be met.[60] However, it appears that even INGOs' best efforts along these lines are insufficient to avoid spattered hands problems. Whatever the explanation for this, the end result is that humanitarian INGOs have a responsibility that they cannot readily discharge. Rather than do-gooding machines or devils, INGOs are thus themselves a kind of moral compromise.

4.3.3 Spattered Hands and Dramatically Distributed Agency

One reason why spattered hands ethical predicaments arise in the first place is that INGOs' agency is dramatically distributed between themselves and actors whose means and/or ends INGOs deplore. Yet unlike slaves, INGOs have significant power over other people—namely, aid recipients and potential recipients—whose well-being depends on how INGOs respond to their agency being dramatically distributed. What are the implications of this state of affairs for INGO political ethics?

Coming to grips with merely distributed agency requires acknowledging that one's agency is intermixed with that of other people and things, without losing sight of one's agency entirely. In Krause's terms, we must recognize that we can have meaningful agency without being entirely sovereign over ourselves.[61] In the case of dramatically distributed agency, however, the

---

[60] Ashley Jackson, "A Deadly Dilemma: How Al-Shabaab Came to Dictate the Terms of Humanitarian Aid in Somalia," *Overseas Development Institute*. December 11, 2013 <http://www.odi.org.uk/opinion/8066-al-shabaab-somalia-negotiations>.

[61] Krause, "Bodies in Action."

challenge is a bit different. The worry is not only about being overtaken by the larger "assemblages" in which one participates;[62] it is also about how to appropriately judge one's moral responsibility under conditions when it can be easy to vastly over- or understate it. On the one hand, aid workers can be so horrified by the gross injustices that they see being perpetrated around them, that they overstate their own or their organization's moral responsibility: they to some extent confuse *contact* with injustice with *causing* injustice. On the other hand, an INGO might reason that: "We find the manipulation of our presence and resources by combatants to be beyond odious. But it is they who are stealing our resources; we are not handing them over willingly. We therefore bear no responsibility for whatever happens as a result of the theft."

I think that INGOs should try to resist both of these logics—that is, both guilt-by-contact and innocence-by-intention. Instead, we should say that when INGOs knowingly but unintentionally contribute to injustices perpetrated primarily by others, they are morally responsible *for those contributions*. That is, they are obliged to explain why those contributions were justified. They are not responsible for everything the primary perpetrator of injustice does, but nor do their good intentions absolve them of responsibility for their own negative effects. Thus, the kind of practical judgment that an INGO must exercise, and the sort of public explaining that it must do to defend its judgments, differ significantly from both that of an individual good Samaritan and a political ruler with dirty hands.

4.4 Conclusion

It is impossible to predict with certainty what would happen to the overall pattern of responses to stay or go questions within the INGO sector if most INGOs were to adopt the spattered hands framework. However, I would speculate that, while attention to rug-pulling and the "downgrading" of contributing to injustice from dirty hands to spattered hands would push INGOs in the direction of staying, the overall effect of INGOs adopting the spattered hands approach would be that INGOs would withdraw more often than they do currently.[63] This would happen because they would discount intentionality and intrinsic-value arguments for staying, make judgments of proportionality that took opportunity costs into account, and actively seek

---

[62] See Jane Bennett, "The Agency of Assemblages and the North American Blackout," *Public Culture* 17.3 (2005): 445–66. See also Krause, "Bodies in Action."

[63] Another powerful factor likely to shape how often INGOs stay and how often they withdraw is what time horizon they utilize.

to combat institutional and psychological sources of bias. Another factor likely to shift INGOs in the direction of withdrawing would be if more INGOs approached their temporally extended responsibilities in a way roughly along the lines of what I have described. If more INGOs did this, donors' expectations might be altered, which in turn would reduce the organizational cost to all INGOs of withdrawing when they judge that they are doing more harm than good.

As I have noted, INGOs facing spattered hands ethical predicaments are usually not second-best actors. In many other contexts, however, INGOs are second-best actors. As such, they face strikingly different ethical predicaments from those examined here. It is to these ethical predicaments—these quandaries of the second-best—that we now turn.

5

The Quandary of the Second-Best

Who elected Oxfam?

—The Economist[1]

On July 21, 2010, the Dodd-Frank Wall Street Reform and Consumer Protection Act, better known as the Dodd-Frank bill, was signed into law by President Obama. Section 1502 of the bill, the Conflict Minerals Provision, requires companies to show that the minerals used in their products did not originate in the Democratic Republic of Congo, or if they did originate in the DRC, that they did not contribute to the conflict there.[2] Support for Section 1502 was spearheaded by the Enough Project, a US-based INGO, and Global Witness, a UK-based INGO. Together with the International Crisis Group's John Prendergast, these two organizations wrote Section 1502.[3] They also helped to shape the lineup of speakers at the Security and Exchange Commission's October 2011 "public roundtable" about rules for implementing the bill.[4]

---

[1] "Angry and Effective," *The Economist*, September 21, 2000 <http://www.economist.com/node/374657>.

[2] U.S. House, 111th Congress, 2nd Session, H.R. 4173, *Dodd-Frank Wall Street Reform and Consumer Protection Act* (Washington, DC: Government Printing Office, 2010), 838–43.

[3] "John Prendergast, the Enough Project, and Global Witness are directly responsible for this completely predictable havoc, as are the American legislators and industry personnel who took their testimony as gospel, let them write section 1502 of the legislation, and ignored dissenting voices in the debate over the minerals" (Laura Seay, "The DRC minerals mess," *Texas in Africa*, August 4, 2011 <http://www.texasinafrica.blogspot.com>). Because this issue is ongoing and contentious, much of the available information comes from blog posts and other unpublished sources.

[4] "[M]embers of Congress like Jim McDermott and their staffs seem to have taken Enough's word at face value, going so far as to let the advocacy organization choose most of the witnesses at hearings on the Dodd-Frank measure, which meant that any dissenting voices—Congolese or American—went mostly unheard" (Laura Seay, "The Dodd-Frank catastrophe," *Texas in Africa*, August 8, 2011 <http://www.texasinafrica.blogspot.com>). Enough claims that it "wasn't involved with this event," but acknowledges that "several members of our team attended the hearing" (John Bagwell, "Hijacking the Congo Conflict Minerals Narrative," *Enough Project*, May 22, 2012 <http://www.enoughproject.org/blogs/hijacking-congo-conflict-minerals-narrative>).

Even before Dodd-Frank was passed, however, many US- and DRC-based academics and activists argued that Section 1502 would have disastrous consequences. They predicted that mining companies in the DRC, anticipating the difficulty and cost of abiding by the new rules, would shift their operations elsewhere, leaving tens of thousands of Congolese miners jobless, and making them, their families, and communities even more destitute than they had been previously.[5] These academics and activists also argued that the bill would not even accomplish its stated objective of reducing conflict in the DRC, because the minerals trade played only a very small role in driving the conflict there.[6] As of 2015, these predicted outcomes seem to have largely come to pass.[7]

Consider another example of advocacy by an INGO.[8] In March 2011, the INGO Oxfam and three Ghanaian NGOs together released a report that they had jointly commissioned, called "Achieving a Shared Goal: Free Universal Health Care in Ghana." The report asserted that "[t]he current health system in Ghana is unfair and inefficient," that Ghana's National Health Insurance Authority (NHIA) had over-stated by 44% the proportion of Ghanaians covered by Ghana's National Health Insurance Scheme (NHIS), and that the scheme should be dismantled and replaced with free-at-point-of-service

---

[5] Congolese civil society organizations estimated that 5–12 million people (miners and their dependents) have been significantly negatively affected by Section 1502 (Laura Seay, "What's Wrong with Dodd-Frank 1502? Conflict Minerals, Civilian Livelihoods, and the Unintended Consequences of Western Advocacy—Working Paper 284." *Center For Global Development*, January 5, 2012 <http://www.cgdev.org/publication/what%E2%80%99s-wrong-dodd-frank-1 502-conflict-minerals-civilian-livelihoods-and-unintended>). See also: David Aronson, "How Congress Devastated Congo," *The New York Times*, August 7, 2011 <http://www.nytimes. com/2011/08/08/opinion/how-congress-devastated-congo.html>; Jason Stearns's response to Aronson, "Thoughts about Conflict Minerals," *Congo Siasa*, August 10, 2011 <http://congo-siasa.blogspot.com>; and Mvemba Dizolele, "Conflict Minerals in the Congo: Let's Be Frank About Dodd-Frank," *Huffington Post*, August 22, 2011 <http://www.huffingtonpost.com/ mvemba-dizolele/conflict-minerals-congo-dodd-frank_b_933078.html>.

[6] Séverine Autesserre, "Dangerous Tales: Dominant Narratives on the Congo and Their Unintended Consequences," *African Affairs* 111(443) (2012): 202–22.

[7] See the sources cited above, especially Seay, "What's Wrong with Dodd-Frank 1502?" The Enough Project disagrees with this assessment (Sasha Lezhnev, "What Conflict Minerals Legislation is Actually Accomplishing in Congo," *Huffington Post*, August 9, 2011 <http:// www.huffingtonpost.com/sasha-lezhnev/what-conflict-minerals-le_b_922566.html>). However, a more recent Enough report on the effects of Dodd-Frank paints an only somewhat positive picture (Fidel Bafilemba, Sasha Lezhnev, and Sarah Zingg Wimmer, "From Congress to Congo: Turning the Tide on Conflict Minerals, Closing Loopholes, and Empowering Miners," *Enough Project*, August 6, 2012 <http://www.enoughproject.org/publications/congress-co ngo-turning-tide-conflict-minerals-closing-loopholes-and-empowering-miners>). While it is impossible to adjudicate definitively among these positions, one reason to give more weight to critics of Section 1502 is that, as Autesserre ("Dangerous Tales") explains, Enough and Global Witness had economic and institutional incentives to accept and perpetuate the idea that conflict minerals are a main driver of the DRC conflict.

[8] By "advocacy" I mean the activities that INGOs themselves describe as "advocacy" or "campaigning." While describing these activities as advocacy is not neutral among possible normative criteria for evaluating them, the term has fewer normative criteria embedded in it than "representation" and "partnership" do.

health care for all, funded primarily by tax revenues.[9] The report also argued that contrary to claims made by the United Nations Development Programme and the World Health Organization, other countries should not adopt Ghana's NHIS as a model.[10]

The "Shared Goal" report generated a "major controversy," both within Ghana and in international development circles.[11] The NHIA slammed the report, arguing that it was a sloppily researched effort by Oxfam to "tarnish a home grown African initiative."[12] But the NHIA did eventually respond to the report's criticisms by altering its methodology for calculating the number of people covered by Ghana's NHIS, which led to a much lower estimate.[13] At the international level, the World Bank issued its own report about Ghana's health care system, partly in response to the "Shared Goal" report. Like the NHIA, the World Bank also repeatedly referred to the "Shared Goal" report as "the Oxfam report," and to the "Shared Goal" report's arguments as "Oxfam's critique," largely ignoring the Ghanaian NGOs that co-commissioned the report.[14]

Over the past few decades, there has been a dramatic increase in advocacy by INGOs working on issues related to inter-group violence, humanitarian disasters, poverty, and injustice, such as the advocacy efforts by Enough, Global Witness, and Oxfam just described.[15] How should these activities be conceptualized and normatively evaluated? What ethical predicaments do INGOs face when they seek to advocate in ways that are consistent with democratic, egalitarian, and justice-based norms? Can we identify better and worse ways—ways that are more rather than less consistent with these norms—for them to navigate these predicaments?[16] This chapter addresses these questions.

[9] Patrick Apoya and Anna Marriott, "Achieving a Shared Goal: Free Universal Health Care in Ghana" (Oxfam International, 2011), 7, 8, and 25 <http://www.oxfam.org/sites/www.oxfam.org/files/rr-achieving-shared-goal-healthcare-ghana-090311-en.pdf>. (The NHIA implied a coverage rate of 62%, but the report argued that it "could be as low as 18%.")

[10] Apoya and Marriott, "Achieving a Shared Goal," 8; George Schieber, Cheryl Cashin, Karima Saleh, and Rouselle Lavado, "Health Financing in Ghana at a Crossroads" (Washington, DC: International Bank for Reconstruction and Development /The World Bank, 2012), ii.

[11] Schieber et al., "Health Financing in Ghana at a Crossroads," 8.

[12] National Health Insurance Authority, "NHIA Position on OXFAM/ISODEC Report on Free Universal Health Care in Ghana," March 17, 2011 <http://www.ghanaweb.com/GhanaHomePage/NewsArchive/artikel.php?ID=205271>.

[13] Schieber et al., "Health Financing in Ghana at a Crossroads," 8.

[14] Schieber et al., "Health Financing in Ghana at a Crossroads," 8–9, 66, 82, 108, 109.

[15] Roger Riddell, *Does Foreign Aid Really Work?* (New York: Oxford University Press, 2007), ch. 17.

[16] This chapter focuses on political advocacy by INGOs on policy issues in wealthy and poor countries. Given this focus, I do not focus only on humanitarian INGOs, even though humanitarian INGOs such as Oxfam and CARE engage in political advocacy. I also do not focus on humanitarian norms. Advocacy aimed at negotiating humanitarian access to groups of civilians in conflict settings raises somewhat different issues. See Claire Magone, Michael Neuman, Fabrice Weissman, and Médecins Sans Frontières (eds.), *Humanitarian Negotiations Revealed: The MSF Experience* (London: Hurst & Co., 2011). Humanitarian INGOs sometimes argue that their

Many democratic theorists have conceptualized INGO advocacy as a paradigmatic example of "non-electoral representation."[17] On this conceptualization, Enough and Global Witness are non-elected representatives of Congolese miners, and Oxfam is a non-elected representative of Ghanaians who lack adequate access to health care. Correspondingly, these INGOs' advocacy efforts should be evaluated based on how well they meet normative criteria of good (democratic) representation, such as being authorized, accountable, and transparent, and deliberating with their "constituents"—or at least being responsive to their preferences. On this conceptualization, in other words, representing democratically simply is what it means for INGO advocates to be democratic.

In sharp contrast to how democratic theorists characterize INGO advocacy, most INGO advocates do not call themselves representatives; in some cases they vehemently reject this label. Many claim instead to be "equal partners" with entities based in the countries about which they are advocating, including domestic NGOs, domestic governments, community-based organizations, and social movements. Thus, neither Enough, Global Witness, nor Oxfam describe themselves as representatives, but Oxfam does describe itself as working "in partnership" with the three Ghanaian NGOs with which it co-commissioned the "Shared Goal" report: ISODEC, Essential Services Platform of Ghana, and the Alliance for Reproductive Health Rights.[18] While democratic theorists are attracted to the representation lens because they see it as specifying relevant democratic norms for INGO advocates,[19] practitioners (and some scholars) like the partnership lens because they see it as specifying relevant egalitarian norms for INGO advocates.[20]

This divergence between how democratic theorists conceptualize INGO advocacy and how many INGO advocates describe themselves raises an

"on the ground" work reduces the likelihood that they will misconstrue the interests of poor and marginalized people, thus distinguishing them from organizations such as Enough and Global Witness, that do not provide aid.

[17] Michael Saward, "Authorisation and Authenticity: Representation and the Unelected," *Journal of Political Philosophy* 17.1 (2009): 1–22; Suzanne Dovi, "Political Representation," in *The Stanford Encyclopedia of Philosophy* (Spring 2014 edition), ed. Edward N. Zalta <http://plato.stanford.edu/archives/spr2014/entries/political-representation/>; Nadia Urbinati and Mark E. Warren, "The Concept of Representation in Contemporary Democratic Theory," *Annual Review of Political Science* 11.1 (2008): 387–412.

[18] See discussion of the "Shared Goal" report on Oxfam's website: <http://www.oxfam.org/en/policy/achieving-shared-goal-ghana-healthcare>. There is a large critical literature about "partnership" in the field of international development. See, for example, Alan Fowler, "Introduction—Beyond Partnership: Getting Real About NGO Relationships in the Aid System," *IDS Bulletin* 31.3 (2000): 1–13; Rita Abrahamsen, "The Power of Partnerships in Global Governance," *Third World Quarterly* 25.8 (2004): 1453–67 and the citations therein.

[19] David Plotke, "Representation is Democracy," *Constellations* 4.1 (1997): 19–34; Nadia Urbinati, "Representation as Advocacy: A Study of Democratic Deliberation," *Political Theory* 28.6 (2000): 758–86.

[20] See discussion of partnership in Chapter 2.

obvious question: who is right? Are democratic theorists guilty of wearing representation-colored glasses—that is, of seeing representation wherever they look, even if it is not the most appropriate conceptualization of the situation at hand? Or are INGOs' claims to be partners rather than representatives merely an effort to avoid being held to the demanding normative standard of "good representative," even though such a standard is in fact appropriate?

There is no denying that INGO advocacy sometimes includes activities that can plausibly be described as representing: although they do not use the term, Global Witness and Enough acted, in effect, as representatives—albeit arguably poor ones—of the Congolese people. Likewise, Oxfam acted in many respects like an equal partner to the Ghanaian NGOs with which it co-commissioned the Shared Goal report. However, I will argue in this chapter that representation and partnership are *both* poor conceptual starting places for normatively evaluating INGO advocacy. In particular, familiar ideas about what it means to be a democratic representative and an equal partner do not provide adequate guidance for understanding what is required for INGO advocacy to be democratic or egalitarian—or just.

The main reason for this is that, as I argued in Chapter 3, humanitarian INGOs are often second-best actors. In the context of advocacy, INGOs are often second-best compared to domestic governments, domestic NGOs, community-based organizations (CBOs), and social movements based in the global South. This means that sometimes the most democratic thing for them to do is *not* to represent as well as possible, but instead to step back and support other advocates. Likewise, sometimes the most egalitarian thing for them to do is *not* to act as equal partners, but rather to step back and let other advocates take the lead.

That is, because they are often second-best actors, INGO advocates regularly face the *quandary of the second-best*: to what extent should they focus on achieving a substantive objective or policy outcome, and work with first-best actors only insofar as doing so is conducive to that goal, and to what extent should they step back and support first-best actors, even if this is likely to delay achieving their substantive policy goals, or reduce their chances for success? This quandary is best seen as arising not from a conflict between substantive outcomes and the intrinsic value of participation on the part of first-best actors, but rather from a conflict between two kinds of substantive outcomes: the specific policy or decision that is being advocated for, and the enhanced capacities, power, connections, etc. of advocates based in the global South.

I argue that given this quandary, we should not conceptualize INGO advocates as representatives or partners and ask whether they represent or engage in partnership well; instead, we should conceptualize INGO advocacy as the *exercise of power*, and normatively evaluate INGO advocates on the basis of how well they *avoid misusing their power*.

This argument has implications not only for the political ethics of INGO advocacy, but also for democratic theory more generally. It highlights tensions between representation and democracy that are very different from those identified by participatory and "strong" democrats.[21] It also offers a counterweight to the recent "representative turn" in democratic theory, by asking not only whether we *can* read particular activities as representation, but also whether we *should* do so: what is revealed and what is elided by the representation lens?[22]

The next two sections (5.1 and 5.2) explain the limitations of the representation and partnership lenses, respectively. Section 5.3 proposes the misuse of power lens as an alternative basis for conceptualizing and normatively evaluating INGO advocacy. I describe four ways in which INGO advocates tend to misuse their power, and propose four corresponding normative principles for identifying and minimizing these misuses in a way that is attentive to the quandary of the second-best.

Throughout, I illustrate my arguments with reference to the two cases of INGO advocacy described above.[23] Neither is an incontrovertible example of INGO advocacy gone wrong—or right. But Oxfam's advocacy on Ghana's NHIS appears to have been more consistent with democratic, egalitarian, and justice-based norms than Enough and Global Witness's advocacy on Section 1502 of the Dodd-Frank bill. One burden of this chapter, then, is to show that the misuse of power lens provides a more perspicacious explanation for why this is so than does viewing INGOs as representatives or as partners.

5.1 INGO Advocacy as Non-Electoral Representation

Since the mid-1990s, democratic theorists have become increasingly interested in political representation in general, and "non-electoral" representation in particular. They regularly cite INGO advocacy as a paradigmatic example of non-electoral representation, and describe INGOs as non-elected representatives and as makers of "representative claims."[24] For example, the

[21] For example, participatory democrats such as Barber argue that representation distances ordinary people from politics and deprives them of its character-building and epistemic benefits. Benjamin R. Barber, *Strong Democracy: Participatory Politics for a New Age* (Berkeley: University of California Press, 2003), 144–7.

[22] Sofia Näsström, "Where is the Representative Turn Going?" *European Journal of Political Theory* 10.4 (2011): 501–10.

[23] I don't claim that these cases are typical of INGO advocacy in general. In social scientific terms, my use of them is "hypothesis-generating."

[24] Michael Saward, *The Representative Claim* (New York: Oxford University Press, 2010). Some right- and left-leaning critics of INGOs, legal scholars, and scholar-practitioners also describe

Stanford Encyclopedia of Philosophy's entry on "political representation" states that, "[g]iven the role that International Non-Governmental Organizations play in the international arena, the representatives of dispossessed groups are no longer located in the formal political arena of the nation-state."[25] Likewise, Urbinati and Warren write that "advocacy" organizations and "international non-governmental organizations" "claim to represent constituencies within public discourse and within collective decision-making bodies."[26]

The theorists making these arguments generally refer to INGO advocacy only in passing, as an example. Their main subject is non-electoral representation, not advocacy. But once INGO advocacy is conceptualized as non-electoral representation, the normative questions that get asked about it are framed in these terms. For example, Michael Saward examines "a set of cases of non-elective representative claims," including those made by advocacy INGOs, and develops "evaluative criteria against which the democratic acceptability of unelected would-be representatives [including these INGOs] might be assessed."[27] For Urbinati and Warren, "the challenges for democratic theory are to understand the nature of these representative claims [including, again, those ostensibly made by INGOs] and to assess which of them count as contributions to democracy and in what ways."[28]

As these quotations suggest, these authors' understandings of both the descriptive content of INGO advocacy and the normative questions that it raises seem to be shaped largely by their prior conceptualization of INGO advocacy as representation and/or as the making of representative claims. But as was mentioned above, advocacy INGOs themselves usually deny being representatives or engaging in representation. In a survey, "less than 10%— of the [I]NGOs examined claimed to be 'speaking for' the South or Southern

INGOs as non-elected representatives. See Paul Wapner, "Introductory Essay: Paradise Lost— NGOs and Global Accountability," *Chicago Journal of International Law* 3 (2002): 155 and other articles in this issue; Erik B. Bluemel, "Overcoming NGO Accountability Concerns in International Governance," *Brooklyn Journal of International Law* 31 (2005–6): 139–206; and Warren Nyamugasira, "NGOs and Advocacy: How Well Are the Poor Represented?" *Development in Practice* 8.3 (1998): 297–308.

[25] Dovi, "Political Representation."

[26] Urbinati and Warren, "The Concept of Representation in Contemporary Democratic Theory," 403. See also Saward, "Authorisation and Authenticity"; Joshua William Busby, "Bono Made Jesse Helms Cry: Jubilee 2000, Debt Relief, and Moral Action in International Politics," *International Studies Quarterly* 51.2 (2007): 247–75; and Laura Montanaro, "The Democratic Legitimacy of Self-Appointed Representatives," *The Journal of Politics* 74.4 (2012): 1094–1107.

[27] Saward, "Authorisation and Authenticity," 1. Saward discusses many types of non-elected actors, including INGOs. See also Montanaro, "The Democratic Legitimacy of Self-Appointed Representatives."

[28] Urbinati and Warren, "The Concept of Representation in Contemporary Democratic Theory," 404. See also Terry Macdonald, *Global Stakeholder Democracy: Power and Representation Beyond Liberal States* (New York: Oxford University Press, 2008), 163.

NGOs..."[29] Jordan and Van Tuijl note that "many NGOs deny the concept of representation, pointing out that local communities, be they in the North or South, are able to adequately represent themselves."[30] Likewise, a recent search of the websites of several major INGOs yielded virtually no references to the word "represent" or its cognates.[31]

What is going on here? While democratic theorists are correct that INGOs sometimes engage in representation, INGOs are correct that their advocacy should not be normatively evaluated primarily through a representation lens—or so I shall argue. There are two main reasons why this is so: INGO advocacy typically involves a range of activities that includes but is not limited to representation, and even when INGOs do engage in representation, they are often second-best actors.

5.1.1 *INGO Advocacy Includes Activities other than Representation*

Even taking into account the existence of a wide range of understandings of what representation is, INGO advocacy typically includes both representing and other activities.[32] If we evaluate INGO advocates based only on how well they represent, we overlook these other activities. This sort of omission should be of great concern to anyone who cares about the democratic and anti-democratic potential of *all* aspects of INGO advocacy, not only representation.

Cases of INGO advocacy often involve one or more of the following four activities, all of which are not, or not only, representation:

(1) Assisting other actors, such as domestic governments, NGOs, and social movements, to better represent poor and marginalized groups (e.g. by providing them with information or connecting them with high-level officials). Oxfam describes this as "supporting organizational and institutional capacity strengthening."[33]

---

[29] Alan Hudson, "NGOs' Transnational Advocacy Networks: From 'Legitimacy' to 'Political Responsibility'?" *Global Networks* 1.4 (2001): 331–52 (338). I doubt that INGOs deny being representatives for legal reasons (e.g. to retain their 501c3 status), because they still make partisan political claims. Also, some INGOs, such as Oxfam America, have separate advocacy arms for precisely this reason.

[30] Lisa Jordan and Peter van Tuijl, "Political Responsibility in Transnational NGO Advocacy," *World Development* 28.2 (2000): 2051–2065 (2053).

[31] A search for "represent," "representation," and "representative" on the web pages of fifteen of the largest humanitarian and development INGOs in August 2012 revealed no instances of INGOs claiming to represent poor and marginalized people.

[32] See Jennifer C. Rubenstein, "The Misuse of Power, Not Bad Representation: Why It Is Beside the Point That No One Elected Oxfam," *Journal of Political Philosophy* 22.2 (2013): 204–30 for a discussion of different conceptions of representation.

[33] Oxfam International, "Working Together: Oxfam's Partnership Principles and Program Standards," February 2012 <http://www.oxfam.org/sites/www.oxfam.org/files/oxfam-partnership-principles.pdf>; also Jordan and van Tuijl, "Political Responsibility in NGO Advocacy."

(2) Pressuring other actors, especially elected officials, to better represent poor and marginalized people.[34] For example, the "Shared Goal" report argues that the current Ghanaian government "came to power in Ghana on a promise to deliver a truly universal health insurance scheme" that "still remain[s] unfulfilled."[35]

(3) Seeking to "improve the workings of the mechanisms and agencies that regulate and frame the behavior of political representatives."[36]

(4) Altering the participants in, or the content of, public debate. While representation can do this (e.g. by "calling forth" a constituency), the participants in and content of a debate can also be altered in other ways.[37] Global Witness and Enough's efforts to shape the lineup of speakers at the SEC's roundtable on implementing Section 1502 of Dodd-Frank is an example. This category of advocacy activity also includes "helping to bring together different actors to work on common problems," "generating and sharing knowledge," "promoting innovation and alternative solutions that may be brought to scale,"[38] and engaging in witnessing or *témoignage*.

In short, INGO advocacy regularly includes assisting other actors to represent, pressuring other actors to represent, improving the institutional context in which representation occurs, and altering the participants in and content of public debate. All of these activities can be more or less democratic, but none of them are (only) representation. They are also not an exhaustive list of advocacy activities other than representation. We therefore need normative criteria for evaluating INGO advocacy that are relevant to as many INGO advocacy activities as possible, including but not only representation (however defined).

---

[34] An INGO that pressures elected representatives on behalf of a group can also be described as representing that group, but the "pressuring" description foregrounds different features of the activity than does the representing description: in particular, it foregrounds the distinctive strategies associated with effectively pressuring of others.

[35] Apoya and Marriott, "Achieving a Shared Goal," 8.

[36] Enrique Peruzzotti, "Civil Society, Representation and Accountability: Restating Current Debates on the Representativeness and Accountability of Civic Associations," in *NGO Accountability: Politics, Principles and Innovations*, ed. Lisa Jordan and Peter van Tuijl (Sterling, VA: Earthscan, 2006), 47. Montanaro, "The Democratic Legitimacy of Self-Appointed Representatives," cites Oxfam's claim that it "seek[s] to influence the powerful to ensure that poor people can ... have a say in decisions that affect them" as evidence that Oxfam is a self-identified representative. I am arguing that there is, at least potentially, an important normative difference between engaging in representation oneself and helping to ensure that poor people can have a say in decision that affect them (for example, by setting up a meeting between poor people and their formal elected representative).

[37] Cf. Montanaro, "The Democratic Legitimacy of Self-Appointed Representatives"; Saward, *The Representative Claim*.

[38] Oxfam International, "Working Together."

5.1.2 INGO Advocates Are Often Second-Best Representatives

I have argued that INGO advocacy should not be conceptualized only as the activity of representing because it includes a range of activities in addition to representing. But what about when INGO advocates clearly *are* engaged in representing, for example, cases in which their activities are consistent with all extant criteria for determining when representation is occurring? In those cases, should INGOs be normatively evaluated based on how well they represent? I think the answer in this case is still "no."

This is because INGOs are often second-best representatives in relative terms and mediocre representatives in absolute terms. While I will focus on INGOs as second-best actors, their second-best status is a more serious concern because they are also mediocre, or worse, in absolute terms. A first reason why INGOs are second-best actors is that, unlike democratic governments and at least some NGOs and CBOs based in poor or disaster-affected countries, INGOs do not operate under the threat of formal or informal sanction by the people most directly affected by their advocacy. This means that INGO advocates often suffer no negative consequences for representing badly. As Michael Edwards writes:

> What if the [I]NGOs who protested so loudly in Seattle turn out to be wrong in their assumptions about the future benefits that flow from different trading strategies—who pays the price? Not the [I]NGOs themselves, but farmers in the Third World who have never heard of Christian Aid or Save the Children, but who will suffer the consequences for generations.[39]

Second, because they are based elsewhere, INGO advocates often lack a nuanced understanding of the political, social, economic, or religious dimensions of the issues they address (this might have been the case with Enough and Global Witness).[40] Third, unlike many NGOs and social movements based in the global South, most INGOs are headquartered in Northern countries and their high-level managers and decision-makers are mostly white people from those countries. When these INGOs represent people living in Southern countries, they can, despite the sincere good intentions of the individuals involved, reproduce or evoke patterns of domination and usurpation by colonial and imperial powers.[41] Another implication of INGOs being poor

[39] Michael Edwards, *NGO Rights and Responsibilities: A New Deal for Global Governance* (London: Foreign Policy Centre, 2000), 19. Also see Clifford Bob, "NGO Representation and Accountability: A Skeptical View," NGOs, International Security and Global Governance, Johns Hopkins University, October 9, 2007 <http://ssrn.com/abstract=1023021>. In "Political Responsibility in NGO Advocacy," Jordan and van Tuijl describe local NGOs in India having the capacity to influence international activists by threatening to cut them off from important information, but such cases are rare.

[40] Jordan and van Tuijl, "Political Responsibility in NGO Advocacy."

[41] This division of advocacy groups between "Northern" and "Southern" is an oversimplification. For example, Justice Africa is based in London, but is "run by, for and with Africans and African communities; guided by the Pan-African slogan: *'Nothing for me without me'*" (Justice

descriptive or "mirror" representatives of the people for whom they advocate is that they fail to provide the epistemic, psychological, symbolic, and other benefits that such representation can provide.[42]

Despite these serious limitations, INGO advocates are in other ways very able representatives, and advocates more generally: they often have sources of funding that domestic NGOs lack, and connections, experience, expertise, and technical capacities that many social movements based in the global South do not have. They can also be less corrupt than domestic NGOs and governments. Nonetheless, the four shortcomings just mentioned—lack of accountability to those most affected, limited understanding of the situation "on the ground," a tendency to evoke colonial and imperial relationships, and lack of descriptive representation—are still prevalent among INGOs, and indeed are closely connected to basic features of INGOs, such as their reliance on donations. Insofar as INGO advocates have these limitations, they are likely to be second-best representatives. As a result, being democratic, for INGO advocates, often means *not* representing (or engaging in other forms of advocacy) as well as possible themselves, but rather stepping back and supporting first-best representatives/advocates, such as domestic governments, domestic NGOs, or social movements.[43] Evaluating INGO advocates based only on how well they represent excludes this possibility.

A proponent of viewing INGOs as representatives might object as follows: Why not say that INGO advocates should represent as well as possible (and be evaluated on the basis of how well they represent) when they are engaged in representation and first-best representatives? They could then be evaluated on other bases when they are engaged in activities other than representing or when they are second-best representatives. The problem with this strategy is that INGOs' status as second-best actors is not only often difficult to assess and the subject of disagreement; it is also, at least potentially, in flux. As a result, INGOs can never fully "settle into" the role of (first-best) representative. Even when no first-best representative is apparent, even when an INGO does not see how it could help create one, the ethics of the second-best suggests that INGO must remain vigilantly attuned to the *possibility* that a first-best representative might emerge

Africa, "About Us" <http://www.justiceafrica.org/about-us/> italics in original). The inequalities at issue here can be material as well as symbolic, if jobs, prestige, and expertise associated with advocacy flow to advocates from wealthy countries.

[42] Jane Mansbridge, "Should Blacks Represent Blacks and Women Represent Women? A Contingent 'Yes'," *The Journal of Politics* 61.3 (1999): 628–57; Anne Phillips, *The Politics of Presence* (New York: Oxford University Press, 1995). See also Linda Alcoff, "The Problem of Speaking for Others," *Cultural Critique* 20 (1991–2): 5–32.

[43] See Suzanne Dovi, "In Praise of Exclusion," *The Journal of Politics* 71.3 (2009): 1172–86. Dovi discusses the ethics of stepping back in the context of formal political offices in the US.

and/or that it could support one coming into being.[44] In short, while an INGO might be second-best only some of the time, the possibility that it might be second-best changes its ethical situation all of the time. As Sudanese academic and activist Abdullahi An-na'im commented to a group of MSF aid workers, "international advocacy is extremely important, but as we do that we should develop local capacity to displace it...Local capacity should be promoted to the extent possible in every respect."[45] This is a very different orientation from that of the INGO that sees itself as a first-best representative and therefore throws itself wholeheartedly into representing as well as possible.[46]

I have argued that for the purposes of normatively evaluating INGO advocacy, we should not conceptualize INGO advocates as representatives because INGO advocacy includes activities other than representation, and because when INGOs do engage in representation, they are often second-best representatives. As a result, what it looks like for them to be democratic is very different from what it looks like for a first-best representative to be democratic.

5.2 INGO Advocacy as Equal Partnership

As a normative standard, "equal partnership" can be applied to a wide range of INGO advocacy activities. It therefore avoids the first problem with the representation lens described above (that it fails to offer leverage on the full range of activities that comprise INGO advocacy). However, the partnership lens does run into the second problem described above: like the representation lens, it also fails to account for INGOs often being second-best actors. As I explain at the end of this section, it also has a third problem that the representation lens does not have.

According to the ordinary, everyday meaning of "partnership," which I will call the "complementarity" conception, being a good partner means

---

[44] While in both cases there is a need for vigilance about whether and when to withdraw, this is very different from spattered hands ethical predicaments: in the quandary of the second-best the main reason for an INGO to pull back is that some other actor would do whatever it is doing better; in spattered hands predicaments the main reason for an INGO to withdraw is that its negative effects are greater than its benefits. The presence of other actors who could fill in (without undermining the political effect of withdrawing) would count in favor of withdrawing, but would not be the primary motivating factor.

[45] Nathan Ford and Richard Bedell (eds.), *Intentions and Consequences: Human Rights, Humanitarianism and Culture* (Amsterdam: MSF, 1999), 27.

[46] Stepping back and supporting first-best actors might seem unnecessary for humanitarian INGOs, such as MSF, that speak out against gross violations of human rights that they witness directly. But it is still appropriate for INGOs that do this sort of work to consult widely and carefully with those affected, regarding the possible effects of speaking out. For an example of what happens when INGOs do not do this, see Magone et al. (eds.), *Humanitarian Negotiations*, 45–6.

treating one's partner(s) as equal(s) and working with them on equal terms. Even if there is a division of labor in which partners perform different roles, they all have equal standing. The complementarity conception of partnership thus embodies what, in Chapter 2, I called "participation equality." The complementarity conception can be found in Oxfam International's "Partnership Principles":

> Oxfam believes it is only through the collective effort of many actors (civil society, state, private sector and others) that this goal [of reducing poverty and injustice] can be achieved. Each of these actors has a role to play in accordance with its responsibility, legitimacy, its capacities and strengths...These relationships are not about side-lining...others; *they seek instead to foster complementarity and to harness the added value each may bring.*[47]

However, as I also argued in Chapter 2, participation equality is not the only, or necessarily the most normatively important, interpretation of equality in the context of INGOs. The relevant kind of equality might instead be what I called "political equality," or the idea that individuals and organizations in society at large should have a chance to help shape outcomes that will significantly affect them. If political equality is the kind of equality that should animate INGO advocacy, then pursuing the complementarity conception of partnership might be relevantly *in*egalitarian, because it gives large, Western-based INGOs an equal say, when they should instead have less say than domestic advocates.

The idea that political equality ought to be a goal of partnership is evident in Oxfam Canada's Partnership Policy. In contrast to the complementarity conception of partnership described above, Oxfam Canada's policy features what I will call the "redundancy" conception of partnership:

> Whatever can be done with sufficient quality, effectiveness and efficiency by local organizations must be done by them...Every effort will be made to live up to the aspiration embodied in OI Program Standard 6 which states that "effective partnering is a fundamental strategy through which *Oxfam seeks to become redundant.*"[48]

Unlike the complementarity conception, which promotes participation equality, the redundancy conception of partnership promotes political

---

[47] Oxfam International, "Working Together" (my italics). This passage is also in Oxfam Canada, "Partnership Policy" (February 25, 2011 <http://www.oxfam.ca/our-work/our-approach/partnership-policy>). See also Jordan and van Tuijl's discussion of "cooperative" advocacy in "Political Responsibility in NGO Advocacy."

[48] Oxfam Canada, "Partnership Policy" (my italics). All but the last sentence of this passage can also be found in Oxfam International's Partnership Policy. The fact that the last sentence refers to an OI document suggests that OI also recognizes the attractiveness of the redundancy conception.

equality. In so doing, it acknowledges Oxfam's status as a second-best actor—with regard to not only representation, but also a wide range of other activities ("*whatever* can be done...by local organizations must be done by them"). Rather than complement local organizations indefinitely, the redundancy conception suggests that Oxfam should continually support other actors and reduce its own involvement, until it eventually becomes redundant. The redundancy conception therefore acknowledges the comparative advantage of other types of actors over INGOs, in terms of the issues discussed above (accountability, local knowledge, etc.). It also acknowledges that the differing strengths and capacities of INGOs and domestic actors are sometimes not happy coincidences to be exploited (e.g. "harnessing the added value each may bring"), but rather effects of injustices that should be remedied. For example, an INGO's inability to decipher an article in a local Indian newspaper and a local Indian NGO's inability to decipher a highly technical World Bank report are in a sense symmetrical problems that seem to call for partnership as a solution. But they are also the result of historic and ongoing inequalities that partnership does not address.[49] Insofar as the redundancy conception implies that Oxfam should leave the scene entirely, it might go beyond what political equality demands in the context of advocacy. But the broader point is that if we prioritize political equality over participation equality, the dominant, "complementarity" conception of partnership looks much less appealing on egalitarian grounds.

The complementarity conception of partnership does have one big advantage over the redundancy conception, however: while the complementarity conception is based on the ordinary language meaning of partnership, the redundancy conception redefines partnership so dramatically that it is hardly recognizable. We do not typically think of partnership as a situation in which one partner strives to become redundant. So insofar as we reject the complementarity conception of partnership as normatively inadequate, we in effect reject partnership overall. While perhaps better than the status quo, it is insufficient as a normative ideal for humanitarian INGO advocacy.[50]

A final shortcoming of the partnership lens, which I discussed extensively in Chapter 2, is that partnership as it is understood in the INGO world pertains primarily to interactions between actors, not to political, economic, or social structures. This means that even the most equal

---

[49] Cf. Jordan and van Tuijl, "Political Responsibility in NGO Advocacy."

[50] One crucial question that this raises is whether the pursuit of participation equality can also promote political equality, even if participation equality is insufficient.

partnership (in the complementarity and even redundancy sense) can persist alongside deep structural inequalities.

It looked at first as if holding INGO advocates to the standard of "democratic representative" would ensure that they were sufficiently democratic advocates, while holding them to the standard of "equal partner" would ensure that their advocacy was sufficiently egalitarian. But closer examination suggests that because INGO advocacy includes activities other than representing, we need a conception of INGO advocacy that is *more general* than representation. Because when INGOs engage in representation (and other advocacy activities) they are often second-best actors, we also need a conception that, unlike both the representation and partnership lenses, *acknowledges the distinctive ethical challenges faced by second-best actors*. Finally, because INGO advocacy takes place in the context of deep structural inequalities, we need a conception of INGO advocacy that, unlike the partnership lens, is *attentive to structural inequalities*.

5.3 INGO Advocacy as the Exercise of Power

I think we can go a considerable way toward meeting these three desiderata if, for the purpose of normative evaluation, we conceptualize INGO advocacy not as representation or partnership, but rather as *the exercise of power*. Correspondingly, the normative standard to which INGO advocates should be held is *not misusing their power*. This focus on the misuse of power avoids the shortcomings of the representation and partnership lenses described above: it accommodates a wide range of INGO advocacy activities; it is sensitive to INGOs being second-best actors; and it is attentive to structural inequalities.

As we will see, the breadth of the misuse of power framework is one of its strengths. But in order for it to be useful, it needs to be internally disaggregated: we need to identify the different kinds of power associated with INGO advocacy, understand what it looks like for INGOs to misuse those forms of power, and show how this framework is helpful for navigating the quandary of the second-best. In the rest of this section, I argue that compared to the representation and partnership lenses, the misuse of power lens provides a more nuanced and penetrating account of how INGO advocacy can enact and support—or undermine—not only democratic and egalitarian norms, but also justice-based norms. I focus on four ways in which INGO advocates tend to misuse their power, and propose four corresponding normative principles for avoiding these misuses, presented in roughly decreasing order of importance.

5.3.1 *Misuse of Power #1: Significantly Undermining the Basic Interests of Poor and Marginalized People*

Perhaps the most obvious way for INGO advocates to misuse their power is by undermining the interests of poor and marginalized people. Correspondingly, perhaps the most obvious specification of the normative requirement that INGOs avoid misusing their power is that they should not undermine the interests of poor and marginalized people. Most policies and practices of coercive institutions—including policies and practices advocated for by INGOs—benefit some poor people and undermine the interests of others. As Riddell notes, "in most cases [of advocacy], some poor people will tend to benefit, either relatively or absolutely, from the consequences of changes in the external policy regime, and some will tend to be adversely affected."[51] A criterion that prohibited INGOs from supporting *any* policy that might make *any* poor or marginalized person even a little bit worse-off would therefore likely exclude advocacy that is on the whole beneficial to poor and marginalized people. So by the *basic interests principle* I will mean that: (a) INGO advocates should not significantly undermine the basic interests of any poor or marginalized individual; and (b) the anticipated net benefits of the policies for which INGOs advocate, together with their advocacy itself, should outweigh the anticipated net negative effects of the policies for which they advocate and their advocacy itself, for poor and marginalized people.

The problem, of course, is that it can be difficult to judge whether a particular instance of INGO advocacy has, in fact, significantly undermined the basic interests of poor and marginalized people. For example, while the evidence available in 2015 suggested that Enough and Global Witness's advocacy on Section 1502 of Dodd-Frank violated the basic interests principle, this assessment was contested and might turn out to be incorrect as events unfold and/or as new information becomes available.

One seemingly promising way to get around this difficulty is to treat due diligence as a proxy for compliance with the basic interests principle. That is, even if it is difficult to tell whether an INGO has actually undermined the basic interests of poor and marginalized people, we can ask whether it took reasonable precautions to avoid doing so. However, determining what counts as due diligence by INGO advocates can also be difficult. For example, on its website, Global Witness posted or linked to several reports about the situation in the DRC, including a report summarizing a survey of the residents of seven mining communities.[52] If Global Witness did violate the basic interests

---

[51] Riddell, *Does Foreign Aid Really Work?*, 300–1.

[52] Global Witness, "Artisanal Mining Communities in Eastern DRC: Seven Baseline Studies in the Kivus," August 22, 2012 <http://www.globalwitness.org/library/artisanal-mining-communities-eastern-drc-seven-baseline-studies-kivus>.

principle, then either its seemingly extensive research did not amount to due diligence, or due diligence is a poor proxy for complying with the basic interests principle in this case.[53] In the absence of clear information about an INGO's effects, the fact that it failed to engage in due diligence is a serious mark against it, while the fact that it did engage in due diligence is not enough to tell us that it complied with the basic interests principle.

I argued in Chapter 3 that INGO advocacy is governmental when it helps to shape coercive policies and practices in a way that goes beyond simply persuading elected leaders to do something. The more that an INGO's advocacy functions as a form of governance, the greater the risk that it will violate the basic interests principle. However, even INGOs whose advocacy cannot be considered a form of governance can violate this principle.

5.3.2 Misuse of Power #2: Displacing Poor and Marginalized Groups and Their (More) Legitimate Representatives

Suppose that Enough and Global Witness turn out to be correct about the effects of Section 1502. We would then have to conclude that the policies that these INGOs advocated did not significantly undermine the basic interests of poor and marginalized people. But would it follow from this that Enough and Global Witness did not misuse their power? No. This is because, as I noted above, these organizations wrote the text of Section 1502 and shaped the lineup of speakers at the SEC hearings about the bill. Regardless of whether the policies they supported significantly undermined the basic interests of vulnerable people, this constituted a misuse of power on democratic procedural grounds.

This type of misuse of power is difficult to see if we use the representation lens: the representation lens tells us that Enough and Global Witness represented Congolese mining communities poorly, and implies that the solution to the problem is to either make Enough and Global Witness better representatives, or replace them with better ones. Now consider an alternative account of why Enough and Global Witness's actions were objectionable: by writing Section 1502 and shaping the lineup of speakers at the SEC roundtable, Enough and Global Witness misused their power by *displacing* other actors. On this view, the problem is not that Enough and Global Witness were poor representatives; it is that they pushed aside other actors that, if given

---

[53] Due diligence is also a poor proxy for not undermining basic interests when actors have an incentive to undertake a particular course of action, regardless of the consequences. Seay ("What's Wrong with Dodd-Frank 1502?") and Autesserre ("Dangerous Tales") argue that this was the case with Enough and Global Witness.

the chance, would likely have done a better job of representing Congolese miners—actors that, had they been allowed to participate *alongside* Enough and Global Witness (and the speakers they helped select), would have, at least potentially, mitigated their negative effects.

In other words, the representation lens only enables us to say that Enough and Global Witness failed to fulfill the (positive) duties of the role of representative—a role that they never claimed to occupy and would likely resist. In contrast, the idea that INGOs misused their power by displacing other actors suggests that Enough and Global Witness violated a *negative* duty by blocking (more) democratically legitimate representation by others. On this view, the problem is not only, or even primarily, that Enough and Global Witness's statements and actions amounted to bad representation: we do not even need to make a judgment on this issue. Rather, all we have to say is that these INGOs—together with legislators and industry representatives—displaced, and thereby helped to silence, *other* voices that could have contested their version of events.[54] This account is not only immune from the "but we never claimed to be representatives" objection; it also offers a more perspicacious description of the problem and gestures toward possible solutions. In particular, it suggests how INGOs might participate constructively in a deliberative democratic process without themselves being good representatives or undermining effective representation by others.

INGOs' displacement of first-best advocates can have at least three kinds of negative effects. First, it can have bad epistemic effects: the knowledge and perspective of those who are displaced never get on the table, which leads to incomplete information and ultimately to policies that undermine the basic interests of vulnerable people—that is, displacement can collapse into violations of the basic interests principle. This appears to have happened in the case of Enough and Global Witness. As Seay writes:

> Many of the problems with Section 1502 and its unintended consequences were anticipated by Congolese civil society leaders and scholars and could have been avoided had their perspectives been integrated in the advocacy process [of US-based organizations] before strategies were released and advocacy activities had already been determined.[55]

Second, displacement can make it more difficult for actors that have the potential to be first-best representatives, such as domestic NGOs based in poor countries, to hone their skills. For example, the Congolese civil society leader Eric Kajemba stated that: "[t]here are NGOs here in the East [of the

---

[54] Seay, "What's Wrong with Dodd-Frank 1502?" and Seay, "The Dodd-Frank Catastrophe."
[55] Seay, "What's Wrong with Dodd-Frank 1502?"

DRC]—BEST, Pole Institute, there are many organizations working on this. I agree, we have problems, but some are trying to do good work."[56] By helping to displace these and other Congolese NGOs from participating in debates about Section 1502, Enough and Global Witness not only deprived US lawmakers of these NGOs' expertise; they also made it more difficult for these NGOs to gain the experience and connections that might have helped them overcome the "problems" to which Kajemba refers.

Third, displacement can prevent the involvement of actors whose involvement is valuable for symbolic reasons. For example, it might be symbolically valuable to audiences in the DRC, and even the US, for Congolese civil society actors to play a role in debates about US policy explicitly aimed at reducing conflict in the DRC.

While Enough and Global Witness appear to have actively displaced Congolese civil society organizations, Oxfam appears not to have actively displaced the Ghanaian NGOs. Insofar as the Ghanaian NGOs were displaced, this was due to the indirect and joint effects—some intended, some not—of Oxfam, Ghana's NHIA, the World Bank, and other entities. Historical conditions also played a role: the history of British colonialism in Ghana provided a rhetorical opening for the NHIA to attack the "Shared Goal" report as neo-colonial by attributing it to Oxfam.[57] The ethical question, then, is not whether Oxfam intentionally displaced the Ghanaian NGOs, but rather whether the outcome of the Ghanaian INGOs being displaced could have been predicted, and whether Oxfam should have done more to avoid this outcome.

The answer to the first question is probably "yes": the literature on INGO partnerships (discussed in Chapter 2) suggests that underlying structural inequalities usually bubble to the surface, in some form or another. The answer to the latter question, however, is by no means clear. Even though the "Shared Goal" report was repeatedly publicly characterized as the "Oxfam report" in prominent venues, and even though, as Duncan Green reports, "The [Ghanaian NGO] partners were actually pretty hacked off at this being described as an 'Oxfam report', and rightly so,"[58] officials from the Ghanaian NGOs participated actively in discussion about the report, including in the comments sections of prominent international

---

[56] Interview with Eric Kajemba (translated from French), conducted by Jason Stearns. <http://congosiasa.blogspot.com/2011/08/interview-with-eric-kajemba-on-conflict.html>.

[57] The NHIA stated that it "hereby serves notice to Oxfam that its parochial agenda cannot succeed in an era that 'divide and rule' has been banished into the annals of history never to be resurrected again in an independent nation such as Ghana" (NHIA, "NHIA Position on OXFAM/ISODEC Report on Free Universal Health Care in Ghana").

[58] Duncan Green, "From Poverty to Power—Really CGD? Really? The Perils of Attack Blogs," March 15, 2011 <http://oxfamblogs.org/fp2p/really-cgd-really-the-perils-of-attack-blogs/>.

development blogs that, in the blog posts themselves, sidelined their contribution.[59] While it is possible that Oxfam's involvement made it more difficult for the Ghanaian NGOs to develop their capacities, it is also possible that working together improved the skills of all the parties (including Oxfam). Moreover, while the effects of Oxfam's participation on actual policy outcomes is uncertain, it almost certainly created more public discussion of the "Shared Goal" report, both within Ghana and internationally, than there would have been if Oxfam hadn't been involved.[60]

Even if it is not clear whether some other course of action by Oxfam would have been better all things considered, what is clear is that any ethical analysis of INGO advocacy must be attuned to the kind of subtle displacement effect that seems to have occurred in this case. That is, we must understand displacement as encompassing both activities directly and intentionally undertaken by a small number of identifiable actors serving a conventional governance function, such as Global Witness and Enough writing Section 1502 of Dodd-Frank and helping to shape the lineup of speakers about the bill, and the indirect and (sometimes) unintended effects of many different actors interacting under conditions of inequality, such as the effective sidelining of the Ghanaian NGOs from public recognition of their role in generating the "Shared Goal" report.

Given these negative effects of displacement, I propose a *minimize displacement principle*: INGOs should minimize the extent to which they displace (or enable the displacement of) first-best advocates for vulnerable groups, taking into consideration other ethical constraints.[61] This principle directly achieves the second of our three desiderata: acknowledging the ethical implications of INGO advocates being often second-best. Because of the "taking into consideration of other ethical constraints" clause, this principle does not direct INGOs to always prioritize supporting first-best actors over achieving their substantive goals when these aims conflict. However, unlike the representation and partnership lenses, it acknowledges this conflict and captures the ethical and political value of not displacing.

While the main strength of the minimize displacement principle is that it meets our second desideratum, it goes some way toward meeting the first and third as well: it is relevant to a wide range of INGO advocacy activities: those in which INGOs are potentially second-best actors. It also addresses structural inequalities that make it difficult for nascent first-best advocates to more fully develop their capacities.

---

[59] Amanda Glassman, "Really Oxfam? Really?" Center for Global Development <http://www.cgdev.org/blog/really-oxfam-really>.

[60] Shang-Quartey, personal communication.

[61] Sharon R. Krause, "Bodies in Action: Corporeal Agency and Democratic Politics," *Political Theory* 39.3 (2011): 299–324. For a discussion of distributed agency and the distinction between distributed agency and dramatically distributed agency, see Chapter 4.

5.3.3 *Misuse of Power #3: Cultivating and Retaining the Capacity for Arbitrary Interference*

What if, instead of helping to write Section 1502 and shaping the lineup of speakers at the hearings about it, Enough and Global Witness had declined, citing other commitments—but had promised lawmakers that they would write legislation for them on future occasions? One might think that in this (counterfactual) case, Enough and Global Witness would not have misused their power. I agree that they would not have significantly undermined the basic interests of poor and marginalized people or displaced first-best actors. But by not questioning the legitimacy of the request, they would have gone some way toward retaining their *capacity* to displace or otherwise arbitrarily interfere with first-best representatives of vulnerable groups. In so doing, they would have misused their power in a third way, albeit one that is considerably milder and more passive than the two misuses of power just described.

By "capacity to arbitrarily interfere," I mean the capacity (i.e. the power) to take actions that significantly affect others, without being pressured to ensure that those actions "track" the interests and preferences of those significantly affected.[62] If Enough and Global Witness had declined to help write Section 1502 in the way described above, they would still have had the capacity to interfere arbitrarily with the Congolese mining communities and with domestic NGOs based in the DRC. This capacity *on its own* appears to have had real effects: as Congolese civil society leader Eric Kajemba stated, "we are not very happy with Global Witness or Enough, but we feel they are very influential, and we are ready to work with them."[63] On one plausible reading of this statement, Kajemba is suggesting that the Congolese NGOs were only working with Enough and Global Witness because they were worried about what Enough and Global Witness would do otherwise because they are very powerful. That is, it was these INGOs' *capacities*—not only what they actually did—that constrained the Congolese NGOs.

The capacity to arbitrarily interfere is objectionable on egalitarian grounds because when A has the capacity to interfere arbitrarily with B, B has an incentive to "toady" and "fawn" to A, in order to stay on A's good side.[64] In his well-known elucidation of this idea, Philip Pettit focuses on cases in which the threatened interference is an intentional or quasi-intentional effort to make other people's lives worse.[65] In contrast, when INGOs interfere

---

[62] "Track" here means "take into account" not "act consistently with"; Philip Pettit, *Republicanism: A Theory of Freedom and Government* (New York: Oxford University Press, 1997), 26.

[63] Interview with Eric Kajemba by Jason Stearns, my italics.

[64] Pettit, *Republicanism*, 5.

[65] Pettit, *Republicanism*, 52–4, 272. Pettit seems to think that he must limit his focus to intentional or quasi-intentional interference because non-volitional events such as natural disasters

arbitrarily with poor and marginalized groups or domestic NGOs, they usually do not intend to make anyone's lives worse. But INGOs' capacity to interfere arbitrarily still creates the kind of dynamic that seems to be in play in the DRC case: civil society leaders such as Kajemba proclaim themselves ready to work with INGOs they do not like, because they are worried about what these INGOs will do otherwise.

Thus, the capacity to arbitrarily interfere can include the capacity to displace, which in turn can lead to coerced "partnerships," in which NGOs that wish not to be displaced accept working with actors, or under conditions, that they would not accept otherwise. These are misuses of power that are, again, entirely overlooked by the representation and partnership frameworks. Thus, a third normative principle for evaluating INGO advocacy is that INGOs should *minimize their capacity to interfere arbitrarily with vulnerable groups and those groups' (more) legitimate representatives*, again bearing in mind other ethical constraints. This principle suggests a significant role for third parties or institutions in constraining INGOs. It can also be applied to a wide range of advocacy activities. It is also attentive to INGOs' status as second-best actors and to structural inequalities.

Can INGOs really be deemed morally responsible for having the *capacity* to interfere arbitrarily, as opposed to actually doing so? I think that they can be, insofar as they actively cultivate and/or passively but knowingly retain this capacity. For example, while US politicians and industry leaders bear some responsibility for Enough and Global Witness's capacity to help write Section 1502 of the Dodd-Frank bill and influence the lineup of speakers at the SEC hearings about the bill, it appears that Enough and Global Witness also sought to retain their capacity to do these things. They could have done otherwise, for example by encouraging the SEC to interview as wide a range of experts on the issue as possible, including Congolese civil society leaders who disagreed with them.

In contrast to Enough and Global Witness, Oxfam does not seem to have had the capacity to interfere arbitrarily with the Ghanaian people or Ghanaian NGOs. This appears to be largely because Ghana is a stable democracy with a vibrant and reasonably inclusive civil society. The "Shared Goal" report was actively debated and criticized, not taken as marching orders by Ghanaian NGOs, the Ghanaian people, or the Ghanaian government (quite the contrary!). In other words, there were strong democratic civil society and institutionally based constraints on Oxfam's capacity to influence domestic

---

do not respond to toadying or fawning in the way that a slave-owner or abusive husband might. But this excludes the category of unintentional harm by volitional actors. Cf. Sharon R. Krause, "Beyond Non-Domination Agency, Inequality and the Meaning of Freedom," *Philosophy & Social Criticism* 39.2 (2013): 187–208.

public policy in Ghana. In contrast, while the US is also a democracy with a vibrant civil society, Enough and Global Witness were able to exercise an outsized influence on policy, while legitimate representatives of Congolese miners and Congolese activists with opposing viewpoints were largely excluded.

The democratic constraints on Oxfam's advocacy in Ghana that reduce its capacity for arbitrary interference are, again, difficult to see through a representation lens. While the representation lens directs our attention to issues of authorization and accountability, Oxfam was not formally authorized by or accountable to the Ghanaian people. But other actors—including Ghanaian government officials and Ghanaian NGOs—contested, diluted, contextualized, and qualified Oxfam's claims in ways that constrained Oxfam's power and rendered the effects of its advocacy reasonably consistent with democratic norms, even in the absence of formal (or informal) authorization and accountability mechanisms. No one elected Oxfam, but Oxfam's power to shape Ghanaian domestic public policy was constrained in other ways. Focusing on power, including the capacity for arbitrary interference, rather than on representation, helps us to recognize this.

5.3.4. *Misuse of Power #4: "Low-balling"*

Oxfam's advocacy has thus far fared well in our analysis: while it might have contributed somewhat to the displacement of Ghanaian NGOs, it seems not to have violated the basic interests principle. In addition, as I just argued, Oxfam was constrained from interfering arbitrarily with Ghanaians affected by Ghana's NHIS. But what should we make of the circumstances surrounding the commissioning and release of the "Shared Goal" report? The agreement between Oxfam and the Ghanaian NGOs was that Oxfam would fund the report, but that all four organizations would release the report together, on equal terms.[66] However, as we have seen, a good deal of the public discussion and rhetoric surrounding the report, both inside and outside of Ghana, failed to recognize the Ghanaian NGOs' formal role in, and substantive contributions to, the report.

The literature on INGO–NGO "partnerships" predicts that because Oxfam paid for the report and had the capacity to fund future joint projects, it would have more power than the Ghanaian NGOs in determining the scope of the report and the issues it addressed.[67] An official from Oxfam-Ghana denied that such power dynamics existed. As she described it, "round table discussions were held with various stakeholders in health, trades unions, civil

---

[66] Shang-Quartey, personal communication and email correspondence.
[67] See Chapter 2 and footnote 18 above. This literature also suggests that the power dynamic between INGOs and NGOs might have influenced what NGO officials were willing to say to me.

society etc. Ideas were shared, discussed and interrogated at various stages of the research process." As a result, the report "was handled equally" and was "fairly ghananian [sic]."[68] An official from a Ghanaian NGO agreed with this assessment in some respects, but was more circumspect. This official noted that it was difficult, for both the Ghanaian NGOs and Oxfam, to retain their identities as individual organizations while working together, and suggested that a correct model for Oxfam would be to "lead from behind."[69]

Without trying to definitively characterize the relationship between Oxfam and the Ghanaian NGOs, I want to investigate the implications of one possibility, hinted at by the Ghanaian NGO official's comments. This is the possibility that, while the Ghanaian NGOs viewed their arrangement with Oxfam as the best available option under the circumstances, they would not have accepted it under less constrained conditions. In particular, they would not have pursued it if they had been able to fully fund and publicize the report on their own, or if they had been able to pursue other projects that they found more worthwhile.

Suppose, then, that the Ghanaian NGOs accepted Oxfam's offer, but that this offer was the most appealing of the Ghanaian NGOs' options in part due to structural and/or historic injustices, such as the history of British colonialism in Ghana. Philosophers call offers such as this "mutually advantageous exploitative" (MAE) offers. An MAE offer is one in which "*A* gets *B* to agree to a mutually advantageous transaction to which *B* would not have agreed under better or perhaps more just background conditions..."[70] Because MAE offers stand at some remove from other forms of exploitation, I will here call them "low-ball" offers.[71] Low-ball offers can result from the capacity to arbitrarily interfere and can pave the way for displacement, but they are not the same as either of these.

In using this term, I do not mean to imply that Oxfam acted in a narrowly self-interested way (as the term "low-ball" might suggest in the context of an offer to, say, purchase a house or car). Rather, a low-ball offer made by an INGO might be strategic but other-regarding (if the INGO wanted to retain power to achieve a particular substantive policy goal) or it might be unintentional (for example if it arose from a complementarity rather than redundancy conception of partnership). The salient issue here is not, in any case, about intentions; it is about benefiting from a structural situation in which actors accept offers that they would not accept under fairer circumstances.

---

[68] Clara Tigenoah, email correspondence.   [69] Interviewee, personal communication.
[70] Alan Wertheimer and Matt Zwolinski, "Exploitation," in *The Stanford Encyclopedia of Philosophy*, ed. Edward N. Zalta, Spring 2013 <http://plato.stanford.edu/archives/spr2013/entries/exploitation/>. Oxfam benefits because of the legitimacy conferred by, and insider knowledge of, the Ghanaian NGOs.
[71] I thank Suzanne Dovi for suggesting this term.

Low-ball offers present a seeming paradox. They are structurally very similar to price gouging, and it is widely accepted that price gouging—for example, charging $100 for a $15 shovel after a snowstorm—is unethical, because it involves reaping a windfall profit at the expense of someone who is especially vulnerable through no fault of her own. But someone who accepts a low-ball offer is presumably better off than she would have been without the offer—otherwise she would not have accepted it. Assuming that Oxfam is under no obligation to make the Ghanaian NGOs any offer at all, how could it be unethical for it to make them an offer that, if accepted, would make the Ghanaian NGOs better off than they would have been without the offer?[72]

I think the answer to this question is that, by entering into what philosophers call a "special relationship" with the Ghanaian NGOs (by making them an offer), Oxfam takes on a responsibility to treat the Ghanaian NGOs in a particular way.[73] This is why Oxfam does not have a duty to make an offer to the Ghanaian NGOs, but if it does make them an offer, it should consider whether the offer takes advantage of historic and ongoing injustices in ways that make things worse for the Ghanaian NGOs than they could otherwise reasonably be.[74] If it does, it is a potential misuse of power on Oxfam's part. The representation and partnership lenses offer little or no traction on this issue.

In light of the exploitation inherent in low-balling, I therefore propose that INGOs should adopt a principle of *wariness about making low-ball offers*.[75] As this principle acknowledges, low-ball offers are not necessarily unjustified, because they can contribute to INGOs achieving valuable substantive outcomes. The main strength of this principle is that it addresses issues of structural inequality. Although it can be difficult to tell what counts as a low-ball offer (because making this assessment requires describing, counterfactually, what the world would look like if particular injustices had not taken place), egregious cases would presumably be easier to identify.

5.3.5. *Avoiding the Misuse of Power*

Conceptualizing INGO advocacy as the use of power, and evaluating INGO advocacy according to how well it avoids the misuse of power, meets the three desiderata for conceptualizing and normatively evaluating INGO advocacy

---

[72] I thank Michael Kates for helpful discussion of this issue.

[73] Cf. Karen Stohr, "Kantian Beneficence and the Problem of Obligatory Aid," *Journal of Moral Philosophy* 8.1 (2011): 45–67.

[74] An example of a non-low-ball offer in this context would be one that gave the Ghanaian NGOs more say than Oxfam, on account of their knowledge of the situation in Ghana and/or closer ties to the population.

[75] Of course, the best way to reduce low-ball offers is to reduce the circumstances of inequality that make them more likely to be offered and accepted.

discussed above. The basic interests principle, minimize displacement principle, and minimize arbitrary power principle are applicable to a wide range of INGO advocacy activities. The minimize displacement and minimize arbitrary power principles reflect INGOs' status as second-best actors; these two principles and the wariness about low-ball offers principle are sensitive to structural inequalities. Together, these four principles help to specify what it means for INGO advocates to avoid misusing their power. Because they are the most relevant to INGOs' status as second-best actors, the displacement and arbitrary power principles, in particular, offer some guidance regarding how INGOs might navigate the quandary of the second-best—that is, how INGOs might decide when and how much to pursue a given activity themselves, and when and how much to step back and make way for first-best actors. Rather than pursue an ideal of good representation or equal partnership, these two principles suggest that INGOs should avoid displacing or dominating first-best actors.

Together, these four principles also suggest what it might look like for INGO advocacy to be consistent with democratic, egalitarian, and justice-based norms. For INGO advocates, being just means, among other things, not undermining the basic interests of poor and marginalized people and being wary of making low-ball offers that exploit historic or ongoing injustices. Being democratic means minimizing the extent to which they displace poor and marginalized groups and those group's (more) legitimate representatives; being democratic also means not cultivating or retaining the capacity to interfere arbitrarily with these groups. Finally, for INGO advocates, being egalitarian means not displacing first-best actors, minimizing their own capacity to interfere arbitrarily with first-best actors, and, again, being wary of making low-ball offers.

The requirement that INGOs avoid misusing their power is likely to be quite demanding. Complying with the four principles outlined above would require many INGOs to significantly alter their current advocacy practices. Given this, it is also worth recalling the role of these principles in the broader argument of this chapter: they are *possible* specifications of what it means for INGOs to avoid misusing their power, not an exhaustive account: INGOs almost certainly misuse their power in ways other than those discussed here; the misuses of power discussed here are also not salient in all cases.

There are also other standards relevant to normative evaluation of INGO advocacy that do not involve the misuse of power, most notably whether INGOs are effective at achieving their (legitimate) objectives.[76] In addition, while I have presented these principles in what I take to be roughly descending order of importance, this is not a lexical ordering. For example, severe displacement of first-best advocates might be more objectionable than a modest violation of the

---

[76] The four principles discussed here are derived from an analysis of only two cases. These principles could be expanded or altered based on analysis of additional cases.

basic interests principle. Moreover, acting consistently with these principles has costs, and the principles say nothing about how these costs should be traded off against compliance with the principles.

In presenting the quandary of the second-best as a quandary—that is, as an ethical predicament in which it is not obvious what INGOs should do—I mean to acknowledge that there are situations in which INGOs *are* justified in misusing their own power in order to achieve some substantive policy outcome or prevent gross abuses of power by others. For example, if Ghana's National Health Insurance Scheme really is much less effective than Ghana's National Health Insurance Authority claims, and if other countries really are on the verge of adopting versions of this scheme, then perhaps some displacement of Ghanaian NGOs is a reasonable price to pay to ensure that the truth about Ghana's National Health Insurance Scheme emerges. However, the broader upshot of this chapter, and in particular the example of Section 1502, suggests why we should be extremely wary of this logic: Global Witness and Enough could argue that they slightly misused their own power over Congolese NGOs and the Congolese people in order to prevent far greater abuses of the Congolese people by armed groups. But in so doing, they helped to silence the very activists and scholars who were arguing that reducing the trade in conflict minerals would in fact have little effect on the violence in the DRC. In other words, the quandary of the second-best really is a quandary: there are weighty reasons for INGOs to advocate as effectively as possible themselves and weighty reasons for them to step back and support first-best advocates. However, in clarifying those reasons, and in particular, in elucidating the range of ways that not stepping back can function as a misuse of power, the account offered here pushes more in the direction of "supporting first-best advocates" than do the representation and equal partnership lenses.

5.4 Conclusion

Although INGO advocates sometimes engage in representation and act as partners, being democratic, for them, does not mean simply representing well, and being egalitarian is not merely a matter of being an equal partner. Rather, because they face the quandary of the second-best, consistency with democratic, egalitarian, and justice-based norms is most precisely and relevantly cashed out in terms of not misusing power. This includes, but is not limited to, not undermining basic interests, not displacing first-best actors, not cultivating a capacity to exercise arbitrary power, and not making low-ball offers.

This, then, is why the *Economist*'s question "Who Elected Oxfam?", and the broader focus on representation that this question precipitated, are at least to some degree misplaced: the normative challenges posed by INGO advocacy are far more diverse—but also addressable in a wider variety of ways—than this question suggests. The question implies that bad representation is the problem, and elections, or other functionally equivalent mechanisms for achieving good democratic representation, are the solution. But as we have seen, Global Witness and Enough did not only represent badly; they undermined the basic interests of poor and marginalized people, and cultivated the capacity to interfere arbitrarily with Congolese NGOs. Oxfam (possibly) and Global Witness and Enough (almost certainly) displaced poor and marginalized people and/or their (more) legitimate representatives. Oxfam might have made a low-ball offer to Ghanaian NGOs that took advantage of historic injustice. These issues go far beyond bad representation. Yet possible strategies for addressing them go far beyond elections.

When one has a hammer, everything can look like a nail. Likewise, when one studies representation, everything can look like representation. I have argued that democratic theorists of representation need to take off their (our) representation-colored glasses and look anew at advocacy through the lens of the misuse of power—especially governmental power—and not only representation. In so doing we will not only see important aspects of INGO advocacy that are not representation; we will also see representation itself in a new light.

The previous chapter and this one have focused on basic service provision in conflict settings and advocacy on policy issues, respectively. The importance of these activities, and the fact that they cost money to undertake, raises another question: on what basis should INGOs allocate resources among these, and other, activities? That is, how should INGOs make large-scale decisions about resource use? What ethical predicaments do they face in making these decisions, and what would it look like for them to navigate these predicaments in ways that are consistent with democratic, egalitarian, humanitarian, and justice-based norms? We turn next to these questions.

6

The Cost-Effectiveness Conundrum

It's still just a drop in the bucket and that's why it has to be an act of resistance because if you don't do it as an act of resistance, it's kind of futile.

—Kenny Gluck, MSF-Holland[1]

In 2000, the town of Gulu, in northwest Uganda, was struck by an Ebola epidemic.[2] The INGO Médecins Sans Frontières, which had been running a basic health program in the area for several years, responded to the epidemic aggressively, providing clinical care to approximately 400 people affected by the disease at the two area hospitals. After the epidemic ended, MSF estimated that it had helped to increase survival by about 5%. That is, it had helped to save about twenty lives.[3] But during the time that MSF's resources and those of the two hospitals were being used to treat Ebola (which is highly contagious), area residents who had other serious health concerns, such as diarrhea, measles, and life-threatening obstetric complications, did not get the care that they needed.[4]

Defending MSF's decision to respond to the Ebola outbreak, one MSF staffer explained that

> The public health response was probably being dealt with in the traditional (local) way by shutting people away in the barn and not feeding them or looking after them. Such a response traditionally would probably have broken the

---

[1] Interview conducted in 2002 by the author; on file with the author.

[2] Nathan Ford and Richard Bedell (eds.), *Justice and MSF Operational Choices* (Amsterdam: MSF, 2002). The rest of my account draws on this source. See also Peter Redfield, *Life in Crisis: The Ethical Journey of Doctors Without Borders* (Berkeley: University of California Press, 2013), 157–9. Redfield notes that MSF was one of three organizations (the others were the CDC and WHO) that had expertise in dealing with Ebola.

[3] This calculation assumes that the "5%" mentioned is 5% of 400 people, rather than a 5% improvement in the survival rate. But either way the number of lives saved was relatively small.

[4] Another negative side effect of MSF addressing the Ebola virus was an increase in nosocomial infections among local medical staff.

epidemic as quickly as anything that we did, but the motivation for MSF was the alleviation of individual suffering. Alleviation of suffering, and dying in dignity was enormously important. We know we saved very few lives.[5]

Another MSF employee expressed greater misgivings about MSF's decision, asking "[h]ow would you explain to a villager from the outskirts of Gulu the choice MSF made in addressing the problem of Ebola but not the health problems in his village?"[6] This question could be asked not only on behalf of villagers living on the outskirts of Gulu, but also on behalf of any potential recipient of MSF's services who was passed over due to the organization's decision to address the Ebola outbreak: how can MSF justify using its limited resources to prevent twenty early deaths from Ebola when it could have instead used those same resources to prevent, for example, 200 early deaths from measles, malaria, and diarrhea?

Humanitarian INGOs such as MSF do not have enough resources to try to assist all of the people they could potentially try to assist.[7] These INGOs must therefore make difficult decisions about which issues to take on and which to ignore, which groups to work with and which to pass over. As I and others have documented elsewhere, these decisions are usually informed by a diverse array of practical and normative considerations.[8] This chapter examines an aspect of these decisions that has received little attention, yet is incredibly important, both in practical terms and because of what it tells us about humanitarian INGOs as actors: how much weight should INGOs put on considerations of cost-effectiveness in their large-scale decisions about resource use? (By "cost-effective" I mean doing whatever they do at the lowest cost possible, so as to have more resources available to do more.)

At first glance, it might seem obvious that INGOs should try to be as cost-effective as possible, or at least weigh cost-effectiveness very heavily. Yet there is profound (though often implicit) disagreement about this issue among INGOs, political philosophers, and scholars of development and humanitarian aid. We can discern at least three distinct positions:

1. Humanitarian INGOs should provide humanitarian (though not development) aid on the basis of need alone. This *need principle* is a core feature of classical humanitarianism, codified in numerous INGO statements of

---

[5] Ford and Bedell (eds.), *Justice and MSF Operational Choices*, 26.

[6] Ford and Bedell (eds.), *Justice and MSF Operational Choices*, 26.

[7] Even INGOs that have sufficient funds can face other constraints, such as enough qualified staff and volunteers.

[8] Jennifer C. Rubenstein, "The Distributive Commitments of Humanitarian INGOs," in *Humanitarianism in Question: Politics, Power, Ethics*, ed. Michael Barnett and Thomas Weiss (Ithaca, NY: Cornell University Press, 2008), 215–34; Redfield, *Life in Crisis*; Lisa Fuller, "Justified Commitments? Considering Resource Allocation and Fairness in Médecins Sans Frontières-Holland," *Developing World Bioethics* 6.2 (2006): 59–70.

principle and codes of conduct. It leaves little or no room for considerations of cost-effectiveness.

2. In all of their work, humanitarian INGOs should seek to alleviate as much "morally important harm" (e.g. unwanted premature death, disability, severe suffering) as possible. This *harm minimization principle* has been elucidated and endorsed by some consequentialist philosophers and development economists (some INGOs mention it as well, but typically only in passing). It directs INGOs to weigh cost-effectiveness very heavily. (I use the term "harm minimization principle" because I draw heavily on an account that uses this term, but it can be easily misunderstood. To be clear: it refers, in this context, to minimizing outcomes such as unwanted premature death, disability, and severe suffering *no matter how they were caused*; it does not refer to INGOs minimizing the harm that they themselves cause or to which they contribute; it should not be confused with the "do no harm" principle discussed in Chapter 4.)

3. In their work, humanitarian INGOs should "refuse" to accommodate the consequentialist logic of cost-effectiveness, and focus instead on symbolic, political, or principled actions, such as helping Ebola victims "die with dignity." This *ethics of refusal* is most closely associated with MSF.[9] Like the need principle, it puts very little weight on cost-effectiveness, but it is much more explicitly political than the need principle.

Which of these approaches provides the best basis for INGOs' large-scale decisions about resource use? I will argue that while need (or a similar concept) should play a role in these decisions, the need *principle* should be rejected because it is a poor instantiation of egalitarian, democratic, justice-based, and (perhaps surprisingly) humanitarian norms. That is, if INGOs wish to make large-scale decisions about resource use in a way that is consistent with any or all of these norms, complying with the need principle is not the way to do it.

The harm minimization principle and the ethics of refusal, both of which take need into account, are more promising. However, both are based on incomplete "maps" of the moral terrain of INGOs' large-scale decisions about resource use. As a result, they do not acknowledge the extent to which these decisions require political judgment: while the harm minimization principle replaces political judgment with technical judgment, the ethics of refusal replaces political judgment with political reflex.

---

[9] Because this is MSF's principle, and MSF does humanitarian and advocacy work but not development, the question of whether this principle also extends to development work has not arisen.

This chapter therefore proposes a more complete map of the terrain of INGOs' large-scale decisions about resource use, and describes a mode of political judgment suitable for navigating it. This map suggests that in making large-scale decisions about resource use, humanitarian INGOs face what I call the *cost-effectiveness conundrum*. Navigating this conundrum requires a form of political judgment that I call the *ethics of resistance*. I will argue that the ethics of resistance provides a basis for recognizing the relevance of, and enacting, humanitarian, democratic, egalitarian, and justice-based norms that is superior to the need principle, the harm minimization principle, and the ethics of refusal. Because it is a form of judgment rather than a set of rigid rules, the ethics of resistance accommodates both the diversity of situations in which INGOs find themselves and the diversity of INGOs themselves.

While scholars of aid, journalists, and other commentators have noted seeming inequities in how aid resources are allocated *overall*—for example, that the humanitarian system provided an average of $2,670 in aid per person to victims of the Indian Ocean tsunami in 2004, but only $53 per person to people affected by the conflict in the Democratic Republic of Congo (DRC) in 2009[10]— the question of how *individual* INGOs do or should make large-scale decisions about resource use has received far less attention than the issue of aid's unintended negative effects (discussed in Chapter 4). Yet, INGOs' large-scale decisions about resource use do not seem to be significantly less important for the well-being of poor and disaster-affected people than aid's unintended negative effects. So why is there so much more interest in the latter?

One possible explanation is the widely shared assumption that INGOs are apolitical and non-governmental. If one makes this assumption, then aid's unintended negative effects appear to be surprising, and so deserving of study: why would mere apolitical helping have unintended negative effects? Conversely, INGOs' large-scale decisions about resource use appear to be their own business, and so not an appropriate subject for normative criticism. In contrast, if we take INGOs to be highly political and sometimes somewhat governmental, as I have argued we should, the disparity between these issues disappears: it is important (but no longer shocking) that INGOs have unintended negative effects, while INGOs' large-scale decisions about resource use appear to be a matter of public significance.[11]

---

[10] Lydia Poole, "GHA Report 2012" (Wells, UK: Development Initiatives, 2012), 32.

[11] With a few exceptions, discussed below, the only aspect of INGOs' large-scale decisions about resource use discussed with any frequency is the proportion of resources INGOs spend on overhead/administrative costs versus program costs. However, this is widely recognized by aid scholars to be a meaningless or even counterproductive statistic. Among other things, some administrative spending, for example on research into the political situation in an area where an INGO is working, is necessary to minimize unintended negative effects. See Leif Wenar, "Poverty is No Pond: Challenges for the Affluent," in *Giving Well: The Ethics of Philanthropy*, ed. Patricia Illingworth, Thomas Pogge and Leif Wenar (New York: Oxford University Press, 2010), 104–32.

The next section delineates the types of large-scale decisions about resource use that are the main subject of this chapter. Section 6.2 describes the need principle, the harm minimization principle, and the ethics of refusal. Section 6.3 evaluates these approaches normatively. Section 6.4 introduces the cost-effectiveness conundrum and explains the ethics of resistance as a form of political judgment suitable for navigating this conundrum. Section 6.5 concludes by elucidating some broader implications.[12]

6.1 INGOs' Large-Scale Decisions about Resource Use

By "large-scale decisions about resource use,"[13] I mean decisions that INGOs make, typically at their headquarters, about what major initiatives to begin, continue, or end, including decisions about where to work, which groups to try to assist, and what themes or issue areas to address. Because most humanitarian INGOs do development aid, advocacy, and/or other activities in addition to humanitarian aid, these decisions often involve trade-offs within and among these different activities. They also include one-off decisions about procedures for decision-making that shape the results of more frequent decisions. For example, a one-time decision to organize pots of money by region rather than issue-area can influence allocative outcomes by affecting which projects get traded off against each other. These large-scale decisions can be contrasted with more fine-grained decisions about how to allocate resources among individuals, families, or organizations within a community (the latter type of decisions are not the subject of this chapter).

Some aid practitioners might object to this entire line of inquiry, as follows: "Between the demands of our donors, the constraints imposed by our mandates, and our existing commitments, we do not have the leeway to make these sorts of decisions. We are not just sitting in an office with a pile of money and a globe, deciding what to spend where!" It is certainly true that none of the humanitarian INGOs discussed in this book make large-scale decisions about resource use without any external constraints. But all humanitarian INGOs have *some* discretion over their use of resources.

---

[12] Most of the examples and much of the secondary literature discussed in this chapter focuses on MSF. This is because there is more information available about MSF's large-scale decisions about resource use than there is about such decisions made by other INGOs. Because MSF is so large, its large-scale decisions about resource use are normatively important in their own right. However, my argument is meant to apply to all large mainstream humanitarian INGOs based in wealthy Western countries that rely on donors for funds.

[13] I primarily use this phrase, rather than "distribution" or "allocation," because the latter terms imply a kind of rationalist logic that the ethics of refusal, in particular, rejects, such that using these terms consistently would seem to "stack the deck" against the ethics of refusal.

More precisely, as I will now suggest, they have enough discretion for it to be plausible to see their decisions about resource use as an ethical and political issue.

With regard to donor demands, INGOs such as MSF, that receive most of their funding from "unrestricted" individual donations, have more leeway in deciding how to use their resources than do INGOs that receive a much higher proportion of their funding from government grants or contracts, such as CARE. However, even INGOs that rely heavily on government grants or contracts exercise discretion when deciding which grants to apply for and which contracts to bid on. These INGOs can, and sometimes do, seek to "educate" their governmental and institutional funders with regard to why some constraints and requirements are especially onerous or counterproductive. Moreover, when INGOs publicly defend their large-scale decisions about resource use, for example, when MSF publishes a list of "top ten under-reported humanitarian stories," this can function discursively to shape donors' beliefs and perceptions, and thereby alter the ways in which donors constrain INGOs' large-scale decisions about resource use in the future.

An INGO's mandate is, among other things, a public promise about the basic content and scope of its aims and activities. INGOs' mandates can limit their large-scale decisions about resource use in the short term. But mandates are not as constraining as they might initially seem, especially in the medium to long term. To the contrary, as the dramatic expansion of, and profusion of new activities by, CARE, Oxfam, Save the Children, and MSF over the last forty to sixty years suggest, INGOs' mandates can change significantly over longer time frames. Finally, INGOs' existing commitments to current aid recipients function as constraints, insofar as they give INGOs strong reasons to not drop everything they are doing and use their resources in a radically new way. However, decisions to respect those reasons are still *decisions*: they can be decided otherwise.[14]

In short, even though INGOs are constrained to some extent by donor demands, their own mandates, and their commitments to current aid recipients, and even though INGO decision-makers often *feel* very constrained, most large humanitarian INGOs have enough control over their resources in the short term, but especially in the medium to long term, that it makes sense to ask: on what basis should they make large-scale decisions about resource use? In particular, what role should considerations of cost-effectiveness play in these decisions?

---

[14] Another seeming constraint on INGOs' decisions about resource use are their organizational cultures. For example, aid practitioners at MSF-Holland frequently discussed whether a given project "was" MSF (fieldwork conducted by the author; Fuller, "Justified Commitments?"). But organizational cultures do not impose external constraints. They are perhaps difficult, but not impossible, to change.

6.2 The Need Principle, the Harm Minimization Principle, and the Ethics of Refusal

Before addressing these questions, I first want to say more about why they are important. Cost-effectiveness might initially seem like a mere technical consideration, separable from the more politically and ethically significant matter of the substantive content of INGOs' decisions about resource use. If this were the case, we might think that INGOs should first choose what activities to undertake or what goals to pursue, and then decide how, or whether, to undertake those activities or pursue those goals cost-effectively. But cost-effectiveness cannot be separated neatly from substance; an INGO's decisions about how much to emphasize cost-effectiveness influences the substance of its large-scale decision-making about resource use in at least two ways.

First, a commitment to cost-effectiveness can shape which activities INGOs undertake and which goals they pursue within a predetermined range of acceptable activities and goals. For example, if an INGO aims to prevent unwanted premature death, and commits to pursuing that goal cost-effectively, it cannot prevent just any unwanted premature deaths; it must focus on those that it can prevent most cheaply. This might mean working only in peaceful areas rather than situations of violent conflict, or working in just a few countries rather than many countries. In other words, a commitment to cost-effectiveness entails that whatever type(s) of "fruit" an INGO has agreed to pick, it must focus on the lowest-hanging fruits of those type(s).[15] Thus, the more broadly an INGO's activities or goals are defined (the more type(s) of fruit it has agreed to pick and the more fruits of each type there are), the more potential its commitment to cost-effectiveness has to shape what it ends up doing.

In addition to shaping which activities and objectives an INGO pursues within a predetermined range, a commitment to cost-effectiveness can also put pressure on that range itself. For example, suppose that an INGO commits to saving lives in emergencies as cost-effectively as possible. The commitment to cost-effectiveness will raise the question of why the INGO is limiting itself to emergencies, if it can save lives more cost-effectively (and so save more lives overall) in non-emergency contexts. There might well be a good answer to this question; my point is just that the commitment to cost-effectiveness raises it.

In short, the commitment to cost-effectiveness is not merely a technical add-on; it is not merely an issue of "how" rather than "what." To the

---

[15] This expression is not ideal—INGOs aim to assist human beings, not pick fruit—but I could not think of a clearer way to convey the point.

contrary, it can deeply shape the content of INGOs' activities and aims. It is therefore of first importance how, if at all, INGOs incorporate a commitment to cost-effectiveness into their large-scale decisions about resource use. After briefly summarizing the three approaches to this question outlined above, I will evaluate them on normative grounds.

6.2.1 *The Need Principle*

We turn first to the idea that humanitarian aid (but not development aid) should be allocated on the basis of need alone.[16] This idea is a central tenet of traditional humanitarianism. The Code of Conduct for the International Red Cross and Red Crescent Movement and NGOs in Disaster Relief, which has been signed by hundreds of INGOs and NGOs, states that "[a]id priorities are calculated on the basis of need alone."[17] Likewise, MSF states that it "provides care on the basis of need alone."[18] The United Nations Office for the Coordination of Humanitarian Affairs states that "[h]umanitarian action must be carried out on the basis of need alone, giving priority to the most urgent cases of distress."[19]

Like the principle of do no harm discussed in Chapter 4, the need principle can be interpreted in a narrow, more literal way or in a looser, more figurative way. Taken literally, the need principle is monistic: it states that only one consideration—need—ought to guide *all* INGO decisions about resource use. It therefore leaves no room for other considerations, except perhaps as tie-breakers between equally needy groups.[20] These other considerations might include not only whether a group's needs can be addressed cost-effectively, but also the causes of various needs, historical relationships between particular INGOs and particular groups of intended beneficiaries, and whether there is widespread endorsement of an INGO's presence among those intended beneficiaries.

If we look at statements of the need principle in their broader context, however, it appears that proponents of this principle do not mean it literally. Indeed, the need principle is frequently presented as synonymous with

---

[16] This limitation to humanitarian aid is important to note, because most humanitarian INGOs undertake a range of activities in addition to providing humanitarian aid.

[17] International Federation of the Red Cross and Red Crescent Societies, "The Code of Conduct for the International Red Cross and Red Crescent Movement and NGOs in Disaster Relief" <http://www.ifrc.org/en/publications-and-reports/code-of-conduct/>.

[18] MSF-USA, "History and Principles" <http://www.doctorswithoutborders.org/aboutus/history-and-principles>.

[19] This wording is from the "Fundamental Principles of the Red Cross and Red Crescent"<http://www.ifrc.org/who-we-are/vision-and-mission/the-seven-fundamental-principles/>.

[20] If INGOs lack the tools (or do not want to expend the resources) to determine the relative neediness of different groups, even the literal version of aid based on need alone might be highly indeterminate.

the far less demanding requirement of "impartiality." For example, the context for the quotation from the Red Cross Code cited above is a principle of impartiality which states that "Aid is given regardless of the race, creed or nationality of the recipients and without adverse distinction of any kind. Aid priorities are calculated on the basis of need alone."[21] Here, "aid based on need alone" is presented as a restatement or clarification of the previous sentence; it seems to simply mean aid that is *not* based on race, creed, nationality, etc. This loose interpretation allows INGOs to put as much or as little weight on cost-effectiveness as they wish, so long as they do not violate impartiality.[22] It therefore differs dramatically from the literal interpretation of the need principle, which says that *only* need may be taken into account. In short, like the do no harm principle, the need principle presents a challenge in that the literal interpretation seems clearly untenable, but the looser interpretation is so loose that it is difficult to identify, let alone evaluate, its implications.

In light of these considerations, it seems as if the best interpretation of the need principle is neither the literal version nor the loose version just described, but rather something like "INGOs should place a very heavy emphasis on need." Because it does seem most plausible, I will normatively evaluate this version of the need principle below. However, as it is frequently written and promulgated, the need principle seems to demand either more or less than this. The fact that the need principle is not only ambiguous, but ambiguous between two interpretations that have such dramatically different implications for how much weight INGOs should put on cost-effectiveness, suggests that humanitarians have not paid as much (public) attention as they might to the ethical implications of possible tradeoffs between providing aid based on need and cost-effectiveness.

6.2.2 *The Harm Minimization Principle*

The harm minimization principle states that humanitarian INGOs should work to prevent as much morally important harm as possible.[23] This principle

---

[21] Likewise, the context for the quotation from MSF cited above is: "MSF is neutral. The organization does not take sides in armed conflicts, provides care on the basis of need alone, and pushes for increased independent access to victims of conflict as required under international humanitarian law." The context for the quote from UCHA is that "Humanitarian action must be carried out on the basis of need alone, giving priority to the most urgent cases of distress and making no distinctions on the basis of nationality, race, gender, religious belief, class or political opinions."

[22] Another possible interpretation of the need principle is that it is meant to apply to smaller-scale allocative decisions among individuals, families, or villages in a given area. But this would imply that INGOs were not committed to impartiality among different racial or ethnic groups in different areas, which does not seem plausible.

[23] I follow Pogge in using the term "harm minimization" rather than "doing good." Pogge's well-known argument (in *World Poverty and Human Rights*, 2nd edn. (Malden, MA: Polity Press,

places a heavy emphasis on cost-effectiveness. It incorporates need as a relevant consideration; alleviating severe harm amounts to roughly the same thing as addressing severe need. However, unlike the need principle, the harm minimization principle directs INGOs to pass over those in the greatest need if doing so will enable them to alleviate the most morally important harm overall.

Versions of the harm minimization principle have been articulated by several political and moral philosophers concerned with issues of global poverty, including Peter Singer, Toby Ord, and Thomas Pogge.[24] Effective Altruist "meta-charities" such as Giving What We Can and Givewell have further developed this principle, and have tried to use it to evaluate specific INGOs and guide donors.[25] I will focus on Thomas Pogge's version of this principle, as an especially thoughtful and well-developed example of the genre. Because my aim is to highlight differences with other views, I will interpret the harm minimization principle in the more demanding way suggested by Pogge's initial presentation, rather than the looser way suggested by some of his critics and his responses to those critics.[26]

Pogge argues that "we"—INGOs and their contributors—should pursue "human rights, development, and humanitarian goals"[27] as cost-effectively as possible. (Note the breadth of these goals; this will be important later.) That is, INGOs "that offer to pool money we give them and to make such funds effective toward human rights, development and humanitarian goals" should protect people from as much "serious harm" as possible, where serious harm is defined as "shortfalls persons suffer in their health, civic status ... or

2008) and *Politics as Usual* (Cambridge: Polity Press, 2010)) is that much of the severe poverty and deprivation in the world is due to harms inflicted by people in well-off countries via global institutional arrangements. I do not enter into this debate here. Readers who do not think that these issues are harms can replace "harm minimization" with "maximization of morally important goods" and proceed with the argument. Unlike in his other work, here Pogge uses "harm" to include both misfortunes, and "bads" caused intentionally or unintentionally by human beings (see page 177, note 20).

[24] Peter Singer, *The Life You Can Save: Acting Now to End World Poverty*, esp. 17; Thomas Pogge, "Moral Priorities for International Human Rights NGOs," in *Ethics in Action*, ed. Daniel A. Bell and Jean-Marc Coicaud (New York: Cambridge University Press, 2006), 218–56; Toby Ord, *The Moral Imperative toward Cost-effectiveness in Global Health* (Washington: Center for Global Development, 2013). Development economists make similar arguments, but primarily with regard to development aid, not humanitarian aid and human rights work. They also sometimes make exceptions for "fragile" states on the grounds of "equity" (Deutsche Gesellschaft für Technische Zusammenarbeit "Application of the Performance Based Allocation System to Fragile States," GTZ and the Overseas Development Institute. June 2007 <http://www.odi.org.uk/sites/odi.org.uk/files/odi-assets/publications-opinion-files/230.pdf>).

[25] Giving What We Can <http://www.givingwhatwecan.org>; Give Well <http://www.givewell.org>. So far, Giving What We Can has focused on organizations that undertake one kind of activity, not INGOs that do a wide range of activities, such as Oxfam or MSF.

[26] Lisa Fuller, "Priority Setting in International Non-Governmental Organizations: It Is Not As Easy As ABCD," *Journal of Global Ethics* 8.1 (2012): 5–17; Thomas Pogge, "Respect and Disagreement: A Response to Joseph Carens," in *Ethics in Action*, ed. Bell and Coicaud, 273–8.

[27] Pogge, "Moral Priorities," 219.

standard of living relative to the ordinary needs and requirements of human beings."[28] More precisely:

> Other things being equal, an INGO should govern its decision making about candidate projects by such rules and procedures as are expected to maximize its long-run cost effectiveness, defined as the expected aggregate moral value of the projects it undertakes divided by the expected aggregate costs of these projects. Here aggregate moral value, or harm protection, is the sum of the moral values of the harm reductions (and increases) these projects bring about for the individual persons they affect.[29]

Despite this somewhat dry formulation, this principle has potentially dramatic implications. Complying with it would likely require humanitarian INGOs to fundamentally alter their activities: rather than prioritizing those in the greatest need, they would sometimes be required to deny aid to those in the greatest need. Rather than providing aid in dozens of countries, as most large INGOs do currently, they might have to work in just two or three countries, at least initially. Rather than providing humanitarian and development aid, they might need to focus only on development aid, or only on development aid and aid to victims of "natural" disasters (rather than people affected by violent conflict). Abiding by the harm minimization principle would mean that INGOs could put no independent weight on aiding victims of injustice over victims of misfortune, as some INGOs do currently, and no independent weight on "associative duties" to current aid recipients. That is, values of loyalty, friendship, or solidarity would have no place in INGOs' large-scale decisions about resource use.[30] Perhaps not surprisingly, Pogge reports that when he presented his idea to a room full of aid practitioners, they responded with "all but universal condemnation."[31]

6.2.3 *The Ethics of Refusal*

In the context of international aid, the term "ethics of refusal" is used primarily by MSF, but it describes an orientation that some other INGOs also accept, to greater or lesser degrees.[32] While the ethics of refusal has not been

---

[28] Pogge, "Moral Priorities," 222.

[29] Pogge, "Moral Priorities," 241. Singer focuses on the broad category of "good things that can be done cheaply," in which he includes saving lives, creating participatory associations that improve people's sense of self-worth, and campaigns for legal rights for oppressed groups (Singer, *The Life You Can Save*, 97).

[30] Pogge and Fuller disagree about how much room for discretion Pogge's principle allows. It's possible that the principle strictly interpreted provides more leeway than Pogge's own more empirical discussion of it suggests. I am here recounting possible implications of Pogge's principle that he mentions (or that follow from implications that he mentions).

[31] Pogge, "Moral Priorities," 273.

[32] For a general discussion of the ethics of refusal in anthropological terms, see Redfield, *Life in Crisis*, ch. 6.

articulated as precisely as the need and harm minimization principles, I will here try to offer a coherent reconstruction of the idea, pointing out one especially important ambiguity.

Accepting the Nobel Peace prize on behalf of MSF in 1999, James Orbinski stated that "the *refusal* of all forms of problem solving through sacrifice of the weak and vulnerable" is a "founding [principle] of humanitarian action." Orbinski continued,

> No victim can be intentionally discriminated against, OR neglected to the advantage of another. One life today cannot be measured by its value tomorrow: and the relief of suffering "here," cannot legitimize the abandoning of relief "over there." The limitation of means naturally must mean the making of choice, but the context and the constraints of action do not alter the fundamentals of this humanitarian vision.[33]

This passage might seem puzzling: what else could "the making of choice" (note the impersonal voice) mean, other than abandoning relief in one place to relieve suffering elsewhere? The key to understanding it appears to lie in Orbinski's use of the word "legitimize": his argument is that while MSF makes hard choices in the face of limited resources, these choices are in a sense illegitimate. This is why they must be "refused." One can refuse an illegitimate choice by being unwilling to work within the logic that it presents. Thus, Orbinski elsewhere describes humanitarianism as "a challenge to political choices that too often kill or allow others to be killed."[34] Pragmatically accepting the "lesser evil" in order to maximally alleviate morally important harm constitutes a failure to mount this challenge. As another MSF intellectual luminary, Jean-Hervé Bradol, writes, "humanitarian action, as we understand it, directly challenges the logic that justifies the premature and avoidable death of a part of humanity in the name of a hypothetical collective good."[35]

The ethics of refusal thus describes an approach to large-scale decision-making about resource use that foregrounds the political and expressive dimensions of these decisions. Decisions made on the basis of an ethics of refusal are, at least in part, a type of public claim-making: they do not only *embody* a particular kind of treatment of aid recipients by INGOs; they *demand* a particular kind of treatment of aid recipients by others, such as governments and dominant social groups. Thus, when MSF states that it "rejects the idea that poor people deserve third-rate medical care and strives

---

[33] James Orbinski, "Médecins sans Frontières—Nobel Lecture," July 29, 2014. *Nobelprize.org*. Nobel Media AB 2014 <http://www.nobelprize.org/nobel_prizes/peace/laureates/1999/msf-lecture.html>, my italics.

[34] James Orbinksi, *An Imperfect Offering: Humanitarian Action for the Twenty-First Century* (New York: Bloomsbury Publishing, 2010), 6. My italics.

[35] Cited in Redfield, *Life in Crisis*, 164.

to provide high-quality care to patients,"[36] it is making a public claim about what poor people deserve—not only from MSF, but from their governments and other entities charged with providing them with care.

In addition to acts of public claim-making intended in part to pressure other actors, the ethics of refusal also emphasizes activities the effects of which are difficult if not impossible to measure and commensurate, such as solidarity, speaking out, witnessing or *témoignage*, and maintaining "prox-imity." Thus, explaining why "MSF may choose to stay in a war-torn area assisting displaced persons when it would be more cost effective to work somewhere more peaceful," Lisa Fuller writes that:

> They may do this because they believe that it is morally important to stand in solidarity with vulnerable populations, and/or as a symbolic reminder to the international population that 'these people are still here', that is, that these people matter even though they are no longer in the news. This is because it is part of their mission and organizational identity that they choose to speak out about atrocities and injustices, and that they value maintaining proximity to vulnerable populations.[37]

One type of project that exemplifies the ethics of refusal is what MSF calls "vertical" projects. These projects provide an extremely high level of care to a small number of people, for example, anti-retroviral treatment for people with HIV/AIDS in an area where such treatment is generally not available. One patient described these projects as "Cadillacs for some [patients, instead of] bicycles for all."[38] These projects "refuse" to accommodate themselves to the low level of care that the harm minimization principle and other approaches that emphasize cost-effectiveness are typically seen to support.

In addition to providing a high-level, but costly, type of treatment to relatively small numbers of people, the ethics of refusal can also lead INGOs to work in areas where it is costly for them to work, but where they believe their presence sends an important message. As longtime MSF staffer Kenny Gluck explained:

> We treat tuberculosis in South Sudan. It is incredibly expensive. We fly in the doctors and the nurses, we fly in the labs...a reasonable person thinking with a utilitarian mind will say, "why don't you do that when you're in Uganda, you're practically in the same area, you can treat these people for a tenth of the cost. You'd save ten times more lives with that amount of money." Well, could these people have been stuck in this war zone, facing massacres and mere genocide for fifty years? That's why we're working with them.[39]

---

[36] MSF, "About MSF"<http://www.msf.org/about-msf>.

[37] Fuller, "Priority-Setting in International Non-Governmental Organizations," 12.

[38] Cited in Fuller, "Justified Commitments?," 68. Some aid recipients object that because they are so narrow, these projects seem more aimed at treating diseases than treating people (Abu-Sada, *In the Eyes of Others*, 28).

[39] Interview conducted in 2002 by the author; on file with the author.

Within the ethics of refusal, both vertical projects (projects that provide a high level of care to a small number of people) and the types of projects that Gluck describes (working in an area where it is expensive to work) are defended, in part, on the grounds of the message they send.

This brings us to the ambiguity in the ethics of refusal alluded to above. As just noted, vertical projects are defended not only as providing high-quality care, albeit to a small number of patients, but also as pressuring governments or other actors to discharge (what MSF takes to be) those other actors' responsibilities. As Redfield writes: "By demonstrating what is possible... [such projects]... can highlight the failures of political will behind inadequate health care and remove the excuse that 'it can't be done.'"[40] The ambiguity within the ethics of refusal centers on what happens when the pressuring or advocacy components of vertical projects fail.[41] When the advocacy components of these projects succeed, they can be quite cost-effective, but when they fail, these projects are, on conventional measures, not cost-effective. Are such projects justified? Most accounts of the ethics of refusal seem to suggest that the answer is "yes."[42] However, ambiguity on this point seems to be an implicit acknowledgment that such projects are far more difficult to defend ethically than projects that have beneficial consequences for a larger number of people. It might be helpful for proponents of the ethics of refusal to clarify whether they think that expensive projects that assist a small number of people are justified even if their advocacy component fails, and whether their objection to focusing on overall outcomes is based on the view that such a focus is often self-undermining in practice (e.g. as implied by Bradol's reference to "hypothetical" collective good), or rather that it is more fundamentally misguided.

6.3 Evaluating the Need Principle, the Harm Minimization Principle, and the Ethics of Refusal

With these three approaches to large-scale decision-making about resource use by INGOs before us, our next question is: what should we think of these

---

[40] Peter Redfield, "Doctors, Borders, and Life in Crisis," *Cultural Anthropology* 20.3 (2005): 328–61 (334).

[41] Fuller, "Justified Commitments?", argues that this is a common occurrence.

[42] Rony Brauman defends the "humanitarian model" (which is closely connected to the ethics of refusal) over the "public health model." The humanitarian model, according to Brauman, "asserts that our primary obligation is to give direct medical treatment to people who require medical attention. Essentially, *we should try to treat as much as we can, regardless of what effects this may have in the future*" (Rony Brauman, "Questioning Health and Human Rights," *Medical Rights Dialogue* 2.6 (2005), my italics).

approaches, normatively? To answer this question, we must consider how attractive they are as interpretations or specifications of humanitarian, egalitarian, democratic, and/or justice-based norms. All four of these norms are relevant to INGOs' large-scale decisions about resource use. Humanitarian norms are relevant because in making these decisions, humanitarian INGOs aim, at least in part, to provide life-saving assistance to people in danger of imminent death. Egalitarian norms are relevant because in making these decisions, INGOs have reason to treat all people as moral equals. Justice-based norms are relevant because INGOs' large-scale decisions about resource use are not only large-scale; as I discuss further below, they are often somewhat governmental. Democratic norms are relevant because INGOs' large-scale decisions about resource use affect the life-chances of many people, who should have a chance to have a say in decisions that significantly affect them.

6.3.1 *The Need Principle*

As I noted above, the most plausible interpretation of the need principle is the idea that, in making large-scale decisions about resource use, INGOs should put significant weight on considerations of need: they should not consider only need, but nor should they interpret "aid based on need alone" to mean "aid provided impartially." I will focus on this interpretation here.

The main attraction of the need principle, understood in this way, is that it appears to offer a compelling interpretation of humanitarian and egalitarian norms. In particular, it insists that no one (or, depending on how closely it approximates the literal version of the need principle, almost no one) should be left to die merely because they are expensive to assist. Everyone deserves to have their basic needs met, regardless of everything, including cost. Compliance with this version of the need principle enacts not only the humanitarian value of respect for human life, but also the egalitarian value of equal respect for all human lives. Insofar as the need principle's egalitarianism is based on providing aid based on need regardless of cost, the need principle is more radically egalitarian the more literally one interprets it.

I want to suggest, however, that the need principle is objectionable on justice-based and democratic grounds—as well as, on further inspection, egalitarian and humanitarian grounds. I argued in Chapter 3 that insofar as large-scale decisions about resource use by humanitarian INGOs are governmental, INGOs have justice-based reasons to maximally alleviate morally important harm—that is, to comply with the harm minimization principle. The need principle overlooks this feature of humanitarian INGOs.

It also cedes little ground to democratic norms: while the need principle allows INGOs to incorporate potential aid recipients' views regarding how "need" should be specified, it leaves little (or on the literal version of the principle, no) room for their views regarding whether factors other than need should be taken into account.[43]

In addition to these difficulties, upon further inspection the need principle also has limitations on egalitarian and humanitarian grounds. As noted above, the need principle is egalitarian in that it states that people's basic needs should be met, regardless of how expensive they are to assist. But "expensive versus cheap to assist" is not a particularly salient axis of inequality. For example, sometimes people are especially expensive to assist because they are (or were) previously quite well-off, such that they have few skills for coping in resource-poor environments. In other words, "aid regardless of how expensive people are to assist" is more like "aid regardless of favorite sports team" than it is like "aid regardless of gender, race, religion, or ethnicity": it does not take a stand against a widespread and highly salient form of inequality or oppression. This does not make the need principle inegalitarian, but it suggests that its egalitarianism might be less politically or morally relevant than it initially appears to be.[44] Moreover, even if the need principle treats potential aid recipients as equal *to each other* regardless of how expensive they are to assist, it functions discursively to exacerbate inequalities between aid recipients and potential recipients on the one hand, and INGOs and donors on the other, by portraying the former as needy victims and the latter as apolitical rescuers.[45]

Finally, while the need principle is closely associated with humanitarianism, its commitment to humanitarian norms is undercut by its refusal to take considerations of cost-effectiveness into account: the more literally the need principle is interpreted, the more open it is to the objection that it is more attached to the *idea* of humanity than to assisting actual human beings in their efforts to avoid premature death and suffering.[46]

---

[43] It is worth comparing this argument to the argument about democratic norms in the context of resource provision in conflict zones, discussed in Chapter 4. There, I argued that aid recipients should be able to democratically demand that INGOs leave, but not that they stay beyond whatever period they have promised. Aid recipients should also have a say in how "benefits" and "costs" of aid are conceptualized (which is a broader question than how to conceptualize need). I also argued that some aid recipient preferences, such as preferences that a particular group should be excluded from aid because of its members' race or ethnicity, should be excluded. This last issue is more salient in the context of immediate decisions INGOs face about whether to continue to provide aid or withdraw in specific conflict settings than it is in ongoing, public discussions about the kinds of considerations that should inform INGOs' large-scale decisions about resource use.

[44] One exception to this is when the need principle directs resources to a group that is expensive to assist because of systematic injustices perpetrated against it.

[45] See Chapter 2 for further discussion.

[46] The Red Cross Code comes close to acknowledging this when it states, in its explanation of the principle that includes "aid based on need alone," that "[t]he implementation of such a

I conclude that in making large-scale decisions about resource use, INGOs should take need into account, but they should not provide aid on the basis of need alone—or even make need the overarching basis for their decision-making.

6.3.2 *The Harm Minimization Principle*

The harm minimization principle can be defended in at least three ways. First, it seems to be justifiable on utilitarian grounds. However, if one is not already a utilitarian, this argument on its own is unlikely to carry much weight. Pogge offers a second argument that does not rest on a prior commitment to utilitarianism: INGOs owe it to their donors to act consistently with the harm minimization principle.[47] But as I showed in Chapter 2, many donors do not want INGOs to maximally alleviate harm. They have other aims, such as improving their global reputation or helping victims of a nearby and/or dramatic natural disaster. Likewise, there is no guarantee that discharging donors' negative or intermediate duties on donor's behalf will lead INGOs to comply with the harm minimization principle.

Pogge also implies a third defense of the idea that INGOs are obliged to comply with the harm minimization principle: INGOs *"offer* to pool money we give them and to make such funds effective toward human rights, development and humanitarian goals."[48] Here "offer" seems to have the implication of "promised." But many INGOs do not offer, or promise, to do all of these things. For example, of these three goals, MSF only offers to pursue humanitarian goals.[49] More generally, relying on INGOs' own voluntary descriptions of their activities seems to be a feeble basis for the harm minimization principle, because it invites INGOs to simply clarify that maximally alleviating morally important harm is not their goal.

Another limitation of the "promise" argument emerges when we consider Pogge's comment that, "an INGO field worker who saves five children from a painful diarrhea death when she evidently could, with equal resources and effort, save ten" is "subject to legitimate moral criticism."[50] Suppose that the field worker in this example was called away to a meeting, but the political theorist who had been shadowing her remained on the scene. Would we

---

universal, impartial and independent policy, can only be effective if we and our partners have access to the necessary resources to provide for such equitable relief, and have equal access to all disaster victims."

[47] Pogge, "Moral Priorities."   [48] Pogge, "Moral Priorities," my italics.

[49] As Toby Ord ("Moral Imperative towards Cost-Effectiveness") notes, cost-effectiveness is achieved primarily in the choice of one's activity (e.g. provide guide dogs for the blind versus vitamin treatments to prevent blindness) not in how one pursues a given activity.

[50] Pogge, "Respect and Disagreement."

judge the political theorist any less harshly than the INGO worker if she saved five children when she just as easily could have saved ten?[51] I think that the answer to this question is "no." This suggests that our intuitions about the INGO worker's responsibilities do not derive (fully) from her having made certain promises as part of her professional role, but are based on something more like the "duty of nearby rescue."[52]

Yet the duty of nearby rescue also seems like an inadequate basis for the harm minimization principle for INGOs; indeed, these two normative commitments can pull in opposite directions: while the duty of nearby rescue suggests that the aid worker (or political theorist) should save all ten children in front of them rather than just five, the harm minimization principle says that they should let all ten die in order to save eleven elsewhere.[53]

All of this leaves proponents of the harm minimization principle in an awkward position: they think that humanitarian INGOs have a responsibility to maximally alleviate morally important harm. Yet it is difficult to defend this claim on other than purely utilitarian grounds. However, defending it on purely utilitarian grounds has what are for many people counter-intuitive implications: it suggests that (for example), local arts organizations based in Ethiopia must also dedicate themselves to saving as many lives as possible. On what basis might we say that humanitarian INGOs, but not Ethiopian arts organizations, have a duty to comply with the harm minimization principle? I will suggest below that there is a partial way out of this difficulty, but it involves conceptualizing humanitarian INGOs in a way that proponents of the harm minimization principle have tended not to conceptualize them.

First, though, we need to temporarily put aside the question of whether compliance with the harm minimization principle is morally *required*, to instead ask whether it is even normatively *desirable*. I will argue that while it has attractive features, it also has some significant limitations. First, like the need principle, the harm minimization principle says nothing about democratic norms; it seems to replace democratic deliberation or aggregation

---

[51] Say, by warning them away from playing near a cliff or doing something else that required no expertise.

[52] Richard W. Miller, *Globalizing Justice: The Ethics of Poverty and Power* (New York: Oxford University Press, 2010), ch. 1. I use the term "rescue" here because I am discussing the philosophical idea of the duty of rescue. As I argued in Chapter 2, conceptualizing INGOs as rescuers is objectionable for a host of reasons.

[53] The duty of nearby rescue itself becomes more difficult to defend when it is so demanding: as Miller points out, it is only possible for most of us to imagine endorsing a demanding duty of nearby rescue ex-ante if we anticipate that we will only need to engage in rescue rarely (Miller, *Globalizing Justice*, ch. 1). Likewise, as Neera Badhwar points out, the intuition that many of us have that one "must act" when faced with someone in need of rescue is partly the result of *not* facing these situations constantly (Neera K. Badhwar, "International Aid: When Giving Becomes a Vice," *Social Philosophy and Policy* 23.1 (2006): 69–101).

with a predetermined principle (although the degree to which this is so depends on how the particular components of the principle are specified). Second, a focus on maximally alleviating morally important harm can "wag the dog," so to speak, leading INGOs to prioritize activities that are not only cost-effective, but the cost-effectiveness of which can be cost-effectively ascertained. This, in turn, can lead INGOs to focus on achieving outcomes that are easier to measure—those that are more concrete, isolated, biological, and technical (but not necessarily high-tech)—and de-emphasize the activities the outcomes or effects of which are primarily political, collective, psychological, and/or that contribute jointly to valuable outcomes with many other actors.

Randomized controlled trials and other innovative efforts to measure the effects of various activities and interventions, show some promise in expanding the range of activities that an INGO committed to cost-effectiveness might undertake.[54] However, these approaches still provide little help in measuring "outcomes" such as standing by an abused population, engaging in *témoignage* (witnessing), or helping Ebola patients die with dignity. This is not because the value of these activities is intrinsic. Insofar as these activities are valuable, they are valuable primarily because of their effects, for example, showing members of an oppressed group that they have not been forgotten, and providing comfort to people who are dying.[55] The issue is that the value of these activities is very difficult and expensive—and maybe even impossible—to measure. Given these difficulties, it is easy to see why an INGO that was committed to being, and showing itself to be, cost-effective, would decide to focus on more easily measurable objectives.

For example, both Pogge and the organization Giving What We Can are, in principle, entirely open to INGOs using their resources to maximally alleviate morally important harm via political means: Pogge's definition of harm includes shortfalls in "civic status"; GWWC identifies "political change" as a positive outcome that INGOs might be able to achieve cost-effectively.[56] However, because it is so difficult to measure the effectiveness of efforts to reduce shortfalls in civic status and to achieve political change, Pogge (in his work on the moral priorities of INGOs) and GWWC both end up primarily endorsing projects aimed at improving people's physical health or increasing

---

[54] For a useful brief overview of the vast literature on randomized controlled experiments, see discussion in Wenar, "Poverty is No Pond."

[55] To see that the value of these activities lies at least in part with their effects, notice that it is better for INGOs to help more patients rather than fewer die with dignity, and engage in witnessing on behalf of more rather than fewer oppressed groups.

[56] Giving What We Can, "Political Change," December 2012 <http://www.givingwhatwecan.org/where-to-give/charity-evaluation/political-change>.

their access to financial resources.[57] This dynamic suggests that the more cost-effectiveness is promoted as a standard for large-scale decisions about resource use by INGOs, and the more that funding agencies require proof (especially short-term proof) of cost-effectiveness, the more difficult it will be for INGOs to experiment with activities the cost-effectiveness of which is difficult or impossible to measure. This tendency might even become self-reinforcing, if INGOs were to develop organizational cultures oriented toward such technical projects, and attract the sorts of employees and donors who view them as valuable.

To be clear, the basic health interventions that, at present, appear to align most closely with the harm minimization principle are immensely important; I in no way mean to discount them. My point is only that in choosing the harm minimization principle as a basis for large-scale decisions about resource use, one is, in effect, choosing basic health interventions over those involving politics or the cultivation of collective political agency, due to the relative ease of measuring the former.[58] It is in this respect that the harm minimization principle replaces political judgment with technical judgment.

The better INGOs get at measuring the effects of a wider range of their activities (and measuring them cheaply), the less a focus on cost-effectiveness will push INGOs toward a narrow range of activities, and the less damaging a strong emphasis on cost-effectiveness will be. However, in calibrating our optimism about these prospects, it is useful to recognize that this issue echoes a debate that has been raging among political scientists, in particular, over the last seventy years: a debate between positivists, naturalists, and behavioralists who think that it is possible to identify substantively important and useful probabilistic or determinate rules governing human phenomena, and anti-positivists, some interpretivists, as well as humanists of various stripes, who think that this is a misguided pipe dream.[59] In short, disagreements about the persistence and profundity of the difficulties with the harm minimization principle parallel broader debates in other fields. The history of these other debates suggests that these disagreements are unlikely to be resolved soon.

[57] As of August 2014, Giving What We Can endorses organizations working on malaria, schistosomiasis, micronutrients, and deworming. The latter two organizations work with governments, but in a technical capacity. Givewell endorses the same two organizations working on schistosomiasis and deworming, as well as an organization that provides cash transfers.

[58] While one could argue that people need to be healthy to exercise their political agency, such that a focus on physical health must take priority, it is also the case that supporting people's political agency can help them to take charge of their health and set their own health-related priorities, which could be different from those of an INGO.

[59] See John G. Gunnell, "American Political Science, Liberalism, and the Invention of Political Theory," *American Political Science Review* 82.1 (1988): 71–87; Benjamin R. Barber, "The Politics of Political Science: Theory and the Wolin–Strauss Dust-Up of 1963," *American Political Science Review* 100.4 (2006): 539–45; Sheldon S. Wolin, "Political Theory as a Vocation," *American Political Science Review* 63.4 (1969): 1062–82.

6.3.3 *The Ethics of Refusal*

Unlike both the need principle and the harm minimization principle, the ethics of refusal is intended to promote structural justice, in at least two ways: by refusing to make moral compromises, it takes a stand against the injustices that create the "need" to make those compromises. It also focuses not (only) on INGOs' own decisions, but also on how their decisions can serve to pressure other actors to fulfill their responsibilities.

The main shortcoming of the ethics of refusal is that, by portraying INGOs as activist gadflies, when they are in fact large-scale, formal, and institutionalized actors, it can be romantic and self-indulgent. In particular, it can fail to acknowledge that INGOs' large-scale decisions about resource use are to some extent forms of conventional and global governance. As a result, what Redfield calls MSF's "refus[al of] the responsibility of rule" can slide into a refusal to take responsibility for the governance power that MSF already exercises.[60]

Redfield writes, "[i]nasmuch as humanitarian actors define their ethics around actions and present that action as a response to suffering, they limit the scope of their perceived responsibility and decision-making. The formula is clear: Moral outrage demands response."[61] But when events in many different places prompt outrage, when an INGO's outrage is keyed too closely to a particular set of experiences or narratives (such as the Holocaust), or when a situation is only borderline outrage-inducing, the automaticity of this process flounders, or provides unreliable results. In these cases, INGOs must make judgments and act in ways that are not simply reflexive responses to morally unambiguous emergencies that "demand" action. They instead face what Redfield calls an "expanding uncomfortable component of decision."[62] It is in the context of such decisions that the ethics of refusal seems inadequate, because it constitutes a kind of political reflex, when what is needed is political judgment.

To summarize: neither the need principle, the harm minimization principle, nor the ethics of refusal offers an adequate account of what it means for INGOs to make large-scale decisions about resource use in a way that is consistent with humanitarian, egalitarian, justice-based, and democratic norms. The need principle and the harm minimization principle offer interpretations of humanitarian norms, but the former, especially when it is

---

[60] Peter Redfield, "Vital Mobility and the Humanitarian Kit," in *Biosecurity Interventions: Global Health and Security in Question*, ed. Andrew Lakoff and Stephen J. Collier (New York: Columbia University Press, 2008), 147–71 (162).

[61] Peter Redfield, "The Verge of Crisis: Doctors Without Borders in Uganda," in *Contemporary States of Emergency: The Politics of Military and Humanitarian Interventions*, ed. Didier Fassin and Mariella Pandolfi (Cambridge, MA: Zone Books, 2010), 173–95.

[62] Redfield, "The Verge of Crisis," 191.

interpreted more literally, seems to value the idea of humanity more than actual human lives, while the latter accepts a too-thin conception of humanity as mere biological life. All three principles are in a sense egalitarian: the need principle emphasizes equality among people regardless of how expensive they are to assist; the harm minimization principle acknowledges equality by protecting as many people from as much serious harm as possible; the ethics of refusal pressures others to treat aid recipients as equals. However, none offers a fully adequate picture of equality, or acknowledge the ways in which different kinds of equality can conflict. Only the ethics of refusal says anything about justice-based norms; however, even it engages with issues of justice primarily in the register of political reflex, rather than considered political judgment. Finally, all three approaches say little about democratic norms, although MSF's public discussion of the ethics of refusal and Giving What We Can's discussion of cost-effectiveness could be seen as consistent with the democratic norm of publicity.

6.4 The Ethics of Resistance

One way to characterize the shortcomings of both the harm minimization principle and the ethics of refusal is that they respond to only some important features of the ethical terrain of humanitarian INGOs' large-scale decisions about resource use. That is, they are based on incomplete maps. I turn next to sketching a more complete map. This map shows that humanitarian INGOs face an ethical predicament that I call the cost-effectiveness conundrum. This conundrum arises because of four main features of INGOs' ethical terrain.[63] These features generate responsibilities that pull INGOs in different directions. After describing these features and the responsibilities they generate, I will sketch the ethics of resistance as a form of political judgment suitable for navigating this conundrum.

First, as I argued in detail in Chapter 3, INGOs' large-scale decisions about resource use are sometimes similar to large-scale decisions about resource use made by conventional governments: these decisions fundamentally affect the private and shared interests of many people; they involve issues of public concern, and they are made in an official capacity. For example, in 2012, MSF spent $1.3 billion on mostly health-related activities.[64] This is more than the governments of Botswana, Cameroon, and Côte

---

[63] A fifth feature, moral autonomy, is closer to a moral permission than a moral responsibility.
[64] MSF, "International Financial Report 2012," 5. <http://www.msf.org/sites/msf.org/files/msf_financial_report_interactive_2012_final.pdf>.

d'Ivoire spent on health care ($1.2 billion each), and more than twice what was spent by Benin, Burkina Faso, Burundi, Congo, Chad, and several other countries.[65] While the effects of MSF's decisions about resource use were more geographically dispersed than analogous decisions made by these individual country governments, MSF's decisions were not, as a result, less consequential for the individuals affected. To the contrary, because MSF focuses on providing medical care in places where it is not being provided, its decisions are potentially more consequential than those made by governments. Moreover, while MSF is very large, it is still only one INGO; if one were to take into account the humanitarian INGO sector as a whole, the governmental character of INGOs' large-scale decisions about resource use would be even more pronounced.

The more that INGOs' large-scale decisions about resource use resemble those made by conventional governments, the greater INGOs' responsibility to make these decisions according to the same criteria that governments should use to make these decisions. This means, in particular, putting significant (though not necessarily singular) emphasis on maximally alleviating morally important harm. Here, then, is our partial answer to the question, posed above, about how to defend the intuition that large-scale humanitarian INGOs have some responsibility to maximally alleviate morally important harm, while small arts organizations do not: *humanitarian INGOs' decisions about resource use, but not those of arts organizations, are somewhat governmental.* Like governments, INGOs make these decisions in an official capacity and at a large scale; their decisions also have public effects. When governments play favorites, or when they dither, stonewall, or otherwise act inefficiently in response to emergencies and serious non-emergencies, they appear to be massively disrespecting the humanity of the people significantly affected by their actions. The same point holds for humanitarian INGOs when their large-scale decisions about resource use serve a conventional governance function.

This analogy between conventional governments and INGOs does not mean that INGOs must always maximally alleviate morally important harm, as a straightforward utilitarian argument might suggest. It therefore does not mean that INGOs must radically alter their goals or activities, for example by switching from humanitarian aid to development aid if the latter is more cost-effective. Rather, the analogy to conventional governments suggests that INGOs must maximally alleviate morally important harm when doing so is necessary to avoid massively disrespecting people—for example, when an INGO is clearly serving a conventional governance function, or when

---

[65] World Health Organization, *WHO Global Health Expenditure Atlas* (Geneva: WHO, 2012) (2010 figures).

maximally alleviating morally important harm does not require sacrificing other important goals. One way to cash this out would be to say that when INGOs make large-scale decisions about resource use that are somewhat governmental, the burden falls on them to explain why they are not maximally alleviating morally important harm.

In addition to functioning as a form of conventional governance, INGOs' large-scale decisions about resource use can also function as a form of global governance, most notably by helping to constitute the international humanitarian order. As I argued in Chapter 3, INGOs have a responsibility to try to make the institutions in which they participate at least minimally just. However, because the effects of efforts to promote justice in institutions are difficult to measure, they can be hard to justify in cost-effectiveness terms. For example, a consortium of large British INGOs recently set up the Start Fund, a collective funding mechanism intended to promote faster INGO and domestic NGO responses to rapid-onset and slow-onset emergencies, and to direct resources toward "under-funded" emergencies.[66] The Start Fund is a formal institution; INGOs that make large-scale decisions about resource use in the context of this institution support and/or help to constitute it. On the argument I have been defending, INGOs that are involved in this institution have a responsibility to help ensure that it is just. Insofar as this requires expending resources in ways that do not maximally alleviate morally important harm, INGOs' global governance responsibilities diverge from, and might compete with, their conventional governance responsibilities.

Likewise, in making and publicly defending their large-scale decisions about resource use, INGOs also often exercise discursive power. In particular, INGOs' compliance with the harm minimization principle can function discursively to normalize the "fact" of limited resources and the "necessity" of making pragmatic decisions in the face of those limitations. In contrast, the ethics of refusal does not take existing levels of resource provision as given, nor does it assume that other actors will (continue to) shirk their responsibilities. So insofar as INGOs' decisions about resource use function as a form of discursive power, INGOs have some reason to publicly "refuse" the political and resource-based limits that they confront. Again, however, whatever positive (or negative) effects this refusal has are likely to be difficult to measure. This refusal can therefore conflict with maximally alleviating morally important harm.

Finally, in making large-scale decisions about resource use, humanitarian INGOs are also often second-best actors. This is easiest to see in the context of decisions about resource use that allocate basic services within a country: it is typically the government of that country, not an INGO, that is the

---

[66] See Start Network, "The Start Fund" (2014) <http://www.start-network.org/how/start-fund/>.

first-best actor there (either making decisions about resource use directly itself, or shaping the context in which resources are allocated by markets or civil society). When INGOs make decisions about resource use that cross borders, the first-best actor is more difficult to identify. But even here, the idea that some other actor or state of affairs would be preferable suggests that a more politicized or institution-building approach might be more appropriate for INGOs than one that focused narrowly on technical efforts to directly maximally alleviate harm.

To summarize: insofar as INGOs' large-scale decisions about resource use resemble those of conventional governments, INGOs have ethical responsibilities to comply with the harm minimization principle. Yet insofar as, in making these decisions, they also engage in global governance, exercise discursive power, and/or are second-best actors, they have ethical responsibilities that pull them in a very different direction: roughly speaking, toward the ethics of refusal. Now we can see why both the harm minimization principle and the ethics of refusal are based on incomplete maps of INGOs' large-scale decisions about resource use, and why both imply that there is little need for political judgment: the harm minimization principle overlooks the more explicitly political dimensions of INGOs' decisions about resource use, and so supposes that technical judgments about cost-effectiveness will suffice; the ethics of refusal overlooks similarities between INGOs' large-scale decisions about resource use and decisions about resource use made by conventional governments, as well as INGOs' global governance activities and status as second-best actors, and so supposes that political reflex will suffice.

In contrast to both of these approaches, my proposed alternative, the ethics of resistance, attends to all four features of INGOs' large-scale decisions about resource use just described: conventional governance, global governance, discursive power, and second-best status. The "ethics of resistance" is my term for a type of political judgment that recognizes and seeks to navigate among these different and sometimes conflicting sources of responsibility. It focuses largely on overall consequences, but has an expansive understanding of what consequences matter, and is attentive to the distortions that can result from efforts to measure and commensurate them.

Because INGOs' large-scale decisions about resource use affect many people's basic interests in an ongoing way, there is *prima facie* reason to think that democratic norms are relevant to these decisions. But what would enacting these norms look like? Rather than trying to approximate a referendum among the billion-plus people significantly affected by INGOs' large-scale decisions about resource use, a seemingly more promising method of incorporating democratic norms into these decisions would be to focus on practices of transparency, publicity, public explanation, and mirror representation. The idea here is that INGOs would be responsible for publicly explaining their large-scale decisions about resource use, including but not only with reference to the features of their political and ethical terrain sketched above.[67] They would thereby open themselves to challenge from donors, other INGOs, UN agencies, domestic NGOs, journalists, activists, and aid recipients themselves. If INGOs had more upper-level managers from aid-recipient countries, and consulted regularly with national employees from a range of countries on resource use issues, they would likely receive information and learn from perspectives that would enhance these judgments. In addition, the symbolic and expressive dimensions of their decisions about resource use would have fewer colonial resonances.[68]

Of all the large mainstream humanitarian INGOs, MSF is perhaps the most transparent and self-reflective about its large-scale decisions about resource use. However, to engage in the ethics of resistance, it would need to be clearer still about exactly why, in making these decisions, it directs resources toward, for example, practices of proximity, solidarity, and speaking out, rather than saving as many lives and alleviating as much suffering as possible. If proximity, solidarity, and speaking out are valuable—say, because they convey respect for the people INGOs wish to assist, and foster good relationships with them—how should we think about these values vis-à-vis lives lost, given MSF's large—official—role as a humanitarian actor on the global stage?

Returning to the example of the Ebola epidemic discussed at the outset of this chapter, in order to enact the ethics of resistance, MSF would have to have some sort of substantive reply for the villager living on the outskirts of Gulu who wondered why resources were being devoted to helping people with Ebola die with dignity rather than helping people in his village stay alive. In answering his question, MSF would need to offer an explanation that was framed in terms of the value of the consequences of its activities, broadly understood, and that acknowledged its conventional governance role, global governance role, second-best status, and exercise of discursive power.

Let us return to another example, Kenny Gluck's description of MSF's tuberculosis program in South Sudan cited above. (This is the program that, according to Gluck, saves ten times fewer lives than would a similar program in Uganda.) Gluck defended MSF's decision to work in Sudan on the grounds that the people living there had "been stuck in this war zone, facing massacres and mere genocide for fifty years." This is the beginning of an answer, but the ethics of resistance demands more: what is being accomplished by working in Sudan that would not be accomplished by working in Uganda?

---

[67] This is consistent with, but more specific than, Fuller's proposal for "responsibility for reasonableness" in "Justified Commitments?"

[68] Anne Phillips, *The Politics of Presence* (Oxford: Oxford University Press, 2003); Jane Mansbridge, "Should Blacks Represent Blacks and Women Represent Women? A Contingent 'Yes'," *The Journal of Politics* 61.3 (1999): 628–57.

For example, is MSF's presence psychologically beneficial to the people of Sudan in a way that it would not be to people in Uganda? Is MSF sending a message to the Sudanese government? Is that message having its intended effects? How do we know? Is sending that message worth not trying to save the lives of thousands more people in Uganda?

Just as INGOs that make somewhat governmental large-scale decisions about resource use must explain when those decisions diverge significantly from the harm minimization principle, INGOs and meta-charities such as Giving What We Can that emphasize cost-effectiveness should explain what is potentially being lost or overlooked as a result of their approach—whether what is lost is a more political, activist orientation on the part of INGOs, or attention to their responsibilities to ensure that the institutions in which they participate are just.

One might object to the ethics of resistance by saying, as one MSF employee told me, that MSF does not have a responsibility to allocate its resources in any particular way, because "we are a private organization, like a football club."[69] I have argued here that this is not (fully) the case: insofar as MSF engages in conventional and global governance functions, it is not merely a private organization. But it is not a full-fledged government, either. And this brings us to the final piece of the ethics of resistance. In liberal democracies, at least, governments are supposed to be servants of the people; they have no discretion to take on projects because they find them interesting or moving, or just because they feel like it. They must instead justify their actions and decisions in terms of the public interest, whatever that is taken to mean. In contrast, because INGOs are not full-fledged governments, they do have some discretion along these lines; they have what Lisa Fuller calls "moral autonomy."[70] It is difficult to characterize the extent of this discretion, except to say that it exists, and its scope gets smaller the more like conventional governments INGOs become.

6.5 Conclusion

Is probably preventing, at least temporarily, 10,000 deaths from tuberculosis in Uganda more important than probably preventing 1,000 deaths from tuberculosis in Sudan and standing up against genocide in a way that might help to reduce the likelihood of future genocides? In the face of this kind of question, there is rarely a definitively right or wrong answer; all we can do, I think, is point to answers that reflect more rather than less astute and

[69] José Bastos, interview with the author (2002). Interview on file with the author.
[70] Fuller, "Priority Setting in International Non-Governmental Organizations."

humane ethical and political judgment. Exercising this judgment, which I call the ethics of resistance, and doing so publicly, in conversation with differently situated interlocutors, is, I contend, what it means for INGOs to make large-scale decisions about resource use in a way that is consistent with appropriately specified democratic, egalitarian, humanitarian, and justice-based norms.[71]

This chapter has sketched a map with five features—conventional governance, global governance, discursive power, second-best status, and INGO moral autonomy—that is intended to contribute to such judgment. Because it does not identify one best route across the political and ethical terrain of large-scale decisions about resource use, this map might be cold comfort to aid workers charged with deciding on such routes—not to mention the people who must live with those decisions, or die, at least in part, because of them. But until INGOs have more resources—or until the issues they seek to address are resolved or addressed in some other way—this is, I think, the best we have. Our dissatisfaction should lead us to not only continue the debate about how INGOs should make large-scale decisions about resource use, but also try to make these decisions unnecessary, or at least less tragic.

One practical consideration that INGOs must incorporate into their large-scale decisions about resource use is whether a given activity will enable them to attract new donors and retain current donors. It is not only, or even primarily, INGOs' "on the ground" activities that attract and retain donors, however—it is also how INGOs, the issues they address, and the people they wish to assist, are portrayed. These portrayals are the subject of the next chapter.

---

[71] How would widespread uptake of the ethics of resistance shift the overall allocation of aid by the INGO sector? Any answer must necessarily be speculative. However, I suspect that there would be at least some movement in the direction of cost-effectiveness, because divergences from cost-effectiveness that are justified only on the basis of geographic spread would likely not withstand scrutiny, nor would vertical projects with no effective advocacy component.

7

The Moral Motivation Tradeoff

Bored with pictures of starving children?
—Oxfam advertisement (1966)[1]

On May 28, 2003, the British newspaper the *Daily Mirror* published a photograph of the Irish rock musician Bob Geldof handing a baby, Mekanic Philipos, to the baby's mother, Bezunesh Abraham, at the Yirba therapeutic feeding center near Awasa, Ethiopia (Fig. 7.1).[2] The photograph, directly beneath the headline "SORT IT OUT," portrays Geldof as a sun-dappled savior, beneficently delivering the malnourished Mekanic into the arms of his disconsolate mother. In so doing, it evokes racial and gender hierarchies, as well as colonial relationships. It quickly became the "defining image" of Geldof's trip.[3]

Geldof's visit to Yirba had been arranged by Save the Children and UNICEF as part of a publicity tour meant to put "Africa" more squarely on the agenda of an upcoming G8 summit.[4] At the time of the visit, Save the Children and UNICEF had policies prohibiting the use of images like the *Daily Mirror* photograph in their own fundraising materials. As John Graham, program director for Save the Children UK in Addis Ababa, stated,

> [The photograph] is not an image we like. In fact, we try to avoid it as much as possible. You won't see any of that on our literature but we do work with

[1] Oxfam Newspaper advertisement, "Bored with pictures of starving children?" 1966. Reproduced with the permission of Oxfam GB, Oxfam House, John Smith Drive, Cowley, Oxford, OX4 2JY, UK. <http://www.oxfam. org.uk">. Oxfam GB does not necessarily endorse any text or activities that accompany the materials.
[2] David Clark, "Representing the MAJORITY WORLD: Famine, Photojournalism and the Changing Visual Economy." PhD dissertation, Durham University, 2009. <http://etheses.dur. ac.uk/136/>, 156.
[3] Clark, "Representing the MAJORITY WORLD," 161. The story behind the photograph is complicated: Geldof actively tried to avoid holding babies to avoid photos such as this from being taken (he was caught off-guard when a UNICEF official handed Mekanic to him). As I discuss further below, Abraham said that she was not embarrassed by the photograph and had no objection to it being published. See Clark, "Representing the MAJORITY WORLD."
[4] Clark, "Representing the MAJORITY WORLD," 154–5.

Figure 7.1 Bezunesh Abraham and Bob Geldof, *Daily Mirror*, May 28, 2003. Image: Antony Njuguna, Reuters. Caption from Reuters: BOB GELDOF HOLDS A MALNOURISHED CHILD AT A FEEDING CENTRE IN ETHIOPIA. Irish rock star Bob Geldof (R) holds Mechanic [*sic*] Philipos a malnourished one-year-old boy from her [*sic*] mother at Yirba feeding centre in Awasa, 300 km south of Addis Ababa, Ethiopia, May 28, 2003. Geldof, who organized the world's biggest rock concert in 1985 to help Africa's starving, is visiting Ethiopia to highlight a looming humanitarian crisis. Aid agencies estimate 14 million Ethiopians are at risk of starvation after the worst drought in nearly two decades.

therapeutic feeding and we do have children that look like that and, I tell you, it opens the pockets and that's the reality you are forced into.[5]

Thus, while both Save the Children and UNICEF refused to use images like the *Daily Mirror* photograph in their own materials, both organizations were willing to facilitate the dissemination of such images in newspapers. Indeed, both organizations "expressed delight at the outcome of [Geldof's] visit, reporting financial and political gains that would not have come otherwise."[6]

In other words, Save the Children finds images like the *Daily Mirror* photograph so objectionable that it refuses to use them in its own literature, but it is willing to facilitate the publication of such images elsewhere, because they prompt people to donate. Yet publishing the photograph of Abraham and Geldof in the *Daily Mirror* might well have been more detrimental, in terms of contributing to skewed perceptions of "Africa" on the part of people elsewhere, than publishing the photograph in Save the

[5] Cited in Clark, "Representing the MAJORITY WORLD," 64.
[6] Clark, "Representing the MAJORITY WORLD," 162.

Children's own materials. Not only was the photograph disseminated more widely than it would have been in a Save the Children advertisement, but functioning as a news photograph gave it an air of objectivity and authority that it would not have had in a fundraising brochure.[7]

Save the Children's decision to facilitate the creation and dissemination of the photograph of Abraham and Geldof was a response to a tradeoff that virtually all humanitarian INGOs regularly face: raise as much money as possible, or limit what I will call their "portrayal-related practices" (creating, disseminating, and/or helping to create or disseminate visual images) on ethical grounds.[8] This chapter examines this conflict with particular reference to images of famine and severe poverty. What is at stake in this conflict? How should INGOs navigate it? More generally, what does it look like for INGOs to engage in portrayal-related practices in a way that is consistent with democratic, egalitarian, humanitarian, and justice-based norms?

Many INGOs and INGO critics share a set of assumptions about this issue. These assumptions, which I will refer to collectively as the "standard view," consist of four main ideas: (1) INGOs face a dilemma of need versus dignity. (2) This dilemma pertains solely to images in INGOs' own materials. (3) The appropriate response to this dilemma is to develop criteria for distinguishing ethical from unethical images. (4) These criteria are best expressed in the form of guidelines, rules, or codes of conduct for individual INGOs or the humanitarian INGO sector.

This chapter challenges all four components of the standard view. I will argue that (1) rather than a dilemma of need versus dignity, INGOs face a more internally variegated set of predicaments that I call the *moral motivation tradeoff*. (2) This tradeoff extends to all of INGOs' portrayal-related activities, not only the images in their own materials. (3) INGOs' portrayal-related practices should be treated holistically, as opposed to giving a "thumbs up" or "thumbs down" to individual images. (4) Efforts to address normative shortcomings in INGOs' portrayal-related practices should include not only rules or codes of conduct, but also creative practices. These practices include *diluting* INGOs' images with images created by other types of actors and institutions, and INGOs themselves engaging in *critical visual rhetoric* by using potentially objectionable images to grab viewers' attention and draw them into a more nuanced understanding of the issues. Some INGOs have facilitated or engaged in versions of both of these strategies, so in proposing them I am reconstructing, developing, and defending ideas that are immanent in some INGOs' existing practices.

---

[7] While the *Daily Mirror* is more of a tabloid than a "serious" news outlet, the image was also published in the *International Herald Tribune*, which is a more serious news outlet (Clark, Representing the MAJORITY WORLD," 163).

[8] See Chapter 3 for a discussion of discursive power.

The standard view, and in particular the idea that INGOs face a dilemma of need versus dignity, suggests that INGOs face a corresponding conflict between humanitarianism (which pertains to need) and justice (which pertains to dignity). In contrast, the perspective of the moral motivation tradeoff dislodges this tight one-to-one correlation between humanitarianism and need and justice and dignity, and enables us to see what is going on in these situations in a more nuanced way: sometimes INGOs' portrayal-related practices generate a tradeoff between different *kinds* of justice, or between promoting justice and avoiding enabling physical harm, or between raising money *and* empowering the individual pictured, on the one hand, and perpetuating false perceptions in donor countries, on the other. By giving us a more nuanced understanding of what is at stake in these predicaments, the perspective of the moral motivation tradeoff helps us to notice and evaluate possible strategies for reducing these tradeoffs that the need versus dignity conception elides (strategies such as dilution and critical visual rhetoric).

While dilution and critical visual rhetoric have the potential to reduce the moral motivation tradeoff, especially in the medium to long term, they cannot eradicate the tendencies that underlie it. While well-meaning individuals are often perceived as "good" donors, compared to more bureaucratic or self-interested institutional donors, a more general upshot of this chapter is that relying on even individual donors, especially those who live in donor countries, is a serious moral hazard for INGOs. This is, in part, because the kinds of images that motivate individuals to donate to humanitarian INGOs systematically undermine their understanding of the issues (especially famine and severe poverty) that INGOs use their donations to address.

The previous three chapters of this book have addressed familiar themes in contemporary liberal political theory: the provision of basic services, advocacy, and large-scale decisions about resource use. I argued that existing concepts and frameworks that theorists often use to address these themes, such as ideas about dirty hands, representation and partnership, and need and harm minimization, are inadequate "maps" of the terrain of humanitarian INGO political ethics. I therefore tried to provide better maps. This chapter, in contrast, addresses an issue about which contemporary liberal political theorists have said relatively little. While the ethics of images is a major theme in media studies and cultural studies, within political theory it has been taken up primarily by scholars who are self-consciously working at the intersection of political theory and other disciplines,[9] as well as by scholars of the politics of recognition (who have tended not to focus on

---

[9] Within political theory, see, for example, James Johnson, " 'The Arithmetic of Compassion': Rethinking the Politics of Photography," *British Journal of Political Science* 41.3 (2011): 621–43; Mark Reinhardt, "Theorizing the Event of Photography—The Visual Politics of Violence and Terror in Azoulay's Civil Imagination, Linfield's The Cruel Radiance, and Mitchell's

the sort of tradeoffs that INGOs confront).[10] As a result, while I draw on recent political theoretical work in political theory on "political rhetoric" to develop my account of critical visual rhetoric, this chapter says less than previous chapters about the limitations of existing political theoretical maps. Rather, my quarrel is with the "standard view" sketched above. Political theorists might well accept the standard view—indeed, I imagine that many do—but the standard view is not a distinctively political theoretical set of ideas.

As I noted in Chapter 1, INGOs are sometimes seen as angels or do-gooding machines on the one hand, or evil corporations or naïve miscreants, on the other. Anyone who accepts one of these characterizations is unlikely to recognize the force of the ethical conflicts discussed in this chapter.[11] If INGOs are do-gooding machines that reliably transform donations into lives saved, then (it would be very easy to think) they should raise as much money as possible, even if this means using very degrading or otherwise harmful images. Conversely, if INGOs are doing more harm than good, there is no reason for them to stay in business at all, let alone fund themselves by creating and circulating objectionable images. But if, as I have suggested, most humanitarian INGOs are neither do-gooding machines nor devils, then we cannot dismiss questions about the ethics of their portrayal-related practices, either by saying, "Of course they should do whatever is necessary to raise more funds!" or "Of course they should avoid all objectionable images!" We must instead work through the ethical conflict as a real conflict, with good arguments on both sides.

The next section describes the "standard view" outlined above and explains its limitations. Section 7.2 introduces my alternative view, which centers on the moral motivation tradeoff. Section 7.3 examines several possible ways of

---

Cloning Terror," *Theory & Event* 16.3 (2013); Mark Reinhardt, "Painful Photographs: From the Ethics of Spectatorship to Visual Politics," in *Ethics and Images of Pain*, ed. Asbjørn Grønstad and Henrik Gustafsson (New York: Routledge, 2012), 33–57; Mark Reinhardt, Holly Edwards, and Erina Dugganne (eds.), *Beautiful Suffering: Photography and the Traffic in Pain* (Chicago: University of Chicago Press, 2007). For theoretically informed work by scholars whose institutional location is outside of political theory, see Sharon Sliwinski, *Human Rights in Camera* (Chicago: University of Chicago Press, 2011); David Campbell, "Geopolitics and Visuality: Sighting the Darfur Conflict," *Political Geography* 26.4 (2007): 357–82; and David Campbell, "Salgado and the Sahel: Documentary Photography and the Imaging of Famine," in *Rituals of Mediation: International Politics and Social Meaning*, ed. François Debrix and Cynthia Weber (Minneapolis: University of Minnesota Press, 2003), 69–96.

[10] For example, Charles Taylor et al., *Multiculturalism: Examining the Politics of Recognition*, ed. Amy Gutmann (Princeton, NJ: Princeton University Press, 1994); Nancy Fraser, "Rethinking Recognition: Overcoming Displacement and Reification in Cultural Politics," in *Recognition Struggles and Social Movements: Contested Identities, Agency and Power*, ed. Barbara Hobson (Cambridge: Cambridge University Press, 2003), 21–34.

[11] Likewise, if one views the use of some images as morally prohibited regardless of their effects, then there is no moral conflict to speak of, either. But even people who view the use of some degrading images as morally prohibited are also likely to think that there is a set of images the ethical acceptability of which depends on their effects.

navigating the moral motivation tradeoff, focusing on strategies of dilution and critical visual rhetoric. Section 7.4 concludes by discussing how INGOs' reliance on donors shapes them as political actors.

7.1 The Standard View and Its Limitations

I turn first to describing and normatively evaluating the standard view. I will also offer some anecdotal evidence that this view is widely held. This evidence is admittedly weak: as far as I have been able to determine, there have not been many efforts to empirically measure acceptance of the various components of the standard view. But so long as you, the reader, accept some or all of this view, or believe that INGOs accept it, it is worth elucidating its limitations and proposing an alternative.

The first component of the standard view is that humanitarian INGOs face a dilemma of need versus dignity. Indeed, in a handbook for Oxfam photographers, Oxfam states that it faces a "dilemma" of "need vs. dignity."[12] Oxfam is not alone in this perception. Betty Plewes and Rieky Stuart argue that "images of misery and passive victimization generate much more in donations than alternatives [that INGOs] have tested."[13] The epigraph to a report on the ethics of INGOs' use of images is a quotation from an aid practitioner stating that "[t]here is always a tension between the kind of image that brings in the money and one that doesn't demean the subjects of the photo."[14] In a small study, MSF found that "conventional" fundraising campaigns are more effective than other kinds of campaigns.[15] As Redfield sums up, "[w]hatever the ethical qualms they might raise, these images [of "dewy-eyed, nameless children"] seem to work."[16]

Likewise, several codes of conduct and guidelines addressing INGOs' use of images emphasize that "dignity" is the primary register in which images should be ethically evaluated. For example, the Red Cross Code states that its signatories shall "recognize disaster victims as *dignified* human beings,

---

[12] Oxfam UK, "Little Book of Communications." Humanitarian Accountability Partnership International <http://www.hapinternational.org/pool/files/oxfam-gb-little-book-of-communications.pdf>.

[13] Betty Plewes and Rieky Stuart, "The Pornography of Poverty: A Cautionary Fundraising Tale," in *Ethics in Action*, ed. Daniel A. Bell and Jean-Marc Coicaud (New York: Cambridge University Press, 2006), 23–37 (30).

[14] Siobhán McGee, "Report on the Review of the Code of Conduct: Images and Messages relating to the Third World." Presented to Dóchas Development Education Working Group, July 6, 2005 <http://dochas.ie/Shared/Files/7/Siobhan-McGee-Final_Code_of_Conduct_Report.pdf>.

[15] Peter Redfield, *Life in Crisis: The Ethical Journey of Doctors Without Borders* (Berkeley: University of California Press, 2013), 97. The quote about dewy-eyed children is Redfield's characterization.

[16] Redfield, *Life in Crisis*, 97. As I discuss below, research on the "identifiable victim effect" suggests that these images would be even more effective if the children's names were provided.

not hopeless objects."[17] The first "guiding principle" of the Concord Code of Conduct on Images and Messages (henceforth, the Concord Code) states that "[c]hoices of images and messages will be made based on the paramount principles of respect for the *dignity* of the people concerned..."[18]

Even when they do not literally use the term "dignity," critics often argue that the central problem with INGO images is that they undermine dignity. For example, David Campbell writes:

> These images [of "famine iconography"] portray a particular kind of helplessness that reinforces colonial relations of power. With their focus firmly on women and children, these pictures offer up icons of a feminized and infantilized place, a place that is passive, pathetic, and demanding of help from those with the capacity to intervene.[19]

Not all critics pose the problem as a simple conflict of need versus dignity. Some offer up a laundry list of objections to INGO images. For example, Rotimi Sankore suggests that threats to dignity are just one of several interconnected "bads"[20] associated with INGO images:

> Increasingly graphic depictions of poverty projected on a mass scale by an increasing number of organisations over a long period cannot but have an impact on the consciousness of the target audience. That is the desired objective. But there can also be unintended consequences. In this case, the subliminal message unintended or not, is that people in the developing world require indefinite and increasing amounts of help and that without aid charities and donor support, these poor incapable people in Africa or Asia will soon be extinct through disease and starvation. Such simplistic messages foster racist stereotypes, strip entire peoples of their dignity and encourage prejudice.[21]

I will argue below that a central problem with the need versus dignity framework is that it conflates distinct issues that should be disaggregated. Sankore's list avoids this problem to some extent. But not just any disaggregation will do: objections to the use of INGOs images need to be disaggregated

---

[17] International Federation of the Red Cross and Red Crescent Societies, "The Code of Conduct for the International Red Cross and Red Crescent Movement and NGOs in Disaster Relief" <http://www.ifrc.org/en/publications-and-reports/code-of-conduct/>, my italics.

[18] CONCORD, "Code of Conduct on Images and Messages." 2006. <http://www.concordeurope.org/component/k2/item/download/82_8ea8cdb1b7d1bf965513bf2a01054935>, punctuation altered slightly, my italics.

[19] Campbell, "Salgado & the Sahel," 70.

[20] I use this (admittedly awkward) term, rather than "negative effects," in order to also include the idea that these images might be intrinsically objectionable, apart from their effects.

[21] Rotimi Sankore, "Behind the Image: Poverty and 'Development Pornography'." *Pambazuka News*, April 21, 2005 <http://www.pambazuka.org/en/category/rights/27815>. See further citations in Clark, "Representing the MAJORITY WORLD" and David Campbell, "The Problem with Regarding the Photography of Suffering as 'Pornography'." *David Campbell*, January 21, 2011 <http://www.david-campbell.org/2011/01/21/problem-with-regarding-photography-of-suffering-as-pornography/>.

in a way that enables us to better characterize the issues at stake and recognize possible ways of navigating them. While Sankore's laundry list approach is rhetorically effective, it does not do this. Thus, both the reductive focus on need versus dignity and more expansive laundry list approaches such as Sankore's fall short in the same way: they do not provide a conceptually and normatively useful disaggregation of objections to INGOs' use of images.

The second component of the standard view is that it focuses narrowly on INGOs' own materials—their fundraising literature, advertising campaigns, websites, etc.—not on their role in facilitating the publication of images elsewhere.[22] That is, the standard view excludes activities such as Save the Children facilitating the *Daily Mirror* photograph discussed above. For example, the Red Cross Code states that "[i]n *our* information, publicity and advertizing activities, we shall recognize disaster victims as dignified human beings, not hopeless objects."[23] The Concord Code states that it applies to INGOs and their "relevant suppliers, contractors and media," but it excludes facilitating the publication of photographs elsewhere. Overall, the Concord Code gives the impression that its subject matter is INGOs "choos[ing]," "avoid[ing], and "us[ing]" images—not facilitating these activities by others.

The third component of the standard view is that the central locus of concern should be on individual photographs, and, ethically speaking, whether they should get a "thumbs up" or "thumbs down." To clarify, while the second component of the standard view is that it focuses on photographs in INGOs' *own* materials as opposed to those in other outlets, the third feature is that it focuses on the normative content of individual *photographs*, as opposed to looking holistically at how all of the images and words that an INGO disseminates function together. For example, the Concord Code states that *"[c]hoices of images* and messages will be made based on..." and "we strive to: *Choose images* and related messages based on values of..."[24] The Concord Code thus directs our attention to individual images and the question of whether they should be chosen or not, rather than the collective effects of INGO images and the question of how their negative effects might be mitigated. One exception to the focus on giving individual images a thumbs up or thumbs down is that INGO codes of conduct frequently discuss how photographs are taken, especially the need for full, free, and informed consent from the individuals pictured. However, there is far less emphasis on what INGOs do with photographs once they elicit such consent.

---

[22] McGee, "Report on the Review of the Code of Conduct," 21.
[23] The International Federation of Red Cross and Red Crescent Societies, "Code of Conduct," my italics.
[24] CONCORD, "Code of Conduct on Images and Messages."

The fourth component of the standard view is that ethical concerns about INGOs should be practically expressed in the form of rules or codes of conduct to guide INGOs, rather than in the form of other activities or initiatives. Of course, many activities and initiatives can be squeezed into the imperative form of a code of conduct after the fact (e.g. "signatories will undertake initiative X or build institution Y"). However, if one starts with the question, "what rules should we promulgate in our code of conduct?" the results are likely to be far more constrained than they would be if one took a more open-ended approach that asked what INGOs might do to reduce the negative discursive effects of their activities. With this brief account of the standard view before us, I turn next to elucidating the shortcomings of each of its four components.

7.1.1 *Shortcomings of the Standard View*

The limitations of the need versus dignity framework include both problems with the need side of the equation and problems with the dignity side. As we saw in Chapters 4 and 5, INGOs are not always effective at using the funds they raise to meet needs, even when that is their intent. The "need" part of the need versus dignity framework elides this fact, thereby creating a false sense of certainty that, whatever its downsides, the use of objectionable images will at least enable INGOs to meet needs.[25] In addition, many INGOs have, at least in principle, replaced the "need-based" approach to humanitarian and development aid with an approach based on rights. For example, while Oxfam tells its photographers that it faces a dilemma of need versus dignity, its webpage states that it "takes a rights-based approach to its development, humanitarian and campaign work."[26] In other words, by its own account, Oxfam does not (only) face a dilemma of need versus dignity; it also faces a dilemma of *rights* versus dignity: in order to raise money to help people secure their rights, it must use images that undermine their dignity.

Compared to the difficulties with the need side, the difficulties with the dignity side of the equation are more significant. As I noted above, the "bads" associated with INGOs' portrayal-related practices are frequently not disaggregated in a conceptually useful way. Instead they are either collapsed into the single issue of undermining dignity or offered up as a laundry list of objections. But in order to address the ethical issues associated with INGO images, we need to disaggregate them more systematically. In particular, we can identify three

---

[25] By "objectionable" here, I mean "images to which some people object." I do not mean that they should not be used all things considered (that is one of the issues under consideration here). I use the more general term "objectionable" rather than a more specific term such as "degrading" because as we will see, people sometimes object to images for reasons other than that they find them degrading.

[26] Oxfam UK, "Our Work" <http://policy-practice.oxfam.org.uk/our-work>.

categories of concerns. These categories are neither jointly fully comprehensive nor entirely mutually exclusive, but they show that there are at least three largely distinct types of issues at stake.

First are *portrayal-based harms to the individuals pictured.* Photographs and videos, both in INGOs' own materials or facilitated by INGOs but published elsewhere, can harm the specific individuals they literally portray. For example, they can physically endanger individuals by exposing their location to enemies or angering family members.[27] They can cause the individuals portrayed to be socially ostracized, or to feel embarrassed or ashamed. Of course, sometimes individuals have no objection to appearing in INGO fundraising materials or newspapers; this seems to be how Buzanesh Abraham felt about the photograph in Fig. 7.1.[28]

The second category of concerns about INGOs' use of images involves *offense to connected third parties*, by which I mean individuals who are not directly portrayed in INGO images, but are somehow connected to them. Connected third parties include:

(a) Aid recipients who happen not to have been photographed, but who perceive themselves as saliently similar to the individuals photographed.

(b) Non-aid recipients who perceive themselves as saliently similar to the individuals photographed. These perceptions of similarity might be based on attributes such as ethnicity, nationality, race, or religion, or on having been affected by the same event or issue.

(c) People, such as elites in aid-recipient countries, who do not perceive themselves as saliently similar to the individuals photographed, but believe that others perceive them that way.

---

[27] Dóchas, "A Guide to Understanding and Implementing the Code of Conduct on Images & Messages." Dublin: Dóchas, April 2008 <http://www.dochas.ie/Shared/Files/5/Guide_to_Code.pdf>, 10, 12. This is structurally similar to the type of negative effects that characterize spattered hands ethical predicaments (an INGO contributes knowingly but unintentionally to harms perpetrated primarily by others), but the benefit of using the image is unlikely to be proportional to the negative effects, and so would lead to an INGO being guilty, not having spattered hands.

[28] Clark interviewed her three weeks after the photograph was taken:

Clark: What is your opinion of this picture?
Abraham: I give thanks to God for this picture because it helped save the life of my son.
Clark: Were you aware of the picture being taken and that it might be published worldwide?
Abraham: Yes I knew, because they explained to us before they came to visit us what would happen.
Clark: Do you feel embarrassed by this picture at all?
Abraham: No, I don't feel embarrassed, why should I?

(Clark, "Representing the MAJORITY WORLD," 164). While there are few systematic studies of this topic, Clark reports wide variation in how aid recipients feel about having their images used in INGO fundraising campaigns and in the media.

(d) People, again such as elites or activists in aid-recipient countries, who feel deep solidarity with the individuals photographed.

How seriously should we take claims of offense made by members of these groups—especially (d)? People are offended by all sorts of things, including gay marriage. As this example suggests, just because someone is offended by a given practice does not mean that the practice should be prohibited. But unlike individuals who are offended by gay marriage, connected third parties generally have good *prima facie* reason to be offended: their offense arises from a desire to be perceived as capable, dignified human beings.[29] These feelings of offense might not end up outweighing other considerations. But they are more than sufficient to support taking the concerns of offended connected third parties seriously. (Recall that all we are doing here is conceptually disaggregating different kinds of objections to INGOs' portrayal-related practices.)

The third kind of objection to INGOs' use of some kinds of images involves the *negative effects of discursive power*. As I discussed in Chapter 3, when INGOs create, circulate, or facilitate the creation and circulation of images on a large scale, they exercise discursive power. That is, they help to create and sustain shared meanings. As Cameron and Haanstra write, "The faces of development that development organisations present to Northern publics can be understood as an important component of the discursive creation of the 'Third World' and the distinction between North and South..."[30] INGOs' discursive effects include at least two categories:[31]

(a) Direct effects on donor country publics. These effects might include contributing to the development of particular beliefs, attitudes, or orientations on the part of members of these publics. These effects can be significant, especially when people in donor countries lack personal experience or other sources of information to contextualize or counterbalance INGO portrayals.

(b) Indirect effects on people in aid-recipient countries, via individuals in donor countries. People in aid-recipient countries can be

---

[29] For US-based readers, it might help to reflect here on whether you would be offended if a Chinese or Saudi Arabia-based INGO used an image of a partially clothed 4-year-old American girl to raise funds for victims of Hurricane Katrina from publics in China or Saudi Arabia.

[30] John Cameron and Anna Haanstra, "Development Made Sexy: How It Happened and What It Means," *Third World Quarterly* 29.8 (2008): 1475–89 (1476).

[31] A third category is direct discursive effects on offended connected third parties; that is, on people who reject INGO images as offensive but whose perceptions are also affected by these images.

negatively affected by the actions that people in donor countries undertake, or do not undertake, in response to INGO images.[32]

Let me say more about these two types of effects and how they are related. While empirical evidence is limited, it seems likely that INGOs' portrayal-related practices contribute to people in donor countries[33] developing (a) inaccurate perceptions about, (b) inappropriately patronizing attitudes toward, and/or (c) counterproductive ideas about how to "help" severely poor and/or famine-affected people. For example, a close-up photograph of a wide-eyed, dejected child with a distended belly, dressed in rags and staring plaintively at the camera, might be effective at raising funds, but it will likely leave viewers who lack other reliable sources of information about these issues with the (usually) mistaken impression that the child's suffering is fundamentally due to a lack of material resources, that she has no family or community to care for her, and/or that she needs an outsider to "save" her, perhaps by sending food or shoes. These inaccurate perceptions, inappropriate attitudes, and counterproductive ideas can then, in turn, have indirect negative effects in aid-recipient countries, by reducing tourism and foreign investment[34] and undermining those countries' ability to develop "a stronger voice in global decisionmaking processes."[35] Yet another indirect negative effect of INGOs' exercise of discursive power is that it contributes to the mistreatment, in donor countries, of immigrants from aid-recipient countries.[36]

In short, while the standard view states that INGOs face a dilemma of need versus dignity, I have argued that the "dignity" side of the equation is better understood as involving three sets of issues, all of which can, but do not necessarily, involve dignity: harm to the specific individuals photographed, offense to connected third parties, and the direct and indirect negative effects of the exercise of discursive power.

---

[32] Insofar as people in aid-recipient countries have other sources of information about the issues that INGOs address, INGOs exercise less discursive power over them than they do over people in donor countries. Likewise, insofar as donor country publics have more information about earthquakes and tornadoes than they do about famine and severe poverty, INGOs have less discursive power to shape their understandings of the former issues than the latter.

[33] These images are seen by people all over the world, but they are aimed primarily at countries where INGOs raise most of their funds.

[34] For example, Ethiopian tourism commissioner Yusuf Abdullahi Sukkar reports that tourism in Ethiopia seems to be inversely related to media coverage that suggests or is interpreted to suggest that famines are occurring (even when there is no famine) (Clark, "Representing the MAJORITY WORLD," 65). Ironically, Bob Geldof stated that "[He does] not understand why Ethiopia is not one of the biggest tourist destinations in the world...It is so beautiful and it is so historic and I really never understand why people are not coming here." Cited in Clark, "Representing the MAJORITY WORLD," 64.

[35] Oxfam, "Little Book of Communications." See also Clark, "Representing the MAJORITY WORLD," 66–7.

[36] Plewes and Stuart, "The Pornography of Poverty," 24.

The second component of the standard view, which I shall now contest, is its focus on INGOs' own materials. As the opening anecdote of this chapter suggests, INGOs do not only create and use images themselves, they also facilitate the creation and dissemination of images in other outlets. If we are interested in ethical issues surrounding INGOs and visual portrayals, it is essential to look beyond INGOs' own fundraising materials, to their role in facilitating the publication of images elsewhere. That is, we must study not only INGOs' own images, but their portrayal-related practices more generally.

Humanitarian INGOs regularly provide journalists and photojournalists with transportation, lodging, food, water, information, translation, companionship, access to facilities (e.g. hospitals), and introductions to local people. Some INGOs even allow photojournalists to "embed" with them, in a way that is somewhat similar to how photojournalists embed with military units.[37] Photojournalists benefit from the support and insight that INGOs provide, INGOs benefit from the free publicity that comes from being featured in news articles. As one photojournalist put it:

> [L]et's be real—there's only two kinds of people that go to conflict zones and places in crisis and that's the NGOs and the journalists. We're in bed with each other. You can't operate without them. Any conflict, any crisis, you're going to have to deal with an NGO. That's just fact.[38]

One indication of the scale of INGOs' cooperation with photojournalists is that the elite photo agency VII's online archive contains more than a thousand photographs taken at MSF program sites, as well as hundreds of photographs taken in or around programs run by other INGOs, including Merlin, IRC, Save the Children, and Oxfam. The online archives of two other prominent photo agencies, Magnum and Panos, also feature hundreds of photographs taken at INGO project sites, including projects run by MSF, Save the Children, World Vision, and Oxfam.[39]

---

[37] For a description of, and vociferous objection to, embedding photojournalists with INGOs, see James Johnson, "Photographer Embedded With NGO Reproduces 1970s Famine Photos," *Notes on) Politics, Theory & Photography*, July 24, 2008 <http://politicstheoryphotography.blogspot.com/2008/07/photographer-embedded-with-ngo.html>. While more formal practices of embedding appear to be more recent, close cooperation between INGOs and photojournalists is nothing new. Oxfam and World Vision facilitated the creation of the famous video of the 1984 Ethiopian famine by the journalist Michael Buerk and videographer Mohammad Amin, and employees of Save the Children and MSF are featured in the report itself. Clark, "Representing the MAJORITY WORLD," 142–5.

[38] James Estrin, "When Interest Creates a Conflict," November 19, 2012 <http://lens.blogs.nytimes.com/2012/11/19/when-interest-creates-a-conflict/>.

[39] The micro-politics of who controls the images that are created and disseminated in these partnerships deserves further study. INGOs sometimes impose strict requirements on photographers. See Marco Ryan, "On Assignment with The Asia Foundation in Laos." *marco ryan photography: Frankfurt* <http://www.marcoryanphotography.com/on-assignment-with-the-asia-foundation-in-laos/> and Judith Gelman Myers, "NGOs to the Rescue." *PopPhoto*, December 16,

INGOs also help to shape portrayals of famine and severe poverty in the mainstream media in other, even more indirect, ways. In particular, INGOs help to create and sustain the narratives, visual and otherwise, that newspaper photo editors seek to evoke when they choose which photographs to publish, regardless of whether the creation of those photographs was facilitated by INGOs. Likewise, some of the most important instances of portrayals of famine over the past fifty years were the result of joint INGO–government initiatives.[40] To sum up: humanitarian INGOs are imbricated in a global system of visual meaning-making, especially around issues of famine and severe poverty. As a result, they play an integral role in the circulation of images that are viewed by much larger audiences than images in INGOs' own materials. Any effort to reckon with the ethics of INGOs' visual portrayals must address this role.

The third component of the standard view is that it focuses on giving a thumbs up or thumbs down to individual photographs in isolation, rather than considering INGOs' images more holistically and understanding how they function. Yet just as it would be arbitrary to evaluate the discursive effects of individual elements within a single photograph (e.g. this person, that door), rather than the discursive effects of the photograph as a whole, it is also arbitrary to evaluate the discursive effects of a single photograph, as opposed to an INGO's discursive effects more generally.

Indeed, the effects of any given photograph depend on both the immediate context and the broader universe of images that form the backdrop against which it is viewed: an image of an African child dressed in rags with a distended belly and flies around her eyes functions as it does, in part, because it is one of a vast number of similar images that circulate regularly— alongside a relative dearth of images of happy, healthy, well-dressed African children playing, studying, or pursuing hobbies. In other words, no image is stereotypical on its own; an image can only be stereotypical in virtue of the existence of other, similar, images. We should therefore not look at INGO images in isolation from either the slightly broader communication strategies of which they are a part (including photographs, text, and videos) or the much broader social and political contexts in which they circulate.

The fourth and final component of the standard view is that it focuses primarily on rules, guidelines, and codes of conduct for INGOs as the

2008 <http://www.popphoto.com/how-to/2008/12/ngos-to-rescue>. In other cases, photographers have more autonomy. For example, in the acknowledgments to *Congo: Forgotten War*, the photographers of VII thank MSF for allowing them to "tell the story of the DRC in our own way," although it is notable that VII thought it appropriate to thank MSF for this (rather than assuming it as a given).

[40] For example, the famous Buerk/Amin video of the 1984 Ethiopian famine was created for an appeal of the Disaster Emergency Committee. The DEC, founded in 1963, is a group of fourteen large British humanitarian organizations. Whenever it launches a joint emergency appeal, the BBC airs a television special about the issue hosted by a celebrity in at least one prime-time time slot after the news. Disasters Emergency Committee, "Corporate Supporters." Updated October 10, 2012 <http://www.dec.org.uk/about-dec/corporate-supporters>.

appropriate practical output of ethical reflection on the issue of INGO images. Existing rules and codes appear to have played some role in reducing the number and severity of objectionable images used by mainstream INGOs. However, this rule-based approach has significant limitations. First, although rules or guidelines might alter an organization's practices, or even its culture or sensibility, absent the threat of sanction for violations, guidelines do not alter underlying incentives: INGOs still have an incentive to use the images that generate the most money, which means that they have an incentive to push the boundaries of, or find loopholes in, their own rules. (We saw this with Save the Children facilitating the publication of photographs in a newspaper that it would not publish in its own materials.) Other examples of such loophole-finding include replacing "negative" images of pain and suffering with "positive" images of cute smiling children, and replacing images of helpless-seeming aid recipients with images of heroic expatriate aid workers.[41] While the latter types of images in both of these examples technically comply with rules against degrading images (as "degrading" is typically understood), they still reinforce harmful stereotypes. Finally, a focus on compliance with rules or codes of conduct diverts attention away from the possibility that more promising solutions to the problems created by INGO portrayals might lie not with INGOs themselves, regardless of what rules they follow, but rather with other actors, institutions, or states of affairs, that INGOs could potentially support.

7.2 An Alternative Approach: The Moral Motivation Tradeoff

In light of the foregoing limitations of the standard view, I turn now to sketching an alternative. Rather than a dilemma of need versus dignity, I will suggest that we should view INGOs as instead facing a *moral motivation tradeoff*. At the heart of this tradeoff is the observation that the photographs that most effectively motivate people in donor countries to donate to INGOs are also *systematically* likely to have negative discursive effects. These images also sometimes harm the individuals photographed and offend connected third parties. However, these effects are less systematically tied to features of photographs that also make those photographs more effective at raising funds.[42]

The term "moral motivation tradeoff" avoids both of the problems with "need" described above: it does not assume that INGOs will be able to meet

---

[41] Kate Manzo, "Imaging Humanitarianism: NGO Identity and the Iconography of Childhood," *Antipode* 40.4 (2008): 632–57; Cameron and Haanstra, "Development Made Sexy."
[42] The relationship between effectiveness at fundraising and offense to connected third parties is closer than the relationship between effectiveness at fundraising and harm to individuals.

needs with the funds that they raise, nor does it assume that they will try to meet needs, rather than, for example, help people to secure their rights. The *moral* motivation tradeoff also reflects the idea that the tradeoff does not arise as the result of just any fundraising effort; it is limited to efforts that function by motivating individuals through appeals to moral reasons, broadly construed—as opposed to, say, self-interest. "Moral motivation *tradeoff*" also avoids the problems with "dignity" described above. In particular, by referring to a tradeoff, rather than one thing "versus" another, it leaves room for the three sets of concerns discussed above (harm to individuals pictured, offense to connected third parties, and negative effects of discursive power). Finally, while it suggests that there is a conflict or tension, the term "tradeoff," unlike the term "dilemma," the term "tradeoff" does not suggest that all available options are necessarily equally bad.

What features of images both motivate individual donors to donate and have negative discursive effects? While it must be taken with a grain of salt,[43] social psychology research on the "identifiable victim effect" and related phenomena suggests that the most effective fundraising photographs for humanitarian INGOs are close-up images of dejected-looking individuals, especially women or children,[44] without background statistical information about the larger issues affecting them.[45] Images of crowds, or even of two people, appear to be less effective at eliciting donations than

[43] This research program is itself in some ways shaped by the phenomena that it purports to explain. For example, Slovic (see note 45 below) frames his research as helping to explain why outsiders do not respond more quickly or aggressively to genocide, but most of the studies he summarizes do not look at responses to intentional violent harm, but rather an (apparent) need for basic resources such as food. Images that depict direct violent harm—while they could well have other problems—might avoid some of the discursive pitfalls described here. For example, they might be exploitative or voyeuristic, but they might not portray people as lacking in agency. Moreover, Slovic's main dependent variable, and that of some other researchers in this area, is how much money people donate. If the outcome of interest had instead been learning more, writing a letter, joining a protest march, or working for a political candidate, the sorts of images that would be deemed effective might have been very different.

[44] One might think that the effectiveness of these images in raising funds is about to wear off, and that "compassion fatigue" (see Susan D. Moeller, *Compassion Fatigue: How the Media Sell Disease, Famine, War, and Death* (New York: Routledge, 1999)) is about to commence in earnest. There is evidence to suggest otherwise. As early as 1966, Oxfam was already running advertisements asking if readers were "Bored with pictures of starving children?" Yet almost twenty years later, in 1984, admittedly more dramatic versions of those same types of images in the Buerk/Amin report generated a tremendous outpouring of donations (Clark, "Representing the MAJORITY WORLD," 145). This response was unprecedented at the time, but modest compared to later disasters. Moreover, while there is some annual variation, the number of people who donate to INGOs and the amount that is donated have risen steadily since the mid-1980s.

[45] Paul Slovic, "'If I Look at the Mass I Will Never Act': Psychic Numbing and Genocide," *Judgment and Decision Making* 2.2 (2007): 79–95. The mechanism here appears to be that people like to solve the "whole" problem, and if you situate an individual aid recipient in a broader context of other similarly situated individuals, it becomes clear that one donation is not going to solve the whole problem. When subjects are told that background statistical information

images of a single person.[46] Likewise, images of individuals looking happy are less effective than images of individuals looking neutral or downcast.[47] Indeed, a study of efforts to raise money for people with handicaps found that

> images which elicit the greatest commitment to give money are those most closely associated with feelings of guilt, sympathy and pity and are negatively associated with posters which illustrate people with a mental handicap as having the same rights, value and capability as non-handicapped persons.[48]

As I noted above, while they might be effective at raising funds, these types of photographs can have all three kinds of negative effects described above. However, the connection between the very features of these images that motivate people to donate, and the "bads" that result from the dissemination of these images, is tightest for the exercise of discursive power. For example, the fact that a photograph shows a close-up image of a single individual rather than a group *both* makes that photograph a more effective fundraising tool *and* contributes to a misperception of famine-affected people as outside of politics. That the very same feature has both of these effects is at the heart of the moral motivation tradeoff.

The second component of my alternative to the standard view is that the moral motivation tradeoff arises in the context of a wide range of INGO portrayal-related practices, not only the images in their own materials. Both sides of the moral motivation tradeoff—the fact that particular images are effective at raising funds from morally motivated donors and the harmful effects of those images—are present, even when the images are published in newspapers rather than INGOs' own materials. Indeed, all three sets of concerns discussed above are just as likely to arise, indeed they might be more likely to arise, if a given image is published in newspapers than if it is published in an INGO's own materials. It is therefore hard to see how an INGO could be less blameworthy for intentionally facilitating the publication of a

suppresses donations, they do not donate more in response to an image with background statistical information; they merely donate less in response to the single individual with no statistical information (Slovic, "Psychic Numbing and Genocide").

[46] Slovic, "Psychic Numbing and Genocide," 91. Other possible explanations for the identifiable victim effect include that the distress of the identifiable victim is more *vivid* than the distress of the statistical victim; that there is more *certainty* that the identifiable victim will die or suffer severe harm unless she receives aid; and that in the case of the identifiable victim the event prompting the need for assistance has already happened (*"ex-post evaluation"*). See Karen Jenni, and George Loewenstein, "Explaining the Identifiable Victim Effect," *Journal of Risk and Uncertainty* 14.3 (1997): 235–57.

[47] Deborah Small, "Sympathy Biases and Sympathy Appeals: Reducing Social Distance to Boost Charitable Contributions," in *The Science of Giving: Experimental Approaches to the Study of Charity*, ed. Daniel M. Oppenheimer and Christopher Y. Olivola (New York: Psychology Press, 2011), 149–60.

[48] Caroline B. Eayrs and Nick Ellis, "Charity Advertising: For or Against People with a Mental Handicap?" *British Journal of Social Psychology* 29.4 (1990): 349–66 (349).

degrading image in a newspaper than it would be for publishing that same image in its own materials.[49]

The third and fourth components of my alternative view do not emerge directly out of the moral motivation tradeoff, but they complement it. The third is the idea that we should look beyond individual photographs (whether in INGOs' own materials or in other outlets) and toward how sets of images work together. The fourth is that, in thinking about possible strategies for reducing the moral motivation tradeoff, we might do well to look beyond rules and codes of conduct, and toward alternative forms of creative action and institution-building. I turn now to these alternative forms, showing that the most effective strategies involve moving beyond individual photographs.

7.3 Strategies for Navigating the Moral Motivation Tradeoff

I will distinguish among possible strategies based on how "costly" they are to INGOs, in terms of images forgone; that is, to what extent does a given strategy for minimizing negative effects prohibit images that are likely to be effective for raising funds? I will also distinguish among these strategies based on which of the three aforementioned sets of concerns they address. We will see that while harm to individuals photographed is, at least in principle, reasonably easy to address, the issues of offense to connected third parties and the negative effects of discursive power are much more challenging. I will suggest that two strategies, dilution and—especially—critical visual rhetoric, are most promising for addressing these issues. However, the fact that even these strategies have significant limitations suggests that INGOs' reliance on individual donors for funds is likely to be a source of deep moral compromise, absent very significant changes on the part of both INGOs and their donors.

Perhaps the most obvious strategy for navigating the moral motivation tradeoff is to give individuals who are, or would be, recognizable in any given photograph a *veto* over the creation and dissemination of that photograph. This strategy addresses the first set of issues discussed above: harm to the specific individuals portrayed. It requires that INGOs obtain, in advance, full, free, and informed consent from individuals who are or would be recognizable in a photograph, to both take and use their photograph.[50] Requirements along these

---

[49] The fact that, in the newspaper case, the INGO achieved the outcome jointly with others does not lessen its moral responsibility, any more than working with accomplices makes a bank robber less guilty.

[50] On the difficulties with and complexities of informed consent, see Onora O'Neill, "Some Limits of Informed Consent," *Journal of Medical Ethics* 29.1 (2003): 4–7; Neil Manson and Onora O'Neill, *Rethinking Informed Consent in Bioethics* (Cambridge and New York: Cambridge

lines are uncontroversial and already included in many INGOs' image-related rules and guidelines. I will assume that INGOs should adopt them.

Because some individuals, such as Buzanesh Abraham, are (apparently) willing to give full, free, and informed consent to INGOs and photojournalists to take and use their photograph, abiding by this requirement does not appear to be very costly to INGOs, in the sense of significantly curtailing the set of images they can use. Indeed, the most interesting aspect of the veto strategy is not the question of whether INGOs should adopt it (they should), but rather the fact that it addresses only one of the three sets of concerns described above: an image might avoid harming the individuals literally pictured in it, but also offend connected third parties and have negative discursive effects. Efforts to address the latter two sets of concerns therefore need to look beyond the veto strategy.

One possibility is to complement the veto strategy with another seemingly attractive strategy: *hiring local photographers*. But while it might benefit local photographers and their families economically, and in some cases reduce the grating symbolic politics of white expatriates taking pictures of non-white aid recipients, there is little reason to think that this strategy would result in very different photographs from the ones taken by expatriate photographers. Locally hired photographers, operating (as most do) with the same knowledge about aid narratives and a similar incentive structure to European or American photographers, would likely take very similar photographs. D. J. Clark shows that this was the case for the photograph of Abraham and Geldof discussed above.[51] While the "cost" of this strategy for INGOs in the form of forgone images would therefore again be low, and while it might have other beneficial effects, it would also not address any of our three main sets of concerns.

In contrast, a *ban* on objectionable images, if it could be enforced, would avoid offense to connected third parties and the negative effects of discursive power. (It would not necessarily address harm to the individuals pictured, because even an image that did not appear objectionable could endanger the individual pictured.) However, the difficulty of enforcing compliance, together with disagreement about what kinds of images should be banned, would make a ban difficult to implement. Banning images could also end up directing donations to poor-quality INGOs that refused to adhere to the ban.[52] A widely accepted *voluntary scheme* analogous to "fair trade" coffee might also be effective, and would not require forcing recalcitrant INGOs to

University Press, 2007); Tom L. Beauchamp, "Informed Consent: Its History, Meaning, and Present Challenges," *Cambridge Quarterly of Healthcare Ethics* 20.4 (2011): 515–23.

[51] Clark, "Representing the MAJORITY WORLD," 122–8.

[52] A ban would also be more effective if it was endorsed by both the broadcast media and INGOs; such an approach would need to walk the line between avoiding negative effects and not impinging on press freedom.

obey: INGOs could sign up to a set of principles governing the use of images, and receive some form of public recognition in return. But as with an enforced ban, some entity would have to police individual images and decide whether they were acceptable. Both an enforced ban and a voluntary scheme would also be very costly in terms of donations to INGOs (unless, of course, INGOs could find other equally motivating images, or persuade donors to donate without the use of such images, in which case there would be much less need for a ban).

Another strategy—one with a much lower cost in images forgone—would be for an INGO to act as a *buffer* between its donors and aid recipients. For example, World Vision's website features close-up photographs of individual smiling children whom visitors to the website are invited to sponsor. These are exactly the sort of context-less, infantilizing, depoliticizing images that critics of INGO imagery rail against. World Vision's website states in large letters that: "Sponsoring a child is the most powerful way *you* can fight poverty." One has to scroll down and click on a tab to find out that rather than providing goods and services to individual sponsored children, "World Vision plans and works alongside community members to help build healthy communities for children."[53]

World Vision thus recognizes that assisting only individual sponsored children is divisive and inefficient. But rather than try to explain this to donors, it takes advantage of donors' interest in "identifiable victims."[54] In this way, World Vision acts as a buffer against the preferences (for apolitical and individually oriented projects) that the visual strategy of its own website calls forth. It is easy to see why this is manipulative and therefore harmful to donors. But the moral motivation tradeoff approach also helps us to see exactly how it is harmful to people in aid-recipient countries. The buffer guards aid recipients against *one* indirect negative discursive effect of these images: donors' ill-conceived ideas about how to "help" (in this case, by sponsoring individual children). But it does not guard against other direct and indirect negative discursive effects of these images, such as contributing to the development of patronizing attitudes or inaccurate perceptions in donor countries, which in turn can have the indirect negative effects on aid-recipient countries described above, for example reduced investment and tourism. Nor, of course, does the buffering strategy do anything to address offense to connected third parties.[55] Again, what is striking about the buffering strategy is how few problems it solves.

---

[53] See World Vision's "Sponsor Child" webpage <http://www.worldvision.org/>.

[54] Slovic, "Psychic Numbing and Genocide."

[55] It is worth noticing here that while this buffering strategy differs in degree from what many INGOs usually do when they use images of context-less, sad-looking individuals to elicit donations but then use the money they raise in a politically savvy way that promotes rights and dignity, it is not so different in kind. My thanks to Colin Kielty for this observation.

We have been looking for a strategy or set of strategies that address the three sets of concerns described above, without too much sacrifice in terms of fundraising for INGOs. We saw that veto is low cost but only addresses harm to individual pictured; hiring local photographers is low cost but addresses none of these concerns (although it might have other beneficial effects); an enforced or voluntary ban would address both offense to connected third parties and the negative effects of discursive power, but it would be costly for INGOs and very difficult to implement. Finally, in addition to being manipulative, buffering might avoid one or more indirect negative discursive effects, but not all indirect discursive effects and not direct discursive effects.

We therefore need to cast a wider net, looking beyond bans, voluntary schemes, and other rules or policies that might appear in an INGO code of conduct. One seemingly more promising strategy is what I will call *dilution*. The goal of this strategy is to create a universe of images diverse enough that INGO portrayals would not reinforce harmful and inaccurate stereotypes, or at least would do so to a lesser degree. Rather than reducing the creation and circulation of some kinds of images by INGOs, the dilution strategy focuses on *increasing* images created by other actors with other perspectives and incentives. It is because of INGOs' tendency to exploit loopholes in rules that these other images must be created and circulated not by INGOs themselves, but by other kinds of actors, such as, for example, the members of the Drik photo agency in Bangladesh. As Shahidul Alam, creator of the Drik photo agency writes, "We have no problems with others telling the story. Our own perceptions need to be challenged. It is the *monopoly* that the West has had on our storytelling that we question."[56]

I argued in Chapter 3 that the appropriate normative standard for evaluating an INGO's exercise of discursive power is that it should not constrain other actors from critically analyzing and, if they choose, altering their own perceptions and assumptions. Dilution would accomplish this by depriving INGOs' images of at least some of their force, by counterbalancing them with other images. Moreover, consistent with Alam's position, the dilution strategy does not reflect an assumption that INGOs should exercise *no* discursive power, nor that INGOs' exercise of discursive power can never serve a useful purpose.

When it comes to shaping the perceptions of people in donor countries about poor and famine-affected people and the challenges they face, humanitarian INGOs are surely second-best actors: their primary aim is to raise funds, not create accurate or humane portrayals. Yet it appears that

---

[56] Quoted in James Estrin, "Wresting the Narrative From the West." My italics. *New York Times Lens Blog*, July 19, 2013 <http://lens.blogs.nytimes.com/2013/07/19/wresting-the-narrative-from-the-west/>.

there is no one (type of) first-best actor for serving this role—not local photographers, and not even aid recipients themselves. What is first-best in this situation, as Alam also implied, is an institutional context in which a diverse array of differently situated actors, with different experiences, identities, and incentives, contribute to the shaping of shared perceptions. These are some of the reasons why dilution is an appropriate strategy for addressing the moral motivation tradeoff.

Some INGOs, most prominently MSF and Oxfam, have engaged in something like dilution: they have set up partnerships with more artistically oriented photographers to make photographic books and exhibits about the issues that they address and the people with whom they work. For example, Oxfam worked with the British fashion photographer Rankin to create a book of photographs, *We are Congo*, that depicts ordinary Congolese people looking happy or content against a plain white background.[57] Likewise, MSF has a formal partnership with the photo agency VII (mentioned above). They jointly produced a book, *Congo: Forgotten War*, along with several other books and educational campaigns.[58] Although these appear to be promising and valuable efforts to raise money and awareness that also break out of the usual visual tropes of INGO fundraising materials, they are not examples of full-fledged dilution, because the books are not entirely independent of INGOs' influence and have very limited circulation.

Another way to implement the dilution strategy would be to combine it with the fair trade model discussed above to yield something like a "cap-and-trade" scheme for INGO photographs: a limited number of potentially offensive images (not vetoed by the individuals photographed) would be allowed to be published. INGOs and other media outlets participating in the scheme would bid for the chance to use these images; the money raised would be donated to the Drik photo agency, PhotoVoice, Sudden Flowers (the latter two of which are discussed below), or similar endeavors.[59] Such a scheme would reduce the number of degrading images in circulation and ensure that the only degrading images that were published were those that (INGOs thought) would be most effective at raising funds. It would also dilute the

[57] For excerpts from Oxfam's *We Are Congo* photo book, see <http://www.editorialdesign served.co/gallery/Oxfam-We-Are-Congo/752449> and <http://www.thefullservice.co.uk/project/ oxfam-congo-design/>. While such images are arguably objectionable, they are objectionable in a different way than standard INGO images, and so can serve to counterbalance them.

[58] See MSF's *Congo: Forgotten War* website at <http://www.doctorswithoutborders.org/events/ exhibits/forgottenwar/> and <http://www.pillandpillow.com/msfCongo/mainEng.html>. Other examples of such joint book projects going back to the 1980s are discussed in Campbell, "Salgado and the Sahel."

[59] See the Drik, PhotoVoice, and Sudden Flowers websites at <http://drik.net/>, <http://www. photovoice.org/>, and <http://www.ericgottesman.net/Sudden-Flowers-the-book/SUDDEN-FLOWERS/1/caption/>, respectively.

negative discursive effects of the images that were published, by supporting alternative portrayals.

Despite its advantages, the obvious problems with the cap-and-trade version of the dilution strategy bring out the limitations of the dilution strategy more generally. Most importantly, while it addresses the issue of negative discursive effects, the dilution strategy does not address the issue of offense to connected third parties. Offense is not only a matter of how many instances of a particular kind of image are in circulation; it is also relational: people are offended, at least sometimes, by an INGO's willingness to use a particular image. The fact that an INGO paid to use a degrading image in the context of a cap-and-trade scheme would, one suspects, not make a connected third party feel any less offended.

Another strategy, one that might address both the offensiveness issue and the discursive power issue, without giving up too much in the way of effective fundraising, is what I will call *critical visual rhetoric*. The idea here is that INGOs can use a two-step process to alter the meaning and effects of the images that they use in a way that not only reduces negative discursive effects, but also is at least potentially responsive to the concerns of connected third parties who might otherwise find those images offensive. More specifically, INGOs can use potentially objectionable images to grab the attention of viewers in donor countries and get them to make an initial donation (step 1). This is the "visual rhetoric" part. But rather than stopping there, they can use other images, text, or other features of a given image to draw viewers into a more nuanced understanding of the issues at hand (step 2).[60] This is the "critical" part. (While these two steps can occur almost simultaneously, it is useful to distinguish them conceptually.)

This two-step process is not a new idea: in the same booklet for photographers in which Oxfam describes the "dilemma" of "need vs. dignity," it also suggests a way out of this dilemma: "Potential supporters can be 'hooked' by strong images of the inspiring people we work with and the things they do. And then motivated to act, to give, and to be passionate about Oxfam."[61] But what the Oxfam booklet does not acknowledge is that the "strong" images that "hook" people are often the same images that it

---

[60] As I was finishing the research for this book, Sullivan et al. published a study suggesting that this two-step process faces an additional challenge: overly simplified narratives, such as the initial Kony2012 video, prompt moral outrage, but this outrage diminishes with the passage of time and with acknowledgment of the complexities of the situation (Daniel Sullivan, Mark J. Landau, and Aaron C. Kay, "When Enemies Go Viral (or Not)—A Real-Time Experiment During the 'Stop Kony' Campaign," *Psychology of Popular Media Culture*, April 14, 2014). This research suggests the importance of more in-depth study of alternatives to moral outrage as a source of political motivation, and how acknowledgment of complexity can be made consistent with the persistence of moral outrage.

[61] Oxfam, "Little Book of Communications."

elsewhere described as generating the need versus dignity dilemma. In other words, even with the two-step process, there is still moral compromise: critical visual rhetoric still involves INGOs using images that, all else being equal, it would be better for them not to use. The difference is that these images are part of a broader strategy that connected third parties might endorse, because it is aimed at not only raising money, but also increasing understanding.

Engaging in critical visual rhetoric responsibly and effectively would require that INGOs try to discern *exactly* what features of images grab viewers' attention and prompt them to donate; for example, that only a single individual is portrayed rather than several people, and avoid objectionable features that do not promote donating, such as images that show someone who is naked or extremely bedraggled. For the most part, as we will see, successful strategies of critical visual rhetoric involve photographs with particular kinds of captions, organized groups of photographs, and videos—not individual photographs with standard captions in isolation.

The two-step process of critical visual rhetoric that I am describing can be usefully compared to *political* rhetoric, as recently "revived" by political theorists.[62] Several political theorists have recently sought to recuperate "good" rhetoric from its Habermasian and Rawlsian detractors, who have found rhetoric unreasonable, manipulative, or coercive.[63] However, these theorists have focused primarily on verbal rhetoric—on *"speech* designed to persuade"— rather than on visual images, which are my main focus here.[64] What I am calling critical visual rhetoric also differs from (verbal) political rhetoric in three additional ways.

First, investigations of verbal rhetoric have focused primarily on the relationship between two parties: the speaker and her audience. The salient question is whether a speaker can engage in rhetoric without manipulating, coercing, or disrespecting her audience. In the context of INGO portrayals, in contrast, there are (at least) four parties: the "speaker"—or in this case, the visual portrayer (the INGO), the audience (including but not only people in donor countries), the subject (the individuals or groups literally portrayed), and connected third parties. The question for INGOs is not only how to

---

[62] Bryan Garsten, "The Rhetorical Revival in Political Theory," *Annual Review of Political Science* 14 (2011): 159–80.

[63] Simone Chambers, "Rhetoric and the Public Sphere: Has Deliberative Democracy Abandoned Mass Democracy?" *Political Theory* 37.3 (2009): 323–50.

[64] Bryan Garsten, *Saving Persuasion: A Defense of Rhetoric and Judgment* (Cambridge, MA: Harvard University Press, 2009), 5. There is a large literature on visual rhetoric in media studies and American studies but it is less helpful for my purposes than the recent literature on rhetoric in political theory. See Lester C. Olson, Cara A. Finnegan, and Diane S. Hope, *Visual Rhetoric: A Reader in Communication and American Culture* (Los Angeles: Sage, 2008); Robert Hariman and John Louis Lucaites, *No Caption Needed: Iconic Photographs, Public Culture, and Liberal Democracy* (Chicago: University of Chicago Press, 2007).

avoid manipulating their audience, but also how to treat those they portray and connected third parties.[65]

Second, proponents of verbal rhetoric have focused primarily on enabling people who are formally members of a polity to effectively participate in that polity's political life. According to theorists such as Iris Young, James Bohman, and Lynn Sanders, verbal rhetoric helps members of marginalized groups to get their voices heard.[66] These scholars argue that one benefit of recognizing the legitimacy of rhetorical speech, for example passionate pleas, angry outbursts, testimony, jokes, and stories, is that people who are, or who are perceived by others to be, less adept at rational deliberation (or whom the boundaries of "rational deliberation" have been designed to exclude) can nonetheless convey their perspectives and opinions to their fellow citizens on more equal footing.

While critical visual rhetoric can help with this project, it is also, and indeed perhaps better, suited for another population: people who are not recognized as formal members of a polity, especially those whose very existence goes unnoticed. These are people who do not have a recognized-in-principle-but-denied-in-practice political right to a say in a polity's collective decisions, but do still have a moral right to have their concerns heard, or their suffering or outrage acknowledged. For these groups, it is not enough for others to recognize their style of self-expression or communication as legitimate. This is because their right to voice their opinion is not recognized in the first place. Indeed, no one is paying them one iota of attention. For them, word-based communication is frequently not enough to get noticed. Without photographs or video, their claims are likely to be—literally—overlooked.

Photographs and video, therefore, can help groups succeed at the initial and necessary—albeit insufficient—task of getting noticed. But not just any photographs or videos will suffice. To get attention, images cannot merely contain information. Formally excluded and invisible groups have no voice or institutional recourse to effectively demand, "look at these photos!" The photographs themselves must make this demand. The 1984 Ethiopian famine, the torture of prisoners at Abu Ghraib, and even factory farms in the US, are all examples of cases in which "the facts were known" long before

---

[65] In this respect, the relationship resembles a relationship of representation, with a representative, a represented, and an audience. (But cf. Michael Saward, *The Representative Claim* (New York: Oxford University Press, 2010)). Of course, verbal rhetoric can also be disrespectful of third parties, although this danger is mentioned less often in discussions of verbal rhetoric than it is in discussions of visual rhetoric.

[66] Young, "Communication and the Other"; James Bohman, *Public Deliberation: Pluralism, Complexity, and Democracy* (Cambridge, MA: MIT Press, 2000); Lynn M. Sanders, "Against Deliberation," *Political Theory* 25.3 (1997): 347–76. See also John S. Dryzek, "Rhetoric in Democracy: A Systemic Appreciation," *Political Theory* 38.3 (2010): 319–39.

visual images became publicly available. But it took images to compel (so to speak) a public response. As Donald Rumsfeld said about Abu Ghraib, "it is the photographs that give one the vivid realization of what actually took place. Words don't do it."[67] Thus, one can imagine a process in which critical visual rhetoric about a particular group opens the door for verbal rhetoric by members of that group themselves.[68] In cases of famine, in particular, visual manifestations of the problem generally arise too late, such that relying on visual images alone can lead to a delayed response.[69]

The third main difference between verbal political rhetoric and critical visual rhetoric involves how they function. Garsten describes (verbal) political rhetoric as a process of meeting people where they are, or "engag[ing] with others wherever they stand and [beginning] our argument there," even if the people we wish to engage with are "opinionated, self-interested, sentimental, partial to their friends and family and often unreasonable."[70] To illustrate this strategy, Drzyek and Garsten offer, respectively, the examples of trying to persuade a religious person of the merits of religious toleration by drawing on arguments from within that person's religion, and defending civil rights legislation to Southern white supremacists in a drawl that signifies "I am one of you."[71] The corollary to this approach in the context of visual rhetoric—that is, the visual version of meeting people where they are—is the use of images that are in some respects clichéd or stereotypical. The clichéd and stereotypical qualities of these images make them legible by repeating back to people things they (think they) know. In both contexts, the two crucial questions are: how far does the rhetorician have to go in repeating back some version of the ideas that she wishes to overturn in order to bring her audience along with her, and do the benefits of doing so outweigh the negative effects?

Let me turn now to some examples of more and less successful critical visual rhetoric. A first example is a photograph that, *taken on its own*, fails the first step of critical visual rhetoric. (As I discuss below, seen in its larger context it appears to be far "more effective." This photograph, "My Favorite

---

[67] *Washington Post*, "Rumsfeld Testifies Before Senate Armed Services Committee," May 7, 2004 <http://www.washingtonpost.com/wp-dyn/articles/A8575-2004May7.html>.

[68] This is not to say that words are always more precise than images; in the wake of Hurricane Katrina, labels on images of whites "collecting supplies" and blacks "looting" highlighted in dramatic fashion how words can distort as well as clarify.

[69] Clark, "Representing the MAJORITY WORLD," 151. This is also the case with violent conflict: images of children who have been gassed or gravely injured by bombs might prompt a response, but the response is too late for those children.

[70] Garsten, *Saving Persuasion*, 3 and 4; Dryzek, "Rhetoric in Democracy": "Crucially, rhetoric recognizes the situated character of its audience" (320).

[71] Examples from Dryzek, "Rhetoric in Democracy" and Garsten, *Saving Persuasion*, 193–4, respectively.

Figure 7.2. "My Favorite Things." Tenanesh Kifyalew and Eric Gottesman, 2004

Things," depicts an HIV-positive 12-year-old girl from Addis Ababa, Tenanesh Kifyalew (Fig. 7.2).[72]

Tenanesh created this photograph in the context of a small photography program in Ethiopia called Sudden Flowers that gave children from different backgrounds cameras to document and reflect on their lives.[73] As the caption suggests, this photograph shows Tenanesh posing with some of her favorite things. While she did not press the button on the camera, she controlled the contents and composition of the photograph.

In that it empowers its subject and defies outsiders' paternalistic assumptions about African children with HIV, this photograph (again, taken on its own) is normatively very attractive. The image is strikingly like that of a middle-class 12-year-old in the contemporary US; it is the kind of image that many people in the US might have in the family photo album in their basement. For better or worse, looking at the photograph on its own leads the distant viewer to see Tenanesh as just another 12-year-old. This is in part because the photograph depicts material items—couches, a television, a

---

[72] I thank Eric Gottesman for an extremely helpful conversation about this photograph.
[73] Gottesman and Sudden Flowers, *Sudden Flowers.*

teddy bear—that audiences (in the US, at least) do not associate with "AIDS in Africa."

The limitation of the photograph as a piece of critical visual rhetoric, then, is that it does not demand to be seen. It is too familiar; it does not grab the viewer and confront her with suffering or injustice. The fact that Tenanesh is not the needy victim that many distant viewers expect makes it hard for them to understand how to orient themselves to the photograph. Even scholars who like the photograph of Tenanesh for all the reasons just enumerated admit that it "cannot appeal to the same mass audience" as more conventional images of pain and suffering.[74] So even though it had other socially and politically beneficial effects, on its own Tenanesh's photo appears to not function effectively as a piece of critical visual rhetoric aimed at distant audiences uninterested in HIV in Africa.[75]

In contrast, consider a photograph of a young woman, Florence, and her 2-month-old daughter, Ssengabi, sitting outside of Florence's home in Gwanda, Uganda.[76] At the time this photograph was taken, both Florence and Ssengabi were HIV positive. The photograph portrays both of them largely as victims—and in particular, as famine victims. By portraying HIV using famine imagery fairly early on in the AIDS epidemic, the photograph spoke a language that viewers familiar with famine iconography already knew, telling them that something was gravely wrong.

In addition to adhering to conventions of famine iconography that make it easily legible to outsiders, the photograph has aesthetic features that draw the viewer in, including its formal composition of vertical rectangles of different widths and tones, Florence's extraordinarily long arm, and the light on Ssengabi's abdomen. The photograph is also surprising and disturbing because it defies widely shared ideas about maternal care and attention: rather than cradling Ssengabi toward her, Florence seems to be letting her head roll back, unsupported. In that this photograph focuses primarily on one person,

[74] Roland Bleiker and Amy Kay, "Representing HIV/AIDS in Africa: Pluralist Photography and Local Empowerment," *International Studies Quarterly* 51 (2007): 139–63 (158).

[75] Indeed, Eric Gottesman—the photographer who organized and ran the Sudden Flowers project with a local NGO, Hope for Children—noted that editors, creative directors, and donors are not highly responsive to this kind of image. Thus, it would be difficult to raise funds for the Sudden Flowers project using the very images that emerged out of it (Eric Gottesman, personal communication, August 2014).

[76] This photograph, taken by Ed Hooper in 1986, can be found in Bleiker and Kay, "Representing HIV/AIDS in Africa," and in Paula A. Treichler, *How to Have Theory in an Epidemic: Cultural Chronicles of AIDS* (Durham, NC: Duke University Press, 1999), 107. The main reason it is not reprinted here is because I was unable to secure permission from the photographer in a timely manner. But in retrospect, I am glad that the permission did not come through in time: even though Florence gave her permission for the photo to be taken, and was paid, Hooper later expressed "misgivings" about his encounter with her (Treichler, *How to Have Theory in an Epidemic*, 108), which in turn makes me hesitant to circulate the photograph further—even though Florence and Ssengabi are both deceased and the interested reader can easily find the image online.

portrays her largely as a victim, uses a familiar language, and is aesthetically interesting and surprising, it meets viewers who do not already care about Florence or HIV where they are, and is therefore an effective first step in the process of critical visual rhetoric.

The problem with the photograph of Florence and Ssengabi is that it does not take the second step of helping to create a deeper, more critical understanding. To be sure, there are elements in the photograph that subvert its more obvious meanings: Florence is looking upward, but not at the camera. Her visage is steely, or even angry; she appears to be preoccupied with her own thoughts. And although she is thin, she does not look particularly weak. But while it might serve to subtly jar our sensibilities, none of this is enough to take viewers significantly beyond the stereotypes to which the image appeals.

Indeed, it is very difficult (although presumably not impossible) for any single image to engage effectively in the two-step process of critical visual rhetoric. If we want to find examples of INGOs using critical visual rhetoric to overcome, or at least reduce, the moral motivation tradeoff, we need to look to some examples of portrayal-related practices that move beyond the single, traditionally captioned image. A first example is from the PhotoVoice project in Afghanistan called "Visible Rights."[77] These photographs were taken by Afghan young people participating in a program somewhat similar to the one in which Tenanesh participated.

Some of the photographs are quite stereotypical: they show children, up-close or in medium range, alone or in small groups, looking passive and bedraggled. But the captions, which describe the photographs from the joint perspective of the photographer and the individuals pictured, offer insights that distant viewers are likely to find both surprising and illuminating. For example, one photograph (Fig. 7.3a) looks down on a little girl with a dirty face in a ragged dress. Distant viewers will likely imagine that the child faces a life of miserable drudgery (and perhaps she does). But the caption states: "My name is Gulalay. My father is disabled...I am happy. I am studying in the 2nd standard in school." Another (Fig. 7.3b) shows four unkempt-looking children in front of a pile of garbage. The caption states that "[t]hese 4 children...are collecting rubbish (bits of paper) to make a fire for cooking...They are not begging but working for themselves. They have their own income. The small sister is Maree and she loves to have fun with her toys." Unlike the text accompanying similar photographs in Slovic's experiments on the

---

[77] PhotoVoice, "Visible Rights—Afghanistan" <http://www.photovoice.org/projects/international/visible-rights-afghanistan-2010>. See also Michael J. Shapiro, *The Politics of Representation: Writing Practices in Biography, Photography, and Policy Analysis* (Madison: University of Wisconsin Press, 1988), 162, for a discussion of how words can help to shape how an image is interpreted.

Figure 7.3a. Article 24: You have the right to good quality health care, clean water, nutritious food and a clean environment. "My name is Gulalay. My father is disabled. I have one brother and I sell plastic bags and get 30 afs per day. I am happy. I am studying in 2nd standard in school."
Credit: © Abdul Rahman 2010 / MSPA / PhotoVoice

identifiable victim effect (which led to a decrease in donations from study participants), the text accompanying these images does not tell the viewer that the individuals pictured are one of many statistical victims; it instead gives the viewer a (slightly) deeper glimpse into how the individuals pictured perceive their own lives.

Looked at in the broader context of the Sudden Flowers project and book, the photograph of Tenanesh discussed above also succeeds as a form of critical visual rhetoric, but uses roughly the opposite strategy. While in the PhotoVoice images, clichéd images of suffering are paired with surprising and humanizing text, in the Sudden Flowers project, a humanizing image is paired with text that, while by no means clichéd, serves to alert us to the extreme difficulty and direness of Tenanesh's situation.[78]

[78] This text includes a transcript of a phone conversation between Eric Gottesman and Tenanesh—the last time they spoke before she died—in which she and her family asked Eric to send $200 so they could buy medicine and a refrigerator in which to store it (Gottesman and Sudden Flowers, *Sudden Flowers*).

Figure 7.3b. Article 2: You have the right to be treated fairly. "These four children are brothers and sisters. They are collecting rubbish to make a fire for cooking. Their father died and they are living in their uncle's home. Their mother makes bread to sell. They are not begging but working for themselves. They have their own income. The small sister is Maree and she loves to have fun with her toys."
Credit: © Sesai 2010 / MSPA / PhotoVoice

Another possible example of critical visual rhetoric can be found in the series of images in Sebastião Salgado's book of photographs, *Migrations*.[79] James Johnson argues that Salgado helps readers overcome our faulty "arithmetic of compassion" (our tendency to care more about one person than many) by interspersing photographs of individuals with photographs of larger and larger groups. Yet while the issue of how Salgado's images function and what they mean is a matter for critical reflection, the question of how viewers *respond* to Salgado's images is largely empirical. While Johnson does not provide direct empirical evidence for his claims, his reading of Salgado suggests how photographs such as the one of Florence and Ssengabi—photographs that attract viewers' attention and subtly disrupt their assumptions, but do not draw them into radically new ways of thinking—might be combined with other photographs to help generate a more critical and politicized orientation toward issues of famine and severe poverty.[80]

[79] Johnson, "'The Arithmetic of Compassion': Rethinking the Politics of Photography." For another positive critical appraisal of Salgado's work, see Campbell, "Salgado and the Sahel."
[80] Ingrid Sischy, "Photography: Good Intentions," *The New Yorker*, September 9, 1991, 89–95 (95), disagrees, describing Salgado's work as "emotional blackmail fuelled by a dramatics of art

A six-minute video about malnutrition in Burkina Faso from MSF's "Starved for Attention" campaign (produced in partnership with the photo agency VII, mentioned above) also meets the viewer where she is and draws her in, but does so via a different and more sophisticated pathway than Johnson traces in Salgado's work.[81]

The video begins, after a few opening shots, with familiar and stereotypical scenes: crowds of women at an intensive nutritional feeding center, children with distended bellies (Fig. 7.4a). The next scenes are also familiar images of crowds at an outpatient treatment center. But the film quickly focuses on one woman, Natasha, and her life at home with her young son, Alexi. Natasha's athletic bearing and mellifluous voice, together with the striking composition of the still photographs in the video, draw the viewer in, as do the familiar-but-different National Geographic-type scenes of Natasha preparing food, gathering firewood, and caring for Alexi. Yet by the end of the video, when we see a close-up image of Natasha sitting on the ground, alone, looking pensively off into the distance (Fig. 7.4b), we are able to see the agency in her stillness, because we perceive her as a thinking human being: "I think about my children, and myself also, my life," she says, "about how I will continue my life…"

In itself, *Starved For Attention* does not prompt the viewer to adopt an explicitly political orientation to Natasha's situation, nor does it offer significant insight into the broader structural and political forces shaping her life and limiting her options. Instead, the video is clearly intended to prompt viewers to read more about MSF's campaign, which is about the need to reform food aid policies so that they provide people with necessary micronutrients, not simply enough calories. Yet the video does seem to overcome the moral motivation tradeoff to a significant degree: it grabs the viewer's attention and orients us with conventional images. It then keeps our attention with features that social psychologists suggest elicit donations (a focus on a single, downcast-looking woman with her child). However, because we see Natasha

direction." Some critics have argued that even though Salgado's work shows large numbers of people, it depoliticizes them by making them tools for his aesthetic purposes.

[81] Another compelling example of critical visual rhetoric is a short video by Save the Children meant to raise awareness (and funds) about the Syria crisis. It shows a "second-a-day" in the life of an English girl while England is being affected by a fictional crisis similar to the crisis in Syria. The video utilizes all of the strategies noted above: it focuses on a single (in this case, also white and middle-class) little girl, with no background statistics. It meets viewers where they are by only asking them to extend their sympathies to a British girl, rather than a Syrian girl. While it is not clear how much money it raised, the video has been watched 30 million times on YouTube. It creatively avoids the problem of directly portraying poor or disaster-affected people. However, as the headline of one commentary about the video noted, the video "is shocking, until you see a real Syrian child refugee" (Natalie Jennings, "Save the Children 'Second a Day' ad is shocking, until you see a real Syrian child refugee," *Washington Post*, March 6, 2014 <http://www.washingtonpost.com/blogs/worldviews/wp/2014/03/06/save-the-children-second-a-day-ad-is-shocking-until-you-see-a-real-syrian-child-refugee/>).

Figure 7.4a, b. Stills from "Starved For Attention: A Mother's Devotion." Jessica Dimmock/VII and MSF

going about her daily routine and hear her expressing herself thoughtfully, we do not see her as a helpless victim.

The video also engages in its own, more subtle politics. Rather than exploiting familiar oppositions of individual versus group, passive versus active, sympathy versus solidarity, and charity versus politics, as Salgado does on Johnson's reading (by moving us simultaneously from the first term in each pair to the second), the MSF video subverts these oppositions, by taking us from images of passive crowds that seem to ask for sympathy to an encounter with an individual, sitting still on the ground, who engages our capacity for judgment with her own. The MSF video thus contests the idea that stillness—especially poor individuals' stillness—reflects a lack of agency. This is crucial, because to see someone's stillness as a lack of agency is to deny their interiority altogether. While Salgado's images exploit the familiar associations of individual–charity–emotion and groups–politics–deliberation, the MSF video deconstructs them, and in this way opens up new possibilities for configuring attentiveness and solidarity.

Critical visual rhetoric is thus one possible way for INGOs to raise funds while also minimizing the negative discursive effects of their portrayals and addressing at least some of the objections of connected third parties. That said, critical visual rhetoric is morally risky. Consider, in this vein, newspaper columnist Nicholas Kristof's response to a reader who complained that Kristof frequently portrays Africans as nameless victims and white Americans and Europeans as heroes. "The problem that I face..." Kristof writes,

> is that frankly, the moment a reader sees that I'm writing about Central Africa, for an awful lot of them, that's the moment to turn the page. It's very hard to get people to care about distant crises like that. One way of getting people to read at least a few grafs in is to have some kind of a foreign protagonist, some American who they can identify with as a bridge character. And so if this is a way I can get people to care about foreign countries, to read about them, ideally, to get a little bit more involved, then I plead guilty.[82]

Kristof is basically describing a verbal version of critical visual rhetoric. Likewise, the skeptical questions that his response provokes are precisely the questions that we should also ask about any given instance of critical visual rhetoric: Is Kristof underestimating his audience? How do we (and Kristof) know that people won't pay attention or respond to stories or images that are unfamiliar? Is more attention to a story with an American protagonist better than less attention to a story with an African protagonist? Could there be some other way of getting people's attention? To what extent is Kristof relying on these rhetorical strategies out of habit, or knowledge of what has worked in the past, rather than on rigorous study of alternatives? For critical visual rhetoric to be even potentially normatively acceptable, INGOs must continually ask themselves these kinds of questions.

There are several possible ways for INGOs to manage the moral risks associated with critical visual rhetoric, although not avoid them completely. One is to insist that there can be no division of moral labor: a given INGO cannot claim that it is doing step 1 and leave other INGOs or other actors to do

---

[82] Nicholas Kristof, "Westerners on White Horses..." July 14, 2010 <http://kristof.blogs.nytimes.com/2010/07/14/westerners-on-white-horses/>.

step 2. That is, an INGO cannot do only the "attention grabbing" part and leave others to do the "drawing viewers into a more critical understanding" part of critical visual rhetoric. Second, INGOs can be publicly self-reflective. While Kristof's public explanation of his decision to use American protagonists is admirably frank, it does not go far enough. If Kristof is going to use an American protagonist in a column about Central Africa, why not also use a Central African protagonist—and/or explain the use of the American protagonist in the column itself? Likewise, INGOs that use critical visual rhetoric should explain what they are doing as transparently as possible. With regard to both Kristof and INGOs, there is no reason to think that such explanation would make the rhetorical strategy any less effective.

7.4 Conclusion

When INGOs contemplate using objectionable portrayals of famine and severe poverty to raise funds, it is tempting to view the ethical predicament they face as a dilemma of need versus dignity. I have argued that this framing—together with the other assumptions that comprise what I called the "standard view"—is a mistake. The ethical issues at stake are far more variegated, and possibilities for addressing (albeit not eliminating) them are far more expansive, than the need versus dignity framing allows.

More generally, the need versus dignity framing implies that INGOs face a conflict between humanitarianism and justice. But once we break away from this framing, we see that the ethical predicaments that INGOs face in the context of their portrayal-related practices often do not align in this way. For example, INGOs' portrayal-related practices can pit different aspects or strands of justice against each other, as when INGOs use images that undermine dignity to fund rights-promoting activities. Likewise, INGO portrayals can support the agency of the individuals pictured and INGOs' humanitarian aims, even as they grate on the sensibilities of connected third parties, as in the case of the photograph of Buzanesh Abraham. Instances of critical visual rhetoric can promote equality by drawing donor country publics into a more sophisticated understanding of a particular issue, thereby reducing their sense of superiority or moral innocence, while at the same time offending elites and other connected third parties in aid-recipient countries. Viewing INGOs' portrayal-related activities through the lens of the moral motivation tradeoff brings these more complicated configurations of underlying values into view.

Whether or not dilution and critical visual rhetoric are possible on any scale, and whether or not they can do anything to help dissolve the moral motivation tradeoff, are in part empirical questions. But even if they succeed, these strategies are unlikely to dissolve the tradeoff completely. This is because neither strategy addresses the fundamental problem built into the structure of INGOs as actors: their very existence depends on voluntary contributions from individuals whose lives and experiences are far removed from those of the people INGOs wish to assist. Even when individuals in donor countries only want to help—perhaps, especially, when all they want to do is help—they tend to be motivated to donate by images that cast the relationship between themselves and aid recipients as highly depoliticized and unequal. That is, the images that motivate them to donate in response to issues of famine and severe poverty undermine their understanding of these very issues.

This means that while INGOs' responsibilities to their donors are less demanding than the "agents for donors" conception discussed in Chapter 2 (INGOs do not have a moral responsibility to act on their donors' preferences or discharge their donors' moral responsibilities on their donors' behalf), they are more demanding than simply being honest and transparent. INGOs also have a more expansive duty to donor country publics, and by extension people indirectly affected by the perceptions of donor country publics, to exercise their discursive power in ways that support other actors' capacity for critical reflection.

In the next chapter, I will argue that there are also things that donors themselves can do to help defuse the moral motivation tradeoff. Ultimately, however, the problem is neither that INGOs have failed to hit on just the right kinds of images to "rope in" donors, nor is it that donors have failed to develop just the right configuration of moral sentiments to render them appropriately responsive to less objectionable images. Rather, the problem is that INGOs rely on money and goodwill from some to aid distant others. Thus, one important question to ask about strategies for navigating the moral motivation tradeoff is to what degree they further entrench, or help to chip away at, this state of affairs.

8

Conclusion: *Political* Political Ethics

We do surgery. We do medicine. We do clean water. We don't do justice.[1]

—ICRC official

What kind of actors are humanitarian INGOs? The large-scale, Western-based, donor-funded humanitarian INGOs that are the main subject of this book are, of course, extremely diverse.[2] Among other things, as one Italian aid worker put it to me, they have different "souls." But as the foregoing chapters suggest, they also share certain features in common, features that make it plausible to characterize them as a distinctive type of actor—and indeed, a distinctive type of political actor. While examining the ethical predicaments that INGOs face helps us to see what kinds of actors INGOs are, the type of actor that INGOs are, in turn, helps to generate the distinctive ethical predicaments they face.

It would be satisfying if we could characterize INGOs by drawing a neat equivalence between them and some other type of actor or figure, if we could say that humanitarian INGOs "are" this or that. But part of what makes humanitarian INGOs distinctive—and by extension, part of what makes the ethical predicaments they face distinctive—is their in-betweenness. On the one hand, the ongoing programs of large-scale, professionalized, donor-funded humanitarian INGOs are a far cry from the one-off, small-scale, spontaneous acts of helping that we associate with the individual good Samaritan. Also unlike individual good Samaritans, INGOs regularly have ongoing relationships with entire populations, exercise coercive power over them, and help to shape the background conditions against which they live. That is,

---

[1] Quoted in Colin Nickerson, "Relief workers shoulder a world of conflict; Aid agencies encounter growing dangers as nations withhold peacekeeping troops," *Boston Globe*, July 27, 1997. The ICRC is not an NGO, but has played a central role in shaping the tradition of classical humanitarianism to which some INGOs adhere.

[2] As I explain below, the title of this chapter is a reference to Jeremy Waldron's article, "*Political Political Theory*."

because they are highly political and sometimes somewhat governmental, humanitarian INGOs are in many respects more like conventional governments than they are like individual good Samaritans.

But on the other hand, humanitarian INGOs are certainly not conventional governments, either. Their governance activities are less comprehensive, coercive, and long-term than those of conventional governments and powerful global governance actors. They also lack many of the basic features of conventional governments that enable conventional governments to govern in ways that are consistent with democratic, egalitarian, and justice-based norms, such as being authorized by and accountable to those they serve, having a reliable source of funding, and having a monopoly on the legitimate use of force. Humanitarian INGOs, in other words, are between Samaritans and states.

Humanitarian INGOs do not only govern *less* than well-functioning democratic governments and some other global governance actors; they also, generally speaking, govern *less well*. As a result, other identifiable actors often have the potential to govern (and undertake other activities) better than INGOs. In other words, INGOs are often second-best actors. In addition, despite their efforts to stay above the fray, INGOs often find themselves having unintended negative effects that are political themselves and/or occur as a result of political processes or dynamics. This, then, is how I proposed that we conceptualize humanitarian INGOs for the purposes of developing an account of humanitarian INGO political ethics: as between Samaritans and states, and more specifically, as sometimes governmental, highly political, and often second-best.

There are, of course, other ways to characterize humanitarian INGOs. As I argued in Chapter 2, we could conceptualize them as rescuers of the people they aim to assist, partners of domestic NGOs, agents for their donors, or agents for their intended beneficiaries. We could develop a normative account of INGOs that focused on making them more accountable to their intended beneficiaries, or on promoting adherence to the traditional principles of classical humanitarianism. Or we could describe them as neo-colonial, or importantly similar to multinational corporations.

All eight of these approaches offer valuable insights into, or raise important questions about, humanitarian INGO political ethics. The map of humanitarian INGO political ethics offered in this book incorporates many of these insights and responds to these questions. First, it reflects the moral urgency of protecting individual lives that is central to the rescuer conception. However, it does this by emphasizing that INGOs engage in conventional governance to some degree, and therefore sometimes have a responsibility to allow their hands to be spattered. By construing INGOs as (to some extent) governors rather than as rescuers, my map figures aid recipients as "citizens" rather than helpless victims.

The account of humanitarian INGO political ethics offered in this book also embraces the commitment to equality that motivates the partnership conception. However, it does this by developing the concept of the second-best and the corresponding notion of political equality (equal say for those equally affected), rather than focusing on the shallower and less structural conception of equality suggested by the partnership approach, participation equality (equal participation for anyone willing to help).

Like the conception of INGOs as agents for their intended beneficiaries and the idea that INGOs should be accountable to their intended beneficiaries, my account of humanitarian INGO political ethics is highly attuned to democratic norms. I argue that even when aggregative decision-making procedures are impossible to implement or inconsistent with other important aims such as public safety, democratic norms of publicity, transparency, deliberation, public reason-giving, and after-the-fact sanctioning are highly relevant to INGOs. This does not imply that an INGO complying with such norms would be first-best compared to a democratic government).

It is not an attack but a critique.

While in previous chapters I have been critical of traditional humanitarian principles, such as "aid based on need alone," my account of humanitarian INGO political ethics does not ask INGOs to directly contravene these principles (in part, admittedly, because the principles turn out to be quite ambiguous). Jumping off from the notion that INGOs are agents for their donors, I argued (in Chapter 7) that INGOs' responsibilities to their donors are less demanding than they would be if INGOs were agents for their donors, but more demanding than simply fulfilling contractual obligations: INGOs also have duties to exercise their discursive power in a way that supports, or at least does not hinder, donors' ability to exercise their own critical capacities. Finally, later in this chapter I will argue that my account of humanitarian INGO political ethics can be put into conversation with the more fundamental criticisms of INGOs suggested by analogies to MNCs and neo-colonial governments.

[In addition to the middle ground between Samaritans and states] humanitarian INGOs also occupy another in-between position: they exercise tremendous power over aid recipients, potential recipients, and (sometimes) domestic NGOs, while at the same time, donors, host governments, and combatants exercise tremendous power over *them*. For example, in spattered hands situations, INGOs are manipulated by combatants at the same time as they provide essential services to aid recipients; in the moral motivation tradeoff, INGOs are at the mercy of donors for funds, while at the same time they have the power to shape perceptions of aid recipients in donor countries.)

CATCH 22? – probs not

This dynamic is not unique to INGOs: wielding power over some, while others wield power over you, (is the story of middle managers and babysitters) everywhere. I emphasize it, however, because it is a central part of what shapes the ethical predicaments that INGOs face, and so humanitarian INGO political ethics, yet it is often overlooked. Critics who accuse INGOs of neo-colonialism often overstate their power, while some defenders of INGOs, especially those who portray INGOs as good Samaritans or do-gooding machines, understate their power. Yet to understand humanitarian INGO politics, it is crucial to see them as both very powerful and highly constrained, simultaneously.

Finally, humanitarian INGOs are—to perhaps stretch the image of in-betweenness past its breaking point—"in between" other INGOs. That is, the terrain between Samaritans and states is crowded. Humanitarian INGOs compete with each other for publicity, moral authority, and funds. While competition can support innovation and help prevent extreme concentrations of power, it can also stymie innovation and be extremely costly, especially if INGOs must follow the latest trend and compete with each other in order to attract funds. Insofar as competition among INGOs makes cooperation more difficult, it contributes to spattered hands problems, the moral motivation tradeoff, and the quandary of the second-best (because it is easier to get funding to "do something" than to step back).

With this picture of humanitarian INGOs as political actors before us, I now want to step back a bit and examine, in a more general way, what this picture suggests about how INGOs should navigate the ethical predicaments they face.

Being morally motivated actors dedicated to saving lives and alleviating suffering—or more generally, having "good intentions"—is central to humanitarian INGOs' self-understanding and public self-presentation. But the fact that humanitarian INGOs operate in highly politicized contexts means that they—and their observers—should not put too much emphasis on their intentions. Intentions matter, to be sure. But an INGO with "good intentions" merely *wants* to navigate the predicaments it faces in an ethical way. This is very different from having the capacity to do so, much less actually doing so. The less powerful INGOs are and the less predictable their surroundings, the less likely it is that they will be able to effectively act on their good intentions—that is, the weaker the link between their intentions and effects will be. While good intentions might be *necessary* for INGOs to act ethically, they are far from sufficient.

While outside observers often focus on INGOs' good intentions, conceptualizing INGOs' activities as intrinsically valuable (regardless of their effects) is a persistent theme among aid workers. It might initially be difficult for some non-aid workers to see this conception as plausible. However, it becomes far more comprehensible once we understand that for aid workers on the ground, not acting can amount to knowingly allowing people to die, or abandoning them. Given a choice between not acting (understood as allowing people to die or abandoning them), and acting, acting often seems like the better option, even if it is not certain that acting will have positive effects.

However, I have suggested that because INGOs are highly political and somewhat governmental, this is generally not the choice they face. When INGOs act, they might have good effects or no effects—or they might cause harm and/or contribute to injustice. Likewise, by withdrawing, INGOs do not necessarily abandon people. In addition they might make a political statement, pressure others, or use their resources more effectively elsewhere. As Rony Brauman, a founder of MSF, writes:

> deciding to act means knowing, at least approximately, why action is preferable to abstention. Any plan of action must incorporate the idea that abstention is not necessarily an abdication but may, on the contrary, be a decision.[3]

Thus, in navigating the ethical predicaments they face, INGOs should put the most emphasis not on their intentions or the intrinsic value of their actions, but rather on their overall effects. However, because there are different and incommensurable sources of value in the world, a focus on consequences does not mean that all humanitarian action must be directed toward achieving a single best outcome, whatever that might be. While it is possible to distinguish between more and less important outcomes, such distinctions ought to be the subject of ongoing deliberation and debate, and need not be the same everywhere.

In addition, while INGOs should focus on outcomes, they should be wary of putting too much emphasis on easy-to-measure outcomes. Because INGOs are often second-best actors, a crucial part of their role is in supporting or pressuring other actors to fulfill whatever functions they themselves had been serving. Yet the effects of these efforts are notoriously difficult to measure. So are the effects of other activities that also have real value, such as *témoignage* (witnessing), developing solidaristic relationships with local activists, and easing the fear and loneliness of a person who is dying. While having effects that can be measured easily and cheaply is, all else equal, a mark in favor of a particular activity, large-scale humanitarian INGOs have good reason to avoid becoming merely highly efficient technical service providers.

The normative arguments developed in Chapters 4–7 explain what this kind of focus on consequences broadly construed looks like in the context of the more specific ethical predicaments that INGOs face. In Chapter 4, I argued that INGOs providing basic services in conflict settings should withdraw when the negative effects of their presence and activities outweigh the benefits. However, when the benefits outweigh the negative effects, they

---

[3] Rony Brauman, "Refugee Camps, Population Transfers, and NGOs," in *Hard Choices: Moral Dilemmas in Humanitarian Intervention*, ed. Jonathan Moore (Lanham, MD: Rowman & Littlefield, 1998), 177–94 (192–3). But cf. Brauman, "Questioning Health and Human Rights" (*Medical Rights Dialogue* 2.6 (2005)) for an argument that pulls in a somewhat different direction.

should, in some cases, grudgingly allow their hands to be spattered. Likewise, in Chapter 5 I argued that rather than representing as well as possible themselves, INGO advocates should focus on not misusing their power. (Here, "misuse" is understood largely in terms of avoiding negative effects, for example by not undermining the basic interests of poor and marginalized groups or displacing their first-best representatives.) In Chapter 6, I argued that in making large-scale decisions about resource use, INGOs should engage in an "ethics of resistance" that puts significant weight on cost-effectiveness, but is also attentive to the harder-to-measure political effects of these decisions. Finally, in Chapter 7 I argued that critical visual rhetoric can help INGOs navigate the moral motivation tradeoff in a way that raises funds while minimizing the direct and indirect negative effects of their discursive power.

8.1 Bringing the Four Maps Together

For reasons of conceptual and analytic clarity, the previous four chapters examined the problem of spattered hands, the quandary of the second-best, the cost-effectiveness conundrum, and the moral motivation tradeoff separately. But of course, INGOs often face several of these predicaments simultaneously. I turn now to describing some of the intersections among these predicaments, drawing on the example of the Rwandan refugee camps in Zaire discussed in Chapter 4.

The humanitarian INGOs working in the Rwandan refugee camps in Zaire after the 1994 Rwandan genocide faced a wrenching question: should they continue to provide aid, knowing that in so doing they were encouraging civilians to stay in an insecure location and helping the militarized groups in the camps to re-group, or should they instead withdraw, thereby avoiding contributing to injustices perpetrated primarily by others—but also depriving thousands of people of the goods and services they needed to survive? Various approaches to navigating this predicament—the principle of do no harm, the concept of complicity, the doctrine of double effect, and the theory of dirty hands—all overlook salient features of it. I therefore proposed a new map, one that characterizes the INGOs in this situation as facing the problem of spattered hands.

The spattered hands framework draws our attention to the ways in which humanitarian INGOs that provide basic services in conflict settings sometimes engage in conventional governance, albeit to a limited degree. I argued that the more that basic service provision by INGOs serves a conventional governance function, and in particular, the more that INGOs' departure would "pull the rug out from under" their intended beneficiaries, the more responsibility they have to continue providing aid, even when doing so means contributing to injustices perpetrated primarily by others—that is, the more responsibility they have to allow their hands to be spattered.

For many expatriate aid workers in the Rwandan refugee camps in Zaire, the question of whether their organization should stay or go was an extremely salient concern. But it was not the only ethical predicament they faced. They also faced a second, less obvious predicament. The militarization of the camps not only contributed to the problem of spattered hands; it also made working in the camps very expensive: a great deal of INGO aid was stolen, and protecting aid workers and preventing more theft required paying exorbitant prices for security-related goods and services.[4] Insofar as the humanitarian INGOs in the camps could have used these resources to address more suffering, death, or political exclusion elsewhere, they faced the cost-effectiveness conundrum: how much should considerations of cost-effectiveness have influenced their decision about whether to withdraw from the Rwandan camps?

While it is difficult to know for certain, it appears that viewing the situation in the Rwandan camps in Zaire from the perspective of the cost-effectiveness conundrum offers a somewhat stronger justification for withdrawal than does viewing the situation from the perspective of the spattered hands problem alone. While the spattered hands framework emphasizes INGOs' governmental role in providing basic services, the ethics of resistance emphasizes that in making large-scale decisions about resources use, INGOs are not only engaging in a conventional governance activity; they are also exercising discursive power. Insofar as withdrawing would have sent a more powerful message than staying in the camps, layering the cost-effectiveness conundrum on top of the spattered hands framework seems to push the relevant considerations further in the direction of withdrawing.

In order to raise money during and after the Rwandan genocide, INGOs had to present themselves and their activities in a way that would motivate people to donate, even though the situation was complex and morally ambiguous. The INGOs working in the camps thus had to navigate a version of the moral motivation tradeoff: how could they portray the situation in a way that would effectively raise funds, while not misleading donor country publics or having other negative discursive effects? One way for the INGOs to have done this would have been to engage in critical visual rhetoric: using dramatic images to grab the attention of potential donors and then drawing them into a deeper awareness of the complexities of the situation.[5]

---

[4] Fiona Terry, *Condemned to Repeat? The Paradox of Humanitarian Action* (Ithaca, NY and London: Cornell University Press, 2002), 185.

[5] For example, the active response to the cholera epidemic by some governments also served as a smokescreen to distract from their unwillingness to intervene to stop the genocide itself. Terry, *Condemned to Repeat?*, 171. While the moral motivation tradeoff is starkest in the context of severe poverty and famine, it is likely to have some relevance for the situation in the

The situation faced by the humanitarian INGOs in the Rwandan refugee camps in Zaire is a paradigmatic example of the spattered hands problem. Upon closer inspection, however, the cost-effectiveness conundrum and moral motivation tradeoff also come into view. However, the quandary of the second-best was not present—indeed, the situation was so wrenching, in part, because the INGOs in the camps were not second-best actors. Had they been, they would have had to continually face the quandary of the second-best, and ask themselves: to what extent should we act ourselves, thereby potentially displacing first-best actors or enabling them to shirk, and to what extent should we step back and support or encourage first-best actors?

In thinking about the ethical predicaments that humanitarian INGOs face as overlapping rather than discrete phenomena, three broader points stand out. First, in order to understand what is at stake in these predicaments, it is crucial to characterize them correctly. In other words, it is necessary to use the right map. We should not assume that arguments and concepts familiar from the study of more conventional political actors, such as dirty hands, representation, or harm minimization, can be extended easily to INGOs.

Second, navigating the ethical predicaments that INGOs face almost always requires some moral compromise; such compromises become even more intricate (if not necessarily more wrenching), when different predicaments are layered on top of each other. The question INGOs generally face is not how they can avoid all negative effects or objectionable outcomes, but rather which is the "least bad" option.

Third, also because the ethical predicaments that INGOs face overlap and intersect in complicated ways, humanitarian INGO political ethics is as much a matter of developing the appropriate virtues and capacities for judgment, for example an ethos of equanimity for navigating spattered hands ethical predicament and an ethics of resistance for navigating the cost-effectiveness conundrum, as it is about abiding by particular rules or principles. Maps not only aid our judgment about what route to take in particular circumstances, they can also help us better understand what kinds of judgment we need to cultivate.

8.2 Implications for Donors

What are the implications of this account of humanitarian INGO political ethics for donors to INGOs? In an essay entitled "Poverty is No Pond"

Rwandan camps, especially insofar as the issue for which funding was being requested was sickness rather than violent harm.

(a reference to Peter Singer's famous analogy between saving a toddler drowning in a pond and donating to an aid organization), Leif Wenar argues that

> You [a person living in a wealthy country] are not in a situation analogous to knowing that you can save a child drowning in a shallow pond. Closer is this: if you hand cash to a stranger he may—along with other strangers hired by other people—try to save some children who have fallen into a lake. Yet it looks like these strangers can only get to the lake by pushing through a crowded rave on a pier with no railings.[6]

Wenar's analogy to a rave is misleading, both because it suggests that the people potentially negatively affected by aid are having a great time at a wild dance party, and because it portrays them as the opposite of intentional, strategic actors.[7] Nonetheless, Wenar's more general point, about the disanalogy between the situation actually faced by donors and Singer's image, is crucial. Wenar offers several suggestions for how individuals wishing to donate to INGOs might proceed in light of this disanalogy: they might do their own research about one particular type of intervention, or try to incentivize INGOs to undertake more reliably cost-effective projects. At the very least, Wenar argues, well-off individuals should consider their own views about harm and uncertainty, and ensure that those views inform their decisions about donating to INGOs.[8]

These suggestions are sensible. But they are based on a description of the general challenges that INGOs face, not the specific ethical predicaments they must navigate. While the donor who wishes to save the children in Wenar's lake faces an ethical predicament of sorts—should she direct the stranger to whom she has handed cash to race as fast as possible to save the children or slow down to avoid knocking the ravers into the lake?—Wenar's substantive suggestions focus only on harm and uncertainty in general terms, not on the substance of any particular ethical conflict.

In contrast, because it offers a detailed account of these ethical conflicts, the map of humanitarian INGO political ethics developed in this book enables us to build up a much richer account of the political and ethical position of individual donors to humanitarian INGOs. Before turning to the details of this account, however, yet another analogy helps to convey its overall upshot. In Chapter 7, I argued that we should view INGOs that raise funds from donor country publics as roughly analogous to candidates for elected office that raise money

---

[6] Leif Wenar, "Poverty is No Pond: Challenges for the Affluent," in *Giving Well: The Ethics of Philanthropy*, ed. Patricia Illingworth, Thomas Pogge and Leif Wenar (New York: Oxford University Press, 2010), 104–32 (127).

[7] David Keen, *The Benefits of Famine: A Political Economy of Famine and Relief in Southwestern Sudan, 1983–1989* (Chichester and Princeton, NJ: Princeton University Press, 1994).

[8] Wenar, "Poverty is No Pond."

from individuals outside of their district (i.e. from individuals who are not their constituents). Likewise, we should view donors to INGOs as analogous to *donors* to these candidates.[9] That is, because INGOs are not do-gooding machines, donating to INGOs is not analogous to putting coins in do-gooding machines. Instead, donors to INGOs, like donors to candidates for elected office outside of their district, are taking a moral risk: the actors they support might end up causing harm, despite their good intentions. As a result, there is a need for careful oversight of INGOs, just as there is of candidates. However, because donors to a given INGO are not most affected by that INGO's actions (just as outside donors to a candidate are not most affected by her actions), there is a significant worry about donors' illegitimate influence.

With this analogy in mind, we can now turn to the substantive account of the donor-INGO relationship that this analogy is intended to capture, an account that diverges dramatically from how the relationship between individual donors and INGOs is often conceptualized. Imagine a donor who had previously viewed INGOs as do-gooding machines, but has since decided that INGOs are better understood as occupying the middle ground between Samaritans and states. What might this donor do differently, and how might she think differently, with regard to donating to INGOs?

Rather than expecting that her financial contribution will be transformed automatically into (what she sees as) good outcomes, this donor recognizes that humanitarian INGOs often operate in contexts in which good intentions often do not lead to good outcomes. As a result, she is highly skeptical of claims that "saving lives is easy." Just as political candidates who make pie-in-the-sky promises are often deemed too naïve to hold political office, so INGOs that claim that saving lives is easy might be deemed too naïve (or insufficiently forthcoming) to deserve funding, unless they offer rigorous empirical documentation of their claims.

Our donor also acknowledges that, in addition to not always achieving its intended positive effects, aid often has unintended negative effects. As a result, she is not scandalized or horrified upon hearing of those negative effects. Rather, she demands that the INGOs she funds provide a regular public accounting of why they chose to accept whatever negative effects they accepted (along the lines of the public accounting discussed in Chapter 4), as well as an explanation of cases in which they reduced or altered aid provision in order to avoid having negative effects.

Recognizing the complexity of the ethical issues that INGOs face and the importance of contextual judgment in dealing with those issues, our donor

---

[9] To make the analogy more apropos, we should say that INGOs are like candidates who receive both funding and votes from people outside their district (i.e. the aid recipients "in their district" cannot vote them out of office).

focuses more on asking INGOs to justify and explain specific decisions after the fact, than on demanding that they adhere to strict rules or principles determined in advance. Nonetheless, she asks INGOs to give a general indication of how they understand and orient themselves toward particular ethical predicaments. For example, will a given INGO refuse to contribute to injustices perpetrated primarily by others under any circumstances, even if this means withdrawing aid, or is it willing to consider contributing to injustice in order to continue providing aid? How has a given INGO prepared itself to address these sorts of predicaments? For example, has it sought to cultivate equanimity? While an INGO's ethos and capacities for judgment can be difficult to discern, our donor looks for evidence of these (or their absence) in public statements by high-ranking individuals within an INGO or in an INGO's institutional design, for example procedures for shared decision-making among aid workers in the field and managers at headquarters, and ongoing practices of consultation with aid recipients and potential recipients.

Our donor also uses different criteria for measuring INGO success than many INGOs and donors do currently. She rejects as irrelevant the proportion of spending on overheads versus program costs (a rejection that is widely shared among aid professionals, as I discussed in Chapter 6). She is also skeptical of, but does not reject outright, another measure that is more widely accepted: outcomes per dollar spent.[10] Her skepticism is based on the worry, described in previous chapters, that too much focus on quantifiable outcomes might divert INGOs' energies toward more technical activities and away from harder-to-quantify initiatives aimed at goals such as political empowerment. For this same reason, our donor is also open to other ways of reporting or explaining the effects of INGOs' activities, such as narrative description. However, she remains cognizant of the tendency to overvalue outcomes that are explained in narrative terms and/or that focus on a single individual, due to the identifiable victim effect and related phenomena.

Finally, our donor understands that while donating might be uplifting, energizing, and even morally good, it is not ever *only* those things. It is morally risky: by donating, she might contribute to harm or injustice. Donating is not a politics-free zone.

This account of donating might seem dauntingly difficult, and oddly alien from how we usually think about, say, texting $10 to Haiti relief. However, it is not rocket science. It seems to me to be roughly in the same ballpark, difficulty-wise, as buying a car or choosing where to go to college. Making such decisions will become easier if more "meta-charities" that are willing and able to

---

[10] See Jeri Eckhart Queenan, "Global NGOs Spend More on Accounting Than Multinationals," *Harvard Business Review*, April 2013 <http://blogs.hbr.org/2013/04/the-efficiency-trap-of-global/>.

do some of the legwork for individual donors come into being. Moreover, while the assumption that donating *will* be easy emerges out of a prior conception of INGOs as apolitical, the assumption that donating *should* be easy, such that when it is not we feel vaguely put-upon, emerges out of a conception of donating as supererogatory, as above and beyond the call of duty. Insofar as donating is a duty rather than an optional act of charity (as scholars such as Peter Singer and Thomas Pogge have argued), then the assumption that donating should be easy (where "should" means something that is owed to us), must also be cast aside.

8.3 Specifying Democratic, Egalitarian, Humanitarian, and Justice-Based Norms for Humanitarian INGOs

In exploring what it might look like for humanitarian INGOs to navigate the ethical predicaments they face in ways that are consistent with democratic, egalitarian, humanitarian, and justice-based norms, I have sought to not only offer normative insights into INGOs, but also broaden our understanding of what it looks like to enact, promote—and undermine—these norms in the contemporary world.

With regard to egalitarian norms, I argued that a familiar and widely endorsed conception of equality, equal partnership, is a rather shallow interpretation of the norm of equality for humanitarian INGOs. Equal partnership is insufficient because it does not address underlying structural inequalities between INGOs and domestic NGOs. As a result, the pursuit of equal partnership in the form of "participation equality" (an equal role for all who can contribute) can undermine what I call "political equality", or equal opportunity to shape outcomes on the part of everyone who is significantly affected by the issue at hand.

Like the ICRC official cited in the epigraph of this chapter, many humanitarian INGOs claim not to "do" justice, at least in their humanitarian work. But I have argued that justice-based norms are still relevant to them, in several respects. In the context of spattered hands problems, continuing to provide aid, rather than pulling the rug out from under people, can be the more just thing for INGOs to do. However, continuing to provide aid can also entail contributing unintentionally to injustices perpetrated primarily by others. In short, when it comes to ensuring that people have the basic goods and services they need to survive, sometimes the most just course of action for an INGO to take also requires contributing to violent harm or intimidation perpetrated by others. All forms of justice do not necessarily go together.

Justice-based norms are also relevant to INGOs because INGOs help to constitute the institution of the international humanitarian order. As a result, they have a responsibility to help ensure that that institution is just. "We don't do justice" is not a valid excuse for INGOs that participate actively in, and benefit from, this order. So while "independence" from donors and abusive host governments might be valuable or even necessary for INGOs to act ethically, claims of independence should not be a smokescreen for INGOs to deflect their responsibilities for ensuring that the international humanitarian order that they help to shape and from which they benefit, is just. Even if this responsibility is overridden by other, more pressing responsibilities, it matters that it exists and is overridden, as opposed to not existing at all.

If the salient logistical hurdles could be overcome, such that a democratically legitimate majoritarian decision-procedure could be implemented, should aid recipients have the right to democratically determine how aid is utilized? That is, on what grounds do INGOs (those that have not been given express permission to operate by a legitimate and competent host government) claim the right to engage in governance functions? Is this simply a matter of might makes right—whoever has the capacity and willingness to govern gets to do so? This is certainly a worrying proposition: just as earning (or inheriting) a lot of money should not be a direct path to formal political office,[11] the ability to attract donations from third parties should not be a direct path to informal governmental power. Thus, aid recipients (and others significantly affected by aid provision) ought to have the right to expel INGOs, so long as they can do so on the basis of a reasonably legitimate democratic procedure—that is, one that includes adequate information, meaningful alternatives, and protection for the rights of numerical minorities. However, aid recipients should not be able to compel INGOs to continue providing aid (beyond what an INGO has promised to provide), because this biases aid provision too strongly in favor of those who currently receive aid and against those who have thus far been passed over, and leaves INGOs with virtually no autonomy.

In contexts of extreme social breakdown, when majoritarian decision-procedures are impossible to implement, do democratic norms have any relevance to INGOs? Even in these circumstances, I argued, democratic norms are highly relevant to INGOs: when INGOs enact norms of transparency, publicity, deliberation, descriptive or "mirror" representation, and reason-giving, they can contribute meaningfully to giving poor and

---

[11] Michael Walzer, *Spheres of Justice: A Defense of Pluralism and Equality* (New York: Basic Books, 1983).

disaster-affected people a greater sense of dignity and more control over their lives—even though such efforts are still, typically, second-best.

Humanitarian norms articulate the (now) widely accepted idea that there is something distinctively valuable about human beings, such that everyone deserves to have their basic needs met and their dignity respected, simply in virtue of being human. But these norms can also cast individuals as suffering victims rather than active subjects, displace more political (in the narrow sense) responses to large-scale social problems, and provide a smokescreen for actors with partial agendas to portray themselves as responding to objective and universal biological needs. In short, it is hard to imagine an appealing ethical perspective that had no version of humanitarian norms. Yet at the same time, these norms seem to undermine much of what humanitarians hold dear.

In response to this paradox, the account of humanitarian INGO political ethics offered in this book suggests that many of the problems with humanitarian norms can be mitigated if these norms are complemented with other norms. For example, as I argued in Chapter 6, it is entirely appropriate for INGOs to put some weight on considerations of need when making large-scale decisions about resource use. The difficulty arises with the strict, apolitical monism of the traditional humanitarian principle of "aid based on need alone." In other words, it is not humanitarian norms per se that are the problem; it is humanitarian norms unconstrained by attention to issues of justice, democracy, and equality.

8.4 Toward a *Political* Political Ethics

An oft-heard objection to the study of political ethics is that because it focuses on feasible ways for existing actors to respond to concrete problems that they currently face, it is biased toward the status quo. In particular, this allegation goes, studying political ethics can blunt our critical sensibilities, leading us to overlook issues that can only be addressed through more profound structural transformation. By directing our attention narrowly and pragmatically to what is possible here and now, the study of political ethics encourages us to develop a sort of tunnel vision, and in so doing, turn a blind eye to deeper, larger-scale injustices. On this view, studying humanitarian INGO political ethics is akin to ignoring why the *Titanic* sank, and instead making a detailed study of the oars on its lifeboats.[12]

---

[12] With this analogy to the *Titanic*, I do not deny that in some respects, as Charles Kenny argues, some issues related to severe poverty are "getting better" (*Getting Better: Why Global Development Is Succeeding—And How We Can Improve the World Even More* (New York: Basic Books, 2012)). But as Thomas Pogge argues (and Kenny to a significant extent acknowledges), things are

I have sought to resist this tendency toward tunnel vision by developing an account of political ethics for humanitarian INGOs that is oriented outward in three ways: toward other actors and institutions, toward diverse and complementary sources of knowledge about INGOs and the issues they address, and toward the future. This outward orientation helps to make my account a more political sort of political ethics, in the sense of being attentive to political institutions, actors, policies, and events in the world, rather than focusing narrowly on the ethical betterment of one type of actor.[13]

The first way in which the account of humanitarian INGO political ethics offered here is oriented outward is that I have tried to situate humanitarian INGOs in the context of other actors. I have done this most pointedly through the concept of the second-best and by emphasizing the collective action problems that INGOs face: what a given INGO ought to do sometimes depends crucially on what other actors are doing and on what they have the potential to do.

My account of humanitarian INGO political ethics is also outwardly oriented in the sense that it is meant to work alongside of, rather than replace, other forms of knowledge about INGOs. The map analogy is crucial here. Maps can, of course, be used to exert control, rationalize, and otherwise replace more discursive, disorderly forms of knowledge.[14] Insofar as this is the case, the map analogy utilized in this book might seem worrisome. However, if we take as our paradigmatic map the open-source, crowd-based, mapping platform known as Ushahidi, mapping is a much more attractive metaphor for political ethics. Ushahidi is a platform that allows anyone to upload information to maps using a mobile phone. The maps are publicly available, in real time, on Ushahidi's website. Ushahidi was first used to document post-election violence in Kenya in 2008. Since then, it has been used to enhance relief efforts in the aftermaths of the 2010 Haiti earthquake and Superstorm Sandy in the US, and in dozens of other situations. Ushahidi maps enable anyone who can find and use a cell phone to quite literally help to shape, and, if they have an internet connection, to see, the "big picture"—that is, the map—of a given issue. Ushahidi thus enables people to collectively create useful descriptions of the world that would be very difficult for any one individual or group to create alone. This is precisely the spirit in which I offer the map in this book: while it is itself based on insights from a range of

still quite bad in absolute terms. In addition, they are not getting better as quickly as is possible, or as some would like us to suppose (Pogge, *Politics as Usual: What Lies Behind the Pro-Poor Rhetoric* (Malden, MA: Polity Press, 2010)).

[13] I take this to be roughly in the spirit of Jeremy Waldron, "*Political* Political Theory: An Inaugural Lecture," *Journal of Political Philosophy* 21.1 (2013): 1–23.

[14] James C. Scott, *Seeing Like a State: How Certain Schemes to Improve the Human Condition Have Failed* (New Haven: Yale University Press, 1998).

sources, it is intended to function as part of a larger map, a map informed by the insights and priorities of other individuals and groups, including, especially, aid recipients and others significantly affected by INGOs.

A third and final way in which my account of humanitarian INGO political ethics is outwardly oriented involves its orientation toward the future. An account of humanitarian INGO political ethics could legitimately be accused of tunnel vision if it focused narrowly on humanitarian INGOs as they are currently, without attending to the possibility that they might change dramatically, or even disappear. As a recent report entitled "Humanitarian Futures" observed:

> The *average* life expectancy for a multinational corporation Fortune 500 Company is *less than 50 years*. Many international NGOs are reaching that age. Those readers who are unwilling to contemplate a dramatic scenario should be at least asking some hard questions about the viability of today's NGO business model.[15]

There are other signs that the humanitarian sector is changing: as of 2014, Turkey was hosting tens of thousands of Syrian refugees in camps without the involvement of INGOs.[16] Innovations such as cash transfers (especially using cell phones), the rise of China and to a lesser extent India in Africa, the increasing prominence of for-profit companies in the provision of humanitarian aid, and a variety of other trends, all suggest that the humanitarian INGO landscape of the future will look very different from the landscape of today.

That said, and even though prognostication is a dangerous business, I would hazard that it is unlikely that humanitarian INGOs will disappear or become unrecognizable in the next few decades: historically, they have manifested a remarkable ability to accommodate themselves to changing circumstances. Moreover, with a few blips here and there, the sector as a whole, especially the large, mainstream humanitarian INGOs that are the main focus of this book, have grown consistently over the last forty years. This is so whether growth is measured in terms of number of donors, amount of money raised, number of donations, geographic range, or diversity of INGOs' activities.[17] But given that

---

[15] Randolph Kent, Justin Armstrong, and Alice Obrecht, "The Future of Non-Governmental Organisations in the Humanitarian Sector: Global Transformations and Their Consequences," Humanitarian Futures Programme, King's College London, August 2013.

[16] Mac McClelland, "How to Build a Perfect Refugee Camp," *The New York Times*, February 13, 2014 <http://www.nytimes.com/2014/02/16/magazine/how-to-build-a-perfect-refugee-camp.html>.

[17] "Spending by the international relief and development organization CARE has jumped 65 percent since 1999, to $607 million last year. Save the Children's budget has tripled since 1998; Doctors Without Borders' budget has doubled since 2001; and Mercy Corps' expenditures have risen nearly 700 percent in a decade" (Michael A. Cohen, Maria Figueroa Küpçü, and Parag Khanna, "The New Colonialists," *Foreign Policy*, June 16, 2008 <http://www.foreignpolicy.com/articles/2008/06/16/the_new_colonialists>).

no one knows what the future will bring, it is worth asking: What would be the value of an account of humanitarian INGO political ethics if humanitarian INGOs were to cease to exist, or if it became clear that they should immediately cease to exist? Can an account of humanitarian INGO political ethics contribute to, rather than resist, such a transformation?

One answer to these questions is that if INGOs were to disappear other actors might face versions of the ethical predicaments that humanitarian INGOs face currently. By being as precise as possible about the distinctive features of INGOs that contribute to these ethical predicaments, I hope to have contributed implicitly to clarifying when, if ever, other types of actors might face similar predicaments. Another answer is that the process of INGOs ceasing to exist, were it to happen, would itself raise serious ethical issues. How might a humanitarian INGO (decide to) cease to exist in a way that was consistent with democratic, egalitarian, humanitarian, and justice-based norms? My conceptualization of humanitarian INGOs as second-best actors provides a first step answering these questions, by providing a framework for thinking about the responsibilities that accompany stepping back and supporting first-best actors.[18]

With its emphasis on consequences and moral compromise, rather than intentions, intrinsic value, or moral absolutism, the account of humanitarian INGO political ethics offered in this book is messy and pragmatic. It is neither rousing nor inspiring. Yet this is, I think, as it should be. If any of us (by which I mean any reader of this book not personally affected by the issues INGOs address) wants inspiration to address disasters, global poverty, and other injustices, they—we—should look not to humanitarian INGOs, but rather to poor, marginalized, and disaster-affected people themselves, most of whom—despite being as flawed as anyone else—press forward with their lives, in the face of seemingly unbearable heartbreak, danger, uncertainty, and loss.

When the rest of us see this in any detail—when we hear about the bookish young Sudanese man in the Kiryondongo refugee camp in northern Uganda trying to continue his education—we want to help. But I have argued that the first part of our task is to resist the myth of the do-gooding machine, despite its intoxicating appeal. The second, equally crucial, part of our task is to accept the loss of this myth without becoming

---

[18] It is worth noting that this question is rarely asked, perhaps because ethicists wish to focus on actors or offices that seem entrenched and stable. While this is understandable, it has led to a significant gap in our thinking about political ethics. Especially as political ethicists look beyond formal governance actors and institutions, they are likely to encounter types of actors with shorter life-spans. Accounts of political ethics for these types of actors can, and should, attend to the ethical issues associated with them ceasing to exist. Also relevant here are professional ethics for individual aid workers: what are the ethical challenges associated with working for an organization that is in the process of ceasing to exist, or that should cease to exist?

paralyzed. In particular, we should remember, first, that we are not innocent bystanders, but deeply implicated in many of the issues that INGOs seek to address. Moreover, as I noted above, the only reason we ever expected "helping" to be easy is because we thought of INGOs as apolitical good Samaritans rescuing helpless victims. Knowing, now, that this picture is false, and equipped with what I have argued is a new and better map, we can work, diligently and carefully, to recognize and support the valuable work that INGOs do, criticize them—or look for alternatives—when they fall short, and always remember the much bigger picture of which they, and we, are a part. In so doing, we can play some small role in helping to create a world that supports the young Sudanese man in Kiryondongo, Hutu refugees in Central Africa, survivors of the Haiti earthquake, villagers living on the outskirts of Gulu, Congolese miners, Bezunesh Abraham and her son—and many, many others not mentioned here—in leading the lives they want for themselves.

Postscript to hardcover version (August 2014)

As this book goes to press (August 2014), an Ebola epidemic is raging across several countries in West Africa. Overwhelmed, under-resourced ministries of health in Guinea, Liberia, and Sierra Leone have asked INGOs for help; two of them—Samaritan's Purse and MSF—are playing a major role in addressing the outbreak. Yet not only is it highly plausible that humanitarian INGOs in general have helped to undermine the capacity of the ministries of health in these countries by displacing them, but even Samaritan's Purse and MSF are now stretched to the limit: MSF has stopped accepting donations restricted to the Ebola response, because it does not have any more trained people to send to the field. In an email to contributors, it stated that "the needs are greater than what Doctors Without Borders is able to manage."[19]

It would be perverse and a gross exaggeration to blame these two INGOs in particular, or humanitarian INGOs more generally, for the difficulties faced by these countries in addressing the epidemic. There is, unfortunately, more than enough blame to go around: as Ken Isaacs, a vice president of Samaritan's Purse, said to a US House Subcommittee hearing, "That the world would allow two relief agencies to shoulder this burden along with the overwhelmed Ministries of Health in these countries testifies to the lack of serious attention the epidemic was given."[20] Nonetheless, the outlines of a vicious

---

[19] Email sent to contributors, August 8, 2014.
[20] Denise Grady and Sherri Fink, "Tracing Ebola Outbreak to an African Two Year Old," *The New York Times*, August 10, 2014.

cycle are apparent: INGOs undermine governments' capacity by displacing them, such that INGOs are the only ones that can address a given problem. However, due to INGOs' own limited capacity, they cannot address the problem adequately, either. Despite this, I find it impossible, in the present moment, to regret their presence on the ground and their expertise in the fight against Ebola.

Bibliography

Abrahamsen, Rita. "The Power of Partnerships in Global Governance." *Third World Quarterly* 25.8 (2004): 1453–67. doi:10.1080/0143659042000308465.

Abu-Sada, Caroline (ed.). *In the Eyes of Others: How People in Crises Perceive Humanitarian Aid.* New York: MSF-USA, 2012.

Alcoff, Linda. "The Problem of Speaking for Others." *Cultural Critique* 20 (1991–2): 5–32. doi:10.2307/1354221.

Anderson, Mary B. *Do No Harm: How Aid Can Support Peace—or War.* Boulder, CO: Lynne Rienner Publishers, 1999.

Anderson, Mary B., Dayna Brown, and Isabella Jean. *Time To Listen: Hearing People on the Receiving End of International Aid.* Cambridge, MA: CDA Collaborative Learning Projects, 2012 <http://www.cdacollaborative.org/media/60478/Time-to-Listen-Book.pdf>.

"Angry and Effective." *The Economist*, September 21, 2000 <http://www.economist.com/node/374657>.

Apoya, Patrick and Anna Marriott. "Achieving a Shared Goal: Free Universal Healthcare in Ghana." Oxfam International, March 2011 <http://www.oxfam.org/en/policy/achieving-shared-goal-ghana-healthcare>.

Aronson, David. "How Congress Devastated Congo." *The New York Times*, August 7, 2011 <http://www.nytimes.com/2011/08/08/opinion/how-congress-devastated-congo.html>.

Autesserre, Séverine. "Dangerous Tales: Dominant Narratives on the Congo and Their Unintended Consequences." *African Affairs* 111.443 (2012): 202–22. doi:10.1093/afraf/adr080.

Badhwar, Neera K. "International Aid: When Giving Becomes a Vice." *Social Philosophy and Policy* 23.1 (2006): 69–101. doi:10.1017/S0265052506060031.

Bafilemba, Fidel, Sasha Lezhnev, and Sarah Zingg Wimmer. "From Congress to Congo: Turning the Tide on Conflict Minerals, Closing Loopholes, and Empowering Miners." *Enough Project*, August 6, 2012 <http://www.enoughproject.org/publications/congress-congo-turning-tide-conflict-minerals-closing-loopholes-and-empowering-miners>.

Bagwell, John. "Hijacking the Congo Conflict Minerals Narrative." *Enough Project*, May 22, 2012. http://www.enoughproject.org/blogs/hijacking-congo-conflict-minerals-narrative.

Barber, Benjamin R. "The Politics of Political Science: Theory and the Wolin–Strauss Dust-Up of 1963." *American Political Science Review* 100.4 (2006): 539–45. doi:10.1017/S000305540606240X.

Barber, Benjamin R. *Strong Democracy: Participatory Politics for a New Age*. Berkeley: University of California Press, 2003.

Barnard, Anne. "Complexity of Conflict Leaves Donors Wary of Aiding Syrians." *The New York Times*, March 22, 2014 <http://www.nytimes.com/2014/03/23/world/middleeast/complexity-of-conflict-leaves-donors-wary-of-aiding-syrians.html>.

Barnett, Michael N. *Empire of Humanity: A History of Humanitarianism*. Ithaca, NY: Cornell University Press, 2011.

Barnett, Michael N. "Humanitarian Governance." *Annual Review of Political Science* 16.1 (2013): 379–98. doi:10.1146/annurev-polisci-012512-083711.

Beauchamp, Tom L. "Informed Consent: Its History, Meaning, and Present Challenges." *Cambridge Quarterly of Healthcare Ethics* 20.4 (2011): 515–23. doi:10.1017/S0963180111000259.

Beitz, Charles R. *Political Theory and International Relations*. Princeton, NJ: Princeton University Press, 1999.

Bendell, Jem. "In Whose Name? The Accountability of Corporate Social Responsibility." *Development in Practice* 15.3–4 (2005): 362–74. doi:10.1080/09614520500075813.

Benhabib, Seyla. *Democracy and Difference: Contesting the Boundaries of the Political*. Princeton, NJ: Princeton University Press, 1996.

Bennett, Jane. "The Agency of Assemblages and the North American Blackout." *Public Culture* 17.3 (2005): 445–66. doi:10.1215/08992363-17-3-445.

Binder, Andrea and François Grünewald. "Cluster Approach Evaluation, 2nd Phase: Haiti" (Berlin: Global Public Policy Institute, 2010) <http://www.urd.org/IMG/pdf/GPPi-URD_Haiti_EN.pdf>.

Black, Maggie. *A Cause for Our Times: Oxfam—The First Fifty Years*. New York: Oxford University Press, 1992.

Bleiker, Roland and Amy Kay. "Representing HIV/AIDS in Africa: Pluralist Photography and Local Empowerment." *International Studies Quarterly* 51.1 (2007): 139–63. doi:10.1111/j.1468-2478.2007.00443.x.

Bluemel, Erik B. "Overcoming NGO Accountability Concerns in International Governance." *Brooklyn Journal of International Law* 31 (2005–6): 139–206.

Bob, Clifford. *The Marketing of Rebellion: Insurgents, Media, and International Activism*. New York: Cambridge University Press, 2005.

Bob, Clifford. "NGO Representation and Accountability: A Skeptical View." NGOs, International Security and Global Governance, Johns Hopkins University, October 9, 2007 <http://ssrn.com/abstract=1023021>.

Bohman, James. "International Regimes and Democratic Governance: Political Equality and Influence in Global Institutions." *International Affairs* 75.3 (July 1, 1999): 499–513. doi:10.1111/1468-2346.00090.

Bohman, James. *Public Deliberation: Pluralism, Complexity, and Democracy*. Cambridge, MA: MIT Press, 2000.

Bornstein, Erica and Peter Redfield. *Forces of Compassion: Humanitarianism Between Ethics and Politics*. Santa Fe, NM: School for Advanced Research Press, 2011.

Branch, Adam. "Against Humanitarian Impunity: Rethinking Responsibility for Displacement and Disaster in Northern Uganda." *Journal of Intervention and Statebuilding* 2.2 (2008): 151–73. doi:10.1080/17502970801988057.

Branch, Adam. *Displacing Human Rights: War and Intervention in Northern Uganda.* New York: Oxford University Press, 2011.

Brauman, Rony. "Questioning Health and Human Rights." Carnegie Council, May 6, 2001 <http://www.carnegiecouncil.org/publications/archive/dialogue/2_06/articles/643.html>.

Brauman, Rony. "Refugee Camps, Population Transfers, and NGOs," in *Hard Choices: Moral Dilemmas in Humanitarian Intervention*, ed. Jonathan Moore, 177–94. Lanham, MD: Rowman & Littlefield, 1998.

Brettschneider, Corey L. *When the State Speaks, What Should It Say? How Democracies Can Protect Expression and Promote Equality.* Princeton, NJ: Princeton University Press, 2012.

Brown, Wendy. "'The Most We Can Hope For...': Human Rights and the Politics of Fatalism." *The South Atlantic Quarterly* 103.2 (2004): 451–63.

Bruckner, Till. "Secret NGO Budgets: Publish What You Spend." *AID WATCH*, May 24, 2010. Accessed March 25, 2014 <http://aidwatchers.com/2010/05/secret-ngo-budgets-publish-what-you-spend/>.

Buchanan, Allen and Robert O. Keohane. "The Legitimacy of Global Governance Institutions." *Ethics & International Affairs* 20.4 (2006): 405–37. doi:10.1111/j.1747-7093.2006.00043.x.

Busby, Joshua William. "Bono Made Jesse Helms Cry: Jubilee 2000, Debt Relief, and Moral Action in International Politics." *International Studies Quarterly* 51.2 (2007): 247–75. doi:10.1111/j.1468-2478.2007.00451.x.

Buston, Oliver and Kerry Smith. "GHA Report 2013." Development Initiatives: Global Humanitarian Assistance, 2013.

Cain, Kenneth, Heidi Postlewait, and Andrew Thomson. *Emergency Sex and Other Desperate Measures: A True Story from Hell on Earth.* New York: Miramax, 2004.

Calhoun, Craig. "The Idea of Emergency: Humanitarian Action and Global (Dis) Order," in *Contemporary States of Emergency: The Politics of Military and Humanitarian Interventions*, ed. Didier Fassin and Mariella Pandolfi, 29–58. New York: Zone Books, 2010, 29–58.

Cameron, John and Anna Haanstra. "Development Made Sexy: How It Happened and What It Means." *Third World Quarterly* 29.8 (2008): 1475–89. doi:10.1080/01436590802528564.

Campbell, David. "Geopolitics and Visuality: Sighting the Darfur Conflict." *Political Geography* 26.4 (2007): 357–82. doi:10.1016/j.polgeo.2006.11.005.

Campbell, David. "The Problem with Regarding the Photography of Suffering as 'Pornography'." *David Campbell*, January 21, 2011 <http://www.david-campbell.org/2011/01/21/problem-with-regarding-photography-of-suffering-as-pornography/>.

Campbell, David. "Salgado and the Sahel: Documentary Photography and the Imaging of Famine," in *Rituals of Mediation: International Politics and Social Meaning*, ed. François Debrix and Cynthia Weber, 69–96. Minneapolis: University of Minnesota Press, 2003.

Capacity.org. "Parallel Service Delivery in a Fragile State." October 29, 2010 <http://www.capacity.org/capacity/opencms/en/topics/fragile-environments/parallel-service-delivery-in-a-fragile-state.html>.

CARE. "About Us." <http://www.care.org/about>.

CARE. "Ongoing Crisis in the Horn of Africa." <http://www.care.org/emergencies/horn-of-africa-hunger-crisis>.

CARE. "Support Food Aid Reform." <http://www.care.org/work/advocacy/food-aid>.

Center for Development Alternatives. "The 'Do No Harm' Framework for Analyzing the Impact of Assistance on Conflict: A Handbook." Do No Harm Project (Local Capacities for Peace Project), a project of the Collaborative for Development Action, Inc. and CDA Collaborative Learning Projects, April 2004.

Central Intelligence Agency. "Haiti," in *The World Factbook*. Washington, DC: Central Intelligence Agency. Page last updated on March 27, 2014 <https://www.cia.gov/library/publications/the-world-factbook/geos/ha.html>.

Chambers, Simone. "Rhetoric and the Public Sphere: Has Deliberative Democracy Abandoned Mass Democracy?" *Political Theory* 37.3 (2009): 323–50. doi:10.1177/0090591709332336.

Chatterjee, Deen K. *The Ethics of Assistance: Morality and the Distant Needy*. New York: Cambridge University Press, 2004.

Clark, David. "Representing the MAJORITY WORLD: Famine, Photojournalism and the Changing Visual Economy." PhD dissertation, Durham University, 2009 <http://etheses.dur.ac.uk/136/>.

Coady, C. A. J. "The Problem of Dirty Hands," in *The Stanford Encyclopedia of Philosophy* (Spring 2014 edition), ed. Edward N. Zalta <http://plato.stanford.edu/entries/dirty-hands/>.

Cohen, Michael A., Maria Figueroa Küpçü, and Parag Khanna. "The New Colonialists." *Foreign Policy*, June 16, 2008 <http://www.foreignpolicy.com/articles/2008/06/16/the_new_colonialists>.

CONCORD. "Code of Conduct on Images and Messages." 2006 <http://www.conordeurope.org/component/k2/item/download/82_8ea8cdb1b7d1bf965513bf2a01054935>.

Coole, Diana. "Rethinking Agency: A Phenomenological Approach to Embodiment and Agentic Capacities." *Political Studies* 53.1 (2005): 124–42. doi:10.1111/j.1467-9248.2005.00520.x.

Cooley, Alexander and James Ron. "The NGO Scramble: Organizational Insecurity and the Political Economy of Transnational Action." *International Security* 27.1 (2002): 5–39. doi:10.1162/016228802320231217.

Crane, Andrew, Dirk Matten, and Jeremy Moon. "Stakeholders as Citizens? Rethinking Rights, Participation, and Democracy." *Journal of Business Ethics* 53.1–2 (2004): 107–22.

Crewe, Emma and Elizabeth Harrison. *Whose Development? An Ethnography of Aid*. London: Zed Books, 1998.

Cullity, Garrett. "Compromised Humanitarianism," in *Ethical Questions and International NGOs*, ed. Keith Horton and Chris Roche, 157–73. Dordrecht: Springer, 2010.

Debrix, François and Cynthia Weber. *Rituals of Mediation: International Politics and Social Meaning*. Minneapolis: University of Minnesota Press, 2003.

Deutsche Gesellschaft für Technische Zusammenarbeit (GTZ). "Application of the Performance Based Allocation System to Fragile States." GTZ and the Overseas Development Institute. June 2007 <http://www.odi.org.uk/sites/odi.org.uk/files/odi-assets/publications-opinion-files/230.pdf>.

Deveaux, Monique. "The Global Poor as Agents of Justice." *Journal of Moral Philosophy*. Available online July 2013. doi:10.1163/17455243-4681029.

De Waal, Alexander. *Famine Crimes: Politics & the Disaster Relief Industry in Africa*. Bloomington: Indiana University Press, 1997.

Disasters Emergency Committee. "Corporate Supporters." Updated October 10, 2012 <http://www.dec.org.uk/about-dec/corporate-supporters>.

Disch, Lisa. "Toward a Mobilization Conception of Democratic Representation." *American Political Science Review* 105.1 (2011): 100–14.

Dizolele, Mvemba. "Conflict Minerals in the Congo: Let's Be Frank About Dodd-Frank." *Huffington Post*, August 22, 2011 <http://www.huffingtonpost.com/mvemba-dizolele/conflict-minerals-congo-dodd-frank_b_933078.html>.

Dóchas. "A Guide to Understanding and Implementing the Code of Conduct on Images & Messages." Dublin: Dóchas, April 2008 <http://www.dochas.ie/Shared/Files/5/Guide_to_Code.pdf>.

Donini, Antonio, Larissa Fast, Greg Hansen, Simon Harris, Larry Minear, Tasneem Mowjee, and Andrew Wilder. "Humanitarian Agenda 2015: Final Report: The State of the Humanitarian Enterprise." Feinstein International Center, 2008.

Dovi, Suzanne. "Guilt and the Problem of Dirty Hands." *Constellations* 12.1 (2005): 128–46. doi:10.1111/j.1351-0487.2005.00406.x.

Dovi, Suzanne. "Political Representation," in *The Stanford Encyclopedia of Philosophy* (Spring 2014 edition), ed. Edward N. Zalta <http://plato.stanford.edu/archives/spr2014/entries/political-representation/>.

Dovi, Suzanne. "In Praise of Exclusion." *The Journal of Politics* 71.3 (2009): 1172–86. doi:10.1017/S0022381609090951.

Drik. "About Us." <http://drik.net/>.

Dryzek, John S. "Rhetoric in Democracy: A Systemic Appreciation." *Political Theory* 38.3 (2010): 319–39. doi:10.1177/0090591709359596.

Dryzek, John S. and Simon Niemeyer. "Discursive Representation." *American Political Science Review* 102.04 (2008): 481–93. doi:10.1017/S0003055408080325.

Duffield, Mark. *Development, Security and Unending War: Governing the World of Peoples*. Cambridge: Polity Press, 2007.

Dugger, Celia W. "CARE Turns Down Federal Funds for Food Aid." *The New York Times*, August 16, 2007, sec. International/Africa <http://www.nytimes.com/2007/08/16/world/africa/16food.html>.

Eade, Deborah and Ernst Ligteringen (eds.). *Debating Development: NGOs and the Future*. Herdon, VA: Stylus Publishing, 2001.

Eayrs, Caroline B. and Nick Ellis. "Charity Advertising: For or Against People with a Mental Handicap?" *British Journal of Social Psychology* 29.4 (1990): 349–66. doi:10.1111/j.2044-8309.1990.tb00915.x.

Edmonds, Kevin. "Beyond Good Intentions: The Structural Limitations of NGOs in Haiti." *Critical Sociology* 39.3: 439–52. doi:10.1177/0896920512437053.

Edwards, Michael. "'Does the Doormat Influence the Boot?': Critical Thoughts on UK NGOs and International Advocacy." *Development in Practice* 3.3 (1993): 163–75. doi:10.1080/096145249100077281.

Edwards, Michael. *NGO Rights and Responsibilities: A New Deal for Global Governance*. London: Foreign Policy Centre, 2000.

Estrin, James. "When Interest Creates a Conflict." *New York Times Lens Blog*, November 19, 2012 <http://lens.blogs.nytimes.com/2012/11/19/when-interest-creates-a-conflict/>.

Estrin, James. "Wresting the Narrative From the West." *New York Times Lens Blog*, July 19, 2013 <http://lens.blogs.nytimes.com/2013/07/19/wresting-the-narrative-from-the-west/>.

European Commission Directorate-General for Humanitarian Aid. "Humanitarian Protection: DG ECHO's Funding Guidelines." Brussels, April 21, 2009 <http://ec.europa.eu/echo/files/policies/sectoral/Prot_Funding_Guidelines.pdf>.

Evans, Gareth. *The Responsibility to Protect: Ending Mass Atrocity Crimes Once and For All.* Washington, DC: Brookings Institution, 2008.

Falconer, Bruce. "Armed and Humanitarian." *Mother Jones*, May 19, 2008 <http://www.motherjones.com/politics/2008/05/armed-and-humanitarian>.

Farmer, Paul. "Five Lessons From Haiti's Disaster." *Foreign Policy*, November 29, 2010 <http://www.foreignpolicy.com/articles/2010/11/29/5_lessons_from_haitis_disaster>.

Farr, James, John S. Dryzek, and Stephen T. Leonard. *Political Science in History: Research Programs and Political Traditions.* Cambridge: Cambridge University Press, 1995.

Farrell, Jodi Mailander. "New York Is Awash in Photojournalism—but Is It Art?" *PopMatters*, October 22, 2007 <http://www.popmatters.com/article/new-york-is-awash-in-photojournalism-but-is-it-art/>.

Fassin, Didier. *Humanitarian Reason: A Moral History of the Present.* Berkeley: University of California Press, 2012.

Fassin, Didier. "Moral Commitments and Ethical Dilemmas of Humanitarianism," in *In the Name of Humanity: The Government of Threat and Care*, ed. Ilana Feldman and Miriam Iris Ticktin, 238–55. Durham, NC: Duke University Press, 2010.

Fassin, Didier and Mariella Pandolfi. *Contemporary States of Emergency: The Politics of Military and Humanitarian Interventions.* Brooklyn, NY: Zone Books, 2010.

Feldman, Ilana and Miriam Iris Ticktin. "Government and Humanity," in *In the Name of Humanity: The Government of Threat and Care*, ed. Ilana Feldman and Miriam Iris Ticktin, 1–26. Durham, NC: Duke University Press, 2010.

Feldman, Ilana and Miriam Iris Ticktin (eds.). *In the Name of Humanity: The Government of Threat and Care.* Durham, NC: Duke University Press, 2010.

Ferguson, James. *The Anti-Politics Machine: 'Development,' Depoliticization, and Bureaucratic Power in Lesotho.* Minneapolis: University of Minnesota Press, 1994.

Ferguson, James. "Seeing Like an Oil Company: Space, Security, and Global Capital in Neoliberal Africa." *American Anthropologist* 107.3 (2005): 377–82. doi:10.1525/aa.2005.107.3.377.

Ford, Nathan and Richard Bedell (eds.). *Intentions and Consequences: Human Rights, Humanitarianism and Culture.* Amsterdam: MSF, 1999.

Ford, Nathan and Richard Bedell (eds.). *Justice and MSF Operational Choices.* Amsterdam: MSF, 2002.

Fowler, Alan F. "Authentic NGDO Partnerships in the New Policy Agenda for International Aid: Dead End or Light Ahead?" *Development and Change* 29.1 (1998): 137–59. doi:10.1111/1467-7660.00073.

Fowler, Alan. "Introduction—Beyond Partnership: Getting Real About NGO Relationships in the Aid System." *IDS Bulletin* 31.3 (2000): 1–13. doi:10.1111/j.1759-5436.2000.mp31003001.x.

Fraser, Nancy. "Rethinking Recognition: Overcoming Displacement and Reification in Cultural Politics," in *Recognition Struggles and Social Movements: Contested Identities, Agency and Power*, ed. Barbara Hobson, 21–34. Cambridge: Cambridge University Press, 2003.

Fuller, Lisa. "Justified Commitments? Considering Resource Allocation and Fairness in Médecins Sans Frontières-Holland." *Developing World Bioethics* 6.2 (2006): 59–70. doi:10.1111/j.1471-8847.2006.00139.x.

Fuller, Lisa. "Priority Setting in International Non-Governmental Organizations: It Is Not As Easy As ABCD." *Journal of Global Ethics* 8.1 (2012): 5–17.

Garsten, Bryan. "The Rhetorical Revival in Political Theory." *Annual Review of Political Science* 14 (2011): 159–80. doi:10.1146/annurev.polisci.040108.104834.

Garsten, Bryan. *Saving Persuasion: A Defense of Rhetoric and Judgment*. Cambridge, MA: Harvard University Press, 2009.

Geuss, Raymond. *Philosophy and Real Politics*. Princeton, NJ: Princeton University Press, 2008.

GiveWell. "Charity Reviews and Recommendations." *GiveWell* <http://www.givewell.org/>.

Giving What We Can. "Political Change." December 2012 <http://www.givingwhatwecan.org/where-to-give/charity-evaluation/political-change>.

Glassman, Amanda. "Really Oxfam? Really?" Center for Global Development <http://www.cgdev.org/blog/really-oxfam-really>.

Global Humanitarian Assistance. "GHA Report 2009." Development Initiatives, United Kingdom, 2009 <http://www.globalhumanitarianassistance.org/wp-content/uploads/2009/07/GHA-Report-2009.pdf>.

Global Humanitarian Assistance. "GHA Report 2010." Development Initiatives, United Kingdom, 2010 <http://www.globalhumanitarianassistance.org/wp-content/uploads/2010/07/GHA_Report8.pdf>.

Global Witness. "Artisanal Mining Communities in Eastern DRC: Seven Baseline Studies in the Kivus." August 22, 2012 <http://www.globalwitness.org/library/artisanal-mining-communities-eastern-drc-seven-baseline-studies-kivus>.

Goodin, Robert E. "Enfranchising All Affected Interests, and Its Alternatives." *Philosophy & Public Affairs* 35.1 (2007): 40–68. doi:10.1111/j.1088-4963.2007.00098.x.

Gourevitch, Philip. "Alms Dealers." *The New Yorker*, October 11, 2010 <http://www.newyorker.com/arts/critics/atlarge/2010/10/11/101011crat_atlarge_gourevitch?currentPage=all>.

Grady, Denise and Sherri Fink. "Tracing Ebola Outbreak to an African Two Year Old." *The New York Times*, August 10, 2014.

Green, Duncan. "From Poverty to Power – Really CGD? Really? The Perils of Attack Blogs." March 15, 2011 <http://oxfamblogs.org/fp2p/really-cgd-really-the-perils-of-attack-blogs/>.

Gunnell, John G. "American Political Science, Liberalism, and the Invention of Political Theory." *American Political Science Review* 82.1 (1988): 71–87. doi:10.2307/1958059.

Haiti Grassroots Watch. "The 'Cluster' System in Haiti." *Ayiti Kale Je—Haiti Grassroots Watch*, Dossier 1, Story 4, October 12, 2010 <http://haitigrassrootswatch.squarespace.com/dossier1story4/>.

Hall, Rodney Bruce and Thomas J. Biersteker. *The Emergence of Private Authority in Global Governance*. New York: Cambridge University Press, 2002.

Hariman, Robert and John Louis Lucaites. *No Caption Needed: Iconic Photographs, Public Culture, and Liberal Democracy*. Chicago: University of Chicago Press, 2007.

Harrell, Eben. "CARE Turns Down U.S. Food Aid." *Time*, August 15, 2007 <http://content.time.com/time/nation/article/0,8599,1653360,00.html>.

Harvey, Paul and Jeremy Lind. "Dependency and Humanitarian Relief: A Critical Analysis." London: HPG Report 19, July 2005.

Haviv, Ron, Gary Knight, Antonin Kratochvil, Joachim Ladefoged, James Nachtwey, de.MO, and VII Photo Agency. *Forgotten War: Democratic Republic of the Congo*. Millbrook, NY: de.MO, 2005.

Held, David. "From Executive to Cosmopolitan Multilateralism," in *Taming Globalization: Frontiers of Governance*, ed. David Held and Mathias Koenig-Archibugi, 160–86. Malden, MA: Polity Press, 2003.

Held, David and Mathias Koenig-Archibugi (eds.). *Taming Globalization: Frontiers of Governance*. Malden, MA: Polity Press, 2003.

Held, David, Anthony McGrew, David Goldblatt, and Jonathan Perraton (eds.). *Global Transformations: Politics, Economics and Culture*. Stanford, CA: Stanford University Press, 1999.

Hendrie, Barbara. "Knowledge and Power: A Critique of an International Relief Operation." *Disasters* 21.1 (1997): 57–76. doi:10.1111/1467-7717.00044.

Hoksbergen, Roland. "Building Civil Society through Partnership: Lessons from a Case Study of the Christian Reformed World Relief Committee." *Development in Practice* 15.1 (2005): 16–27. doi:10.1080/0961452052000321541.

Honig, Bonnie. *Emergency Politics: Paradox, Law, Democracy*. Princeton, NJ: Princeton University Press, 2009.

Hooker, Brad. *Ideal Code, Real World*. New York: Oxford University Press, 2000.

Hopgood, Stephen. "Saying 'No' to Wal-mart? Money and Morality in Professional Humanitarianism," in *Humanitarianism in Question : Politics, Power, Ethics*, ed. Michael Barnett and Thomas G. Weiss, 98–123. Ithaca: Cornell University Press, 2008.

Hudson, Alan. "NGOs' Transnational Advocacy Networks: From 'Legitimacy' to 'Political Responsibility'?" *Global Networks* 1.4 (2001): 331–52. doi:10.1111/1471-0374.00019.

Human Accountability Project. "2013 Humanitarian Accountability Report." June 2013 <http://www.hapinternational.org/pool/files/2013-har.pdf>.

Illingworth, Patricia. *Giving Well: The Ethics of Philanthropy*. New York: Oxford University Press, 2011.

International Campaign to Ban Landmines. "National Campaigns." <https://www.icbl.org/index.php/icbl/Campaigns>.

International Federation of the Red Cross and Red Crescent Societies. "The Code of Conduct for the International Red Cross and Red Crescent Movement and NGOs in Disaster Relief." <http://www.ifrc.org/en/publications-and-reports/code-of-conduct/>.

International Federation of the Red Cross and Red Crescent Societies. "Fundamental Principles of the Red Cross and Red Crescent." <http://www.ifrc.org/who-we-are/vision-and-mission/the-seven-fundamental-principles/>.

International Rescue Committee. "About the International Rescue Committee." <http://www.rescue.org/about>.

Jackson, Ashley. "A Deadly Dilemma: How Al-Shabaab Came to Dictate the Terms of Humanitarian Aid in Somalia." *Overseas Development Institute*. December 11, 2013 <http://www.odi.org.uk/opinion/8066-al-shabaab-somalia-negotiations>.

Jakobsen, Peter Viggo. "Focus on the CNN Effect Misses the Point: The Real Media Impact on Conflict Management Is Invisible and Indirect." *Journal of Peace Research* 37.2 (2000): 131–43. doi:10.1177/0022343300037002001.

Jean, François and Médecins Sans Frontières (eds.). *Populations in Danger 1995: A Médicins Sans Frontières Report*. Rushcutters Bay, NSW: Halstead Press, 1995.

Jenni, Karen and George Loewenstein. "Explaining the Identifiable Victim Effect." *Journal of Risk and Uncertainty* 14.3 (1997): 235–57. doi:10.1023/A:1007740225484.

Jennings, Natalie. "Save the Children 'Second a Day' ad is shocking, until you see a real Syrian child refugee." *Washington Post*, March 6, 2014 <http://www.washingtonpost.com/blogs/worldviews/wp/2014/03/06/save-the-children-second-a-day-ad-is-shocking-until-you-see-a-real-syrian-child- refugee/>.

Jochum, Bruno. "Perception Project: A Remedy Against Complacency," in *In the Eyes of Others: How People in Crises Perceive Humanitarian Aid*, ed. Caroline Abu-Sada, 100–6. New York: MSF-USA, 2012.

Johnson, James. "'The Arithmetic of Compassion': Rethinking the Politics of Photography." *British Journal of Political Science* 41.3 (2011): 621–43. doi:10.1017/S0007123410000487.

Johnson, James. "Photographer Embedded With NGO Reproduces 1970s Famine Photos," *Notes on Politics, Theory & Photography*, July 24, 2008 <http://politics-theory photography.blogspot.com/2008/07/photographer-embedded-with-ngo.html>.

Jordan, Lisa and Peter van Tuijl. "Political Responsibility in Transnational NGO Advocacy." *World Development* 28.2 (2000): 2051–2065.

Justice Africa. "About Us." <http://www.justiceafrica.org/about-us/>.

Kabamba, Patience. "The Real Problems of the Congo: From Africanist Perspectives to African Prospectives." *African Affairs* 111.443 (2012): 202–22 <http://afraf.oxfordjournals.org/content/early/2012/02/09/afraf.adr080.abstract/reply>.

Keen, David. *The Benefits of Famine: A Political Economy of Famine and Relief in Southwestern Sudan, 1983–1989*. Chichester and Princeton, NJ: Princeton University Press, 1994.

Kennedy, David. *The Dark Side of Virtue: Reassessing International Humanitarianism*. Princeton, NJ: Princeton University Press, 2004.

Kenny, Charles. "Belief in Relief." *The Washington Monthly*, December 2010 <http://www.washingtonmonthly.com/features/2010/1011.kenny.html>.

Kenny, Charles. *Getting Better: Why Global Development Is Succeeding—And How We Can Improve the World Even More*. New York: Basic Books, 2012.

Kent, Randolph, Justin Armstrong, and Alice Obrecht. "The Future of Non-Governmental Organisations in the Humanitarian Sector: Global Transformations and Their Consequences." Humanitarian Futures Programme, King's College London, August 2013.

Keystone Accountability. *Keystone Performance Surveys NGO Partner Survey 2010*. London: Keystone Accountability, 2011 <http://www.keystoneaccountability.org/sites/default/files/Keystone%20partner%20survey%20Jan2011_0.pdf>.

Knox-Clarke, Paul and John Mitchell. "Reflections on the Accountability Revolution." *Humanitarian Exchange Magazine* 52 (Humanitarian Practice Network) (2005) <http://www.odihpn.org/humanitarian-exchange-magazine/issue-52/reflections-on-the-accountability-revolution>.

Krause, Sharon R. "Beyond Non-domination Agency, Inequality and the Meaning of Freedom." *Philosophy & Social Criticism* 39.2 (2013): 187–208. doi:10.1177/0191453712470360.

Krause, Sharon R. "Bodies in Action: Corporeal Agency and Democratic Politics." *Political Theory* 39.3 (2011): 299–324. doi:10.1177/0090591711400025.

Kristof, Nicholas. "Westerners on White Horses…" July 14, 2010 <http://kristof.blogs.nytimes.com/2010/07/14/westerners-on-white-horses/>.

Kristoff, Madeleine and Liz Panarelli. "Haiti: A Republic of NGOs?" Washington, DC: The United States Institute of Peace, 2010.

Kutz, Christopher. *Complicity: Ethics and Law for a Collective Age*. Cambridge: Cambridge University Press, 2007.

Laidler-Kylander, Nathalie and Bernard Simonin. "How International Nonprofits Build Brand Equity." *International Journal of Nonprofit and Voluntary Sector Marketing* 14.1 (2009): 57–69. doi:10.1002/nvsm.353.

Lakoff, Andrew and Stephen J. Collier. *Biosecurity Interventions: Global Health and Security in Practice*. New York: Columbia University Press, 2008.

Large, Tim. "TIP SHEET: How to 'Sell' Forgotten Emergencies." *Thomson Reuters Foundation*, October 5, 2005 <http://www.trust.org/item/20051005114500-7oiru/>.

Lazar, Nomi Claire. *States of Emergency in Liberal Democracies*. Cambridge and New York: Cambridge University Press, 2009.

Leeson, Peter T. "Better Off Stateless: Somalia before and after Government Collapse." *Journal of Comparative Economics* 35.4 (2007): 689–710. doi:10.1016/j.jce.2007.10.001.

Lepora, Chiara and Robert E. Goodin. "Grading Complicity in Rwandan Refugee Camps." *Journal of Applied Philosophy* 28.3 (2011): 259–76. doi:10.1111/j.1468-5930.2011.00536.x.

Lepora, Chiara and Robert E. Goodin. *On Complicity and Compromise*. New York: Oxford University Press, 2013.

Lepora, Chiara and Joseph Millum. "The Tortured Patient." *Hastings Center Report* 41.3 (2011): 38–47. doi:10.1353/hcr.2011.0064.

Lezhnev, Sasha. "What Conflict Minerals Legislation is Actually Accomplishing in Congo." *Huffington Post*, August 9, 2011 <http://www.huffingtonpost.com/sasha-lezhnev/what-conflict-minerals-le_b_922566.html>.

Li, Tania. *The Will to Improve: Governmentality, Development, and the Practice of Politics*. Durham, NC: Duke University Press, 2007.

Lu, Catherine. "World Government," in *The Stanford Encyclopedia of Philosophy* (Fall 2012 edition), ed. Edward N. Zalta <http://plato.stanford.edu/archives/fall2012/entries/world-government/>.

Lucas, J. R. "Against Equality Again." *Philosophy* 52.201 (1977): 255–80.

McClelland, Mac. "How to Build a Perfect Refugee Camp." *The New York Times*, February 13, 2014 <http://www.nytimes.com/2014/02/16/magazine/how-to-build-a-perfect-refugee-camp.html>.

Macdonald, Terry. *Global Stakeholder Democracy: Power and Representation Beyond Liberal States.* New York: Oxford University Press, 2008.

McGee, Siobhán. "Report on the Review of the Code of Conduct: Images and Messages relating to the Third World." Presented to Dóchas Development Education Working Group, July 6, 2005 <http://dochas.ie/Shared/Files/7/Siobhan-McGee-Final_Code_of_Conduct_Report.pdf>.

McIntyre, Alison. "Doctrine of Double Effect," in *The Stanford Encyclopedia of Philosophy* (Spring 2014 edition), ed. Edward N. Zalta <http://plato.stanford.edu/entries/double-effect/>.

Magone, Claire, Michael Neuman, Fabrice Weissman, and Médecins Sans Frontières (eds.). *Humanitarian Negotiations Revealed: The MSF Experience.* London: Hurst & Co., 2011.

Mamdani, Mahmood. *Saviors and Survivors: Darfur, Politics, and the War on Terror.* New York: Pantheon Books, 2009.

Mansbridge, Jane. "Rethinking Representation." *American Political Science Review* 97.4 (2003): 515–28.

Mansbridge, Jane. "Should Blacks Represent Blacks and Women Represent Women? A Contingent 'Yes'." *The Journal of Politics* 61.3 (1999): 628–57. doi:10.2307/2647821.

Mansfield, Edward D., Richard Sisson, and American Political Science Association. *The Evolution of Political Knowledge: Theory and Inquiry in American Politics.* Columbus: Ohio State University Press, 2004.

Manson, Neil C. and Onora O'Neill. *Rethinking Informed Consent in Bioethics.* Cambridge and New York: Cambridge University Press, 2007.

Manzo, Kate. "Imaging Humanitarianism: NGO Identity and the Iconography of Childhood." *Antipode* 40.4 (2008): 632–57. doi:10.1111/j.1467-8330.2008.00627.x.

Mapel, David R. "Revising the Doctrine of Double Effect." *Journal of Applied Philosophy* 18.3 (2001): 257–72. doi:10.1111/1468-5930.00193.

Maren, Michael. *The Road to Hell: The Ravaging Effects of Foreign Aid and International Charity.* New York: Free Press, 1997.

Markell, Patchen. *Bound by Recognition.* Princeton, NJ: Princeton University Press, 2003.

Markell, Patchen. "The Insufficiency of Non-Domination." *Political Theory* 36.1 (2008): 9–36. doi:10.1177/0090591707310084.

Matten, Dirk and Andrew Crane. "What is Stakeholder Democracy? Perspectives and Issues." *Business Ethics: A European Review* 14.1 (2005): 6–13. doi:10.1111/j.1467-8608.2005.00382.x.

May, Larry. *Genocide: A Normative Account.* New York: Cambridge University Press, 2010.

Médecins Sans Frontières. "About MSF." <http://www.msf.org/about-msf>.

Médecins Sans Frontières. "International Activity Report 2012." July 16, 2013 <http://www.msf.org/sites/msf.org/files/msf_activity_report_2012_interactive_final.pd>.

Médecins Sans Frontières. "International Financial Report 2012" <http://www.msf.org/sites/msf.org/files/msf_financial_report_interactive_2012_final.pdf>.

Médecins Sans Frontières. "Top 10 Most Underreported Humanitarian Stories of 2004" <http://www.doctorswithoutborders.org/news-stories/special-report/top-10-most-underreported-humanitarian-stories-2004>.

Médecins Sans Frontières Access Campaign. "About Us." <http://www.msfaccess.org/the-access-campaign>.

Médecins Sans Frontières and VII Photo. "Malnutrition." Starved for Attention Campaign <http://www.starvedforattention.org/about-malnutrition.php>.

MSF-Canada. "We Are Seeing Sick Patients Who, on Top of Being Sick, Are Actually Starving." August 19, 2011 <http://sites.msf.ca/news-media/news/2011/08/we-are-seeing-sick-patients-who-on-top-of-being-sick-are-actually-starving/>.

MSF-Holland. "Justice and MSF Operational Choices." Report of a discussion held in Soesterberg, Netherlands, June 2001.

MSF-Hong Kong. "Democratic Republic of Congo Forgotten War Photo Exhibition." <http://www.pillandpillow.com/msfCongo/mainEng.html>

MSF-USA. "History and Principles." <http://www.doctorswithoutborders.org/aboutus/history-and-principles>.

MSF-USA. "How Programs are Chosen and Implemented." December 31, 2013 <http://www.doctorswithoutborders.org/how-programs-are-chosen-and-implemented>.

MSF-USA. "Impact." <http://www.doctorswithoutborders.org/our-work/impact>.

MSF-USA. "US Annual Report 2012." <http://www.doctorswithoutborders.org/sites/usa/files/attachments/msf_usa_annual_report_2012.pdf>.

Merlingen, Michael. "Governmentality: Towards a Foucauldian Framework for the Study of IGOs." *Cooperation and Conflict* 38.4 (2003): 361–84. doi:10.1177/0010836703384002.

Mill, John Stuart. "On Liberty" in *On Liberty and Other Writings*, ed. Stephan Collini. Cambridge: Cambridge University Press, 1989.

Miller, Richard W. *Globalizing Justice: The Ethics of Poverty and Power.* New York: Oxford University Press, 2010.

Moeller, Susan D. *Compassion Fatigue: How the Media Sell Disease, Famine, War, and Death.* New York: Routledge, 1999.

Montanaro, Laura. "The Democratic Legitimacy of Self-Appointed Representatives." *The Journal of Politics* 74.4 (2012): 1094–1107.

Moore, Jonathan. *Hard Choices: Moral Dilemmas in Humanitarian Intervention.* Lanham, MD: Rowman & Littlefield, 1998.

Moskop, John C. and Kenneth V. Iserson. "Triage in Medicine, Part II: Underlying Values and Principles." *Annals of Emergency Medicine* 49.3 (2007): 282–87. doi:10.1016/j.annemergmed.2006.07.012.

Mouffe, Chantal. "Deliberative Democracy or Agonistic Pluralism?" *Social Research* 66.3 (1999): 745–58.

Myers, Judith Gelman. "NGOs to the Rescue." *PopPhoto*, December 16, 2008 <http://www.popphoto.com/how-to/2008/12/ngos-to-rescue>.

Nagel, Thomas. "The Problem of Global Justice." *Philosophy & Public Affairs* 33.2 (2005): 113–47. doi:10.1111/j.1088-4963.2005.00027.x.

Näsström, Sofia. "Where is the Representative Turn Going?" *European Journal of Political Theory* 10.4 (2011): 501–10. doi:10.1177/1474885111417783.

National Health Insurance Authority. "NHIA Position on OXFAM/ISODEC Report on Free Universal Health Care in Ghana." March 17, 2011 <http://www.ghanaweb.com/GhanaHomePage/NewsArchive/artikel.php?ID=205271>.

Nickel, James W. *Making Sense of Human Rights*. Malden, MA: Blackwell, 2007.

Nickerson, Colin. "Relief workers shoulder a world of conflict; Aid agencies encounter growing dangers as nations withhold peacekeeping troops." *Boston Globe*, July 27, 1997.

Nyamugasira, Warren. "NGOs and Advocacy: How Well Are the Poor Represented?" *Development in Practice* 8.3 (1998): 297–308. doi:10.1080/09614529853594.

O'Connor, Maura R. "Does International Aid Keep Haiti Poor?" *Slate*, January 7, 2011 <http://www.slate.com/articles/news_and_politics/dispatches/features/2011/does_international_aid_keep_haiti_poor/the_un_cluster_system_is_as_bad_as_it_sounds.html>.

O'Dwyer, Brendan. "Stakeholder Democracy: Challenges and Contributions from Social Accounting." *Business Ethics: A European Review* 14.1 (2005): 28–41.

Olson, Lester C., Cara A. Finnegan, and Diane S. Hope. *Visual Rhetoric: A Reader in Communication and American Culture*. Los Angeles: Sage, 2008.

O'Neill, Onora. "Global Justice: Whose Obligations?" in *The Ethics of Assistance: Morality and the Distant Needy*, ed. Deen K. Chatterjee, 242–59. Cambridge: Cambridge University Press, 2004.

O'Neill, Onora. "Lifeboat Earth," in *International Ethics*, ed. Charles Beitz, Marshall Cohen, Thomas Scanlon, and John Simmons, 262–81. Princeton, NJ: Princeton University Press, 1985.

O'Neill, Onora. "Some Limits of Informed Consent." *Journal of Medical Ethics* 29.1 (2003): 4–7. doi:10.1136/jme.29.1.4.

Oppenheimer, Daniel M. and Christopher Yves Olivola. *The Science of Giving: Experimental Approaches to the Study of Charity*. New York: Psychology Press, 2011.

Orbinski, James. *An Imperfect Offering: Humanitarian Action for the Twenty-First Century*. New York: Bloomsbury Publishing, 2010.

Orbinski, James. "Médecins sans Frontières—Nobel Lecture," July, 29, 2014. *Nobelprize.org*. Nobel Media AB 2014 <http://www.nobelprize.org/nobel_prizes/peace/laureates/1999/msf-lecture.html>.

Ord, Toby. *The Moral Imperative toward Cost-effectiveness in Global Health*. Washington, DC: Center for Global Development, 2013.

Oxfam Canada. "Oxfam Canada Partnership Policy." February 25, 2011 <http://www.oxfam.ca/our-work/our-approach/partnership-policy>.

Oxfam International. "Oxfam Annual Report 2012–2013." <http://www.oxfam.org/sites/www.oxfam.org/files/oxfam-annual-report-2012-2013.pdf>.

Oxfam International. "Trade Campaign." <http://www.oxfam.org/en/campaigns/trade>.

Oxfam International. "Working Together: Oxfam's Partnership Principles and Program Standards." February 2012 <http://www.oxfam.org/sites/www.oxfam.org/files/oxfam-partnership-principles.pdf>

Oxfam UK. "Countries We Work In." <http://www.oxfam.org.uk/what-we-do/countries-we-work-in>.

Oxfam UK. "Little Book of Communications." Humanitarian Accountability Partnership International <http://www.hapinternational.org/pool/files/oxfam-gb-little-book-of-communications.pdf>.

Oxfam UK. "Our Work." <http://policy-practice.oxfam.org.uk/our-work>.

Oxfam and Listening Project. "Listening Exercise Report from Tamil Nadu, Southern India" (March 2012).

Perlez, Jane. "Ban on Doctors' Group Imperils Muslim Minority in Myanmar." *The New York Times*, March 13, 2014 <http://www.nytimes.com/2014/03/14/world/asia/myanmar-bans-doctors-without-borders.html>.

Peruzzotti, Enrique. "Civil Society, Representation and Accountability: Restating Current Debates on the Representativeness and Accountability of Civic Associations," in *NGO Accountability: Politics, Principles and Innovations*, ed. Lisa Jordan and Peter van Tuijl, 43–58. Sterling, VA: Earthscan, 2006.

Pettit, Philip. *Republicanism: A Theory of Freedom and Government*. New York: Oxford University Press, 1997.

Phillips, Anne. *The Politics of Presence*. New York: Oxford University Press, 1995.

Phillips, Robert R., Edward Freeman, and Andrew C. Wicks. "What Stakeholder Theory is Not." *Business Ethics Quarterly* 13.4 (2003): 479–502.

PhotoVoice. "About PhotoVoice." <http://www.photovoice.org>.

PhotoVoice. "Visible Rights—Afghanistan." <http://www.photovoice.org/projects/international/visible-rights-afghanistan-2010>.

Pictet, Jean. "The Fundamental Principles of the Red Cross: Commentary." International Committee for the Red Cross Resource Centre, January 1, 1979 <http://www.icrc.org/eng/resources/documents/misc/fundamental-principles-commentary-010179.htm>.

Pitkin, Hanna Fenichel. *The Concept of Representation*. Berkeley: University of California Press, 1967.

Plewes, Betty and Rieky Stuart. "The Pornography of Poverty: A Cautionary Fundraising Tale," in *Ethics in Action*, ed. Daniel A. Bell and Jean-Marc Coicaud, 23–37. New York: Cambridge University Press, 2006.

Plotke, David. "Representation is Democracy." *Constellations* 4.1 (1997): 19–34. doi:10.1111/1467-8675.00033.

Pogge, Thomas W.. "Moral Priorities for International Human Rights NGOs," in *Ethics in Action*, ed. Daniel A. Bell and Jean-Marc Coicaud, 218–56. New York: Cambridge University Press, 2006.

Pogge, Thomas. *Politics as Usual: What Lies Behind the Pro-Poor Rhetoric*. Cambridge: Polity Press, 2010.

Pogge, Thomas W. "Respect and Disagreement: A Response to Joseph Carens," in *Ethics in Action*, ed. Daniel A. Bell and Jean-Marc Coicaud, 273–8. New York: Cambridge University Press, 2006.

Pogge, Thomas W. *World Poverty and Human Rights*, 2nd edn. Malden, MA: Polity Press, 2008.

Polman, Linda. *The Crisis Caravan: What's Wrong With Humanitarian Aid?* trans. Liz Waters. New York: Metropolitan Books, 2010.

Poole, Lydia. "GHA Report 2012." Wells, UK: Development Initiatives, 2012.

Porter, Toby. "An Embarrassment of Riches." *Humanitarian Exchange Magazine* 21 (2002) <http://www.odihpn.org/humanitarian-exchange-magazine/issue-21/an-embarrassment-of-riches>.

Prunier, Gérard. *Darfur: A 21st Century Genocide*. Ithaca, NY: Cornell University Press, 2008.

Purcell, Kristen and Michael Dimock. "Americans Under Age 40 are as Likely to Donate to Japan Disaster Relief through Electronic Means as Traditional Means." *Pew Research Center's Internet & American Life Project*, March 23, 2011 <http://www.pewinternet.org/2011/03/23/americans-under-age-40-are-as-likely-to-donate-to-japan-disaster-relief-through-electronic-means-as-traditional-means/>.

Quarmby, Catherine. "Why Oxfam Is Failing Africa." *The New Statesman*, May 30, 2005 <http://www.newstatesman.com/node/150728>.

Queenan, Jeri Eckhart. "Global NGOs Spend More on Accounting Than Multinationals." *Harvard Business Review*. April 2013 <http://blogs.hbr.org/2013/04/the-efficiency-trap-of-global/>.

Ramachandran, Vijaya. "Is Haiti Doomed to Be the Republic of NGOs?" *Huffington Post*, January 12, 2012 <http://www.huffingtonpost.com/vijaya-ramachandran/haiti-relief-ngos_b_1194923.html>.

Rawls, John. *A Theory of Justice*, revised edn. Cambridge, MA: Harvard University Press, 1999.

Redfield, Peter. "Bioexpectations: Life Technologies as Humanitarian Goods." *Public Culture* 24.1 (2012): 157–84.

Redfield, Peter. "Doctors, Borders, and Life in Crisis." *Cultural Anthropology* 20.3 (2005): 328–61. doi:10.1525/can.2005.20.3.328.

Redfield, Peter. *Life in Crisis: The Ethical Journey of Doctors Without Borders*. Berkeley: University of California Press, 2013.

Redfield, Peter. "The Verge of Crisis: Doctors Without Borders in Uganda," in *Contemporary States of Emergency: The Politics of Military and Humanitarian Interventions*, ed. Didier Fassin and Mariella Pandolfi, 173–95. Cambridge, MA: Zone Books, 2010.

Redfield, Peter. "Vital Mobility and the Humanitarian Kit," in *Biosecurity Interventions: Global Health and Security in Question*, ed. Andrew Lakoff and Stephen J. Collier, 147–71. New York: Columbia University Press, 2008.

Reinhardt, Mark. "Painful Photographs: From the Ethics of Spectatorship to Visual Politics," in *Ethics and Images of Pain*, ed. Asbjørn Grønstad and Henrik Gustafsson, 33–57. New York: Routledge, 2012.

Reinhardt, Mark. "Theorizing the Event of Photography—The Visual Politics of Violence and Terror in Azoulay's Civil Imagination, Linfield's The Cruel Radiance, and Mitchell's Cloning Terror." *Theory & Event* 16.3 (2013) <http://muse.jhu.edu/journals/theory_and_event/v016/16.3.reinhardt.html>.

Reinhardt, Mark, Holly Edwards, and Erina Dugganne (eds.). *Beautiful Suffering: Photography and the Traffic in Pain*. Chicago: University of Chicago Press, 2007.

Riddell, Roger. *Does Foreign Aid Really Work?* New York: Oxford University Press, 2007.

Rieff, David. *A Bed for the Night: Humanitarianism in Crisis*. New York: Simon & Schuster, 2003.

Rieff, David. "Kosovo's Humanitarian Circus." *World Policy Journal* 17.3 (2000): 25–32.

Rieff, David. "The Kouchner Conversion." *Project Syndicate*, August 1, 2007 <http://www.project-syndicate.org/commentary/the-kouchner-conversion/english>.

Rieff, David. *Slaughterhouse: Bosnia and the Failure of the West*. New York: Touchstone, 1996.

Risse, Thomas. "Global Governance and Communicative Action." *Government and Opposition* 39.2 (2004): 288–313. doi:10.1111/j.1477-7053.2004.00124.x.

Risse, Thomas (ed.). *Governance Without a State? Policies and Politics in Areas of Limited Statehood*. New York: Columbia University Press, 2013.

Rosenau, James N. and Ernst Otto Czempiel. *Governance Without Government: Order and Change in World Politics*. New York: Cambridge University Press, 1992.

Rubenstein, Jennifer C. "Accountability in an Unequal World." *The Journal of Politics* 69.03 (2007): 616–32. doi:10.1111/j.1468-2508.2007.00563.x.

Rubenstein, Jennifer C. "The Distributive Commitments of Humanitarian INGOs," in *Humanitarianism in Question: Politics, Power, Ethics*, ed. Michael Barnett and Thomas Weiss, 215–34. Ithaca, NY: Cornell University Press, 2008.

Rubenstein, Jennifer C. "Emergency Claims and Democratic Action," *Social Philosophy and Policy*, forthcoming.

Rubenstein, Jennifer C. "Humanitarian NGOs' Duties of Justice." *Journal of Social Philosophy* 40.4 (2009): 524–41. doi:10.1111/j.1467-9833.2009.01469.x.

Rubenstein, Jennifer C. "The Misuse of Power, Not Bad Representation: Why It Is Beside the Point That No One Elected Oxfam." *Journal of Political Philosophy* 22.2 (2013): 204–30. doi:10.1111/jopp.12020.

Rubenstein, Jennifer C. "Pluralism about Global Poverty." *British Journal of Political Science* 43.4 (2013): 775–97.

Ryan, Marco. "On Assignment with The Asia Foundation in Laos." *marco ryan photography: Frankfurt* <http://www.marcoryanphotography.com/on-assignment-with-the-asia-foundation-in-laos/>.

Sanders, Lynn M. "Against Deliberation." *Political Theory* 25.3 (1997): 347–76.

Sankore, Rotimi. "Behind the Image: Poverty and 'Development Pornography'." *Pambazuka News*, April 21, 2005 <http://www.pambazuka.org/en/category/rights/27815>.

Save the Children, "Interactive Map" <http://www.savethechildren.org/site/c.8rKLIXMGIpI4E/ b.7801347/k.981A/Interactive_Map.htm>.

Saward, Michael. "Authorisation and Authenticity: Representation and the Unelected." *Journal of Political Philosophy* 17.1 (2009): 1–22. doi:10.1111/j.1467-9760.2008.00309.x.

Saward, Michael. *The Representative Claim*. New York: Oxford University Press, 2010.

Scheuerman, William E. "Global Governance Without Global Government? Habermas on Postnational Democracy." *Political Theory* 36.1 (2008): 133–51.

Schieber, George, Cheryl Cashin, Karima Saleh, and Rouselle Lavado. "Health Financing in Ghana at a Crossroads." Washington, DC: International Bank for Reconstruction and Development / World Bank, 2012.

Scott, James C. *Seeing Like a State: How Certain Schemes to Improve the Human Condition Have Failed.* New Haven: Yale University Press, 1998.

Seay, Laura. "The Dodd-Frank Catastrophe." *Texas in Africa.* August 8, 2011 <http://www.texasinafrica.blogspot.com>.

Seay, Laura. "The DRC Minerals Mess." *Texas in Africa.* August 4, 2011 <http://www.texasinafrica.blogspot.com>.

Seay, Laura. "What's Wrong with Dodd-Frank 1502? Conflict Minerals, Civilian Livelihoods, and the Unintended Consequences of Western Advocacy—Working Paper 284." Center for Global Development. January 5, 2012 <http://www.cgdev.org/publication/what%E2%80%99s-wrong-dodd-frank-1502-conflict-minerals-civilian-livelihoods-and-unintended>.

Sen, Amartya. "Equality of What?" In *The Tanner Lecture on Human Values, I,* ed. Sterling M. McMurrin, 197–220. Cambridge: Cambridge University Press, 2011.

Sending, Ole Jacob and Iver B. Neumann. "Governance to Governmentality: Analyzing NGOs, States, and Power." *International Studies Quarterly* 50.3 (2006): 651–72. doi:10.1111/j.1468-2478.2006.00418.x.

Shapiro, Michael J. *The Politics of Representation: Writing Practices in Biography, Photography, and Policy Analysis.* Madison: University of Wisconsin Press, 1988.

Shivji, Issa G. "Silences in NGO Discourse: The Role and Future of NGOs in Africa." *African Development* 31.4 (2006): 22–51.

Shklar, Judith N. *The Faces of Injustice.* New Haven: Yale University Press, 1990.

Shue, Henry. "Torture in Dreamland: Disposing of the Ticking Bomb." *Case Western Reserve Journal of International Law* 37.2/3 (2006): 231–9.

Simmons, A. John. "Ideal and Nonideal Theory." *Philosophy & Public Affairs* 38.1 (2010): 5–36. doi:10.1111/j.1088-4963.2009.01172.x.

Singer, Peter. "Famine, Affluence, and Morality." *Philosophy & Public Affairs* 1.3 (1972): 229–43.

Singer, Peter. *The Life You Can Save: Acting Now to End World Poverty.* New York: Random House, 2009.

Sischy, Ingrid. "Photography: Good Intentions." *The New Yorker,* September 9, 1991, 89–95.

Slaughter, Anne-Marie. *A New World Order.* Princeton, NJ: Princeton University Press, 2005.

Slim, Hugo. "Claiming a Humanitarian Imperative: NGOs and the Cultivation of Humanitarian Duty." *Refugee Survey Quarterly* 21.3 (2002): 113–25. doi:10.1093/rsq/21.3.113.

Slim, Hugo. "Doing the Right Thing: Relief Agencies, Moral Dilemmas and Moral Responsibility in Political Emergencies and War." *Disasters* 21.3 (1997): 244–57. doi:10.1111/1467-7717.00059.

Slim, Hugo. "The Grammar of Aid," Introduction to *Collaboration in Crises: Lessons in Community Participation from Oxfam International's Tsunami Research.* Oxford:

Oxfam International, 2009 <http://www.oxfam.org/sites/www.oxfam.org/files/collaboration-crises-lessons-tsunami.pdf>.

Sliwinski, Sharon. *Human Rights in Camera*. Chicago: University of Chicago Press, 2011.

Slovic, Paul. "'If I Look at the Mass I Will Never Act': Psychic Numbing and Genocide." *Judgment and Decision Making* 2.2 (2007): 79–95.

Small, Deborah. "Sympathy Biases and Sympathy Appeals: Reducing Social Distance to Boost Charitable Contributions," in *The Science of Giving: Experimental Approaches to the Study of Charity*, ed. Daniel M. Oppenheimer and Christopher Y. Olivola, 149–60. New York: Psychology Press, 2011.

Sphere Project. *Humanitarian Charter and Minimum Standards in Humanitarian Response* <http://www.spherehandbook.org/>.

Spielthenner, Georg. "The Principle of Double Effect as a Guide for Medical Decision-Making." *Medicine, Health Care and Philosophy* 11.4 (2008): 465–73.

Start Network. "The Start Fund" (2014) <http://www.start-network.org/how/start-fund/>.

Stearns, Jason. "Thoughts About Conflict Minerals." *Congo Siasa*, August 10, 2011 <http://congosiasa.blogspot.com/2011/08/thoughts-about-conflict-minerals.html>.

Stohr, Karen. "Kantian Beneficence and the Problem of Obligatory Aid." *Journal of Moral Philosophy* 8.1 (2011): 45–67. doi:10.1163/174552411X549372.

Stoianova, Velina. *Private Funding: An Emerging Trend in Humanitarian Donorship*. Wells, UK: Global Humanitarian Assistance, 2012.

Sullivan, Daniel, Mark J. Landau, and Aaron C. Kay. "When Enemies Go Viral (or Not)—A Real-Time Experiment During the 'Stop Kony' Campaign." *Psychology of Popular Media Culture*, April 14, 2014. doi:10.1037/ppm0000031.

Swidler, Ann and Susan Cotts Watkins. "'Teach a Man to Fish': The Sustainability Doctrine and Its Social Consequences." *World Development* 37.7 (2009): 1182–96. doi:10.1016/j.worlddev.2008.11.002.

Taylor, Charles et al. *Multiculturalism: Examining the Politics of Recognition*, ed. Amy Gutmann. Princeton, NJ: Princeton University Press, 1994.

Taylor, Glyn, Abby Stoddard, Adele Harmer, Katherine Haver, Paul Harvey, Kathryn Barber, Lisa Schreter, and Constance Wilhelm. "The State of the Humanitarian System 2012." London: ALNAP/Overseas Development Institute.

Terry, Fiona. *Condemned to Repeat? The Paradox of Humanitarian Action*. Ithaca, NY and London: Cornell University Press, 2002.

Treichler, Paula A. *How to Have Theory in an Epidemic: Cultural Chronicles of AIDS*. Durham, NC: Duke University Press, 1999.

Tvedt, Terje. *Angels of Mercy or Development Diplomats? NGOs and Foreign Aid*. Trenton, NJ: Africa World Press, 1998.

Unger, Peter K. *Living High and Letting Die: Our Illusion of Innocence*. New York: Oxford University Press, 1996.

UNHCR. "Dadaab—World's Biggest Refugee Camp 20 Years Old." *UNHCR*. Accessed April 4, 2014 <http://www.unhcr.org/4f439dbb9.html>.

UNICEF. "UNICEF's Humanitarian Principles." PATH Training Programme, Participant Manual, July 2003 <http://www.unicef.org/pathtraining/Documents/

Session%204%20Humanitarian%20Principles/Participant%20Manual/4.2%20 UNICEF%20Humanitarian%20Principles.doc>.

United Nations Development Programme. "Human Development Indicators, Haiti." Human Development Reports <http://hdr.undp.org/en/countries/pro-files/ HTI>.

United Nations Office for the Coordination of Humanitarian Affairs (OCHA). "Cluster Coordination." <http://www.unocha.org/what-we-do/coordination-tools/ cluster-coordination>.

Urbinati, Nadia. "Representation as Advocacy: A Study of Democratic Deliberation." *Political Theory* 28.6 (2000): 758–86.

Urbinati, Nadia and Mark E. Warren. "The Concept of Representation in Contemporary Democratic Theory." *Annual Review of Political Science* 11.1 (2008): 387–412. doi:10.1146/annurev.polisci.11.053006.190533.

US Department of State. "U.S. Relations With Haiti." Bureau of Western Hemisphere Affairs. Fact Sheet, February 11, 2013 <http://www.state.gov/r/pa/ei/bgn/1982. htm>.

US House, 111th Congress, 2nd Session, H.R. 4173. *Dodd-Frank Wall Street Reform and Consumer Protection Act.* Washington, DC: Government Printing Office, 2010.

Vaux, Tony. *The Selfish Altruist: Dilemmas of Relief Work in Famine and War.* London: Earthscan, 2002.

Waldron, Jeremy. "*Political* Political Theory: An Inaugural Lecture." *Journal of Political Philosophy* 21.1 (2013): 1–23. doi:10.1111/jopp.12007.

Waldron, Jeremy. "Who Is My Neighbor? Humanity and Proximity." *Monist* 86.3 (2003): 333–54. doi:10.5840/monist200386324.

Walzer, Michael. *Arguing About War.* New Haven: Yale University Press, 2005.

Walzer, Michael. "Emergency Ethics," in *Arguing about War*, 33–50. New Haven: Yale University Press, 2004.

Walzer, Michael. "Political Action: The Problem of Dirty Hands." *Philosophy & Public Affairs* 2.2 (Winter, 1973): 160–80.

Walzer, Michael. *Spheres of Justice: A Defense of Pluralism and Equality.* New York: Basic Books, 1983.

Wapner, Paul. "Introductory Essay: Paradise Lost—NGOs and Global Accountability." *Chicago Journal of International Law* 3 (2002): 155.

Washington Post. "Rumsfeld Testifies Before Senate Armed Services Committee." May 7, 2004. World Vision <http://www.worldvision.org/>.

Watkins, Susan Cotts, Ann Swidler, and Thomas Hannan. "Outsourcing Social Transformation: Development NGOs as Organizations." *Annual Review of Sociology* 38: 285–315. doi:10.1146/annurev-soc-071811-145516.

Wenar, Leif. "Poverty is No Pond: Challenges for the Affluent," in *Giving Well: The Ethics of Philanthropy*, ed. Patricia Illingworth, Thomas Pogge, and Leif Wenar, 104–32. New York: Oxford University Press, 2010.

Wertheimer, Alan and Matt Zwolinski. "Exploitation," in *The Stanford Encyclopedia of Philosophy*, ed. Edward N. Zalta. Spring 2013 <http://plato.stanford.edu/archives/ spr2013/entries/exploitation/>.

Williams, Bernard. "Is International Rescue a Moral Issue?" *Social Research* 62.1 (1995): 67–75.

Wolin, Sheldon S. "Political Theory as a Vocation." *American Political Science Review* 63.4 (1969): 1062–82. doi:10.2307/1955072.

World Health Organization. *WHO Global Health Expenditure Atlas*. Geneva: WHO, 2012.

Index

Printed and bound by CPI Group (UK) Ltd, Croydon, CR0 4YY